The Path to the THRONE of GOD

THE SANCTUARY

or

THE GOSPEL ACCORDING TO MOSES

By

Sarah Elizabeth Peck

Author of *God's Great Plan* which has been translated into more than six foreign languages, also fifteen other books used extensively for many years as text books in English speaking church schools.

TEACH Services, Inc.
Brushton, New York

2007 08 09 10 11 12 · 5 4 3 2 1

The author assumes full responsibility for the accuracy of all facts and quotations as cited in this book.

Copyright © 2002 TEACH Services, Inc.
ISBN-13: 978-1-57258-218-7
ISBN-10: 1-57258-218-9
Library of Congress Catalog Card No. 2001093888

Published by

TEACH Services, Inc.
www.TEACHServices.com

Dedicated

To "The Common People" - (Mark 12:37)

By One of Them

KEY TEXT

THUS SAITH THE LORD GOD:
Although I have cast them far off among the heathen, and although I have scattered them among the countries, *yet will I be to them as a little sanctuary* in the countries where they shall come. Ezekiel 11:16

Contents

Section VI–The Church In The Sanctuary

Section VII–The Sanctuary After Redemption

PREFACE

The accompanying study of the sanctuary aims to give the reader an overall view of the entire sanctuary, including the earthly and the heavenly sanctuaries, and reaching its climax in the temple eternal, the earthly model as constructed by Moses, being a type or illustration of both the others. It also aims to make plain that the sanctuary symbolizes not only the redemptive work of Christ, but also the Christian experience of each of His followers, and of the church as a whole.

The book of Exodus wherein the sanctuary building is described in minute and careful detail, is the foundation of this study, an understanding of which is essential to a full and correct comprehension of the sanctuary. In this presentation, the logical order has been followed, taking the court, the holy place, and the most holy place in their divinely revealed and natural sequence.

Following this sequence, the work of Christ as Redeemer is traced when at His birth He entered the court of earth to give His life as a sacrifice for the sins of the world; when at His ascension He entered the holy place of the heavenly sanctuary to act as High Priest; when in 1844 at the end of the 2300 days He entered the most holy place as Judge to begin the Investigative Judgment of the house of God; when this Judgment closes at the beginning of the thousand years He comes as the Bridegroom to receive His bride, the redeemed, and take them to the mansions He has prepared for them; and finally when at the close of the thousand years He returns to this earth to cleanse it from sin and sinners, and create a new heaven and a new earth wherein dwelleth righteousness. All this, and more, is symbolized in the sanctuary as herein presented.

In the same sequence is traced the individual's Christian experience as he moved forward on *The Path to the Throne of God*. Here the sanctuary is shown to illustrate reconciliation and justification in the court where by faith he receives imputed righteousness, sanctification in the holy place, where as the result of a lifelong experience, he by faith gains imparted righteousness, glorification in the most holy place, where he receives his reward, eternal righteousness.

Likewise, this study aims to show that the sanctuary illustrates the four generations of the church as a whole: *first*, the church of the court of the Hebrew church, the first church organized on earth when at Sinai God through Christ spoke His law to Israel on the Sabbath; *second*, the church of the holy place, the Christian church, also founded on the Sabbath, when at Christ's ascension and inauguration God gave the Holy Spirit, Christ's representative, to abide with them forever; *third*, the church of the most holy place, the Remnant church, the last church on earth which began in 1844, having the truth regarding the sanctuary and the Sabbath as its two foundation pillars, which was divinely revealed to the believers; *fourth*, the church of the Firstborn, the church of the temple eternal, which begins at the second coming of Christ and throughout eternity meets for worship around the Throne from one Sabbath to another.

Thus the Sabbath, being the great underlying truth on which every generation of the church is based, furnishes a key to the instruction that, in these closing days of the church on earth, God's messengers are to proclaim the Sabbath more fully.

The writer is persuaded that the spiritual significance of all parts of the sanctuary as herein presented will appeal to all classes of religious people; to the Jews, because first "unto them were committed the oracles of God," Rom. 3:2, as given in the sanctuary; to Catholic Christians, because the priesthood permeates all its parts and services; to Protestant Christians because the everlasting gospel is the keynote of the sanctuary; and even to the heathen, because in practically all, if not all, heathen worship there still remain traces of this divine object lesson.

Although the approach to this subject is different from any that has yet been published, no effort has been made to present new truth that would make the old obsolete, but instead that which will illuminate the old and help the reader to see new beauty in it, and revive in the minds of Bible students and Christian people, generally, truths that have long remained dormant, perhaps because so many excellent books dealing with this subject are no longer obtainable.

Lectures illustrated by a replica model of the sanctuary constructed by Moses have frequently been given by the writer in colleges, schools of lower grades, churches, sanitariums, and elsewhere, and so many college students, church members, and gospel workers have requested written copies of these lectures, that it has been deemed advisable to make them available in printed form. In doing this every effort has been made to make the Scriptures the infallible guide so that the result might be as nearly perfect as is humanly possible. Nevertheless, it is recognized that while all the books written on this subject have been definitely helpful, none have yet appeared in which every single statement met the full approval of every reader, and this book will doubtless be no exception to the rule. But if it will make more clear and beautiful and practically helpful, some of the most fundamental truths of the gospel of salvation as symbolized in the sanctuary—truths vital to all, and especially to those who are looking for the soon coming of Him who is the Antitype of the sanctuary, if it will help the reader to walk with greater joy and assurance on *The Path to the Throne of God*, the author's purpose will have been accomplished.

As the reader meditates on the spiritual truths with which the sanctuary abounds, he will surely have a deeper appreciation of the magnitude, the beauty, and the richness of the plan of redemption as symbolized in this, God's great object lesson, and it is hoped that as he reaches the end of the *PATH TO THE THRONE OF GOD*, he will stand with all the redeemed around the Throne, and join in the mighty chorus of the song of Moses and the Lamb.

—The Author

ACKNOWLEDGMENT

In this discussion of the sanctuary the author is deeply indebted to a number of well-qualified Bible specialists who have read the manuscript and offered many constructive and helpful suggestions, which have contributed much to its present value.

Brief excerpts from Reports of Readers of the Manuscript

From *L. L. Caviness*, Ph.D., for years Head of Department of Biblical Languages, Pacific Union College:

This topic is approached in a very intriguing and interesting manner. I am especially pleased with the way the life of the individual Christian is shown in the sanctuary. We are told that before the end the Sabbath is to be proclaimed with increased power. This has been well presented in this manuscript.

From *Raymond F. Cottrell*, A.M., recently of the Department of Religion, Pacific Union College:

The point that much more attention should be given to the sanctuary is well taken. "The Heavenly Sanctuary" as presented in Chapter 15, is most excellent, with which I heartily concur. The redemptive work of Christ and also the life experience of His followers is clearly set forth.

From *Minnie E. Dauphinee*, well-known dean of women in our colleges and sanitariums:

I do not know how to express my gratitude for the privilege of reading this manuscript. I was thrilled to learn the significance of its various parts, the vails, the pillars, the colors, etc. When one of the secretaries of the General Conference was here and read one of the chapters, he exclaimed, "Why, even the juniors could understand that." But I heard a minister, one of the deepest Bible students, say that he had read the manuscript with great profit, had learned much that he had not known before, and had received great spiritual help.

From *William J. Harris*, Associate Secretary of the General Conference Sabbath School Department:

We in the Department think the manuscript is really outstanding. You have given a marvelous presentation of this important subject. Your approach is very different from any I have read before. It is my personal opinion that it would be very valuable as a topic for Sabbath-school lessons. I know it will be a valuable contribution to the literature of the Advent people.

From *L. H. Hartin*, M.A., Head of Department of Religion, Pacific Union College:

To my mind the approach to this subject is very unique in that the entire building as symbols presents spiritual lessons, for every part of the Building given by God was intended to teach the plan of redemption, a truth that to my knowledge has never before appeared in print. Painstaking effort has been made to follow the Bible closely, and this has been done with commendable accuracy. In Chapter 15, "The Heavenly Sanctuary" has been more clearly presented than I have read in any other work. It is a very informative work, and should be to anyone desiring a fuller understanding of the sanctuary.

From *Winifred L. Holmden*, for years Professor of Ancient Languages in several of our colleges:

I consider the manuscript a masterpiece. I like the logical arrangement, especially the closing chapters, which give the final antitype of the court, the holy place and the most holy place. It is a real inspiration. It has helped me to understand some parts of the Bible that I have never understood before.

From *Elder Ernest Lloyd*, widely known as a former member of the Pacific Press editorial staff:

This manuscript is both informative and inspirational. It is a definite contribution to our denominational literature on this vital subject, and is approached in an interesting and helpful manner. It makes plain the work of our great High Priest in heaven, the life experience of each of His followers, the work of the church as a whole in its relation to the earthly sanctuary, to the heavenly sanctuary and to the temple eternal. Our entire church membership should be given the opportunity of studying this subject as presented in this manuscript.

From *Elder Meade MacGuire*, General Conference Field Secretary:

This manuscript is different from any I have ever read before on the sanctuary. I am looking forward to having the book, so I can read it all through again, for to me it is fascinating. I think it would be good to include in a ministerial reading course. I feel sure the book will accomplish much good. I have read many books on the sanctuary, but I got more information and a fuller understanding of the subject from this than from any other. I hope its publication will go forward without delay.

From *W. G .C. Murdoch*, Ph.D., of the Theological Seminary:

I have very much appreciated reading this manuscript. It is Biblical and orthodox. It is approached in an interesting and helpful manner. I hope that nothing will hinder the bringing of this manuscript to fruition.

From *P. E. Quimby*, Ph.D., for many years in the Dept. of Religion Pacific Union College:

This manuscript occupies a field not entered at all by any other writer. It is most vital to every worker and to every church member. It has clarified many Bible problems for me. It is thoroughly orthodox, and will make an excellent contribution to our literature. It most uniquely combines the Bible and the Spirit of Prophecy. It will bring great light, instruction, emphasis and enthusiasm to a subject that has been greatly neglected. It will strengthen all *readers in the Third Angel's Message. I strongly urge and enthusiastically recommend its publication without delay.*

From *G. A. Roberts*, former president of the Inter-American Division, and more recently connected with the General Conference:

I have given the manuscript a careful reading and now have a deeper and far more comprehensive understanding of the sanctuary. I would not presume to criticize that to which has been given such exhaustive study and research. The explanation of Melchizedek is the clearest I have ever read. Because this generation is so far removed from a knowledge of even a tabernacle, a very full and detailed description as set forth is required. It will greatly deepen the Christian experience of sincere readers, as they view the plan of salvation through the sanctuary.

From *O. H. Shrewsbury*, former missionary in India, now retired chaplain, St. Helena Sanitarium:

Since reading this manuscript, I feel most decidedly that our people should be stirred as to the necessity for the study of the sanctuary. This subject is indeed the "present truth" of "Present Truth." My own life has been lifted to a higher plane through my study of this manuscript. Its reading has led to practical changes in my attitude toward the reality of the intercession of my High Priest in the heavenly sanctuary. In fact, His name as High Priest is now His most meaningful name to me. I believe the reading of this manuscript which has been prepared with such care, may serve to help others as it has me. I hope it will soon be made available to our people. I with others have studied and discussed chapter 16, and we are agreed that this presentation of the two Passover's and Pentecost's of A.D. 31, is plain and Biblically correct.

From *A. J. Wearner*, former Head of Dept. of Religion, Union College, Lincoln, Nebraska:

It would be a rare work that would not somewhere be called in question. Yet I have found nothing out of harmony in this manuscript with what we as a people consider orthodox. As a teacher, I could well assign it as special reading for Bible classes. I consider it of outstanding value. It is not just to read and then lay aside. I look forward to having it in book form. The concluding chapters certainly provide a beautiful and fitting climax. I believe that, when printed, it will be a valuable addition to our already rich Seventh-day Adventist literature.

Aside from the Bible itself, which is our unerring guide, the following sources were used: Looking Unto Jesus, by Uriah Smith, published in 1891; S. N. Haskell's book, The Cross and Its Shadow, published in 1914; F. C. Gilbert's books, Practical Lessons from the Experience of Israel, and Messiah in His Sanctuary; M. L. Andreasen's book, The Book of Hebrews; and The Tabernacle in the Wilderness, 1897, by Marcus Rainsford, an old English writer, whose book is no longer obtainable, and others, especially the writings of Mrs. E. G. White.

KEY TO ABBREVIATIONS OF REFERENCES

AA—The Acts of the Apostles
COL—Christ's Object Lessons
CT—Counsels to Teachers
DA—The Desire of Ages
DR—The Prophecies of Daniel and the Revelation
Ed—Education
EW—Early Writings
FBEncy.—Fausett's Bible Encyclopedia
JFB Com.—Jameson, Fausett, and Brown's Commentary
GC—The Great Controversy Between Christ and
Satan
GW—Gospel Workers
HS—Historical Sketches
LJ—Looking Unto Jesus
LS—Life Sketches
MB—Thoughts from the Mount of Blessing, 1900
edition
MH—Ministry of Healing
MYP—Messages to Young People
PP—Patriarchs and Prophets
RH—Review and Herald
SBDict.—Smith's Bible Dictionary
SC—Steps to Christ
SD—Sons and Daughters of God
SP—Spirit of Prophecy
TM—Testimonies to Ministers
T—Testimonies for the Church
YI—Youth's Instructor

SECTION I

THE IMPORTANCE
OF THE SANCTUARY

CHAPTER 1 PREVIEW

THE SANCTUARY
ONE OF GOD'S LESSON BOOKS

- God's Three Books
- God's First Book, The Book of Creation
- The Sanctuary God's Second Book
- God's Third Book - The Written Word

1

THE SANCTUARY
ONE OF GOD'S LESSON BOOKS

God's Three Books. From the creation of the world to the present time, the one outstanding purpose of Heaven has been to make known to man the character and work of our Creator and Redeemer. To accomplish this, God has given three books to the human family: *first*, the book of creation, His word in nature; *second*, the sanctuary, His Word visualized in an object lesson; and *third*, the Bible, the written Word. The grand central theme of each of these books is the plan of salvation. To study any one of them with any other object in view than to understand God's character and His plan for us is to miss His purpose entirely.

God's First Book, The Book of Creation. The book of nature was given to man while he lived in the Garden of Eden. Through the things that God had made, he was to learn of His omnipotent power, His infinite wisdom, His boundless love and goodness. Before sin marred God's plan, these lessons on His character were perfectly revealed in the beauty and fragrance of the flowers, the singing birds, the gorgeous butterflies, the fruitful trees, the beautiful landscape, the clear, healthful air, the life-giving water, the happy contented beasts of the field, and above all in man, made in God's own perfect image. In earth and sea and sky God's character was manifest. "On every leaf of the forest or stone of the mountains, in every shining star,…God's name was written." "God's glory in the heavens, the innumerable worlds in their orderly revolutions, 'the balancings of the clouds,' the mysteries of light and sound, of day, of day and night, —all were open to the study of our first parents." PP 51. And all revealed the divine character of man's adorable Creator and his marvelous Teacher.

The book of nature is still a parable to teach us of heavenly realities, for "as the earth bringeth forth her bud, and as the garden causeth the things that are sown in it to spring forth; so the Lord God will cause righteousness and praise to spring forth before all the nations." Isaiah 61:11.

After sin marred this fair world, nature everywhere revealed the presence and character of the evil one. "The atmosphere, once so mild and uniform in temperature, was now subject to marked changes." PP 61. Satan had become "the prince of the power of the air" [Eph. 2:2], and the terrible conflict between good and evil, between Christ and Satan, was on. This conflict is still on, and this book of nature plainly reveals in death and decay on every hand. To understand this conflict so that we shall line up on God's side is the real objective of true nature study. Unless in our study and teaching of nature, the work of Christ not only as Creator but as Redeemer, is made plain, it cannot truthfully be called *Christian* education, even though it be so labeled.

When Adam and Eve witnessed signs of decay in drooping flowers and falling leaf, we are told that they "mourned more deeply than men now mourn over their dead." PP 62. But they were not left without hope. The book of nature still revealed the love and character of God. In His mercy He has left many of nature's beauties. While nature reveals the presence of the enemy, it also teaches the lesson of redemption. Although death and decay are everywhere manifest, the trees shed their leaves only to put forth new ones in the freshness of the springtime. The plants die only to rise again in fresh verdure at the appointed time. Even man himself as he lays down his life, looks forward to the resurrection, when he shall come forth in immortal youth and glory. Each yearly round demonstrates the spring, summer, autumn, and winter of life, and the resurrection morning. And all show God's gracious care and imperishable love toward all the works of His hand.

"The invisible things of Him from the creation of the world are clearly seen, being understood by the things that are made, even His eternal power and Godhead; so that they are without excuse." Rom. 1:19, 20; 2:13-16; Ps. 19:1-3. In fact, so fully is the plan of redemption made known in the book of nature, that some will be saved who have never known any other book of God. "Among the heathen are those who,…though ignorant of the written law of God,…have heard His voice speaking to them in nature, and have done the things that the law required, … and they are recognized as the children of God." DA 638. Some have never known of the great Sacrifice made for their salvation, and when they see the nail prints in the hands of Christ, they ask, "What are those wounds in Thine hands? Then He shall answer, Those with which I was wounded in the house of My friends." Zech. 13:6. See also PK 376, 377.

The Sanctuary God's Second Book. For about 2500 years the book of creation was man's only lesson book. During this time, he gradually failed to discern the spiritual lessons in nature, until at last the Creator was lost sight of. Then he deified and worshiped the things of nature—the sun, moon, stars, water, earth, and even the animals that God had made for his use. He "worshiped and served the creature more than the Creator," and as a result, his "foolish heart was darkened." Rom. 1:25, 21.

Then God called Abraham away from his idolatrous kindred, that through him and his seed He might reveal to the world His character and His divine purpose. As time went on, the descendants of Abraham were for generations held in Egyptian bondage, where they were fast losing sight of the character of the true God, the Creator, and of the wondrous plan of salvation. Their manner of life made it difficult for them to grasp the grand truths of redeeming love. How were they to be prepared to fulfill Heaven's plan for them?

The Master Teacher knew how. He would teach them through the most marvelous object lesson ever conceived and ever used—the sanctuary. He who knew that nearly ninety percent of what we remember comes through the eyes and the hands, while only about ten percent comes through the ears, emphasized the importance of clearly understanding His plan by appealing first to the ear in giving the most minute and explicit directions for the construction of the sanctuary, next to the eye by showing Moses the pattern, and finally to the hand by instructing the people to unite in its construction. In this masterpiece of true Christian education, this comprehensive textbook of visual education, God demonstrated in perfect detail all the various stages of the plan of redemption, not only for the world as a whole, but for each individual for whom the Lamb of God has given His precious life.

Every step of the way from the moment we enter the gate of the sanctuary and experience justification by accepting the offering made for our sins, typified in the court, through the lifelong process of sanctification, typified in the holy place, into the glory room, the most holy place, where are typified the blotting out of all sin and the granting of life's reward—the entire work of Christ for our salvation is made clear and simple and beautiful and deeply impressive in the book of the sanctuary. It is indeed *The Path to the Throne of God*. And, as in the book of nature each yearly round represents the full span of life, so in His second book, the sanctuary, the complete plan of redemption was repeated in type every year.

Like the book of nature, the book of the sanctuary is for all ages and for people in all walks of life. By means of this divinely planned object lesson, that which otherwise would be a complicated study suited only to the learned, is made plain and simple even to a child.

To the mature Christian student a knowledge of the sanctuary is of inestimable value, because it makes the entire plan of salvation visible in one magnificent view. Through this study he is able to organize and classify his Bible knowledge so that he can see its parts in their proper order and perspective. Indeed, the sanctuary may be compared to a mammoth and limitless filing case, where every essential Bible doctrine has its own place into which it fits perfectly in God's great plan.

When viewed in the light of the sanctuary, the Bible thus becomes a great system of truth, not a scrapbook of disconnected and unrelated fragments. When considered in its fullness, the sanctuary is like a wonderful mosaic of divine revelation; one truth omitted spoils its symmetry; one error introduced mars its perfection. Thus the sanctuary not only illuminates truth, but it reveals error. For this reason the importance of understanding the lessons portrayed in the sanctuary can hardly be overestimated.

A spiritual study of sanctuary is sure to awaken in the Christian student an insatiable longing to delve more deeply into the inexhaustible mine of Bible truth. It will inspire him with a profound love of the truth for these last days. How quickly and how vividly, and how truly will a study of this book of God—the sanctuary—reveal the importance and the eternal perpetuity of the Creator's divine law—the Ten Commandments! Such a study will give the student an experience that will be his anchor through earth's final crisis.

God's Third Book - The Written Word. For about fifteen hundred years the sanctuary was the main book through which God taught His people of His character and the plan of salvation. Not until after the sacrificial lamb met its antitype in the death of the Lamb of God was God's third book, the Bible, completed. Even then it was another fifteen hundred years before the printing press came into use, and the Bible began to be printed in the language of the people, and thus made available to the world.

As in the book of nature and of the sanctuary, so the "grand central theme" of the Bible is Christ and redemption. The Bible is a divine commentary which throws the searchlight of Heaven on the other two books, giving a brilliant illumination to their theme—redemption. While the Bible illuminates the truths worked out in God's wondrous object lesson, the sanctuary, on the other hand the sanctuary is the substructure of the entire Bible. It is not merely a golden thread running throughout the Bible, but it is a complete golden network of truth entering into and binding together into one harmonious whole all parts of Sacred Volume—history and prophecy, poetry and song, law and gospel. It is a visible illumination of all its essential doctrines, giving to each a new and deep significance.

These three books make a vast and complete library of divine revelation, and with them at his command, the student will be enabled to interpret with accuracy not only God's plan for the world as revealed in prophecy, but His plan for himself personally, so that we even more than those who have gone before, shall most surely be "without excuse" Rom. 1:20, if we neglect to study God's three books, and be benefited by their truths.

CHAPTER 2 PREVIEW

THE SANCTUARY,
THE GOSPEL IN THE OLD TESTAMENT

- The Gospel Preached Unto Israel
- By Whom and How Preached
- The Sanctuary a Prophecy of Christ
- The Sanctuary a "Compacted Prophecy"
- Spiritual Significance of the Sanctuary Building
- Individual Christian Experience Taught in the Sanctuary
- The Sanctuary and the Holy Spirit
- The Sanctuary Shows Revelation a Harmonious Whole
- The Sanctuary a Key to Every Doctrine of Salvation
- The Sanctuary Truth Permeates All Scripture
- Four Gospels in Both Old and New Testaments
- The Everlasting Gospel

2

THE SANCTUARY, THE GOSPEL IN THE OLD TESTAMENT

The Gospel Preached Unto Israel. Speaking of the Israelites "that came out of Egypt by Moses," Paul says, "Unto us was the gospel preached, as well as unto them," or, "the gospel was first preached unto them" Heb. 3:16; 4:2,6, margin. Let us not forget that the Israelites had the gospel of Christ preached unto them centuries before it was given to us in the Christian dispensation by New Testament gospel writers.

By Whom and How Preached? Who preached the gospel to Israel? It was preached by Moses. How did he preach it? By means of the sanctuary and its services, a complete system of truth given by God Himself to Israel at Sinai. The sanctuary was for the sole purpose of revealing Christ not only to the Hebrew nation in times past, but to every nation, kindred, tongue, and people to the very end of time, at which time it reaches its climax and reveals the everlasting gospel in its fullness and beauty. Let us ever remember that while the sanctuary *was given* to *ancient* Israel, God's truth there revealed *was written* for *modern* Israel, especially for us "upon whom the ends of the world are come." I Cor. 10:11.

The Sanctuary A Prophecy of Christ. The fact that the gospel was given to Israel through Moses is made plain by Christ Himself as He walked with the two disciples on the way to Emmaeus after His resurrection, when, *"beginning at Moses*...He expounded unto them...the things *concerning Himself."* And later to the eleven He said, "All things must be *fulfilled*, which were written in *the law of Moses*...*concerning Me."* Luke 24:27, 44, italics supplied. Yes, the gospel revealed in the sanctuary was a prophecy concerning Christ, a prophecy that was "fulfilled" in the New Testament gospels. "Through Christ was to be fulfilled the purpose of which the tabernacle was a symbol." Ed. 36. The New Testament is an inspired commentary on the sanctuary of the Old Testament; on the other hand, a spiritual understanding of the sanctuary is essential to a spiritual understanding of the New Testament.

The Sanctuary a "Compacted Prophecy." This prophecy of the gospel, illustrated in the sanctuary and its services, is a complete revelation of the gospel of salvation through Christ. "Christ was the foundation of the Jewish economy. The *whole system* of types and symbols was a *compacted prophecy* of the gospel, a presentation in which were bound up the promises of redemption." AA 14, italics supplied. "In every sacrifice Christ's death was shown. In every cloud of incense His righteousness ascended. By every jubilee trumpet His name was sounded. In the awful mystery of the holy of holies His glory dwelt." Truly, the sanctuary is not only a prophecy of the gospel, but it is a "compacted prophecy." It is literally *packed* with the truths of the gospel.

Spiritual Significance of the Sanctuary Building. Some have thought that, although Christ and the gospel are symbolized in all the services of the sanctuary, it is "absurd" to suppose that the building itself has such significance. Is it absurd? Let us see. F. C. Gilbert, an authority on the Jewish economy says: "Every part [of the sanctuary building] had a special function, and in every way it must be made according to the pattern. Nothing was left for conjecture or supposition; not even the smallest minutia was passed by unheeded." *Practical Lessons from the Experience of Israel*, p. 172.

Here is another, from the *Review and Herald*, June 9, 1949, p. 10: "In types and shadows, each article of furniture, each hanging, every detail of fixture, typified the atonement. Nothing was without spiritual significance." Louise C. Kleuser, Associate Secretary of the General Conference Ministerial Association.

Another: "There was nothing superfluous in its construction,… everything was typical of the heavenly." W. G. C. Murdoch of the Washington Theological Seminary, in *Our Firm Foundation*, Vol I, p. 317.

As we continue our study, this truth will become more and more apparent for we shall find that the boards, the bars, the pillars, the coverings, the embroidery, and the materials used—the fine linen, the blue and purple and scarlet, the wood, the brass, the silver, the gold, the precious stones—all either directly or indirectly represent Christ in some phase of His work for fallen man, and all combine to make the plan of salvation clear, and beautiful, and wonderful.

David had no question on this point. He says, "In His temple *every whit* of it uttereth His glory." Ps. 29:9, margin. Another inspired writer says, "The sanctuary itself [as well as the ministration of the priests] was to serve unto the example and shadow of heavenly things." PP 351-352. "Through Christ was to be fulfilled the purpose of which the tabernacle was a symbol—that glorious building, the walls of glistening gold reflecting in rainbow hues the curtains inwrought with cherubim." Ed. 36. And again, "God designed that the temple at Jerusalem should be a continual witness to the high destiny open to every soul. But the Jews did not understand the significance of the building they regarded with so much pride." DA 161. Let us beware lest, like the Jews, we do not understand the *significance* of the sanctuary *building*. In fact, a spiritual understanding of the sanctuary building as described in the book of Exodus is the true foundation of all sanctuary study. Without this foundation, we cannot so well appreciate the significance of the offerings as recorded in the book of Leviticus, nor can we so well understand the force of the many allusions to the sanctuary which pervade the entire Bible.

Individual Christian Experience Taught in the Sanctuary. Not only was Christ symbolized in all parts of the sanctuary but in it "God desired His people to read His purpose for the human soul." Ed. 36. Another writer puts it this way: "The sanctuary is a dramatized parable of God's dealing with men. To study it is to think

8

God's thoughts after Him. To understand its every detail is to realize to some extent the depths of His wisdom." Robert B. Thurber in *Bible Truth Series*, No. 38. In it is illustrated the complete experience of every true Christian, his reconciliation and justification by faith symbolized in the court, with its *imputed* righteousness, his sanctification by faith in the holy place as a lifelong experience, with its *imparted* righteousness, and his glorification by faith in the most holy place, with its *eternal* righteousness—all are there. The Sanctuary in its fullness is a complete revelation of the gospel of Christ, symbolized for the entire human family. The more fully we understand its details, the more easily and completely shall we comprehend the important closing events now in progress in the heavenly sanctuary—events that most deeply concern our own personal salvation.

The Sanctuary and the Holy Spirit. The sanctuary was not merely the skilled efforts of men who constructed this most wonderful work of art; it was the inspiration of the Holy Spirit working through human instrumentalities. Men called of God were filled "with the Spirit of God" to do this work. Ex. 31:3. Because this work was inspired, we shall find inspired truth not only in the sanctuary as a whole, but in all its parts.

The Sanctuary Shows Revelation a Harmonious Whole. In his book "*Looking Unto Jesus*," pages 56 and 57, Uriah Smith says: "No man can look unto Jesus, and properly understand His position and work, without viewing it in the light of this tabernacle of God, built by Moses in the wilderness—this shadow cast on earth to show forth 'heavenly things'…. This sanctuary is…the great central object in the plan of salvation through Jesus Christ. There is no one object connected with the plan of salvation… in which we see the different subjects of revelation blended together in such a harmonious whole." He further says: The sanctuary "unites the two great dispensations," the Mosaic and the Christian, and shows their relation to each other. It divides with no other subject the high honor of explaining the position and work of our Lord Jesus Christ." The books of Moses, illuminated by this "brilliant lamp," become "animated with life, and radiant with consistency and beauty." Everything connected with the Hebrew worship was suggestive of Christ the Messiah.

More than any other subject, a study of the sanctuary will enable the student "to view the Word as a whole, and to see the relation of its parts." More than any other subject, it will enable him to comprehend "its grand central theme, God's original purpose for the world, the rise of the great controversy, and the work of redemption." Ed. 190.

The Sanctuary a Key to Every Doctrine of Salvation. All the doctrines of salvation through Christ are symbolized in the sanctuary—the gift of God's only begotten Son to the world, His crucifixion, burial, resurrection, and ascension; His work as High Priest, as Judge, and as King Eternal; the work of the angels and of the Holy Spirit.

"There is no other subject which so fully unites all parts of the Sacred Volume into one harmonious whole as this subject of the sanctuary. Every gospel truth centers in the sanctuary service, and radiates from it like the rays of the sun." J. L. Shuler, in *The Great Judgment Day*, p. 51.

The Sanctuary Truth Permeates All Scripture. To every Israelite in Old Testament times and to every true Israelite in the Christian dispensation, the sanctuary was and is the great central object in the plan of salvation. In it, like the spokes of a wheel, all the truths of revelation center in Christ as the hub, thus making a complete circle of gospel truth.

The subject of the sanctuary ramifies and permeates all parts of the Scriptures from Genesis to Revelation. In the Garden of Eden God Himself offered the first sacrifice pointing forward to the sacrifice of His own precious Son on cruel Calvary, and in the skins of which He wrapped His guilty children to protect them from the chill air of transgression. Gen. 3:21. In Revelation, John in his wondrous vision saw the heavenly sanctuary where was revealed the law of God that humanity has violated, Rev. 11:19, while "in the volume of the Book," in Solomon's "Song of songs,"—Solomon carries us forward into eternity, representing the sanctuary as a palanquin, or sedan, in which the "daughters of Zion" go forth to meet their King. Song. 3:6-11. The science of redemption, so marvelously symbolized in God's great object lesson, the sanctuary, is "the key that will unlock the whole treasure house of God's Word." "He who grasps this thought has before him an infinite field for a study,...the study of God's redeemed throughout endless ages." Ed. 126.

A full and spiritual understanding of the sanctuary is the basis of a fundamental and comprehensive knowledge of the Bible, without which we grasp only dimly its great theme—salvation. Is not such a subject worthy of our best mental and spiritual effort?

Four Gospels in Both Old and New Testaments. We usually think of the gospels as the first four books in the New Testament. And these books do present the principles of salvation as demonstrated in the earthly life of Christ. Together they feature His fourfold character:

Christ as King — The Gospel according to Matthew,
Christ as Servant — The Gospel according to Mark,
The humanity of Christ — The Gospel according to Luke,
The divinity of Christ — The Gospel according to John.

But while it is true that the gospel is clearly revealed in the New Testament, we should not lose sight of the fact that it is revealed with equal clearness in the Old Testament. With the book of Genesis as a background and introduction, the next four books written by Moses present in type the work of salvation through Christ. This, *The Gospel According to Moses*, is also in four books:

Christ our Sanctuary —The Book of Exodus,
Christ our Sacrifice —The Book of Leviticus,
Christ our Guide — The Book of Numbers,
Christ our Reward —The Book of Deuteronomy.

In *Exodus*, the gospel is illustrated in the sanctuary itself,—its arrangement, its furniture, and all its parts; in *Leviticus* is illustrated in all the services of the sanctuary; in *Numbers* it is revealed in the wanderings of Israel as Christ in the pillar of fire and cloud guided them through the wilderness to the promised land; in *Deuteronomy*, which, in *Smith's Bible Dictionary*, article *Pentateuch*, is called "the spiritual interpretation and application of the law," is given, as its name indicates, a "repetition of the law" for special emphasis. This final pronouncement of the teachings of the "Gospel according to Moses" was given to prepare Israel to enter the *earthly* Canaan, and it is typical of the final "repetition" and "special emphasis" now given to God's law as a preparation of the Remnant church to leave earth's wilderness and enter the *heavenly* Canaan.

Through the sanctuary of the Old Testament, the gospel is presented in type; the New Testament presents its antitype. The New Testament has its roots deep down in the Old Testament, from which it draws its nourishment and out of which it grows. To belittle or neglect the Old, is to cut the New from its root system, and thus deprive the New of its source of life and power.

"The law [the Old Testament] is the gospel embodied, and the gospel [the New Testament] is the law unfolded. The law is the root, the gospel is the fragrant blossoms and fruit which it bears." COL 128. Without the Old Testament it is impossible to gain a full and correct understanding of the New Testament,—its gospels, the teachings of Paul and the other apostles, or the prophecies of John the Revelator, for all these abound in allusions and references to the sanctuary of the Old Testament. Let us, therefore, beware how we treat this life-giving relationship, for the Old and the New Testaments are God's "two witnesses," which, on severe penalty, we are warned not to "hurt." Rev. 11:3, 5.

The Everlasting Gospel. Many think the books of Moses are uninteresting and monotonous, intended only for ancient Israel, and of no particular value to Christians. Why is this? It is because they have not discerned the life and teachings of Christ in these books that God inspired Moses to write "concerning Himself." Luke 24:27. As we look more closely into this "Gospel According to Moses," as we advance along this *Path to the Throne of God* we shall see that Moses preached the same gospel that John preached: "Behold the Lamb of God, which taketh away the sin of the world." John 1:29. This is the everlasting gospel, the theme of all Scripture, the gospel of salvation for all people in all ages.

CHAPTER 3 PREVIEW

THE SANCTUARY
FOR SPECIAL STUDY IN OUR DAY

- Result of Misunderstanding the Sanctuary
- The Sanctuary to Be Understood by All
- Even Children Should be Taught the Sanctuary
- The Sanctuary Points the Way
- Essential to Faith in Christ
- Sanctuary Study Develops Faith
- Lack of Spiritual Intelligence, a Hindrance
- A Key to Important Prophecies
- It Illuminates God's Last Message
- A Safeguard Against Satan's Deceptions

3

THE SANCTUARY FOR SPECIAL STUDY IN OUR DAY

Result of Misunderstanding the Sanctuary. For many years after the time of the apostles, the study of the sanctuary, God's divine lesson book, was almost entirely neglected, and even those who gave it some attention did not understand its significance.

Had the sanctuary been understood when the second coming of Christ and the cleansing of the sanctuary began to be preached in 1844, God's people would have been saved the consequent ridicule and ignominy that were cast upon it. And, it is safe to add that a revival and correct understanding of this subject in these closing days of the gospel will save God's truth and His people from still further error and disappointment.

The Sanctuary to Be Understood by All. Frequently through the years the importance of giving special attention to a study of the sanctuary has been repeated and emphasized. Take for instance the following, published in 1882: "Such subjects as the sanctuary, in connection with the 2300 days, the commandments of God, and the faith of Jesus...are the *principal subjects* on which the messengers should dwell." EW 63, italics supplied.

Another published in 1888: "The subject of the sanctuary and the Investigative Judgment should be clearly understood by the people of God. *All* need a knowledge for themselves of the position and work of their great High Priest." GC 488.

Such instruction led a few outstanding Bible students, notably Uriah Smith, S. N. Haskell, F. C. Gilbert, M. L. Andreasen, and a few others, to give the church valuable publications that have illuminated the sanctuary of the Scriptures, and unfolded many precious truths.

But for the past half century or more, with few exceptions, a serious study of the sanctuary by church members generally has received but little attention, and in the education of children and young people it has been almost entirely neglected. Therefore, by the church as a whole, it is but dimly understood, and its vital significance but feebly comprehended.

Even Children Should Study the Sanctuary. A study of the sanctuary contains spiritual food for all ages. This subject to which God has given so many chapters in the Scriptures is part of the "all Scripture" which is profitable "that the man of God may be perfect, thoroughly furnished unto all good works." II Tim. 3:16, 17. It is profitable not only to the "*man* of God" but also to the *child*. DA 78, gives us this picture for the children:

"At the age of 12, for the first time the child Jesus looked upon the temple. He saw the white-robed priests performing their solemn ministry. He beheld the bleeding victim upon the altar of sacrifice. With the worshipers He bowed in prayer, while the cloud of incense ascended before God.... Day by day He saw their meaning more clearly. Every act seemed to be bound up with His own life. New impulses were awakening within Him. Silent and absorbed, He seemed to be studying out a great problem. The mystery of His mission was opening to the Saviour."

Even thus in a study of the sanctuary, especially in these closing days of probation, should we who are older contemplate *our* "great problem" that the "mystery" of *our* "mission" may open to us, and "new impulses" awaken within us. It is not to be expected that the child will grasp the full meaning of the sanctuary, but as the consecrated teacher presents the subject in its simplicity, the Holy Spirit will interpret its spiritual truth to his heart, often even more clearly than to the heart of the adult. Let us therefore not deprive the children of a knowledge of the sanctuary truths according to their ability to understand, which is usually greater than grown-ups credit them.

The Sanctuary Points the Way. Why is a correct and more nearly complete understanding of the sanctuary so vital to those who are preparing for the second coming of Christ? Because here, in visible and tangible form, easy to be understood by young and old, learned and unlearned, God has given us in type a symmetrical and complete view of His "way"—the way of salvation, Ps. 77:13, *The Path to the Throne of God*. In the sanctuary David, that hero of faith, that man after God's own heart, saw God's power and glory, Ps. 63:1,2; and he calls upon us to bless God and to praise Him in His sanctuary. Ps. 134: 2; 150:1. Asap, a Levite who wrote several of the Psalms, was one of King David's choir leaders, I Chron. 6:31, 39, and "chief of the singers." Neh. 12:46. Although an inspired seer, 2 Chron. 29:30, he had his perplexities even until his "steps had well nigh slipped," but his problems were solved and his faith restored when he "went into the sanctuary of God." Ps. 73: 2, 17. If more people would follow the example of Asap and King David there would be fewer backsliders in the church today.

Essential to Faith in Christ. Another authority on this subject says that without a knowledge of the sanctuary "it will be impossible for them [church members] to exercise the faith which is essential at this time, or to occupy the position which God designs them to fill. Every individual has .. a case pending at the bar of God. Each must meet the great Judge face to face. How important, then, that every mind contemplate *often* the solemn scene when the Judgment shall sit and the books shall be opened, when, with Daniel, every individual must stand in his lot, *at the end of the days*!" The same writer, continuing says: "The sanctuary in heaven is the very center of Christ's work in behalf of man. It concerns every soul living upon the earth. It opens to view the plan of redemption, bringing us down to the very close of time, and revealing the triumphant issue of the contest between righteousness and sin. It is of the utmost importance that *all* should *thoroughly in-*

vestigate these subjects…. The intercession of Christ in man's behalf in the sanctuary above is as essential to the plan of salvation as was His death upon the cross. By His death He began that work which after His resurrection He ascended to complete in heaven. We must by faith enter within the vail, whither the Forerunner is for us entered. Heb. 6:20. There the light from the cross of Calvary is reflected. There we may gain a clearer insight into the mysteries of redemption. "Jesus has opened the way to the Father's throne, and through His mediation the sincere desire of all who come to Him in faith may be presented before God." GC 488, 489, italics supplied. This "way to the Father's throne" which Jesus has opened for us—*The Path To The Throne of God*—is symbolized in His marvelous object lesson of redemption, the sanctuary, each part of which is like an illuminated signboard pointing the way.

Sanctuary Study Develops Faith. Moses, that great leader of Israel, whom God divinely instructed to build the earthly sanctuary, had such a faith, for of him it is written, "By faith Moses… refused to be called the son of Pharaoh's daughter…Esteeming the reproach of Christ greater than the treasures of Egypt: for he had respect unto the recompense of the reward… By faith he forsook Egypt…for he endured as seeing Him who is invisible." Heb. 11:24-27.

Through a spiritual study of the sanctuary, we too may have the faith that will enable *us* to see "him who is invisible" for He is revealed in all its sacrifices. And as we continue its study we shall be enabled more and more to understand and properly evaluate the "recompense of the reward." With such a faith it will not be difficult to refuse the riches, the honors, the fame of the world, "choosing rather to suffer affliction with the people of God, than to enjoy the pleasures of sin for a season." Without it, "it will be impossible to exercise the faith which is essential at this time, or to occupy the position which God design us to fill." GC 488.

Lack of Spiritual Intelligence, a Hindrance. Andrew Jukes, an old English writer, puts it this way in his book, *The Law of the Offerings*, pages 5, 6:

"I have often been surprised that the inspired parables of the Old Testament [referring to the sanctuary] should have been so neglected. The types [of the sanctuary] are in fact a series of pictures directly from the incomprehensible… These vast and infinite objects He brings before us…with the accuracy of One who views them as they are seen and understood by Himself, and in a way in which they may be seen and understood by us."

This writer ventures further to say that the neglect of a full and earnest study of the sanctuary is due to the fact that this subject "requires more spiritual intelligence than many Christians can bring to it; we know so little [of the things of God] and, what is worse, we do not know our ignorance." Our "infancy in Christ, our lack of growth, hinder our understanding." And we excuse ourselves "under the plea that these things are not important or at least not essential."

What an indictment not only against Christians in general, many of whom are still in darkness regarding the present position and work of our High Priest in the sanctuary above, but even against many—altogether too many—Christians who profess to be looking for His soon return to this earth when His work as Intercessor is finished. To such it is not only an indictment but it should be a challenge.

A Key to Important Prophecies. The relation of the sanctuary to important prophecies is thus expressed by another reliable writer: The sanctuary "is a key to the interpretation of some of the most important prophecies pertaining to the present time. Neglecting to use this, an expositor can hardly come to right conclusions; using it, he can scarcely go astray. It shows our present light, draws out the heart in practical Christianity, points the inquirer the way to Christ, shows on what lines the Judgment proceeds, how and when the work of mercy for this world will close, Christ appear, redemption be completed, and the blessings of the everlasting covenant be secured. Strange [strange indeed] that a subject occupying so important a position in the divine economy should have been so long overlooked. Strange that so few *even now* are found to give it in any degree their attention, still less their study." Uriah Smith in *Looking Unto Jesus*, pp. 57, 58.

It Illuminates God's Last Message. The sanctuary illustrates not only the plan of salvation in general, but it points out the great gospel truths that pertain particularly to our own time and on down to the very end of time. It makes clear God's last message to the world: "The hour of His Judgment is come." Rev. 14:7. It points out both the time and the event that marked the beginning of this message—the time was the end of the 2300 days, the event is the cleansing of the heavenly sanctuary, or the beginning of the Investigative Judgment. Dan. 8:14.

In this movement only—the proclamation of the third angel's message of Revelation 14:6-12—is it made a prominent feature, and by those only who accept and proclaim this message, is it regarded as vital to Christian experience and to a full and broad comprehension of almost, if not entirely, all Bible truth. As a correct understanding of the sanctuary opened up God's last message, and shed a flood of light on all lines of Bible truth due at that time, so at its close a revival of sanctuary study will vitalize Christian experience and strengthen our faith in the *closing* work of God.

In the sanctuary are revealed all the truths that characterize the Remnant church. Here are found the perpetuity of God's law, and the eternal character of the Sabbath, the gift of the Spirit of prophecy, the Judgment of the human family, the second coming of Christ to this earth to take His people to their eternal home. "The recovery of the truth concerning the sanctuary and its cleansing has been the most unique and outstanding contribution of the Remnant church, because in it is brought to view a complete system of truth into which every doctrine of the Bible is integrated and made very present truth to this closing generation of earth's history. When taught in its relation to the sanctuary service, each doctrine will be seen in the light that streams from Calvary and will contribute to a better understanding of Jesus as the central theme of the Scriptures." B. P. Hoffman, in RH, Feb. 3, 1949. Indeed, as some has concisely stated, "The sanctuary is not so much a doctrine as it is a system of standards by which to evaluate the validity of the many accepted beliefs to be found in the Christian church."

A Safeguard Against Satan's Deceptions. "Satan,...the arch deceiver, hates the great truths that bring to view an atoning Sacrifice and an all-powerful Mediator," and he "invents unnumbered schemes to occupy our minds that they may not dwell upon the very work with which we ought to be best acquainted." GC 488.

"In the future, deception of every kind is to arise, and we want solid ground for our feet. The enemy will bring in false theories that there is no sanctuary. This is one of the points on which there will be a departure from the faith." Ellen G. White in RH, May 25, 1905, page 17.

Because the sanctuary so fully reveals the work of Christ in these last days, therefore, as J. E. Fulton has well stated in his book, *The Sanctuary*, page 10: "At no point does Satan seek to obscure our vision and confuse our minds more than in the sanctuary." In a correct understanding and spiritual appreciation of the sanctuary in all its many phases, the subtle work of the enemy is completely unmasked so that none need be deceived. Certainly no hazy knowledge, no indefinite idea, of this most important Bible truth is sufficient now.

SECTION II

PREPARING TO BUILD

CHAPTER 4 PREVIEW

ISRAEL'S PREPARATION FOR SERVICE

- The First Passover
- Deliverance "at Midnight"
- "Out of Egypt the Selfsame Day"
- The Song of Moses
- Arrival at Mount Sinai
- The First Pentecost
- God Speaking His Law
- Moses Given the Judgments and Reading them to Israel
- In the Mount with God
- The "Pattern" Given to Moses
- Exact and Minute Description Given
- "A Shadow of Things to Come"
- God's Final Word to Moses
- His Law Engraved in Tables of Stone

4

ISRAEL'S PREPARATION FOR SERVICE

The First Passover. Preparatory to entering upon the sacred work of constructing the sanctuary, God led the Israelites through experiences designed to strengthen their faith and better qualify them for the task. Chief among these was their miraculous deliverance from Egyptian bondage and idolatry. When the exact time arrived God laid bare His mighty arm to set them free. To mark this great event, in obedience to His command, each household, on the tenth day of Abib (See Appendix page 25), the first month, selected a lamb "without blemish, a male of the first year." The lamb was kept until the fourteenth day of Abib, when it was slain "in the evening"; that is, between three P.M. and sunset, and the blood sprinkled on the door posts of every house where the Israelites were assembled. It was then "roast with fire." "In that night," the early hours of Abib 15, it was eaten with unleavened bread and bitter herbs. Ex. 12:1-9.

The bitter herbs were to be a reminder of their release from bitter bondage; the unleavened bread was "bread of affliction; for thou camest forth in haste;" They were "thrust out." Deut. 16:3; Ex. 12:33, 39. The lamb roasted with fire typified the fiery trials of "the lamb of God," who was "wounded for our transgressions," "oppressed" and "afflicted." Isaiah 53:4-12. The blood put on the doors for the protection of those within, symbolized the blood of Christ, shed to protect them from the power of sin.

This service was called the Passover because, when the Lord smote all the first-born of the Egyptians, He *passed over* the house of Israel where the blood had been sprinkled. It was "for a memorial" to be observed in commemoration of their deliverance. It was to be "an ordinance forever," Ex. 12:14, and throughout eternity those whose sins have been washed away by the blood of Christ, will continue to celebrate their great deliverance.

The Passover was not observed in the wilderness. PP 406, 485; Ex. 12:25; Josh. 5:10. Regarding it, the Lord told Moses, "When ye be come to the land which the Lord will give you…ye shall keep this service from year to year," and when your children ask, "What mean ye by this service?" explain to them its divine significance which even children were to understand. Ex. 12:25-27; 13:10. As we explain these things to our children today, let us make it plain that the plagues sent on Egypt at this time were not against the people but against "all the gods of Egypt." Ex. 12:12. They were designed to teach the Egyptians the power of the true God and the utter helplessness of all false gods, which could not protect even the firstborn dedicated to their idolatrous worship. Ex. 11:4, 5.

Deliverance "at Midnight." It was "at midnight" when all the firstborn of Egypt were slain; "there was not a house where there was not one dead." Immediately all Egypt was aroused, and the king sent Moses an urgent command to leave the land in haste, lest they be all dead men. Ex. 12:29-33. By this time every arrangement had been made for their departure. The people had been "divided into companies under appointed leaders." Every man and woman had visited the Egyptians and "claimed a recompence for their unpaid labor." The Lord gave them such favor in the sight of the Egyptians that they were given jewels of silver and jewels of gold, and whatever they asked. The amount collected was so great that it is written "they spoiled the Egyptians." Ex. 11:2,3; 12:35, 36; PP 281; Ed. 37. The Passover had been observed with loins girded, shoes on feet, and staff in hand, Ex. 12:11, so when Pharaoh issued his command, immediately after midnight, "the bondmen went forth laden with the spoil of their oppressors." God "brought them forth with silver and gold" and Egypt was glad when they departed. PP 281; Ps. 105:37, 38. This fulfilled the prophecy that at the end of their 400 years of affliction, they would come out "with great substance." Gen. 15:13, 14.

Israel "departed from Rameses on the fifteenth day of the first month." Num. 33:3. They went out "by night," they went out "in haste" for the command was urgent. Deut. 16:1; Ex. 12:33. They were "thrust out." Ex. 12:39. But, although thrust out in haste, they went out not in disorder. "Israel went harnessed [in orderly array—*Moffatt*] out of...Egypt." Ex. 13:18.

"Out of Egypt" "the Selfsame Day." It should be clearly understood that the expression "the selfsame day" applies not only to the 430 years sojourning, Ex. 12:40, but also to the 400 years of bondage. Gen. 15:13. Both periods ended on the selfsame day. On that very day God laid bare His arm to fulfill His promise. He brought them forth from Egypt by "strength of hand." Ex. 13:14. God is the "wonderful numberer." Dan. 8:13, margin. He foreknows every event and the exact time when it will occur. He makes no mistakes in His plans.

Arriving at Succoth, they baked unleavened cakes of the dough they had brought with them, for being "thrust out" they had not "prepared for themselves any victual." Ex. 12:39. From Succoth, instead of continuing eastward, the cloud that guided them directed southward to Etham "in the edge of the Wilderness." Ex. 13:20. [This led Pharaoh to conclude that they were "entangled in the land."] From here they were directed to journey to Pihahiroth and encamp by the Sea.

The places along the Red Sea, which is the eastern boundary of Egypt, were fortresses where guards were stationed to signal the approach of danger. "After the Hebrews had been gone from Egypt some days," 1SP 206, these guards sent the warning message to Pharaoh that instead of serving God in the wilderness, as Moses had requested, Ex. 5:1, the people were fled. Ex. 14:5.

Immediately the king's army followed in hot pursuit, planning to recover part of the spoil and, if necessary, destroy some of the people. They overtook Israel at the Sea. Ex. 14:3-9; 15:9.

"The third night after leaving Rameses they [Israel] found themselves walled in on each side by mountain ranges, while the Red Sea lay before them." 4T 21. In spite of apparently insurmountable difficulties, the command of the Lord was, "Go forward." Ex. 14:15.

To make this possible, another mighty miracle was wrought. The guiding cloud passed between the two armies, becoming a pillar of darkness to Pharaoh's army, but of light to Israel. "All that night," Ex. 14:21, God held the waters of the Sea in check and Israel passed over on dry ground. In "the morning watch," [the watch before the dawn—*Moffatt*] the entire army of Pharaoh, attempting to follow, was drowned in the Sea. Ex. 14:10-31.

The Song of Moses. In commemoration of this event Moses, under the inspiration of the Holy Spirit, wrote one of the most remarkable songs on record, a song that still bears his name—"the Song of Moses." That "same day he directed to commit it to memory ... and to teach it to their children and children's children." It was not to be forgotten, for it was to "testify against them as a witness," when they should depart from God. Deut. 31:19-22; PP 467-468; Ed. 39. While it expressed thanksgiving to God for His deliverance, it pointed forward not only to the earthly but also to the heavenly sanctuary. Ex. 15:17, 18.

> "I will sing unto the Lord, for He hath
> triumphed gloriously.
> Pharaoh's chariots and his host...his chosen
> captains also are drowned in the Red Sea."
> "The Lord...is become my salvation: He is my God
> and I will prepare him an habitation.
> **(the earthly sanctuary)...**

> "Thou shalt bring them in and plant them
> in the mountain of Thine inheritance,
> In the place, O Lord, which Thou hast made
> for Thee to dwell in,
> In the sanctuary, O Lord, which Thy hands have
> established."
> **(the heavenly sanctuary)** Ex. 15:1, 2, 4, 17.

All the women led by Miriam, the prophetess, the sister of Aaron, with timbrels in their hands, joined in the grand chorus. Ex. 15:20, 21. Over desert and sea rang the joyous refrain. It would seem that Israel spent most of this wonderful day memorizing and singing this immortal song. It was a day of great rejoicing. Its Antitype, the *Song of Moses and the Lamb*, Rev. 15:2, 3, will be sung around the eternal throne when all the enemies of God's people are destroyed, and His eternal sanctuary is established. PP 467, 468. That will be a day of still greater rejoicing.

Arrival at Mount Sinai. Israel reached Mount Sinai the third month, "the same day;" that is, the third day, Sivan 3. Ex. 19:1 (See Appendix page 25. Here they "camped before the mount," [Ex. 19:2], where they were to remain about one year. After they had camped, they spent the first two days—"today and tomorrow"—Sivan 3 and 4, (See Appencix page 25) washing their clothes and sanctifying themselves. Ex. 19:10, 14. This was the necessary physical and spiritual preparation to meet with God, who on the third day, Sivan 5, after their arrival was to appear in a thick cloud on Mount Sinai and speak His law in their hearing. Ex. 19:9; Deut. 4:10-13.

The First Pentecost. The word Pentecost means fiftieth. It was so named because this ordinance was to be celebrated on the fiftieth day from "the morrow after" the ceremonial sabbath; that is after the day the Passover was eaten. It is also called the Feast of Weeks, because it was "seven Sabbaths...complete," Lev. 23:15, 16, "seven full weeks" [*Moffatt*], a "week of weeks." Ex. 34:22; Deut. 16:9, 10, 16. This first Pentecost fell on Sivan 5, the third day after Israel's arrival at Sinai. Ex. 19:16 (See Appendix page 25). "In the morning" of this day, Ex. 19:16, "Moses brought forth the people out of the camp to meet with God." Which day does the Bible recognize as God's special day? From Genesis 2:3 and Exodus 20:11, we learn that the seventh day is the Sabbath of the Lord thy God. They took their stand at the foot of the mount, outside the "bounds" which God had told Moses to set about it. Ex. 19:12.

Upon the mount a thick cloud rested, and on top "the glory of God was like devouring fire." Ex. 19:9; 24:17. It was like a heavenly pulpit for here "the Father and the Son, attended by a multitude of angels," were present to address the people. PP 304, 339. These angel attendants were "the chariots of God...even thousands of angels. The Lord is among them, as in Sinai." Ps. 68:17. Describing the scene later, Moses said, "He came with ten thousand of saints," Deut. 33:2, and David, in his poetic style, wrote, "He bowed the heavens...and came down." Ps. 18:9. Out of the cloud, lightning flashed and thunders roared and "Mount Sinai was altogether on a smoke because the Lord descended on it in fire; and the smoke thereof ascended as the smoke of a furnace, and the whole mount quaked greatly ... and the trumpet sounded long, and waxed louder and louder," so that all the people trembled. Ex. 19:17-19. This manifestation of divine power and glory indicated that God had something of great importance to say to His people.

God speaking His Law. Out of the cloud, a voice like a trumpet blast was heard. Ex. 19:16. "Christ and the Father, standing side by side...proclaimed God's divine law, the Ten Commandments." HS 231; Ex. 20:1-17. Because of the fiery display about the cloud, Moses fittingly declared, "From His right hand went a fiery law." Deut 33:2. So terrible was the sight and so awe-inspiring God's voice that even Moses said, "I exceedingly fear and quake." Heb. 12:21. Never before, since the voice of the Eternal spoke the worlds into existence, had there been a more sublime scene. The Ten Commandments, spoken by God's own voice from Mount Sinai, Ex. 19:9: 29:22, was Jehovah's fundamental law, the constitution, for the government of the nation and the church which at this time He organized. PP 303. This is the only time that with audible voice God ever addressed His assembled people on earth, an event well calculated to inspire in man the solemnity and sacredness of the law of God, His eternal law that governs the entire universe.

As "the Passover was to be both commemorative and typical, not only point-ing back to the deliverance from [the bondage of] Egypt, but forward to the greater deliverance which Christ was to accomplish in freeing His people from the bondage of sin," PP 277, so also Pentecost was both commemorative and typical. As commemorative, Webster says "it was instituted to be a memorial of the gift of the law on the fiftieth day after Israel's departure from Egypt." To this agree Fausset's Bible Encyclopedia, Smith's Bible Dictionary, Clark's Commentary, and "most of the later Jews." From that time Pentecost was to be an annual reminder of Israel's covenant with God to obey His law, Ex. 19:8; 24:7, and of their sacred obligation to teach it to all the nations; and as typical, it pointed forward to the time when Christ's representative, the Holy Ghost, was to set apart the Christian church to carry to the whole world, to every nation under heaven a knowledge of the law as fulfilled in Jesus Christ, its Author. Acts 2:5-12; Matt. 5:17.

At this first Sabbath morning service at Sinai, the congregation consisted of the entire body of God's chosen people—603,550 men twenty years old and upward, Num. 1:45, 46, besides women, and children under twenty. God Himself was the Speaker; His sermon, brief but emphatic, His eternal law, the Ten Command-ments—spoken in their hearing. Ex. 19:9; 20:22. This memorable occasion was certainly the most outstanding Sabbath morning service ever held on this Earth.

It certainly did not take a long time for God to speak the Ten Command-ments—His "ten words," as Rotherham has literally translated Deut. 4:13 from the Hebrew, for anyone can read them audibly, slowly, and with appropriate emphasis in much less than ten minutes. But the fiery display on the mountain, the roaring of thunder, and the majesty of God's voice, so terrified the people that they urgently requested Moses "Speak thou with us and we will hear, but let not God speak to us lest we die." Ex. 20:19.

God heard their cry. Although He had more to say to them that morning, He listened to their request and in His compassion and tender mercy, did not chide them for their fear. He understood their distress as He always understands us in trouble. God did not ignore their plea, but instead of speaking to them direct, He called Moses to Him. After giving him specific directions for building an altar He said unto Moses, "Thus thou shalt say unto the children of Israel… These are the judgments which thou shalt set before them." Ex. 20:22; 21:1. This change in chapters well illustrates the fact that the division of the Bible into chapters is manmade and not inspired, these judgments being merely a continuation of the narrative of Chapter 20.

Moses Given the Judgments and Reading Them to Israel. God dictated these judgments to Moses who wrote them in a book. They are recorded in Exodus 21, 22 and 23.

These civil laws were called judgments because they were to guide Israel to manifest justice in matters regarding their relation to one another. Moses read these civil laws to the most influential of the people who promised or covenanted to obey. Thus ended this never-to-be-forgotten Sabbath Day. Ex. 24:3-7.

In the Mount with God. "Early in the morning," Sivan 6, (See Appendix next page) an altar was built under the hill, according to the directions God had given Moses. On it sacrifices were offered, and the covenant duly ratified. Ex. 20:24-26; 24:4-8. The glory of God, which to Israel looked like blazing fire, still rested on the top of the mount, and for six days the cloud covered it. Ex. 24:16, 17 (See Appendix next page). During this time, Moses with seventy elders and a few others whom God called, went into the cloud where they spent the time in heart-searching, meditation, and prayer. To Moses this was a time of preparation for closer communion with God. Ex. 24:9. While all the people saw the glory of God, to these chosen ones was given a closer view. The God of Israel was above them. Under His feet they saw "as it were a paved work of a sapphire stone [a sky-blue stone, one of the most valuable and lustrous of the precious gems], and as it were the body of heaven in his clearness." Ex. 24:1, 3, 10.

At the close of the six days, "on the seventh day, Sivan 12 (See Appendix next page) [which was the Sabbath, PP 313], Moses, at the divine call, went alone into the midst of the cloud where God was. Since it is true that the seventh day, Sivan 12, the day Moses went into the presence of God, was the Sabbath, is it not equally true that the previous seventh day, the day God spoke His law from Sinai, was the Sabbath? Moses remained in the mount forty days and forty nights, Ex. 24:18. During this time he received the tables of stone and complete directions for making the sanctuary, the earthly dwelling place for God.

The Pattern Given to Moses. The earthly sanctuary was to be a "pattern of the things in the heavens" Heb. 9:23, "a figure for the time then present" of "a greater and more perfect tabernacle, not made with hands." Heb. 9:9-11. It was to be "a miniature representation," God also gave Moses detailed instructions for building the sanctuary. "Moses wrote all the directions in a book, and read them to the most influential of the people." 1SP 269. For our learning, they are recorded in the book of Exodus, chapters 25 to 31 inclusive.

The words "representation" and "book" as here used agree perfectly with the translation of the word "pattern" in *Exodus* and in *Hebrews* as given by Hebrew and Greek scholars; namely, that the word "pattern" indicates a *model*, though it may also include a *book*. "He [God] presented before Moses a miniature model of the heavenly sanctuary, and commanded him to make all things according to the pattern shown him in the mount." 1SP 269. This makes it doubly plain that when Moses was in the mount, God showed him a miniature *model*, "a figure" of the heavenly sanctuary, and then dictated instructions which he wrote in a *book* as a guide in the construction of the earthly sanctuary. In this sense, both the *model* and the *book* were the *pattern*.

Exact and Minute Description Given. Bible expositors in general agree that the *services* of the sanctuary illustrates the work of Christ in the plan of salvation. As already noted, the various parts of the *building* itself also symbolized His re-

APPENDIX

ABIB

Sun	Mon	Tue	Wed	Thu	Fri	Sab
						1
2	3	4	5	6	7	8
9	10	11	12	13	14	15
16	17	18	19	20	21	22
23	24	25	26	27	28	29
30						

ZIF

Sun	Mon	Tue	Wed	Thu	Fri	Sab
	1	2	3	4	5	6
7	8	9	10	11	12	13
14	15	16	17	18	19	20
21	22	23	24	25	26	27
28	29					

SIVAN

Sun	Mon	Tue	Wed	Thu	Fri	Sab
		1	2	3	4	5
6	7	8	9	10	11	12
13	14	15	16	17	18	19
20	21	22	23	24	25	26
27	28	29	30			

Abib 14	—	Passover: Ex. 12:2; 13:4; GC 399
Sivan 3	—	Sinai Encampment: Ex. 19:1
Sivan 5	—	Law Given: Ex. 19:10, 11, 16; Ex. 20:17
Sivan 12	—	Moses Called into cloud after six days preparation. Ex. 24:12-18; PP 313.

demptive work. If this be not true, why did the Divine Architect give so much space in the inspired Word to such a minute description of each part of this spiritual object lesson? Why did He require such exactness of detail, such skill, such wisdom and perfection in the execution of His plan? And why was He so particular to admonish Moses, and frequently to repeat the command, "Look that thou make them after the pattern which was showed thee in the mount?" Ex. 25:9, 40; Heb. 8:5. Eighteen times in Exodus 39 and 40, it is stated that the *details of the sanctuary building* were made "as the Lord commanded Moses."

Not only the services of the sanctuary but "the sanctuary itself ... was to serve unto the example and shadow of heavenly things." Heb. 8:5; PP 351. Therefore the Lord, through Moses, gave the most definite instruction concerning every part.

Jamieson, Fausset, and Brown Commentary states it this way: "It is impossible to account for the circumstance of God's descending to such minute details, except on the assumption that the tabernacle was to be of a typical character." By way of emphasizing its fullness of spiritual meaning, A. T. Pierson, an eminent Bible student and writer says: "Typical structure and furniture are shown in the tabernacle, the description of which, with its contents and ritual, occupies more room in the Bible than any other single object or subject in the Old or New Testaments, and there must be a reason for it. Every detail of the tabernacle is described, and seven times in all is reference made to the pattern shown in the Mount, to emphasize the fact that in no respect, however, minute, was that pattern to be disregarded. Ex. 25:9, 40; 25:30; 27:8; Num. 8:4; Acts 7:44; Heb. 8:5; I Chron. 28:11, 12, 18, 19." (*God's Living Oracles*, p. 130).

What does all this mean? Is it not that God would thus emphasize the *importance of its study*? Moreover, in the space thus occupied many things are repeated. Surely God does not multiply words without a purpose. "Every word of God is pure." Prov. 30:5. "The words of the Lord are pure words; as silver tried in a furnace of earth, purified seven times." Ps. 12:6. Why then this repetition? Why did God repeat Pharaoh's dream about the years of plenty and the years of famine? "That the dream was doubled unto Pharaoh twice." We are told, "It is because the thing is *established by God*." Gen. 41:32, italics supplied. The dream contained information vital to the *physical and temporal* life of the king and the nation, and the sanctuary contains truth that is vital to our *spiritual and eternal* life. In repeating, God would have these truths to be "established." For this reason the student must dig, and dig deep, to find the hidden treasures wrapped up in the sanctuary.

"A Shadow of Things to Come." The sanctuary has been fittingly called "a shadow picture of Christ." Paul speaks of it as "a shadow of things to come; but the body is of Christ." Paul speaks of it as "a shadow of things to come; but the body is of Christ." Col. 2:17. Christ is indeed the key to these types, as He is the key to the whole Bible. With this key in the hand of faith, our study will be richly rewarded.

The sanctuary is not only a shadow picture of Christ, it is a shadow picture to teach us about God the Father, the Holy Spirit, and the angels as ministering spirits in their work to save us. It also represents the experience of every true believer as well as of the church in all its generations; all compose the "building fitly framed together unto an holy temple in the Lord...for an habitation of God through the Spirit." Eph. 2:21, 22; a dwelling place of God, a "temple of the Holy Ghost." I Cor. 6:19.

God's Final Word to Moses. During the forty days that Moses was in the mount, nothing regarding the building of the sanctuary was left to his imagination or devising. Every detail was divinely dictated. At the end of this time, he was to return to the people and communicate the instruction to them. But! Wait a moment! God has one final word of great importance—a command that involves life or death to His people. In their ardor to see the work go forward, they might forget, so He sent a warning that not a stroke of even so sacred a work as building a dwelling place for God, was to be done on the Sabbath. "Verily," He emphasized, "My Sabbaths ye shall keep, for it is a sign between Me and you throughout your generations; that ye may know that I am the Lord that doth sanctify you. Ye shall keep the Sabbath therefore; for it is holy unto you: every one that defileth it shall surely be put to death; for whomsoever doeth any work therein, that soul shall be cut off from among his people!" Ex. 31:13, 14. This was the climax of that long and very important interview between God and Moses.

His Law Engraved in Tables of Stone. Although Israel had seen the glory of God that rested on Mount Sinai, and had heard His voice as He spoke His law, God "did not...trust His precepts to the memory of a people who were prone to forget His requirements, but wrote them upon tables of stone." PP 364. When He "had made an end of communing with Moses upon Mount Sinai," He gave unto him these "two tables of testimony; tables of stone, written with the finger of God." Ex. 31:18. This "testimony" was the Ten Commandments. Ex. 34:28.

On what kind of stone did God write the Ten Commandments? The only stone mentioned in the description of His presence on Mount Sinai is the precious "sapphire stone," a blue sapphire stone, like "the body of heaven in his clearness." Ex. 24:10. How fitting that on the stone which formed the "paved work"—the pavement or foundation under the feet of God—when He spoke His law, the eternal God should write His eternal law, which is the foundation of His eternal throne! And how fitting that it should be a *blue* stone, a color indicating obedience to heavenly truth! Num. 15:36-40.

"The tables were the work of God, and the writing was the writing of God, graven upon the tables." Ex. 32:15, 16. "Graven," that is, cut or carved in sunken pattern, impressed deeply or indelibly similar to cloisonne work for which Chinese artists have been famous. What excellent illustration this indelible writing is of the indelible character of God's law! It cannot be erased; it cannot be changed; it is the writing of God.

"And Moses turned, and came down from the mount, and the two tables of the testimony were in his hand." Ex. 32:15. When, because of the apostasy of Israel, these tables were broken, Moses, at the command of God, "cut two tables of stone, like the former ones." Then, "early in the morning" he went up into Mount Sinai "… and took in his hand the two tablets of stone." Upon them God condescended to write again "the words that were on the former tablets." Ex. 34:1, 2, 4 *Moffatt*. Is not this a marvelous illustration of God's patience and mercy toward these who break His law?

CHAPTER 5 PREVIEW

"THAT I MAY DWELL AMONG THEM"

- Our Father's Longing Desire
- What Is a Sanctuary?
- A "Little Sanctuary" in Our Hearts
- Oneness with God
- Dwelling with God Eternally

5

"THAT I MAY DWELL AMONG THEM"

Our Father's Longing Desire. "Let them make Me a sanctuary that I may dwell among them." Ex. 25:8. How lightly we read the pathetic words, "that I may dwell among them." Yet what a volume of pent-up love and yearning for His wayward children do they contain! A simple little story may help us to feel the depth of tenderness wrapped up in those few words—"that I may dwell among them."

Bobby had been a very naughty boy. For three successive days he had absented himself from school without his parents' permission or knowledge. Fearing he might be ill, the teacher called to inquire. The parents were amazed and deeply grieved that their child had deceived them. They were at their wits' end to know how to train him so that eventually he would grow up to noble manhood. Some punishment must be administered. The parents talked it over and decided to deprive him of his liberty for three days, the same length of time that he had abused his liberty. During this time he was confined in the attic, where he could think quietly by himself. There he was given a comfortable bed, and at meal times Daddy carried his food to him. Night came, and Bobby was tucked into bed. Then the parents retired; but not to sleep. The father tossed from side to side. He was thinking of little Bobby alone in the attic.

"What's the matter, John?" asked the mother; "Why don't you go to sleep?"

"I can't," said the father, "I think I'll go up and stay with Bobby."

So up the attic stairs he went. He opened the door. There was Bobby, wide awake, sobbing softly to himself. The father crept under the bed covers by the side of his child. He put his arms around him and kissed the tears away. All he could say was:

"Daddy loves you, son; Daddy wants you to be a good boy." Their tears mingled. The naughty but now penitent child began to realize that wrongdoing does not pay. Each night the fond father chose Bobby's bed in the attic to his own comfortable bed. He could not enjoy his own pleasant room while Bobby must stay in the attic. At last the three days were over; Bobby had learned his lesson, and was restored to his place in the family.

So it is with our heavenly Father. Because of the leprosy of sin we have been isolated—separated from His presence. But His great heart of Father love yearns after His wayward children. "All heaven took a deep and joyful interest in the creation of the world and of man. Human beings were a new and distinct order. They were made 'in the image of God.'" Gen. 1:27. *Review and Herald*, Feb. 11, 1902. Quoted in *SDA Commentary*, Vol. I, p. 1081. Though sin has marred the Creator's work, the Father cannot endure to be separated from those whom He created in His own image. He must be with them. But how? In the person of His Son, Jesus our Redeemer, He issues the loving command, "Let them make Me a sanctuary, that I may dwell among them"—a sanctuary that will show them the way back to the Father's throne.

What Is a Sanctuary? A sanctuary is a place set apart for a sacred purpose. Sometimes a person reserves a room in his home for his own personal use, a place where he may get away from the distracting activities and cares of life and be alone for quiet thought and study. He calls this room his *sanctum*. The word "sanctuary" contains the same thought as "sanctum," which literally means "holy." If the person wishes to emphasize the fact that his sanctum is strictly private, he speaks of it as his *sanctum sanctorum*, which literally means "holy of holies." Webster says: "A sanctuary is a sacred place of refuge and protection." God invites us to make Him our Sanctuary, our place of refuge and protection, where we may flee for quiet communion with Him.

A "Little Sanctuary" in Our Hearts. As the setting up of the sanctuary at Sinai marked a new era in Israel's experience, so when the sanctuary is set up in our hearts, it will make a new era in our Christian experience. Indeed, the Lord has promised that in all our heart wanderings far off among the heathen, He will be to us "as a little sanctuary" in the countries of our captivity and sojourn. Eze. 11:16. How beautiful the figure, that with God's sanctuary in our hearts as "the chapel of His presence," we shall be safe from the snares and pitfalls of the enemy!

Oneness with God. "That I may dwell *among them*." Ex. 25:8. The actual thought in this text, we are told, is that I may dwell *in them*. God's desire is to dwell in His followers. "As thou, Father, art in Me, and I in thee, that they also may be one in us." John 17:21. "Christ became one flesh with us, in order that we might become one Spirit with Him." DA 388. Even as in Christ "dwelleth all the fullness of the Godhead bodily," so God longs to dwell *in* His people, "that they may be made perfect in one." John 17:23. This is the very closest relationship possible, a relationship found in the expression, "that I may dwell among them."

In the sanctuary building, this unity of God and His people is illustrated by the fact that its various parts symbolize not only Christ but also what His followers should be. And so, as we study, "we walk together, My Lord and I." Enoch walked with God until God took him to heaven, and the sanctuary teaches us that we must walk with Him on earth before He can take us to live with Him in Heaven. The language of our heart must be:

> "O let me walk with thee, my God,
> As Enoch walked in days of old."

"He that sanctifieth and they who are sanctified are all of one: for which cause He is not ashamed to call them brethren." Moreover, "God is not ashamed to be called their God." Heb. 2:11; 11:16.

Rainsford, an old English writer, speaks of the sanctuary as a pledge of God's purpose to dwell with man; a representation of the true believer as "the temple of the Holy Ghost" I Cor. 3:16; 6:19; of the church "Which is His body, the fulness of Him that filleth all in all" Eph. 1:23; a vivid and unmistakable representation of the way of access for sinners to God—*The Path to the Father's Throne.*

Dwelling With God Eternally. This wondrous object lesson, both as a whole and in its parts, is designed to teach this lesson of oneness with the Father, to illustrate God's everlasting purpose to make the human soul His dwelling place, His temple, His sanctuary. "It is by virtue of this union that we are to come forth from the grave, —not merely as a manifestation of the power of Christ, but because, through faith, His life has become ours. Those who see Christ in His true character and receive Him into the heart, have everlasting life ..." DA 388. The Spirit of God received into the heart by faith is the beginning of the life eternal. Then will be completely fulfilled the victorious words of inspiration: "Behold the tabernacle [dwelling place] of God is with men, and He will dwell with them, and they shall be His people, and God Himself shall be with them, and be their God." Rev. 21:3.

CHAPTER 6 PREVIEW

"WILLING-HEARTED" GIVING

- Sabbath Keeping of First Importance
- Christ, or Lucifer?
- Only Willing Gifts Accepted
- Love, Not the Amount, Is True Giving
- Israel's Response
- The Gifts Were of God's Providing
- Unprofitable Giving
- True Generosity

6

WILLING-HEARTED GIVING

Sabbath Keeping of First Importance. When Moses came down from the mount, he gathered all the people together, and his first word to them was, not about the wonderful design of the sanctuary that God had revealed to him— his first word to them was God's last word to him: "These are the words which the Lord hath commanded, that ye should do them," he said. "Six days shall work be done, but on the seventh day there shall be to you an holy day, a Sabbath of rest to the Lord; whosoever doeth work therein shall be put to death." Ex. 35:1, 2. There was no trace of compromise in these words from God; they were straight forward and definite. Everyone that defileth the Sabbath "shall surely be put to death," he "shall be cut off from among His people." Ex. 31:14.

Christ, or Lucifer? Why such a terrible sentence against Sabbath desecration? — Because true Sabbath keeping indicates under whose banner we choose to enlist. Our attitude toward Sabbath observance determines whether we stand under the black banner of the prince of the power of the air, or under the bloodstained banner of Prince Emmanuel. When sin entered the heart of Lucifer, it was over the question of rulership. Why should so beautiful and wise and talented an angel as he be deprived of the throne? Why should Jehovah and not *he* be worshiped? Why should not *his* name be the seal of the divine law—a sign of *his* authority? Lucifer determined that it should be. But he could not destroy the eternal law of God, so he substituted a law of his own, in which he stamped his own mark, or seal. On every hand we see the result of his usurped leadership—war with all its horrible results, crime of every sort, disaster by sea, land, and air; sickness, suffering, deep heart sorrow, and at the end grim death. Under which banner must Israel stand? Proper observance of the Sabbath would decide. Disobedience would automatically cut them off from among God's people. Sabbath desecration puts them under Satan's black banner. Do we realize the supreme sacredness with which God regards the Sabbath day, the seal of His eternal law? Shall we not more sacredly guard its meaningful hours, not doing our own ways, nor finding our own pleasure, nor speaking our own words? Isaiah 58:13.

Only Willing Gifts Accepted. "This is the thing which the Lord commanded," continued Moses. "Speak unto the children of Israel, that they bring Me an offering: of every man that giveth it *willingly* with his *heart* ye shall take an offering." Ex. 35:4; 25:2, emphasis supplied. "Devotion to God, and a spirit of sacrifice were the first requisites in preparing a dwelling place for the Most High." PP 343. No unwilling offering for the building of the sanctuary was to be received, for only a willing gift—a gift of love—could fitly represent God's gift to man. "God so *loved* the world that He *gave*." John 3:16. In the gift of His Son, God gave all. "The Son of God...loved me, and gave Himself for me." Gal. 2:20. God and Christ gave their all willingly and with heartfelt love. Our gifts to God, to be acceptable, must be of the same spirit. If we do less than give our all for Him, do we really appreciate what He has done for us?

Love, Not the Amount, Is True Giving. The amount has nothing to do with true giving. Of the poor widow who cast in two mites, it is said, she "hath cast more in than all they which have cast into the treasury." Why? Because "all they did cast in of their abundance;" but because of her love and devotion, "she of her want [penury] did cast in all that she had, even all her living." Mark 12:43, 44.

A certain church member, when approached to give to the cause of God, once asked: "Must I *always* be giving?" "O, no;" was the response; "give only until God stops giving to you." Someone has retold this experience in verse:

> "What! Give again?" I asked in dismay,
> "And must I keep giving and giving alway?"
> "Oh, no," said the angel, piercing me through,
> "Just give till the Father stops giving to you."

A Christian worker, when in attendance at a large meeting where an appeal for missions was made, said, "Well, brethren, I have $300.00 in the bank; you may have it all." His wife once said, "on his return from a long trip to mission fields, he always came home 'broke,' and often in debt." The needs of the cause of God had so tugged at his heart strings, that he not only gave all, but drew on his future income. Although he owned no home of his own, he did not hesitate to give his all, for he knew that the God whom he served would supply all his "need according to His riches in glory by Christ Jesus." Phil. 4:19.

Like the poor widow and this Christian worker [we too must cast in our all], not "grudgingly or of necessity," but cheerfully, because of our sincere love for God and His work. Unless we are willing to do this, our gifts, however large, are not acceptable to God, and they will accomplish little or nothing in His building.

Israel's Response. When Moses presented to the people God's appeal for gifts with which to build the sanctuary, "they came, both men and women, as many as were willing hearted." "They came both men and women"—literally, "the men over and above the women," "a phraseology which implies that the women acting a prominent part, presented their offerings first, and then were followed by as many of their male companions as were similarly disposed." J.F.B. Com. The women "brought bracelets, earrings, and rings, and tablets, [margin, girdles], all jewels of gold: and every man that offered, offered an offering of gold." Ex. 35:22. They also brought "blue, and purple, and scarlet, and fine linen, and goats' hair, and red skins of rams, and badgers' skins…silver and brass…and shittim wood… And all the women that were wise hearted did spin with their hands, and brought that which they had spun, both of blue, and of purple, and of scarlet [yarn—*Moffatt*] and of fine linen. And all the women whose heart stirred them up in wisdom spun goats' hair. And the rulers brought onyx stones, and stones to be set, for the ephod, and for the breastplate; and spice, and oil for the light, and for the anointing oil, and for the sweet incense … a willing offering unto the Lord…for all manner of work, which the Lord had commanded." Ex. 35:23-29.

Gold or goats' hair,—God will use the least as well as the most expensive gift, if it is brought with a willing heart. Of this great variety of gifts, one tabernacle was to be built—unity in variety. How wonderfully God works with our willing gifts—and with us!

The Gifts Were of God's Providing. Whence all these gifts? Before leaving Egypt, when the people asked the Egyptians a recompense for their unpaid labor, God knew just what materials would be needed in the construction of the sanctuary. He was keeping watch over His own, so that the Egyptians gave the Israelites the very things that would be required. These spoils of Egypt, the gifts of Israel, were therefore God's own providing.

"As all the gifts of Israel were of the spoils of Egypt, so [when we come to God] we have nothing to bring but that which has been used in sinful indulgences when we were in the bondage of sin; but if we bring it willingly, He can refine and purify it, and make of it a place in which the light of the Shekinah may burn brightly, lighting the heart with the glory of God, and sending its effulgent rays out into the darkened world of sin." R.S. Owen in RH, March 26, 1925, page 12.

Unprofitable Giving. Not long before this, the people had brought their golden earrings to Aaron, from which he had made an idol—the golden calf. How much did their gifts at that time count? The calf which he had made was burnt in the fire, then ground to powder and strewn upon the water, which the people drank. So the people kept their gold. Is it possible for God's people now to offer gifts with which to build an idol? If so, such gifts will never direct our steps toward Canaan; they will only turn our hearts to Egypt. Because of Israel's idolatry, three thousand fell of plague, Ex. 32:20, 28, 35, and the gold used to make the golden calf was all wasted; it could not stand the test of fire and the grinding process. I Cor. 3:13-15. Unless our gifts are rightly motivated, we might as well keep our idols of gold and silver; but in so doing we may be assured that in the end our treasures will all be burned, and we ourselves may perish.

True Generosity. After Israel had repented of their idolatry, and were converted, while the building of the sanctuary was in progress, the people, old and young—men, women, and children—continued to bring their offerings, until those in charge of the work, PP 344, said to Moses, "The people bring much more than enough for the service of the work...And Moses...caused it to be proclaimed throughout the camp, saying, Let neither man nor woman make any more work for the offering of the sanctuary. So the people were restrained from bringing. For the stuff they had was sufficient for all the work to make it, and too much." Ex. 36:5-7.

"What a striking contrast," says Allen Moore, "with our present-day methods, when euchre, dances, concerts, and other worldly means are resorted to in order to get money for keeping up the church!" *The Story of the Tabernacle*, p. 59. Shall we not bring our gifts as freewill offerings from the heart, and not because some "benefit" device prompts us to so-called liberality? And shall we not bring our gifts to God while there is still need, for the time is not far distant when He will say, "There is no further need."

CHAPTER 7 PREVIEW

"WISE-HEARTED" WORKERS "CALLED"

- Bezaleel and Aholiab Called "by Name"
- All the "Wise-Hearted" Were "Called"
- Who Was Bezaleel?
- Who was Aholiab?
- Bezaleel and Aholiab as Teachers
- A Model School
- All Talents Are God's Gifts
- Essentials to Successful Service

7

"WISE-HEARTED" WORKERS "CALLED"

Bezaleel and Aholiab Called "by name." The Lord said to Moses, "I have called by name Bezaleel,…and I have given with him Aholiab." It is easy for us to believe that God calls consecrated, godly men to the ministry, or to fill some other position of importance and sacred responsibility in His work. But how about men who work with their hands? Is the work of a carpenter or a worker in metal and stone of sufficient importance for God's notice? This was true of Bezaleel, why not of godly workmen today? Of Bezaleel God said, "I have filled him with the spirit of God, in wisdom and in understanding, and in knowledge, and in all manner of workmanship, to devise cunning works, to work in gold, and in silver, and in brass, and in cutting of stones to set them, and in carving of timber." Ex. 31:1-6.

Aholiab was called of God "to work all manner of work of the engraver … and of the embroiderer, in blue, and in purple, in scarlet, and in fine linen, and of the weaver." Ex. 35:34, 35.

All the Wise Hearted Were Called. Nor were Bezaleel and Aholiab the only ones whom God called to the work of the sanctuary. Those who made the priests' garments were "called" to this work by God, when He said to Moses, "Speak unto all that are wise hearted, whom I have filled with the spirit of wisdom, that they may make Aaron's garments." Ex. 28:3. Women also "that were wise hearted" were laborers together with God. They "did spin with their hands … both of blue, and of purple, and of scarlet, and of fine linen. All the women whose heart stirred them up in wisdom, spun goats' hair." Ex. 35:25, 26. And that which they spun was woven and embroidered by wise-hearted men under the direction of Aholiab, the master weaver and embroiderer, into hangings for the gate, the door, and the vail, and into the first and second coverings of the sanctuary, and for the garments of the priests.

Moreover, God said to Moses, "In the hearts of all that are wise hearted I have put wisdom, that they may make all that I have commanded thee." Ex. 31:6. God puts wisdom in "all who are wise hearted," that is, all who from the heart dedicate their talents to Him.

Who Was Bezaleel? Who were these young men, Bezaleel and Aholiab, whom God called "by name?" The name Bezaleel means *in the shadow of God*. This would suggest that when he was born his parents were suffering the cruelties of Egyptian bondage, and to them it seemed as if they were under a cloud, "in the shadow of God," but their trust was in Him. So they named their child *Bezaleel*.

Bezaleel was of the tribe of Judah, the strongest and most influential of all the tribes. Of Judah it is said, "Thou art he whom thy brethren shall praise." Gen. 49:8. And again, "Judah prevailed above his brethren." I Chron. 5:2. Why was this? It was because of Judah's personal character of justice and unselfishness, and his strict integrity to principle. It is said of him that "more traits are preserved than of any other of the patriarchs, with the exception of Joseph." SB Dict. Judah was the only tribe that was loyal to David when the disruption of Solomon's kingdom took place, and this tribe was the last to be captured by Babylon. I Chron. 9:1

An illustrious line of descendants is the fruitage of a character like that of the tribe of Judah. Daniel, who stood the test of the lion's den at the court of Babylon, and his three worthy companions who stood the test of the fiery furnace, Dan. 3:6, were of the tribe of Judah. Dan. 1:6. Christ Himself was of this tribe; He was the "Lion of the tribe of Judah." Rev. 5:5; Gen. 49:9, 10.

Bezaleel was great grandson of Caleb—which name means *capable*, and this Caleb was the grandfather of Caleb the spy, who with Joshua on their return from spying out the land of Canaan, stood so nobly in the face of unbelief and opposition of all the other spies, and declared with loyalty and courage, "Let us go up at once, and possess it; for we are well able to overcome it." Num. 13:30.

Bezaleel was grandson of Hur—the same Hur who with Aaron stayed up the hands of Moses in the battle with Amalek at Rephidim on their way to Sinai. Jewish tradition is that Hur was the husband of Miriam, the prophetess, who after crossing the Red Sea, led all the women in the joyful song of deliverance in the words: "Sing ye to the Lord, for He hath triumphed gloriously." Ex. 15:21. What famous pedigree Bezaleel had!

Who Was Aholiab? How different was the ancestry of Aholiab! He was of the tribe of Dan. Of their father Dan, it is written: "Dan shall be a serpent by the way, an adder in the path, that biteth the horse heels, so that his rider shall fall backward." Gen. 49:17. And because of this backbiting, criticizing disposition and practice, which he never overcame, the name Dan is omitted from the genealogies of the tribes in I Chronicles, and also from the list of those who are sealed, as given in Revelation 7. If we are ever tempted to "backbite" or speak unfavorably of anyone, or indulge in unkind criticism, we would do well to remember the fate of Dan.

Another glimpse into the character of the tribe of Dan is given in Leviticus 24:10-16. Here is a son of the tribe of Dan whose mother was an Israelite and his father an Egyptian. One day the son strove with a man of Israel in the camp, and in his anger he "blasphemed the name of the Lord, and cursed." To speak lightly or disrespectfully of the name of our Creator and Redeemer, that name "which is above every name," that name at the mention of which "every knee should bow," Phil. 2:9-11, that name which "there is none other name under heaven given among men, whereby we must be saved," Acts 4:12, is regarded by God as one of the chiefest of sins, a sin punishable in a most terrible manner, that of stoning to death. Lev. 24:13-16. Because of this sin, this son of the tribe of Dan was put "in ward," and finally stoned outside the camp. Later it is written of the children of Dan that they set up "Micah's graven image, which he made, all the time that the house of God was in Shiloh." Judges 19:30, 31.

The noble character of Aholiab, though a descendant of the tribe of Dan, shows that no matter what our environment or pedigree, we need not be like those who disobey God, even though our lot may be cast among them.

Aholiab was the son of Ahisamach. And who was Ahisamach? The only record left is that he was the father of Aholiab, surely an honored father of a noble son. Had it not been for his noble son, the name Ahisamach would never have been mentioned in the Bible. Probably both these young men, Bezaleel and Aholiab, had wise, devoted mothers.

The history of Bezaleel and Aholiab furnishes a most excellent demonstration of the truth that "God is no respecter of persons; but in every nation he that feareth Him, and worketh righteousness, is accepted with Him." Acts 10:34, 35.

Bezaleel and Aholiab as Teachers. God put it in the heart of Bezaleel "that he may teach, both he and Aholiab." Ex. 35:54. Why did God thus honor these young men? First, doubtless, because while in Egyptian bondage, not only had their hearts been loyal to God under difficulties, but they had improved their opportunities to learn carving timber, engraving, and setting of stones, embroidery, and weaving. And whatever tasks were given them by their taskmasters, they did with their might and to the best of their God-given ability. Thus they had honored God, and now God honors them. They had improved their opportunities, now God trusts them with greater responsibilities. They had cultivated their talents of heart and mind and hand, and now God gives them greater talents. The fundamental talent of everyone whom God calls to His work is to be "willing" and "wise hearted." It was such workers whom God filled with His Spirit, and "with wisdom of heart." Ex. 31:3; 35:35. Therefore the sanctuary in all its parts was not merely the skilled work of men; it was indeed the inspiration of the Holy Spirit.

A Model School. All the wise-hearted, willing workers participated in this instruction given by Bezaleel and Aholiab. These teachers were "cunning" workmen, wise-hearted men who were "called" of God and daily taught of God. The students also were willing, wise hearted men and women. They were all taught of God. This was a school after God's own plan—an industrial school in which the students learned many spiritual truths from the work of their hands. It was a school in which the hand, the head, and the heart, received symmetrical attention. It was a pattern for all time.

All Talents are God's Gifts. As Bezaleel was a "called" smith and carver of timber, and Aholiab a "called" engraver, embroiderer and weaver, so there are "called" men and women in every other pursuit—called farmers, called merchants, called teachers, called students, called physicians, called nurses, called parents, and every other calling for which God has given special fitness and talent to be used for Him. And all who are "wise hearted" will lay every talent on the altar to be used entirely for God. The "called" worker in any line will do his work thoroughly, painstakingly, honestly, and with wise hearted consecration. There will

40

be no slovenly, dishonest, or careless work, for the Christian worker will constantly remember that he is called of God, and to God he must finally give account.

Anyone who is inclined to boast of his attainments, the Lord challenges with the question, "Who giveth thee power to get wealth?" or to do this or that? Deut. 8:17, 18. "Every man also to whom God hath given riches, and wealth, and hath given him power to eat thereof, and to take his portion, and to rejoice in his labor; this is the gift of God." Eccl. 5:19.

Essentials to Successful Service. It is not clear, then, that if we are to do any work that God can accept—whether it be with timber, or stone, or metal, or making garments, or any other line of work, our *hearts* must be right before God, our *motives* must be wholly unselfish, so that day by day God can fill us with the spirit of wisdom—that wisdom from above which is "first pure, then peaceable, gentle, and easy to be entreated, full of mercy and good fruits, without partiality, and without hypocrisy?" James 3:17. Filled with such wisdom there will be no place for unholy ambition, self seeking, strife, stubbornness, or unfriendliness toward any fellow worker. All will be peace, good will, and absolute honesty. With such God can work, and His work will prosper.

Is it not an encouragement to know that no matter what our ancestry, or how few our talents, if we are faithful in improving our opportunities, loyal to God at all times, willing hearted and wise hearted, God will place us in His work "according to our several ability" to use for Him whatever talent has been entrusted to us. Matt. 25:15. Let us put it down "as a memorial"— something never to be forgotten—that "There is no limit to the usefulness of one who, putting self aside, makes room for the working of the Holy Spirit upon his heart, and lives a life wholly consecrated to God. All who consecrate body, soul, and spirit to His service will be constantly receiving a new endowment of physical, mental, and spiritual power. MH 159.

SECTION III

IN THE COURT

CHAPTER 8 PREVIEW

CHRIST ENTERING THE COURT - THIS EARTH

- The Promised Saviour
- Prophets Foretold His Coming
- Darkness the Result of Formal Sanctuary Service
- "The Fullness of the Time"
- "His Own Received Him Not"
- Heaven's First Celebration of Christ's Redemptive Work

8

CHRIST ENTERING THE COURT— THIS EARTH

The Promised Saviour. In the Garden of Eden the promise was first given of Him who would bruise the head of the serpent, the originator of sin. Gen. 3:15. But though day after day at the gate of Eden, Adam offered the sacrifice that showed his faith in the coming Redeemer, yet the fulfillment of the promise tarried. He lived for nearly a thousand years, and at last died without seeing Him of whom his sacrifices were a type. To Seth, to Enoch, to Methuselah, to Noah, to Shem, and to the other patriarchs, the promise was repeated. Again and again to Abraham, Isaac, and Jacob, God said, "In thee shall all families of the earth be blessed." Gen. 12:3, 28:14. Yet the Saviour did not come. Still the hope of seeing the Son of God walk among the children of men did not die out of the hearts of God's faithful ones. Through the centuries they continued to offer the sacrifices which pointed to the coming Deliverer.

Prophets Foretold His Coming. God sent His prophets to instruct the descendants of Jacob—the nation whom He had chosen to give the message of the coming Redeemer—about the "Star" that should come out of Jacob. Num. 24:17. Micah said that He would be born in Bethlehem. Micah 5:2. Isaiah said that His name should be Immanuel. Isaiah 7:14. Jeremiah told about the terrible slaughter of the little children of Bethlehem in an effort to destroy the Promised One, and of the bitter weeping of the mothers who "refused to be comforted." Jer. 31:15-17. Daniel foretold the exact time when "Messiah the Prince" should come. Dan. 9:25. Not only His birth, but His childhood, His baptism, His later ministry, His triumphal entry into Jerusalem, His betrayal, persecution, and trial, His crucifixion, death, and burial, His resurrection and ascension—all were clearly written in the scrolls of the prophets hundreds of years before He came to the court of earth. At the home fireside, and later in the schools of the prophets, Israel was taught from these scrolls about the coming Redeemer.

Darkness the Result of Formal Sanctuary Service. Day after day and year after year the sacrifices were offered which pointed to the advent of the Saviour, and which were intended to prepare Israel for this marvelous event, but gradually their spiritual significance dimmed or was lost sight of. With many these services became a mere formal round. Even the prophecies, so plain and definite, were misunderstood and misinterpreted. Priests and rulers looked, not for a Saviour from sin who should give His life as a sacrifice, but for a mighty king, who would be their saviour from earthly domination. As the true spiritual meaning of the sanctuary and its services was lost, "darkness covered the earth, and gross darkness the people." Isaiah 60:2. Many were ready to throw away their faith in the sanctuary, which had been given to establish them in their hope. Ezekiel in vision, foreseeing this time, heard the people say in tones of discouragement, "The days are prolonged, and every vision faileth." Eze. 12:22.

"The Fullness of the Time." Finally, "the fullness of the time was come" Gal. 4:4, when the Antitype of the sacrificial lamb was to enter the court of this earth, when the Son of God was to lay aside His divine glory and power, and take upon Himself the weakness of sinful flesh.

Gabriel had appeared to Mary, announcing the arrival of a Son whose name should be called "JESUS…the Son of the Highest." Luke 1:26, 31, 32. "The angel of the Lord" [Gabriel], Luke 1:11, 19, also repeated the news to Joseph, saying, "Thou shalt call His name JESUS; for He shall save His people from their sins," "Emmanuel, which being interpreted is, God with us." Matt. 1:21, 23. All this was a fulfillment of prophecy. Isaiah 7:14. The interest of all Heaven was focused on this momentous event. The angels knew the exact time when His birth would occur, and when the great clock of time struck the hour, Jesus was born in Bethlehem. He, the King of glory, was laid, not in a glorious home such as He had left in heaven, not even in an ordinary earthly dwelling, but in the manger of a stable.

"His Own Received Him Not." When Jesus came to the court of earth to reveal through His own perfect life the character of the Father, and to make plain the plan of redemption as illustrated in the sanctuary and its services, He was robed in the garb of humanity. But though thus concealed, His true nature and mission might have been clearly understood through a spiritual understanding of the sanctuary and the prophecies.

Every angel watched to see how their beloved Commander would be received in the court of earth. Was He given the royal reception from His own people that was His due? Far from it! He who was "in the beginning … with God…came unto His own, and His own received him not." John 1:1, 11. Heaven had done everything possible to prepare God's people for this significant event so that they would be ready to welcome their Saviour. Not only had the prophecies of Daniel foretold the time of His coming, but about a year before He was born Gabriel, had been sent to the temple in Jerusalem to inform the priest, Zacharias, that His coming was at the door. Luke 1:5-19. Nevertheless, when the time came, not a single preparation had been made to welcome Him. It is true that morning and evening the priests offered on the altar the sacrifice that pointed to His coming, but to them this service had become devoid of its real significance.

Heaven's First Celebration of Christ's Redemptive Work. But Jesus was not to be left without a reception. In the fields of Bethlehem, where as a boy David had watched his flocks, shepherds were still watching their sheep by night, possibly some of the very sheep that were to be used as sacrifices in the temple at Jerusalem to prefigure the true Sacrifice. These men were familiar with the prophecies, and "through the silent hours they talked together of the promised Saviour, and prayed for the coming of the King to David's throne." DA 47

Although Jesus received no welcome from those whom He had come to save, all Heaven was alert and eager to do Him honor. It was the heavenly privilege of God's leaders on earth to share with the angels the joy and the honor of announcing the Saviour's arrival. But when the angels saw that the priests and rulers in

Jerusalem had made no preparation to receive their Commander, they, amazed at their indifference, passed by these haughty leaders and appeared to the humble yet devoted shepherds.

As the glory of the Lord shone round about the startled shepherds, "lo, the angel of the Lord [Gabriel] came upon them," and joyfully announced, "Behold, I bring you good tidings of great joy, which shall be to all people; for unto you is born this day in the city of David a Saviour, which is Christ the Lord." Luke 2:9-11.

No longer could the accompanying host of angels remain silent. "Suddenly there was with the angel a multitude of the heavenly host." Luke 2:13. The sky seemed full of these shining beings, and the whole field was lighted up with their glory. "Earth was hushed, and Heaven stopped to listen," DA 47, to the anthem which filled their ears with celestial music:

"Glory to God in the highest,
And on earth peace, good will toward men!"
Luke 2;13, 14, A.V.

As the angels disappeared, the music died away in the distance, the glorious light faded from sight, and once more the plain and the hills were wrapped in the shadows of the silent night. The anthem the angels had sung celebrated the advent of Him whom the sanctuary typified. It was Heaven's first celebration of Christ's sacrificial work for our salvation. God's own little Lamb—a "lamb…without blemish, a male of the first year," Ex. 12:5, had now entered this earth, the court of the heavenly sanctuary, antitype of the court of the earthly sanctuary.

Thrilled with what they had seen and heard, the shepherds said, "Let us now go even unto Bethlehem, and see this thing which is come to pass." And "they came with haste, and found Mary, and Joseph, and the Babe lying in a manger." Luke 2:15-18.

CHAPTER 9 PREVIEW

THE CHRISTIAN ENTERING THE COURT

- The Court and Its Antitype
- The Court Gate
- Significance of Its Colors
- The Four Pillars
- The Gate a Position of Authority
- Christ Our Gate of Refuge
- Christ the Way
- "Come Unto Me"
- Our Behavior Within the Gate

9

THE CHRISTIAN ENTERING THE COURT

The Court and Its Antitype. We now enter directly upon the study of the sanctuary, which consisted of three parts: the court, the holy place, and the most holy place. The court is the first section of our journey along *The Path to the Throne of God*. Christ leads the way, explaining by symbols in His object lesson of redemption how we, His followers, can travel the path successfully. As we enter the court, let us be true disciples—real learners in the school of Christ. In this journey we have nothing to fear for Christ gives us many assuring promises:

"I will teach thee and guide thee with Mine eye." Ps. 32:8
I will guide thee "in judgment." Ps. 25:9
I will guide thee "into all truth." John 16:13
He will "guide our feet into the way of peace." Luke 1:7, 9.
"All the time I will be with you, to the very end of the
world." Matt. 28:20, *Moffatt*.

And so we walk together, my Lord and I.

The court, as well as the sanctuary proper, was a type illustrating in part the redemptive work of Christ. Uriah Smith makes it plain that this earth is the antitype of the court. He says, "The court is the place where the victims were slain whose blood was to be ministered in the sanctuary. The antitypical Victim must die in the antitypical court, and He [Jesus] died on Calvary in Judea." DR 532.

The Court Gate. The entrance to the court of the sanctuary occupied twenty cubits [at least 30 feet] in the middle of the eastern court wall, and on each side of this entrance were fifteen cubits of wall. It was five cubits high, the same as the wall, and was called *the gate*. Num. 4:26. It was a hanging of royal colors, "blue and purple and scarlet, and fine-twined linen, wrought with needlework." Ex. 27:16. This needlework, or embroidery, was done under the direction and instruction of Aholiab, who as we have learned, was cunning, or skillful, in this art. It was "wrought" with thread of pure gold, which made it not only brilliant but very costly. To secure the thread, "they did beat the gold into thin plates, and cut it into wires to work it in the blue, and in the purple, and in the scarlet, and in the fine linen, with cunning work." Ex. 39:3. When completed it was a gorgeous piece of exquisite and durable tapestry reflecting the rainbow colors and, especially in the sunshine, brilliantly illuminated with the inwrought gold.

We are not told what design was worked out in this gold needlework, but since the gate, the entrance to the court; the door, the entrance to the holy place; and the vail, the entrance to the most holy place, all represent Christ in the three divisions

47

of His work for our salvation, it would seem quite probable that the design on all three was similar—cherubim in some form. This is definitely so stated of the vail and the door which was a similar vail. Both vails were embroidered with cherubims like the inner covering that formed the ceiling. Ex. 26:31; PP 347.

Significance of Its Colors. Let us look a little closer that we may think God's thoughts after Him. Did God require these particular colors without a purpose? Did He repeatedly insist upon strict obedience to the pattern without a reason? Most assuredly not. The plan of salvation and the work of Christ which the sanctuary typified mean too much to God as well as to His children for Him to talk at random, or without serious meaning. Let us ever remember that "The words of the Lord are *pure* words: as silver tried in a furnace of earth, purified seven times." Ps. 12:6. These royal colors must have some definite spiritual meaning in this divine object lesson. What is it? White is a symbol of purity and righteousness. Rev. 19:8. Scarlet represents sacrifice. Rev. 19:13. Purple signifies royalty. John 19:2, 3. Blue indicates obedience to the eternal truth of heaven, as shown by God's direction that a ribbon of *blue* should border the uniform to be worn by the children of Israel. Num. 15:37-40. This blue ribbon, from which has come the expression "true blue," was to be a reminder that God's children are to obey all His commandments; they are to be "true blue." As blue mixed with scarlet produces purple, so obedience to God's eternal truth added to sacrifice makes royalty. These significant symbols apply both to Christ and to His followers. The fine white linen represents His righteousness, the blue, the scarlet, and the purple—all royal colors—represent His eternal truth, His sacrifice, His kingship.

The Four Pillars. The gate of the sanctuary court was hung on four pillars, Ex. 27:16,—only four, no more, no less, with the command, "See that thou make it after the pattern," lest thou mar God's great plan. Why four? For the same reason that the vail, which represented His flesh, Heb. 10:20, was hung on *four* pillars, and for the same reason that when He tabernacles on earth, inspiration gave us His life in *four* gospels. As *seven* in the Bible indicates completeness and perfection, so the number *four* in the sanctuary, dictated by God, must have some divine significance. This number occurs in the *four* coverings, the *four* ingredients of the shewbread, the incense, the anointing oil, also in the fourth commandment and in other places, where it always points to Christ. As the number *four* points to Christ, so the multiples of *four*, 12, 24, 48, 60, 12,000, 144,000 are used to indicate special groups of his true followers. Continuing our study, we shall notice that this number four, recurs frequently, and to the spiritual minded the promise is, "The Spirit of truth will guide you into all truth." John 16:13.

The Gate a Position of Authority. In ancient times, the gate of a city was the place where just judgment was dispensed. Deut. 16:18. In summoning one to the gate, no preliminaries were necessary, no writings, no delay. In a short conversation any matter could be stated. Ruth 4:1. The position at the gate was one of prestige, honor, and authority. Among the special purposes for which it was used may be mentioned a place of audience for kings and rulers or ambassadors. How fitting that the gate of the sanctuary, the way to the throne of God, should represent King Jesus, Heaven's Ambassador to me and to you here and now in this earth, He who is "the way, the truth, and the life!" John 14:6.

The gateways of royal palaces were often richly ornamented. Sometimes sentences from the law were inscribed on and above the gates. Deut. 6:9.

Christ Our Gate of Refuge. At the gate of a city of refuge anyone fleeing thither could declare his cause, be admitted into the city, and be given a place to dwell there in safety. Josh. 20:2-4. To such a refugee the gate was as the gate of heaven. When Jacob was fleeing from Esau, the ladder that he saw in his dream reached from earth to heaven, and "the Lord stood above it." When he awoke, he exclaimed, "This is none other... but the gate of heaven." Gen. 28:13, 17. This ladder represented Christ, Gen. 28:12; John 1:51; PP 187, who is our gate to the heavenly city of refuge. Like Jacob's ladder, the gate of the court also represented Christ, the entrance to *The Path to the Throne of God*.

Christ the Way. As the gate was the way, and the only way to the sanctuary court, so Christ is the only way to heaven. In answer to the question of doubting Thomas, "Lord, we know not whither thou goest; and how can we know the way?" Jesus answered, "I am the way, the truth, and the life: no man cometh unto the Father but by Me." John 14:5, 6. In the sanctuary we shall find not only "the way" to Christ, but "the truth," and at the end of the way "the life"—eternal life. David answered this question when he said, "Thy way, O God, is in the sanctuary." Ps. 77:13. "Because strait is the gate, and narrow is the way which leadeth unto life,...few there be that find it." But is it not better to travel with the "few" than to be among the "many" who enter the wide gate, and travel the broad way that leads to destruction? Matt. 7:13, 14. Although "strait is the gate, and narrow is the way, it is a glorious way—a way consecrated by the footprints of Christ who has promised, "Lo, I am with you alway, [all the way and all the time] even unto the end of the world, Amen." Matt. 28:20. So, with Christ as companion and guide, and angels speeding back and forth between heaven and earth ministering to our infirmities, why should we lose our way?

So long as we remain outside the gate, we are "without Christ, being aliens from the commonwealth of Israel, and strangers from the covenants of promise, having no hope, and without God in the world." Eph. 2:12. What a pitiful condition! But God, "who remembered us in our low estate: for His mercy endureth forever" Ps. 136:23, leaves us not alone with our enemy outside the gate. If we will enter, He will listen to our plea for pardon and protection, and will dispense mercy and judgment.

"Come Unto Me." By faith we see Jesus, whom the gate represents, standing at the entrance to the sanctuary court beckoning to all who, like Thomas, know not the way, and calling out "softly and tenderly" in tones that reach to "the ends of the earth" Isaiah 45:22. "This is the way, walk ye in it." Isaiah 30:21.

"Come unto Me, all ye that labor and are
heavy laden." Matt. 11:28.
Come, "kings of the earth, and all people;
Princes and all judges of the earth:
Both young men and maidens;
Old men and children." Ps. 148: 11,12.
Let the children come, for "of such is the
kingdom of heaven." Matt. 19:14.
"Whosoever will, let him come." Rev. 22:17.

"Time is now fleeting, the moments are passing,
Passing from you and from me; ...
Though we have sinned, He has mercy and pardon,
Pardon for you and for me.
Come home, come home;
Ye who are weary, come home!"

— W. L. Thompson

And so I come to the gate, the Lord from heaven —

"Just as I am, without one plea,
But that Thy blood was shed for me,
And that Thou bidst me come to Thee,
O Lamb of God, I come, I come."

Our Behavior Within the Gate. Within the gate of the sanctuary, we are on holy ground. It is important that we "know how... to behave...in the house of God on earth which is the church of the living God." I Tim. 3:15. With humility and becoming decorum we should enter the gate of the court, for in that place of honor, Jesus stands to welcome us to His house. Even at the gate of the house of God on earth we are on holy ground. "There are those who conduct themselves in His house as they would not presume to do in the audience chamber of an earthly ruler. These should remember that they are in His sight whom seraphim adore, before whom angels vail their faces." PP 252.

"To the humble, believing soul, the house of God on earth is the gate of heaven. The song of praise, the prayer, the words spoken by Christ's representatives, are God's appointed agencies to prepare a people for the church above. From the sacredness which was attached to the earthly sanctuary, Christians may learn how they should regard the place where the Lord meets with His people.... Happy are those who have a sanctuary, be it high or low, in the city or among the rugged mountain caves, in the lowly cabin or in the wilderness. If it is the best they can secure for the Master, He will hallow the place with His presence, and it will be holy unto the Lord of hosts." 5 T 491, 492.

CHAPTER 10 PREVIEW

THE COURT AND ITS WALL

- The Two Squares of the Court
  - The Two Centers
  - The Court Hangings
  - The Court Pillars
  - Pillars as a Symbol
  - Significance of Brass
  - Significance of Silver
  - The Redemption Money
- Value of the Silver in the Pillars

10

THE COURT AND ITS WALL

The Two Squares of the Court. The court was an unroofed enclosure one hundred cubits long and fifty cubits wide, or at least seventy-five by one hundred fifty feet, as large as two ordinary city lots. Ex. 27:11-13. *Hastings' Bible Dictionary* divides this space into two squares, each fifty by fifty cubits, with the entrance, of course at the east end. In the eastern square was the brazen altar and the laver, the altar doubtless being located in its center. In the other square was the sanctuary proper, including the holy place and the most holy place. At the center of this square was the ark in the most holy place. The first of these two squares illustrated the work of Christ on earth for our salvation; the second symbolized His work in heaven.

The Two Centers. These two centers, where were located the altar and the ark are most significant. The cross of Christ is typified in the altar on which the sacrifices were offered; His throne is typified in the ark. The cross of Christ, represented in the altar, is the center of Christ's life and of the Christian's life on earth; the throne, represented in the ark, is the center of His life in heaven and of the Christian's future life in heaven. Everything on earth centers in, or rotates around, the cross of Christ. Everything in heaven centers in, or rotates around, the throne of Christ.

The sacrifice of the "Lamb of God" at the altar is the only possible atonement [at-one-ment] for sin, which is the transgression of God's law located in the ark. I John 3:4; Rom. 4:15. It is the only possible way to heaven, where it will be the delight of all to obey God's law because it has been engraved with the Spirit of God in the fleshy tables of their hearts. II Cor. 3:3.

The Court Hanging. The court was enclosed with hangings of fine-twined linen. Ex. 38:16; 27:18. "Fine linen, clean and white" represents "the righteousness of saints." Rev. 19:8. But the righteousness of saints is the robe of Christ's righteousness, purchased for us at infinite cost, and *given* to us "without money" and "without price"—because it is priceless. Isaiah 55:1; 52:3. We are made "white" in the blood of Christ. Rev. 7:14. As the blood of transfusion helps the body to throw off disease, so the blood of Christ cleanses the soul from the leprosy of sin.

The Court Pillars. The linen wall, which was five cubits high, was held up by brass pillars of the same height and five cubits apart. Each pillar was set in a socket of brass. At its top was a "chapiter" or capital, overlaid with silver. Just below the chapiter was a "fillet," or connecting band, on which was a "hook," both of which were also of silver. From these hooks the linen wall was suspended. There were twenty pillars on the north side of the court, twenty on the south side, and ten on each end—sixty in all. Ex. 27:9-10; 38:17, 20. From the top of each pillar a "cord" reached to the ground, where, like a tent rope, it was fastened with "pins," or stakes, also of brass. Ex. 35:18; 27:19.

The size of these pillars, except their height, is not given, but in Solomon's temple "the height of one pillar was eighteen cubits; and a fillet of twelve cubits did compass it; and the thickness thereof was four fingers; it was hollow." Jer. 52:21. These pillars were therefore about twenty-seven feet in height, eighteen feet in circumference, or six feet in diameter, the brass about three inches thick. The pillars for the sanctuary court of the wilderness were much smaller, their height being less than one-third of those in the temple of Solomon. Probably they also were hollow.

Pillars As a Symbol. Exodus 24:3-8 gives us a key to the significance of pillars. After Israel had unanimously covenanted to obey all the words of the Lord that Moses read to them from the book where they were written, he took with him a few representative people and solemnly ratified the agreement by building an altar and *twelve pillars*, "according to the twelve tribes of Israel." Ex. 24:1, 4. This shows that pillars sometimes represent God's obedient children. In Revelation 3:10 we read "Him that overcometh will I make a *pillar* in the temple of my God." Here pillars represent the redeemed.

Both these texts are general, representing all the tribes and all who are finally overcomers. But the sixty pillars of the court wall being definitely numbered, could hardly represent sixty individual overcomers. Moreover, these sixty pillars supporting the court wall formed a protection about the sanctuary. Solomon calls them "threescore men about it, of the valiant of Israel. They all hold swords [the Sword of the Spirit, which is the Word of God], being expert in war [expert in fighting the battles of the Lord with the Word.] Song 3:7, 8. From this, would it not seem that these sixty pillars represent some specially numbered group chosen from the twelve tribes for a special work? The Bible mentions only one such group—the 144,000, which number is a multiple of 60. Rev. 7:4.

Originally, the Levites who camped close about the sanctuary, were divinely appointed to have charge of the tabernacle, I Chron. 23:24, 32, serving in courses "day and night." After redemption, this tribe is numbered among the twelve, Rev. 7:7, and the 144,000 as their successors, serve in the temple "day and night." Rev. 7:15. Just as the sacred enclosure within the sanctuary wall was holy ground within which no one ever entered except the priests, their assistants the Levites, and the sinner who came to offer sacrifice for his sin, so after redemption, in the temple just outside the City, only the 144,000 enter. EW 19. Let us keep this in mind for in our further study, it will come up again.

Significance of Brass. "The brass of the offering [for the sanctuary] was seventy talents, and two thousand and four hundred shekels," which approximately is 9,000 pounds. Ex. 38:29-31, margin. This was used for the 60 brass pillars, the 65 brass sockets [including five for the sanctuary door], the brazen altar and its vessels, the laver, and other parts that were made of brass. If we allow 6,000 pounds for the 60 pillars, each pillar would weigh 100 pounds. While this is only an estimate, it is near enough for us to visualize something of the reality.

Brass signifies strength, stability, endurance, and victory through suffering. Of Asher Moses said, "Thy shoes shall be iron and brass; and as thy days, so shall thy strength be." Deut. 33:25; Micah 4:13. In Zechariah 6:1, 12, Christ, the Branch, is represented by four chariots coming out from between two "mountains of brass"—a fitting symbol of Christ's strength, stability, endurance and victory. These mountains of brass, according to Cruden's Concordance, article *Brass*, are "the immovable decrees of God; the steady execution of His counsels; the inseparable restraints on all empires which God keeps within the barriers of such impregnable mountains that no one can start till He opens the way."

Significance of Silver. In the sanctuary, silver represents redemption through Christ. Every man, from twenty years old and upward, when numbered among the tribes, was required to give a half shekel of silver as "a ransom for his soul," Ex. 30:11-16, the men representing the women and the children in the family. Not that redemption is worth only half a shekel given from time to time, or that it can be purchased with any amount of money; redemption is a free gift of the Redeemer, given "without money and without price" for it is priceless. Isaiah 55:1. A half shekel was valued at 32 cents or about two days' wages. This money was from the spoils of Egypt, and the amount was within the reach of all. It was called the atonement or redemption money, and as the cost of redeeming rich and poor is the same—the blood of Christ—"The rich shall not give more, and the poor shall not give less than half a shekel." Ex. 30:15. Not only are we God's children because we are redeemed, but we are redeemed because we are His children.

The Redemption Money. The redemption money, the half shekel, was used "for the service of the tabernacle" and for the Levites, the ministers of the sanctuary. Ex. 30:16; Num. 7:5. Like the tithe, its payment was not an expression of liberality, but a test of obedience and honesty. Nor was it a voluntary contribution as were other offerings; it was required by the express command of God, and there was no substitute for it. A refusal to pay the atonement half-shekel implied a willful exclusion from the privileges of the sanctuary, as well as exposure to divine *judgment*. Even Christ Himself paid the "tribute money [the temple tax—*Moffatt*]—the "piece of money," a shekel, that Peter at His command took from the fish's mouth. This shekel was the atonement money, sufficient for two—"for Me and thee." Matt. 17:24-27. Not that Christ needed atonement any more than He needed baptism, but He was obedient "for," said He, "thus it becometh us to fulfill all righteousness." Matt. 3:15.

Each man was required to present the atonement money personally whenever the people of Israel were numbered before the Lord for service, God thus writing up His people as they pass before, and as they are seen in Christ. There was no enlistment in the service of God but on this ground. It was required "that there be no plague among them." It was "a memorial unto the children of Israel before the

Lord," a reminder that the ransom of the soul is the gift of Jehovah—He gave His Son that we might have eternal life. It was also to "remind the Eternal," *Moffatt*, of His pledge to ransom every obedient soul. Ex. 30:11-16.

Value of the Silver in the Pillars. At Sinai there were 603,550 men numbered, Num. 1:46, and of the atonement money gathered, 1,775 silver shekels made the chapiters, fillets, and hooks for the sixty pillars. Ex. 38:26, 28. Each pillar was therefore crowned with about twenty-nine and one-half shekels of silver, the value of which at sixty-four cents a shekel would be nearly $19.00. In United States money, the value of the silver in the sixty pillars would thus be well over $1,000.00. And yet our Redeemer, who died to make atonement possible, was sold for thirty pieces, or shekels, of silver, less than twenty dollars, which was "a goodly price," Zech. 11:13, the price of a slave that had been accidentally killed, or killed by a beast. How little, how very little, did Judas value the cost of his redemption! Understanding the meaning of the brass and the silver in the pillars, with what humility and gratitude would the true believer look from the brass sockets and pillars upward to his redemption as memorialized in the silver chapiters, fillets, and hooks!

This shows the brazen altar with its four horns, its grate where was placed the fire for the burnt offering, the compass on which the priest walked when sacrificing, and its approach which was "not by steps." Ex. 20:26. Also one of the several sets of tools—the shovel, the flesh hook, the fire pan; and bowls for various uses. The lamb, symbol of the Lamb of God, is tied to a horn of the altar, waiting to be washed ready for the sacrifice. Every part of this altar was of brass, symbol of victory through suffering.

56

CHAPTER 11 PREVIEW

THE BRAZEN ALTAR

11

THE BRAZEN ALTAR

The Altar Call. We have heard the altar call of Jesus, "Come unto Me." We have entered the gate, and have come to the altar for pardon and acceptance. How sweet are the promises: "If we confess our sins, He is faithful and just to forgive us our sins, and to cleanse us from all unrighteousness." I John 1:9. "Him that cometh to Me I will in no wise cast out." John 6:37.

God Placed His All on the Altar. What is this on the altar? And what does it all mean? It is a lamb "without blemish, a male of the first year." Ex. 12:5. Its innocent life has been sacrificed, and it will soon be entirely consumed by the altar fire. This lamb represents Christ, "the Lamb of God, which taketh away the sin of the world." John 1:29. It represents Jesus who from His first year, and even before His birth, was dedicated by God to be the Saviour of the world. Luke 1:35. He was "the Lamb slain from the foundation of the world." Rev. 13:8. At that time, He gave His life to be completely consumed for our salvation. The fire, which came out "from before the Lord," Lev. 9:24, is of God's own kindling, thus showing that God not only accepts but shares the sacrifice. The fire "shall never go out," Lev. 6:13; it shall burn day and night, representing continual atonement, continual mercy, and continual acceptance for the repentant sinner.

Morning and evening continually, at the stated hour for worship, as the priest places the lamb on the altar, all Israel bowed in prayer with their faces toward Jerusalem, accepting Christ as their sacrifice and dedicating anew their all to live for Him and serve Him. This was the "continual burnt offering." Ex. 29:38-42. It was a "whole burnt sacrifice." Deut. 33:10.

I Surrender All. That the lamb was of the first year suggests the text: "Remember now Thy Creator in the days of thy youth." Eccl. 12:1. When a person decides to become a child of God, he accepts Christ and Him crucified as the offering for his sin. Are we willing to give Him all our sins to be burned on the altar—the sins which He has purchased with His blood—all our follies, all our bad habits, all unprofitable reading, all evil associations, all harmful amusements—everything that spoils or hinders soul growth? Are they all on the altar? Let us give them all up, for they do us only harm. Though the mistakes of our life may be many, and the sins of our heart may be more, let us truthfully say:

> "All to Jesus I surrender,
> I surrender all."

Let us make sure of this, for only thus can God accept the gift or the giver.

But this offering means still more than giving up our sins to be burned. We must give our bodies—our lives, "*a living sacrifice*," Rom. 12:1, —all affections—all must be laid on the altar to be consumed entirely for Him, to be used as He shall direct. Only thus do we truly love God with all our heart, and with all our soul, and with all our mind and with all our strength. "This is the first and great commandment," Mark 12:30; Matt. 22:38. It is the first step on *The Path to the Throne of God*. Nothing but complete consecration can be acceptable. From the depth of our heart, we can then truthfully and gladly sing:

> "All to Thee, my blessed Saviour,
> I surrender all."

If we cannot do this, we are not "worthy" of Him, Matt. 10:38, and of the great sacrifice He has made for us. "No man can succeed in the service of God unless his whole heart is in the work.... No man who makes any reserve can be the disciple of Christ, much less can he be His colaborer." DA 273. He that giveth not all that he hath, "Yea, and his own life also, he cannot be My disciple." Luke 14:26. He *cannot*; it is *impossible*. Giving is the first word in the Christian's vocabulary, and surrender is its synonym. Unless we do this, it will do little or no good merely to have our names on the church record. Are we able to be His disciples? Satan will whisper the words of unbelief, "You can't!" But, reaching upward the hand of courageous faith, let us answer, "I can!" "I can do all things through Christ which strengtheneth me." Phil. 4:13.

The Christian Soldier's Strength. Christ has chosen us to be soldiers, and each one can be "a good soldier of Jesus Christ." II Tim. 2:3, 4. In this warfare we have nothing to fear, for—

"*God is able* to make all grace abound toward you." II Cor. 9:8

"*He is able* to succor them that are tempted." Heb. 2:18

He "will not suffer you to be tempted above that ye are able; but will with the temptation also make a way to escape, that *ye may be able* to bear it." I Cor. 10:13.

"*He is able* also to save them to the uttermost." Heb. 7:25.

"*Our God whom we serve is able to deliver us*." Dan. 3:17

"He is able even to subdue all things unto Himself." Phil. 3:21

"*He is able* to do exceeding abundantly above all that we ask or think." Eph. 3:20.

He "is able to keep you from falling, and to present you faultless before the presence of His glory with exceeding joy." Jude 24.

Through "the word of His grace, [*God*] *is able* to build you up, and to give you an inheritance among all them which are sanctified." Acts 20:32.

With such a galaxy of assurances—and there are many more—can we not respond—

"*I know* whom I have believed, and *am persuaded* that *He is able* to keep that which I have committed unto Him against that day." II Tim. 1:12.

I am "*fully persuaded* that, what He has promised, *He is able* also to perform." Rom. 4:21, Italics supplied.

Reconciliation. After entering the gate, the altar experience is the next step on the *Path to the Throne of God*. Without it we shall continue to follow "fleshly lusts, which war against the soul." I Peter 2:11. We shall continue to "love the world" and "the things that are in the world." We do not truly love God, and under such circumstances His law becomes a yoke of bondage. I John 2:15, 16.

But when at the altar we surrender all, when we yield all our powers of body, mind, and soul, to live for Him and to labor for Him, we are no longer at enmity with God. God "hath reconciled us to Himself by Jesus Christ"—"reconciled by the death of His Son... by whom we have now received the atonement," the at-one-ment. II Cor. 5:18; Rom. 5:10, 11. "You that were sometime alienated and enemies in your mind by wicked works, yet now hath He reconciled in the body of His flesh through death." Col. 1:21, 22. Now we are no longer His enemies, but His friends. Reconciliation brings harmony with God and with all His requirements, so that the follies we once loved, we now hate.

The Altar and the Vessels Thereof. Ex. 27:1-8; 38:1-7. Look now at the altar itself. "Five cubits was the length thereof, and five cubits the breadth thereof; it was four square; and three cubits the height thereof." Ex. 38:1. It was "hollow with boards" overlaid with brass. At the four corners thereof were *four horns* of the same.

"To the midst of the altar"—half way between the top and the bottom—was "a grate of network of brass." At the four corners of the grate were four rings of cast brass, to be places for the staves. The staves also were of wood overlaid with brass. Just above the grate was "the compass of the altar." Ex. 27:5; 38:4. The Bible does not say what this compass was nor what it was for but, according to the best information now available, it seems to have been a narrow platform encompassing the altar, on which the priests walked when placing the firewood and arranging the parts of the sacrifice. As the feet of Christ were "like unto fine brass," Rev. 1:15, so the feet of the earthly priests walked on a platform of brass. The approach to the compass was not by steps, Ex. 20:26, but by a sloping ascent to the altar on the south side. Aaron "came down" from offering. Lev. 9:22. In its making, every detail of the altar was to be exactly "as it was showed" to Moses "in the mount." Ex. 27:2, 6-8.

All the vessels thereof were of brass, "his pans to receive his ashes, and his shovels, and his basins, and his fleshhooks and his firepans." Ex. 27:3. Some of the basins were doubtless for washing the sacrifices, others for receiving the blood to be ministered in the sanctuary. The shovels were used to remove the ashes from the altar and the grate; the fleshhooks for handling the sacrifice, the firepans, or brazen censers, held the sacred fire when the altar was carried from one place to another in the wilderness wanderings. J.F.B. Com. on Ex. 27:3. As brass represented suffering, so the altar as a whole was a symbol of Christ and Him crucified. In its parts several symbols are worthy of attention: the wood, the height of the grate, the four horns, and the brass.

The Boards of the Altar. The altar was made "hollow with boards." The staves and the horns were of the same. Wood in the sanctuary represents humanity—either our humanity or the humanity of Christ, or both—usually both. Our humanity with all its mistakes is called "wood, hay, and stubble." "Every man's work shall be made manifest: for the day shall declare it, because it shall be revealed by fire; and the fire shall try every man's work of what sort it is." I Cor. 3:12, 13. How thankful we should be that the wood of which the altar was made was completely overlaid and protected with brass, because the path to victory not only for Christ but for His followers leads through suffering. "Yea...all that will live godly in Christ Jesus shall suffer persecutions." II Tim. 3:12. As the brass protected the boards from being consumed by the fire, so Christ will be our companion and protector all the way to the throne of God. He will never leave us nor forsake us.

Height of the Grate. This presents another interesting thought in the salvation that Christ is working out for man. The height of this network of brass on which the atonement offerings were laid to be consumed, is the same as the height of the mercy seat—one and one-half cubits. God's mercy is as great as His justice. In Christ "mercy and truth are met together; righteousness and peace have kissed each other." Ps. 85:10.

The Four Horns of the Altar. Horns are the chief weapons and ornaments of animals that possess them. Hence, the word *horn* is often used to signify strength, honor, and victory. SB Dict. As *strength*, Moses' prophecy concerning Joseph reads: "His horns are like the horns of unicorns; with them he shall push the people together to the ends of the earth." Deut. 33:17. As *honor*, Job says, "I have sewed sackcloth upon my skin, and defiled my horn in the dust." Job 16:15.

As *power* and *victory*, Daniel gives us an illustration with the ram and the goat. The ram with two horns did "according to his will, and became great," and the goat with "a notable horn between his eyes" "smote the ram, and brake his two horns!" so that "there was no power in the ram to stand before him." Dan. 8:4-7. When Israel forsook God, Jeremiah said, "He hath cut off in His fierce anger all the horn of Israel." Lam. 2:3. When Joab was in trouble, he "fled unto the tabernacle of the Lord, and caught hold on the horns of the altar." I Kings 2:28. This was like taking hold on Jehovah's strength for protection. And of Christ it is written, "He had horns coming out of His hand: and *there* was the hiding of His *power*." Hab. 3:4.

When the sacrifice, which represented Christ, was brought into the court, it was bound "with cords, even unto the horns of the altar." Ps. 118:27. Likewise, if our sacrifices are bound to the horns of the altar, the power of Christ will make them acceptable and effectual. As the gate with its "four" pillars represented Christ in His gracious invitation "Come unto Me," so the *four horns* of the altar, reaching out in four directions, represent His worldwide invitation and the power of His sacrifice to provide salvation to the four corners of the earth.

The Brass of the Altar. While, as already noted, brass is a symbol of strength and endurance, it also signifies condemnation or judgment. In the curses, or judgments, for disobedience, God says to Israel, "If ye will not...hearken unto Me, then I will make your earth as brass:...for your land shall not yield her increase." Lev. 26:18-20. "Thy heaven that is over thy head shall be brass." Deut. 28:23. Equally fruitless will be our service for Christ, if the love of God is not our inspiring motive. "Though I speak with the tongues of men and of angels, and have not love, I am become as sounding brass." I Cor. 13:1.

Brass also represents victory through suffering and sacrifice. At the altar Christ won the victory through sacrifice. He was made "perfect through sufferings," Heb. 2:10,—not perfect in character, for He was always that, but perfect as our Redeemer. Since "He Himself hath suffered being tempted, He is able to succor them that are tempted. Only thus could He sympathize with those who fall under temptation; only thus could He be made "a merciful and faithful High Priest," Heb. 2:17, 18, the Captain of our salvation.

Brass and "Fine Brass"." Brass, which is an alloy of copper and zinc, is formed only in a furnace, a "furnace of earth." It is written, "I have chosen thee in the furnace of affliction." Isaiah 48:10. When John saw Christ officiating as our High Priest in the heavenly sanctuary, His feet appeared "like unto fine brass, as if they burned in a furnace." Rev. 1:15. Fine brass, mentioned only twice in the Scriptures, was brass of so superior quality that its value was greater even than gold. How infinite in value was the fine brass that illustrates the feet of Christ, as for us He walked on this earth through the fiery furnace of affliction! Who, more than our Redeemer, suffered the just for the unjust? The entire fifty-third chapter of Isaiah is a vivid picture of Christ, the "man of sorrows," the man who was "acquainted with grief," He was "wounded for our transgressions," who was "bruised for our iniquities," He on whom the Lord hath laid "the iniquity of us all," and who finally, though "He had done no violence, neither was any deceit in His mouth," yet "He made His grave with the wicked." Only "fine brass" could illustrate the sufferings of Christ. It is even written, "It pleased the Lord to bruise Him"—Isaiah 53:10—even His own beloved Son. Why all this? —It was for me; it was for you.

"With His stripes we are healed."
"Christ was treated as we deserve,
that we might be treated as He deserves."

"He was condemned for our sins, in which He had
no share, that we might be justified by His
righteousness, in which we had no share."
"He suffered the death which was ours,
that we might receive the life which was His.
'With His stripes we are healed.'" DA 25.

How meaningful that the altar on which was offered the symbol of the Lamb of God should be an altar of brass!

As we stand before this altar, let each one ask himself, "Can I be a partaker with Him of His sufferings?" Christ vanquished the enemy, and we too may be overcomers if we never forget that "In all their afflictions He was afflicted, and the angel of His presence saved them." Isaiah 63:9. Although Christ was made an offering for sin, victory is His. As a result of His sacrifice, "He shall see His seed, He shall prolong His days…He shall see of the travail of His soul, and shall be satisfied." Although He made His grave with the wicked, God will "divide Him a portion with the great, and He shall divide the spoil with the strong." Isaiah 53:10-12. Christ not only Himself suffered death at the altar, but there He tasted death for every man. Heb. 2:9; there He "exhausted death." This is strength! This is stability! This is endurance! This is victory!

Meeting Encouragement Under Trial. As we enter into His suffering, how inspiring are these words: "God never leads His children otherwise than they would choose to be led, if they could see the end from the beginning, and discern the glory of the purpose which they are fulfilling as co-workers with Him. Not Enoch, who was translated to heaven, not Elijah, who ascended in a chariot of fire, was greater or more honored than John the Baptist who perished alone in the dungeon." "Unto you it is given in the behalf of Christ, not only to believe on Him, but also to suffer for His sake." Phil. 1:29. And "of all the gifts that Heaven can bestow upon men, fellowship with Christ in His sufferings is the most weighty trust and the highest honor." DA 224, 225.

How, then, should we regard any so-called sacrifice for God? "We are never called upon to make a real sacrifice for God. Many things He asks us to yield to Him, but in doing this we are but giving up that which hinders us in the heavenward way. Even when called upon to surrender those things which in themselves are good, we may be sure that God is thus working out for us some higher good." MH 473, 474.

What encouragement does God give to those who surrender all? "Those who surrender their lives to His guidance and to His service will never be placed in a position for which He has not made provision. Whatever our situation, if we are doers of His word, we have a Guide to direct our way; whatever our perplexity, we have a sure Counselor; whatever our sorrow, bereavement, or loneliness, we have a sympathizing Friend." MH 248-249.

To whom is the most severe discipline given? "The weightier the trust and the higher the service, the closer is the test and the more severe the discipline." Ed. 151.

If God is leading His children, why do trials come upon them? "It is because God *is* leading them that these things come upon them.... The fact that we are called upon to endure trial shows that the Lord Jesus sees in us something precious, which He desires to develop. If He saw in us nothing whereby He might glorify His name, He would not spend time in refining us." "He does not cast worthless stones into His furnace. It is valuable ore that He refines. MH 471. "The trials of life are God's workmen, to remove the impurities and roughness from our character.... Upon no useless material does the Master bestow such careful, thorough work. Only His precious stones are polished after the similitude of a palace." MB 10.

Why does God sometimes permit a crisis to come in His work or in our individual lives? "With nations, with families, and with individuals, He has often permitted matters to come to a crisis, that His interference might become marked. Then He has made manifest that there is a God in Israel who will maintain His law and vindicate His people." COL 178.

What will be our loss if we refuse the discipline that comes with service? "Not even God can make our characters noble or our lives useful, unless we become co-workers with Him. Those who decline the struggle lose the strength and joy of victory. We need not keep our own record of trials and difficulties, griefs, and sorrows. All these things are written in the books, and Heaven will take care of them... If as workers for Christ you feel that you have had greater cares and trials than have fallen to the lot of others, remember that for you there is a peace unknown to those who shun these burdens." MH 487. Worry is blind, and cannot discern the future; but Jesus sees the end from the beginning.... "Our heavenly Father has a thousand ways to provide for us, of which we know nothing." DA 330.

When disappointments come, how will He counterbalance the trial? "Our plans are not always God's plans. He may see that it is best for us and for His cause to refuse our very best intentions, as He did in the case of David. But of one thing we may be assured, He will bless and use in the advancement of His cause those who sincerely devote themselves and all they have to His glory. If He sees it best not to grant their desires, *He will counterbalance the refusal by giving them tokens of His love, and entrusting to them another service*." MH 473, italics supplied.

And lastly, "Beloved, think it not strange concerning the fiery trial which is to try you, as though some strange thing happened unto you; but rejoice, inasmuch as ye are partakers of Christ's sufferings; that, when His glory shall be revealed, ye may be glad also with exceeding joy." I Peter 4:12, 13.

The Laver with its foot located between the Brazen Altar and the door of the Sanctuary. Like the Altar, both were of brass, but unlike the Altar, these were made of the brass looking glasses of the women. Ex. 38:9. Here the Priests washed their hands and their feet before entering upon any sacred service. They washed, not herein, but thereat, with water drawn from the Laver. Failure to be thus cleansed meant death, because the spiritual significance of the sacred service was thus disregarded. Ex. 30:18-21.

CHAPTER 12 PREVIEW

THE LAVER AND HIS FOOT

- The Mirror Laver
- The Laver for Cleansing
- The Two Parts of the Laver
- Justification Began at the Altar
- Justification Continued at the Laver
- Exceptions to the Normal Plan
- Imputed Righteousness and the Second Birth
- The Sons of God
- Adoption Into the Family of God
- The Laver and Feet Washing
- Justification Follows Reconciliation
- Ambassadors for Christ

12

THE LAVER AND HIS FOOT

The Mirror Laver. After giving ourselves in complete consecration to Christ at the altar, we next go to the laver for cleansing. The laver was located between the altar and the door of the holy place, in the first square of the court. Because here was typified Christ's life of humiliation and suffering for our salvation, both the laver and his foot, like everything else in the court, were made of brass. But unlike the rest, these were made of the polished brass mirrors—"the looking glasses of women...which assembled at the door of the tabernacle of the congregation." Ex. 38:8. "These women, like Anna," Luke 2:36, 37, were women of pious character and influence, who frequented the court of the sacred building, and whose parting with their mirrors was a symbol of renouncing the world—renouncing the instrument of personal vanity for the sake of a higher beauty of holiness." JFB Com. A mirror reveals imperfection of uncleanness. God's law is likened to a mirror. "Whoso looketh into the perfect law of liberty...is like a man beholding his natural face in a glass." James 1:25, 23.

The Laver for Cleansing. The laver was not only a mirror to reveal uncleanness, but a bath for the removal of all defilement. The laver held the water, which was supplied from "the rock." Ex. 17:3, 6. Here the priests washed their hands and their feet preparatory to any service at the altar or in the sanctuary. This was very important, a matter of life or death. The penalty for indifference, or failure to obey this divine requirement is twice stated; it was absolute and unconditional—"that they die not." Ex. 30:20, 21. David referred to this cleansing when he said, "I will wash mine hands in innocency; so will I compass thine altar O Lord." Ps. 26:6. No less important is God's command to us: "Be ye clean that bear the vessels of the Lord." Isa. 52:11

The Two Parts of the Laver. Wherever the laver is mentioned, it is always the laver "and his foot also," Ex. 30:18, indicating two distinct parts. No specific description is given as to size or shape of either the laver or his foot, but in Solomon's temple the laver was round, II Chron 4:2. It seems evident that the laver was a bowl of considerable size. Perhaps large enough to hold a day's supply of water. The washing was not in the laver, but at the laver. "Aaron and his sons shall wash their hands and their feet *thereat*," Ex. 30:19, or more literally *therefrom*. This indicates that the water for washing was drawn from the laver by some sort of faucet, and evidently the priests washed in this flowing water.

The foot, in which the later itself rested, received the water actually used in washing. Some pictures represent one priest washing another's feet, using a small basin containing water as if dipped from the laver. This, however, cannot be, for the Bible nowhere mentions any vessels for the laver.

It was the duty of the Levites to keep the laver filled, and to dispose of the water in its foot. Their faithful service kept the laver always full, always ready for immediate use. This unfailing supply of water represented the free and unlimited supply of the cleansing power of Christ's salvation, which was purchased at the altar at such infinite cost.

Justification Begun at the Altar. When the sinner responds to the pleadings and the wooing of the Holy Spirit, he enters the court. Here he sees on the altar a sacrifice, a lamb. This lamb represents Christ, "the Lamb of God which taketh away the sin of the world." John 1:29. "If we confess our sins, He is faithful and just to forgive us our sins." I John 1:9.

When we confess our sins and accept the sacrifice, Christ takes the sin upon Himself and suffers their penalty while the sinner goes free. "If therefore the Son shall make you free, ye shall be free indeed." John 8:36; Gal. 5;1. "He is reconciled [to God] by the death of His son." Rom. 5:10. "Whom God hath set forth to be a propitiation [a reconciliation] through faith in His blood, to declare His righteousness for the remission of sins that are past, through the forbearance of God." Rom. 3:25. This is *the first step* in justification, symbolized in the court of the earthly sanctuary.

Justification Continued at the Laver. Christ is faithful and just not only to forgive our sins but to "cleanse us from all unrighteousness." The only place where cleansing was done was at the laver. Immediately after the death of Christ [symbolized at the altar] were His burial and resurrection, of which baptism is a memorial. Our burial in the water corresponds to the burial of Christ; our rising out of the water corresponds to His resurrection. "Therefore we are buried with Him by baptism into death, that like as Christ was raised up from the dead by the glory of the Father, even so we also should walk in newness of life. For if we have been planted together in the likeness of His death, we shall be also in the likeness of His resurrection: knowing this, that our old man [the man of sin] is crucified with Him, that the body of sin might be destroyed." Rom. 6:6; see Eph. 4:22-24. We are born again of water and of the Spirit, "begotten...unto a lively hope by the resurrection of Jesus Christ from the dead." I Pet. 1:3.

At the altar our past sins are forgiven; at baptism they are washed away, Acts 22:16, and we are cleansed. When we are cleansed—washed, or laved—the righteousness of Christ is imputed to us—declared to be ours. We are then accounted just. Rom. 4:24.

Exceptions to the Normal Plan. The forgiveness of sins symbolized at the altar, and the washing away of sins symbolized at the laver, is the normal procedure. But as the result of sin there are exceptions to God's normal plan. For example, the thief on the cross was not baptized, yet he was accepted by Christ. Luke 23:43. There are others who because of illness or lack of proper instruction, have lacked opportunity and have not been baptized, but will be saved.

Imputed Righteousness and the Second Birth. Imputed righteousness comes to us not because of any good thing that we have done, for "by the deeds of the law shall no flesh be justified." Rom. 3:20. It is a free gift, a gift of grace or divine favor, which we accept by faith through Jesus Christ. Rom. 5:15. "Where is boasting then? It is excluded. By what law? of works? Nay, but by the law of faith." Rom. 3:27. "According to His mercy He saved us, by the washing of regeneration and the renewing of the Holy Ghost." Titus 3:5. According to Webster, regeneration is re-creation, revival, reformation, the entering into a new and spiritual life.

This act of entering into a new and spiritual life is the second birth. This new life, which reflects His righteousness as from a mirror, is a life dedicated to His service. To live this life we will study His Word prayerfully and obey all its requirements cheerfully. To experience true regeneration marks another milestone on *The Path to the Throne of God*.

The Sons of God. Since baptism is the washing away of sin, why then was Christ baptized, for He had no sin from which to be cleansed? Christ was baptized as our example, that He might "fulfill all righteousness." As He rose from the water, a dove [symbol of peace] lighted upon Him, and a voice from Heaven was heard saying, "This is my beloved Son." Matt. 3:15-17. When we are truly baptized, a great peace fills our souls, and we become the sons of God. "Behold what manner of love the Father hath bestowed upon us, that we should be called the sons of God." I John 3:1. When we are truly baptized, we are baptized "in the name [character] of the Father, and of the Son, and of the Holy Ghost." Matt. 28:19. "Beloved, now are we the sons of God, and it doth not yet appear what we shall be; but we know that when He shall appear, we shall be like Him." I John 3:2.

Adoption into the Family of God. The second birth is the requisite for adoption into the family or household of God, and baptism is the adoption ceremony. Then Jesus the Son of God becomes our Elder Brother. Then we are "the sons of God," I John 3:2; John 1:12, 13, "the offspring of God" Acts 17:29, and the Father loves us as He loves His only-begotten Son—incomprehensible but absolutely true. John 17:23. We are children of the King, and our names are registered by our Father's own hand in His family record book, the Book of life. Ex. 32:32. On our part we are to live worthy of royal blood.

"What love, what matchless love, that, sinners and aliens as we are, we may be brought back to God and adopted into His family. We may address Him by the endearing name, 'Our Father,' which is an expression of our affection for Him, and a pledge of His tender regard for and relationship to us. And the Son of God, beholding the heirs of grace, 'is not ashamed to call them brethren.'" 5 T, 739-740.

The Laver and Feet Washing. Washing at the laver in the Mosaic dispensation corresponds in the Christian dispensation not only to the ordinance of baptism, but to the ordinance of feet washing, as instituted by Christ. John 13:12-17. This Christian service is as sacred as was that of olden time.

As failure of a priest to wash before entering upon any service for the Lord meant death, Ex. 30:21, 20, so to Peter's refusal to let Christ wash his feet, Jesus said, "If I wash thee not, thou hast no part with me." John 13:8. "The service that Peter refused was the type of a higher cleansing. Christ had come to wash the heart from the stain of sin. In refusing to allow Christ to wash his feet, Peter was refusing the higher cleansing included in the lower." DA 646. The failure of a priest to wash was as really rejecting the Lord as was Peter's refusal, and the penalty in both cases was the same. With what reverence and humility should we participate in the sacred ordinances that point back to the sacrifice made for us on Calvary, and symbolized at the altar and at the laver!

This Christian ordinance of feet washing provides for continual cleansing. Jesus said to Peter, "He that is washed [laved or baptized] needeth not save to wash his feet." John 13:10. When defilement is contracted in our daily walk, we come again and again in this sacred ordinance, where we renew our baptismal vows and received renewed forgiveness. Then the righteousness of Christ is once more imputed to us, and by faith in Him we are justified.

"This is He that came by water and blood, even Jesus Christ; not by water only, but by water and blood." I John 5:6. Blood refers to the altar of sacrifice, water to the laver of cleansing. John, who was an eye witness of the death of Christ, declares that when one of the soldiers pierced His side with a spear, "forthwith came there out blood and water." John 19:34.

> "Let the water and the blood
> From Thy riven side that flowed,
> Be of sin the double cure,
> Save me from its guilt and power."

This Christian ordinance of feet washing provides for continual cleansing. When defilement is contracted in our daily walk, we come again and again to the laver in this sacred ordinance, where we renew our baptismal vows, and go forth for more efficient service. Jesus said, "He that is washed [laved or baptized] needeth not save to wash his feet." John 13:10.

As in the court of the earthly sanctuary, all the washing and cleansing were done before the sacrifices were slain and the blood was taken into the sanctuary, so all our cleansing must be done here and now, because in heaven there will be no cleansing symbolized by baptism and feet washing. If we are not thus cleansed, we are not prepared to enter the holy place for sanctification.

"We have an altar of sacrifice where Jesus died for all, and by it He became a living laver, 'a fountain opened to the house of David and to the inhabitants of Jerusalem for sin and for uncleanness.' Zech. 13:1, so that we may be cleansed and prepared to pass into the very presence of God. Thus Jesus is the antitype both…of the altar of burnt offering and the laver for cleansing." R.S. Owen in RH, March 26, 1925.

Justification Follows Reconciliation. Repentance with confession and baptism are prerequisites to the remission of sins. Acts 2:38. The former precedes reconciliation and the latter precedes justification. "If, when we were enemies, we were reconciled to God by the death of His Son, [illustrated at the altar] much more, being reconciled, we shall be saved by His life." [illustrated at the laver]. Rom. 5:10. The laver is the complement of the altar; that is, reconciliation, the work begun at the altar, is completed in justification symbolized at the laver.

As Christ "was delivered for our offences, and was raised again for our justification," Rom. 4:25, so in type at the laver we are buried with Christ in baptism, and raised by Him to a new life. By this act we are justified, or accounted just. All our past sins are forgiven, and we are pronounced entirely free from guilt, because the righteousness of Christ has been *imputed* to us—declared to be ours.

Ambassadors for Christ. Being reconciled and fully justified we are "no more strangers and foreigners, but fellow citizens with the saints, and of the household of God." Eph. 2:19. With this new relationship we accept new responsibility. God now commits unto us "the ministry of reconciliation," and we become "ambassadors for Christ," beseeching others "in Christ's stead" to be reconciled to God. II Cor. 5:18-20. Thus from the very beginning of our Christian experience we are to become "laborers together with God." I Cor. 3:9.

CHAPTER 13 PREVIEW

THE PRIEST AND HIS GARMENTS

- Where the Priests Officiated
- The Garments of the Common Priest
- Spiritual Lessons from These Garments
- The Penalty of Disobedience
- The Priesthood a Birthright
- The Ministry of the Priests
- Christ as Antitype of the Priests
- Three Orders of Priests
- The "Order" of Melchizedek
- Christ and Melchizedek
- "After the Similitude of Melchizedek"
- The Redeemed a "Royal Priesthood"
- Preparation for the "Royal Priesthood"

13

THE PRIEST AND HIS GARMENTS

Where the Priests Officiated. During the year, the high priest had duties to perform not only in the court but in the holy place, and on the last day of the year—the day of atonement—his duties led him into the most holy place. Into this apartment he went alone to perform the special services of that day. Heb. 9:7; Lev. 16:17. The common priests conducted their service in the court and in the holy place only. Heb. 9:6. They never entered the most holy place. The Levites, though divinely set apart to assist the priests, never entered the sanctuary itself, except when the camp was moved from place to place, and even then only after all the furniture had been covered. Num. 3:6, 9; 4:15, 20-33. At other times, their service was confined to the court. An ordinary Israelite had access only to the court when he brought his sacrifice for sin. PP 353. During His life on earth, Christ Himself never entered either the holy place or the most holy place, because His work as priest did not begin until His sacrificial work in the court of earth was finished. Then He began His ministry in the holy place of the *heavenly* sanctuary—in "heaven itself." Heb. 9:12, 24.

The Garments of the Common Priest. The garments of priest and high priest differed considerably because they were symbolic of the different duties performed. But all were "holy garments," they were "for glory and for beauty." Ex. 28:2, 40. They were "of fine linen of woven work." Ex. 39:27. They were "whole [that is, woven in one piece] and without blemish;" DA 709; that is, no garment worn was to have a rent or be unclean. Only thus could they represent the pure unblemished character of the heavenly Priest, Jesus Christ their great Antitype. The making of these garments was a sacred task, entrusted only to the "wise-hearted" whom God had "filled with the spirit of wisdom." Ex. 28:3.

"For Aaron's sons thou shalt make coats, and thou shalt make for them girdles, and bonnets." These composed their outer garments. The under garment, or "linen breeches," extended "from the loins even unto the thighs." Ex. 28:40, 42. The girdle was "of fine twined linen, and blue, and purple, and scarlet, of needlework." Ex. 39:29. The coat corresponded to the plain simple coat of Jesus, which was "without seam, woven from the top throughout," John 19:23, 27 —the seamless coat for which, fulfilling prophecy, Ps. 22:18, the heathen soldiers cast lots. The girdle was used to bind up the coat for greater freedom in service. It was uniformly the emblem of readiness for work. Jesus says, "Let your loins be girded about, and your lights burning," Luke 12:35, that is, be always prepared for any service that God requires of you; and be diligent about it. Of Christ it is said, "Righteousness shall be the girdle of His loins, and faithfulness the girdle of His reins." Isaiah 11:5.

At the burning bush, God said to Moses, "Put off thy shoes from off thy feet, for the place wherein thou standest is holy ground." Ex. 3:5. So, as the priests walked on the holy ground of the sanctuary, ministering in the tabernacle and in the court, they wore no shoes. The very ground on which the sanctuary was placed was selected by God, and there His presence was manifested. It was holy ground.

Spiritual Lessons From These Garments. "Everything connected with the apparel and deportment of the priests was to be such as to impress the beholder with the sense of the holiness of God, the sacredness of His worship, and the purity required of those who came into His presence." PP 351. The fine white linen of which these simple beautiful garments were made, is a symbol of righteousness. Rev. 19:8. It represented the beauty of the character of Christ, of whom the priests were a type. Does it not also indicate that the garments of the gospel minister—the earthly representative of Christ—should be spotlessly immaculate, without blemish, and of simple pattern?

The material and simplicity of the priests' garments betokened also the beauty of character of every Christian who is an ambassador for Christ. Simple, modest garments are an index to the "hidden man of the heart," I Peter 3:3, 4, whose adorning is purity, truth, sincerity, unselfishness, and other graces of the spirit. These are holy garments for glory and for beauty, beauty which is immortal. The outward adorning of "broided hair, or gold, or pearls, or costly array" I Tim. 2:9, belongs to "Babylon, the Great, the Mother of harlots and abominations of the earth." Rev. 17:4, 5. They indicate a lack of the true ornaments of heart and life. "When Adam and Eve were created, they were clothed with a covering of light and glory such as the angels wear." SR 21. This beautiful soft "robe of light was a symbol of their spiritual garments of heavenly innocence." COL 310-311. The redeemed will be "arrayed in fine linen, clean and white…[which] is the righteousness of saints." Rev. 19:8.

As the priests' garments were woven in one piece, so Christ's life was riveted to one great purpose, from which nothing ever turned Him aside. Likewise, the Christian's experience must be constant as he goes steadily forward, having as his motto, "This one thing I do." Phil. 3:13. Faith in Christ, not emotions, must hold us true to duty and loyal to God's everlasting truth. Emotions are unstable, up and down, here and there. Guided by them, we shall be "like a wave of the sea driven with the wind and tossed." James 1:6.

As the inner linen garment was "to cover their nakedness" Ex. 28:42, so to those who are preparing for His coming, Christ says, "I counsel thee to buy of Me…white raiment, that thou mayest be clothed, and that the shame of thy nakedness do not appear." Rev. 3:18. Spiritual nakedness implies a departure from loyalty to God, which is spiritual whoredom.

The Penalty of Disobedience. The wearing of these holy garments by the priests "when they come in unto the tabernacle of the congregation [the holy place], or when they come near unto the altar to minister," was a very definite requirement of God, and any failure on the part of a priest to obey meant death. Ex. 28:43.

Why so severe a penalty? Because in that case it would be impossible for the priest to bear the iniquity of the children of Israel, which as Christ's representative was his portion. Num. 18:1. Under such circumstances, "they bear not iniquity and die." They die because they misrepresent Jesus Christ their Antitype. The result to the unfaithful Christian is the same, for if the ambassador for Christ is not clothed with His righteousness, he cannot turn others from their iniquity, but he will lead them astray. As a result, he may cause their eternal ruin, and he may lose his own soul.

The Priesthood a Birthright. From the earliest days among the patriarchs, the priesthood was the birthright of the eldest son. When Esau sold his birthright to Jacob, he forfeited the sacred privilege of the priesthood. In the Levitical priesthood, Aaron, the firstborn of Amram and Jochebed, both of the tribe of Levi, Ex. 6:19, was chosen by God to be high priest. "The priesthood was established to represent the mediatorial character and work of Christ," DA 165, who is the "firstborn of every creature." Col. 1:15.

The Ministry of the Priests. The earthly priests were ordained to offer sacrifices as mediators between God and man. The high priest under God acted not only as intercessor from day to day throughout the year, but he also judged Israel. This God indicated by the Urim and Thummim which rendered the breast plate that he wore a "breastplate of judgment." Ex. 28:29, 30. The high priest's work as judge was manifest especially on the day of Atonement, when God through him judged who were to be "cut off" from Israel—those who had not afflicted their soul or had not observed the other requirements of God for the day, Lev. 23:27-29, and those who were accounted worthy to be retained as God's people.

The priests were also teachers in Israel. Ed. 78. Under God, they also acted as rulers of the nation. Their ministry as rulers continued to the time of Samuel, when they demanded a king that they might be "like all the nations." I Sam. 8:4, 5, 19, 20.

Christ as Antitype of the Priests. On the cross Christ the Lamb of God, John 1:29, offered Himself to take away the sin of the world—Himself the Priest, Himself the sacrifice. At His ascension, He was anointed High Priest in the capacity of Intercessor. All the angels assist in this work for they are "ministering spirits, sent forth to minister for them who shall be heirs of salvation." Heb. 1:14. The Holy Spirit also cooperates, earnestly pleading with fallen man. Rom. 8:26.

Since His ascension, Christ continues Priest "forever" Heb. 6:20, but not always in the same capacity. The Greek word for "forever" here used is the same Greek word as is used in Heb. 7:17, 24, 25, 28. Also Heb. 5:6 and wherever this word occurs it refers to Christ, and means throughout eternity. As on the day of atonement, the typical day of Judgment, the earthly high priest acted as judge of Israel, so during the real day of Judgment, Christ, our heavenly High Priest, acts in the capacity of Judge, judging first the "house of God." John 5:22; I Peter 4:17. When this judgment, called the Investigative Judgment because it is simply to investigate the cases, is finished probation for the human family closes, and His work as Intercessor ends, for mercy is no longer extended to sinners. Then Christ lays off "His priestly attire" and clothes "Himself with His most kingly robes." EW 281. At this time He comes as a Bridegroom to receive His bride, the redeemed. How appropriate for this crowning event of His life of sacrifice He should lay aside His priestly garments and be attired in His most kingly robes. The fact that He lays off His priestly attire does not indicate that He is no longer a Priest for He is a Priest "forever." Being a Priest forever, He continues as Priest-Judge for one thousand years, during which time the wicked are judged. In this Judgment the redeemed are associated, "They shall be priests of God and of Christ a thousand years." Rev. 20:6; Dan. 7:22. After the thousand years He executes the Judgment. Rev. 20:7-13. He still continues as priest but not judge, for the Judgment—investigative and executive—is forever past.

At His ascension, Christ was not only anointed High Priest but He was declared King and crowned the King of Glory. Ps. 24:7-10; Heb. 2:9. At that time, He was seated "on the right hand of God," and ever afterward He "shares the Father's throne." Mark 16:19; DA 832. He is then a Priest-King. As King, He is "the King Eternal" or as Moffatt puts it "The King of Eternity." I Tim. 1:17. As such He will be the Ruler of redeemed Israel.

As Priest, what will be His ministry in the new earth? As antitype of the earthly priests, who were the teachers of Israel, so Christ throughout eternity serves as Master Teacher in the School of the Hereafter. Even while on this earth, He was recognized by learned and by rich as "Master" Teacher, Luke 10:25; Mark 10:17, *Moffatt*; also by Roman officials who declared, "Never man spake like this man." John 7:46. And at the close of His famous sermon on the Mount given especially for the disciples, it is written, "He taught them as one having authority, and not as the scribes." Matt. 5:1, 2; 7:28, 29.

Thus, as Intercessor, as Judge, as King, and as Master Teacher, our heavenly High Priest, is a complete Antitype of the earthly priests.

Three Orders of Priests. From the time sin entered this world, three distinct orders of priests are brought to view in the Scriptures.

First: In the patriarchal period, from Adam to Jacob, every patriarch was the priest of his own household. This may be called the *Patriarchal order* of priests. It continued until, and at least to some extent during, the bondage of Israel in Egypt. Throughout this period, the family altar was the only sanctuary. Before the flood this altar was at the gate of Eden, PP 62, where the Shekinah glory abode, and angels were stationed "to keep the way to the tree of life." Gen. 3:24. Later, the members of each household met for morning and evening worship and for the offering of the sacrifice that expressed their faith in the coming Redeemer.

Second: At the time of their deliverance from Egypt, after Israel had reached Sinai, the Lord chose the tribe of Levi for the service of the sanctuary which was constructed at that time; and He set apart Aaron of the tribe of Levi to be the high priest. Thus the *Aaronic*, or *Levitical*, *order* of priests was established. This signal favor was conferred upon the tribe of Levi because of their loyalty to God when Israel apostatized in the worship of the golden calf. Ex. 32.26. The Levitical order, or the Aaronic priesthood, extended to the cross, and then came to an end. From that time, there has been no divinely appointed order of earthly priests. The earthly priesthood ended at the cross.

Third: At the ascension of Christ the priesthood was transferred to the heavenly sanctuary. Then Christ was anointed High Priest, and the *priesthood of Christ began.*

The "Order" of Melchizedek. At His ascension, Christ was made a Priest forever "after the order of Melchizedek." Heb. 6:20. This translation has led some to suppose that *Melchizedek* was the name of another *order*, or series, of priests. But the Bible nowhere records a series of earthly priests before the cross other than the Patriarchal and the Levitical. Moffatt translates this expression found in Hebrews 5, 6, and 7, "with the rank of Melchizedek." Hebrews 7:15 reads, "After the similitude of Melchizedek." These texts seem to give the correct idea.

Melchizedek and Abraham. Melchizedek is mentioned in only three places in the Bible: Genesis 14:18-20, Psalms 110:4, and Hebrews 5, 6, and 7. He was "king of Salem…and priest of the Most High God" living in the area where Abraham sojourned. Gen. 14:18-20. This was more than four hundred years before the Levitical priesthood was established. He was, therefore, not of the tribe of Levi; nor was he one of the patriarchs. Yet he was a worshiper of the true God. It seems that Abraham was acquainted with Melchizedek and trusted in his righteousness, accepting his kind hospitality as expressed in the bread and wine that Melchizedek brought forth for the refreshment of his army. PP 136. Abraham manifested confidence in Melchizedek's position as "priest of the Most High God" by paying tithe to him. In bestowing the benediction upon Abraham, Heb. 7:6, 7, Melchizedek acknowledged that Jehovah was the source of Abraham's strength and of his victory. Gen. 14:19, 20.

Christ and Melchizedek. "It is evident that our Lord sprang out of Judah," though we would naturally expect Him to come out of Levi whom He Himself had chosen for the priesthood. "And it is yet far more evident: for that *after the similitude* of Melchizedek there ariseth another Priest [Christ] who is made…a Priest forever *after the order* [with the rank—*Moffatt*] of Melchizedek." Heb. 7:14-17, Emphasis supplied.

Melchizedek was made priest "like unto the Son of God"—[resembling God's Son—*Moffatt*]. "He abideth a priest continually," or permanently, as Moffatt has it; that is, without a successor. Heb. 7:3. Christ also had no successor; He was made High Priest "after the power of *an endless life*," or "forever." He was made High Priest with *the rank* of Melchizedek: that is, as Melchizedek was both priest and king, so also was Christ. Thus Melchizedek was a type of Christ.

After the Similitude of Melchizedek. It is not the service of Christ that is after the similitude of Melchizedek [of whose service there is no record], but of

Melchizedek as *priest and king*. The service of Christ is fully typified in the service of the Levitical priesthood as illustrated in the earthly sanctuary. In what particulars, then, was Christ similar to Melchizedek?

1. *In rank*. Melchizedek was "king of Salem" [afterward *Jerusalem*] and "priest of the Most High God." Gen. 14:18. His name by interpretation is "king of righteousness, and after that the king of Salem, which is king of peace." Heb. 7:1, 2. Likewise, Christ is both King and Priest—Priest of the Most High God, and "The Prince of Peace." Isaiah 9:6. He is the King of Righteousness with His throne finally in the *New Jerusalem*. Rev. 21:22.

2. Melchizedek was made priest as he was made king—not by inheritance, as were the Levitical priests, but by *appointment*. Christ also was made Priest, not because His father was priest; but by *appointment*—on the oath of God. Heb. 7:20, 21; Ps. 110:4. This was the fulfillment of the promise to Abraham: "In thee shall all families of the earth be blessed," Gen. 12:3,—the promise of the Redeemer, who would be forever both Priest and King. Thus Christ as our Redeemer is assured to us "by two immutable things"—God's promise and His oath. Heb. 6:12, 17, 18.

3. Melchizedek was not one of the patriarchs; he was not of the Patriarchal order of priests, nor was he a Levite, of the Levitical order. Likewise, Christ was not of either of these orders of priests. "Our Lord sprang out of Judah, of which tribe Moses spake nothing concerning priesthood." Heb. 7:14, 15.

4. Melchizedek was "without father, without mother, without descent," Heb. 7:3, *in the priesthood*. This expression, says Smith's *Bible Dictionary*, is a "Greek idiom," indicating one whose parentage was humble or unknown. There is no record of his genealogy, while a very exact record of the genealogy of both the Patriarchal and Levitical priests was kept, and finally preserved in the Bible. Like Melchizedek, Christ was without *priestly* parentage or pedigree.

5. Melchizedek's priesthood had "neither beginning of days nor end of life." This also, says Smith, is a "Greek idiom," indicating one whose "days"—time of discharging his function as priest—was unrecorded and unknown by humanity. Christ is a Priest "forever with the rank of Melchizedek; that is, He is both Priest and King. *Moffatt*, Heb. 6:20; Ps. 110:4. His days, the time of discharging His function as Priest are known and recorded in the Bible. He was made Priest after the power of an endless life, a time no man can comprehend. Heb. 7:15-17.

6. Both Patriarchal and Levitical priests were changeable; that is, death prevented them from continuing; therefore, their priesthood passed by inheritance from father to son. But Melchizedek did not belong to a *succession* of priests—his priesthood did not pass to a successor, nor did he receive it by inheritance—and in that sense it was unchangeable. Likewise, Christ, "because He continueth ever, hath an unchangeable priesthood." Heb. 7:24.

"He holds His priesthood without any successor, since He continues forever, or "permanently." Moffatt's translation of Heb. 7:3, 23, 24.

7. Melchizedek was an individual priest recognized by God. He was a Canaanite, an ordinary human being living at Salem. But he was *extraordinary* in that, in spite of his Canaanitish pedigree and environment [he was near neighbor of the king of Sodom, Gen. 14:17, 18] yet he was righteous. Christ was taken from among men, Heb. 5:1, from among sinners. He was "made like unto His brethren, that He might be a merciful and faithful High Priest." Heb. 2:17. Until He had partaken of human nature, until He had been tempted in all points like as we are, and in a most unfavorable environment had overcome and was "without sin," He could not be a Priest of the Most High God, because without this experience He could not be "touched with the feeling of our infirmities," Heb. 4:15, nor could He "succor them that are tempted." Heb. 2:18; 4:15. How comforting and how wonderful is the thought that Christ identifies himself with anyone—even a Canaanite—who serves God to the best of his knowledge and ability in righteousness and peace!*

The Redeemed a "Royal Priesthood." Of the redeemed, John says they will be associated with Christ in His priestly work—"Priests of God and of Christ a thousand years." Rev. 1:6; 20:6. Some of these have already entered upon their mission. They are that multitude who "came out of their graves after His resurrection," Matt. 27:50-53; Eph. 4:8, margin, and ascended with Him as the first fruits of His redemption. Rev. 4:4; 5:8-10. Finally, *all* the redeemed, those who have part in "the first resurrection…shall be priests of God and of Christ." Rev. 20:6. Peter calls these a "royal priesthood." I Peter 2:9. To be one with Christ in the priesthood will indeed be a great honor. As "no man taketh this honor unto himself,…so also Christ was glorified by the Father, John 17:4, 5, 24, and the redeemed, His sons and associate priests, when arrayed in fine linen, clean and white, Rev. 19:8, will He glorify. John 17:22, 23.

Preparation for the "Royal Priesthood." Aaron was chosen by God to be the earthly high priest, not only because he was the firstborn, but by virtue of his blood relationship to Moses, who represented God, Ex. 4:16. So Christ was chosen by God to be the *heavenly* High Priest—chosen by God "that said unto Him, Thou art My Son, today have I begotten Thee." Heb. 5:5. As Christ was chosen because of His relationship to God, so the redeemed, as "brothers" of Christ their "Elder Brother" Matt. 12:50, are chosen by God to be priests, by virtue of *their* spiritual relationship to Christ. Rev. 20:6. In the Levitical priesthood, any stranger who could not prove his genealogy direct from Aaron, the high priest, was cast out of

---

*   For further study on Melchizedek see *The Book of Hebrews*, by M. L. Andreasen, pages 245 to
     265; *The Atonement*, by W. H. Branson, pages 43 to 45; *Smith's Bible Dictionary*, article
     Melchizedek; and *Jameson, Faisset*, and *Brown's Commentary* on Hebrews 7.

the priesthood, and was even subject to death. Ezra 2:62; Num. 3:10. Likewise, the Christian who cannot prove his blood relationship to Christ, the heavenly High Priest, can have no part in the "royal priesthood," and will finally be cast out and suffer death.

We have the promise that the redeemed are to be "priests of God and of Christ. Rev. 20:6. Since the priesthood is still a birthright, on what grounds can we claim this promise? How do we get blood relationship to Christ? This is a spiritual relationship, which may be compared to the way in which we get our physical relationship. As the mother gives of her life blood, and travails in pain that her child may be given the *first* birth, so Christ gave His life blood on Calvary that we may experience the *second* birth. We are the purchase of His blood, "bought with a price," "redeemed...with the precious blood of Christ." I Cor. 6:20; I Peter 1:18, 19. It is this that opens to us the door into the family of God—that makes us brothers of Christ, Matt. 12:50, and given us blood relationship to Him. When those for whom Christ has spilled His precious blood that they may be born into His kingdom, regard iniquity in their hearts, He suffers anew the agony of the crucifixion and soul travail. Heb. 6:6. Not until redemption is finished and all sin is eternally destroyed, not until He sees the fruit of the travail of His soul, shall He be satisfied. Isaiah 53:11. Then, by virtue of our spiritual blood relationship to Christ, we shall be eligible to a place in the royal priesthood.

How wonderful is this blood relationship to Christ—human and divine, earthly and heavenly, the mystery of godliness! Thus, like the earthly priests who were *born* into the priestly family, we must be born of water and of the Spirit into the family of God. Then we shall be partakers of the Father's nature, and His name, or character, will be in our foreheads. Ex. 28:36-38; Rev. 14:1. This is "the high calling of God in Christ Jesus," the mark toward which we press for the prize. Phil. 3:14.

CHAPTER 14 PREVIEW

THE GARMENTS OF THE HIGH PRIEST

- His Plain Linen Garments
- The "Broidered Coat"
- The Embroidered Girdle
- The Blue Robe of the Ephod
- Lessons from the Golden Bells
- Lessons from the Pomegranates
- Other Lessons from These Ornaments
- The Ephod
- The Onyx Stones
- The Breastplate of Judgment
- The Order of the Names
- The Urim and the Thummim
- The Breastplate Jewels and the New Jerusalem
- Ephraim and Dan "cut off" —Why?
- Onyx Stones and Breastplate Bound Together
- The "Curious Girdle" of the Ephod
- The Mitre, or "Holy Crown"
- Summary of Priests' Garments

14

THE GARMENTS OF THE HIGH PRIEST

His Plain Linen Garments. The high priest had two sets of garments. One was of plain white linen, Ex. 39:27, 28, like these of the common priest, except the mitre and the girdle. The priests wore "goodly bonnets," Ex. 39:28, while the linen mitre of the high priest was somewhat conical in shape. The girdle of the common priest, being merely to bind about the coat, passed only about the waist. Josephus says that the girdle of the high priest passed over the shoulder, crossed upon the breast, passed under the arms, twice around the body, and tied in front, the ends hanging down to the feet, thus rendering the high priest more venerable.

The high priest wore these plain garments on the day of atonement, when he went into the most holy place to minister for his own sins as well as for those of the people. Then he appeared in the humble character of a suppliant. As he approached into the very presence of God, symbolized in the Shekinah, he did so in pure white linen attire, Lev. 16:2-4, without ornament or ornamentation of any kind—garments befitting reverence and humility. These garments were also the emblem of that perfect purity which was sought by the expiations of that day.

These special garments worn by the high priest on the day of atonement have no counterpart in the work of the heavenly High Priest, because when Christ began His work in the most holy place in the heavenly sanctuary, He went in—not to make atonement for His own sins, for He had none—He went in to make atonement for the sins of the people only. Therefore in this, the antitypical day of atonement, Jesus is represented as clothed "with precious garments," those with "a bell and a pomegranate," and with the breastplate that "glittered like diamonds." EW 251.

The "Broidered Coat." In the high priest's "golden garments" the embroidered coat was worn next over the under garment. Like all the garments of the priest and the high priest, this coat was made of fine linen, and woven in one piece. It was richly embroidered.

In his Bible Dictionary, Smith describes this embroidery as worked in a tessellated manner, in squares such as stones might be set. Webster's Dictionary defines tessellated as formed of little squares, oblongs, or pieces approximating squares like mosaic work. The Hebrew word for embroider in Ex. 28:39 is rendered to interweave colored threads in squares, to encase gems in gold.

This must have been a most beautiful and exquisite type of embroidery requiring special skill and care. The coat extended down to the foot. Rev. 1:13.

"No rent must be made in the priestly robes, for this would mar the representation of heavenly things. The high priest who dared to appear in holy office...with a rent robe, was looked upon as having severed himself from God...He was no longer accepted by God as an officiating priest." DA 709. He [Caiaphas] pronounced sentence upon Christ as a blasphemer, and expressed his horror of this sin by rending his official robe, but in this act he himself was committing blasphemy. Even after the death of Christ, as a fulfillment of prophecy, His garment was not rent. John 19:23, 24; Ps. 22:18.

The Embroidered Girdle. In the East great value was attached to the girdle as being the part of the military dress connected with the sword and bow. This was especially true if it had been worn by a sovereign or his eldest son and heir. When Johnathan gave David his robe, he gave "even to his sword, and to his bow, and to his girdle." I Sam. 18:4. This was not only a ratification of their covenant of brotherhood for life, but also a sign that he had surrendered to David his royal inheritance.

A girdle of sackcloth was expressive of sorrow; a girdle of leather, such as was worn by Elijah and John the Baptist, expressed deep humility. The girdle was also a symbol of strength and victory. Ps. 18:39, 40. Rich girdles were sometimes given as rewards to soldiers. Paul referred to this custom when he said, "Have your loins girt about with truth." Eph. 6:14.

Thus we see that the girdle was expressive of various emotions and meanings; the deeper and more exalted the idea to be expressed, the richer and more elaborate the girdle. The girdle worn by the high priest to bind about his embroidered coat was made "of fine twined linen, and blue, and purple, and scarlet," beautifully and fittingly decorated with "needlework." Ex. 28:39; 39:29.

As elsewhere, the pure white linen symbolized spotless righteousness, and being "fine twined" it was righteousness of the highest order, even the righteousness of Christ. The blue, and scarlet, and purple corresponded to these royal colors in the sanctuary itself, indicating obedience to divine truth, complete and unselfish sacrifice, and kingly royalty. All these were characteristics of the great Antitype, Jesus Christ, our High Priest.

A high priest less perfectly clothed could not represent Christ as our sin bearer. Therefore of Joshua the high priest, who was clothed with "filthy garments," the Lord commanded, "Take away the filthy garments from him. And unto him He said, Behold, I have caused thine iniquities to pass from thee, and I will clothe thee with change of raiment…And the angel of the Lord stood by." Zech. 3:3-7. Filthy garments represent sin, in this case evidently the sin of Israel which the high priest by virtue of his office must bear, Num. 18:1, while the pure white linen symbolized the righteousness of Christ with which the high priest must be clothed to bear the sins of Israel.

The Blue Robe of the Ephod. This was the garment worn next over the embroidered coat. It was "of woven work, all of blue," this color, as always, being a symbol of heavenly truth, or of heaven itself. Like the embroidered coat, it was in one piece. It had no sleeve, but only slits in the sides for the arms to come through, and an opening in the top for the head. Upon the hem of the robe were fastened bells of pure gold, between which were "pomegranates of blue, and purple, and scarlet, and twined linen;" both were expressive of the character and work of our heavenly High Priest. Ex. 28:31-35; 39:22-26. The Bible does not tell us how many of these ornaments there were, but Jewish tradition has it that there were 72 bells. Others state that there were 72 ornaments in all—36 of each, which seems more reasonable. However, as someone has wisely said, "It is more modest to be silent where God is silent, than to indulge ourselves in boundless and groundless fancies."

Lessons from the Golden Bells. What do the bells and the pomegranates signify? Because these were equal in number, someone has suggested that they well illustrated the lesson that in our Christian experience there should be as much fruit as sound, or profession. At any rate, the bells were not made of "sounding brass," symbol of lack of love, I Cor. 13:1, but of pure gold, representing great value. The bells also had a special purpose on the day of atonement, their joyful sound indicating to the people that the high priest had finished his work in safety, and that God had accepted the sacrifice for their sins.

Lessons from the Pomegranates. Why did God command that the alternate ornament be a pomegranate instead of some other fruit? The pomegranate is a round fruit about the size of an apple. Its purplish-red shell is completely packed with seeds, each of which is encased in a sack of blood red, delicious but sometimes bitter juice. Each fruit is a veritable "seed basket" of "precious seed." "The seed is the Word of God." Luke 8:11. By actual count one pomegranate of ordinary size contained approximately 650 seeds, suggesting at least that the Word of God is literally packed with precious promises. The blood red juice suggests the blood of Jesus Christ, which cleanseth from all sin. The fine-twined linen in royal colors of blue and purple and scarlet, of which these ornaments were made, has the same significance here as elsewhere in the sanctuary—heavenly truth, royalty, and sacrifice.

Not only is the scarlet indicative of the sacrificial character and work of Christ, but also the sacrifice of His followers even to death itself which is often necessary in order to carry the truth of God to those in darkness. The linen represents not only the righteousness of Christ, but the righteousness required of those whom God calls to His work. "Be ye clean, that bear the vessels of the Lord." Isaiah 52:11. They sow the precious seed beside all waters, bringing things new and old out of God's Word. "He that goeth forth and weepeth, bearing precious seed [margin, seed basket], shall doubtless come again with rejoicing, bringing his sheaves with him." Ps. 126:6.

Other Lessons from These Ornaments. The bells and pomegranates were not on the coat of white linen, nor were they on the golden ephod; they were on the blue robe, *blue*, a symbol of God's eternal truth. How beautiful is the thought expressed in the pomegranate seed baskets, as hour by hour the high priest went about his daily duties, officiating in behalf of the repentant sinner and dispensing "seeds" of hope and cheer, comfort and instruction from God's Word, that wonderful "seed basket!" With what joy does he take from his "seed basket" and give to the repentant sinner this seed of encouragement: "The blood of Jesus Christ His Son cleanseth us from all sin;" I John 1:7; and another: "Thy faith hath made thee whole; go in peace." Mark 5:34; "Sin no more, lest a worse thing come upon thee." John 5:14.

Then as the sinner receives the Word into his heart, and the joyful sound of the golden bells is heard, comes that inspiring seed: "Joy shall be in heaven over one sinner that repenteth." Luke 15:7. As the golden bells on the hem of the high priest's robe "all of blue," sound out their joy, the response is taken up by the angels in heaven as they sweep the strings of their golden harps. How this does bring back from memory's hall that little child's song:

> "Ring the bells of heaven,
> There is joy today,
> For the wand'rer now is reconciled."

And then the chorus:

> "Glory! Glory! how the angels sing!
> Glory! Glory! how their loud harps ring!"

If you have never heard a group of innocent little children with their sweet voices singing that song, you have missed a heavenly thrill.

The Ephod. The ephod, which was worn outside the blue robe, was the peculiar official garment of the high priest of Israel. The word *ephod* is sometimes translated apron, being shorter than the blue robe, and sleeveless. PP 351. It was the most costly and the most magnificent of his garments, being made entirely of "gold, blue, and purple, and scarlet, and fine twined linen," Ex. 39:3, every thread of which represented the perfect character of Christ. This gorgeous material richly embroidered with real gold thread identified the high priest personally and officially with the gate of the court, the door of the tabernacle, the vail, and the beautiful inner covering of the sanctuary, all of which were of the same costly material and skillful workmanship as the ephod. This, perhaps, accounts in part at least for the fact that at his death the dress of the high priest passed on to his successor. Ex. 29:29.

The Onyx Stones. The front and the back of the ephod were clasped together at the shoulders with two onyx stones, on each of which were engraved six of the names of the tribes of Israel. Ex. 28:10, 39:6. These onyx stones were nearly white with pink streaks like agate. They were enclosed in ouches, or rosettes, of gold, and the names were "graven as signets are graven." Ex. 39:3-7. A signet is a seal used by a sovereign in sealing official documents. It gives validity to the document and represents the authority of the government over which the officer rules. Likewise, the names graven on these onyx stones indicated that those thus represented were officially set apart and sealed to become loyal servants of their heavenly Sovereign.

Badges of honor and authority are often worn on the shoulders of government officials, or others who have won distinction. As the Messiah was to bear the government upon His shoulder, Isaiah 9:6, so the shoulder stones of the high priest expressed God-given honor and responsibility. The burden bearing shoulder signifies submission to servitude. Issachar "bowed his shoulder to bear, and became a servant unto tribute." Gen. 49:15. The onyx stones fastened to the shoulder of the ephod indicated that the high priest was to bear the physical burdens of Israel, even as the heavenly High Priest carries our burdens; "Cast thy burden upon the Lord, and He shall sustain thee." Ps. 55:22, is no idle promise, and for any of us to be a burden bearer for God is a high and heavenly honor.

The names of Israel in the onyx stones were engraved "according *to their birth*," Ex. 28:10, Reuben, the eldest to Benjamin the youngest. As these were borne on the shoulders of the lambs of the flock and those newly born into the family of God. Luke 15:4-6. These names represent the new recruits who are preparing to respond to the call of their mighty General for reinforcements to His loyal army represented in the breastplate jewels. Both the onyx stones and the breastplate jewels were engraved "for a memorial," something that God will never forget. "Yea, they may forget, yet will I not forget thee," for "I have graven thee," not upon the precious stones, but that which is infinitely more precious, "upon the palms of my hands." Ex. 28:12, 29; Isaiah 49: 15, 16. God will never forget those who are preparing for His service, or those who are actually engaged in it. This is the promise of the Lord to Zion.

The Breastplate of Judgment. Like the ephod, the breastplate was made of gold, blue, and purple, and scarlet, and fine-twined linen. This richly embroidered piece of brocade when doubled was foursquare, measuring a span, approximately nine inches each way. Within its border "in ouches [rosettes] of gold," Ex. 39:13, were set four rows of precious stones, three in each row. On each of these stones was engraved the name of one of the twelve tribes. Ex. 28:15-21. They glistened like diamonds, reflecting the light, and magnifying the names engraved upon them. EW 251. These jewels, each measuring nearly two by three inches, were not only of external splendor, but precious stones of great intrinsic value. Hebrew writers say that the ensign or banner of each tribe bore the same color as that of the precious stones representing that tribe in the breastplate of the high priest.

"Aaron shall bear the names of the children of Israel in the breastplate of judgment [or justice] upon his heart, when he goeth in unto the holy place, for a memorial [a reminder] before the Lord continually." Ex. 28:29. Just so day by day "continually" Christ, our heavenly High Priest is reminded of His own. He "bears upon *His* heart the name of every repentant, believing soul." PP 351. He "continually" thinketh upon every "poor and needy" one. Ps. 40:17. He bears not only our physical burdens, but all our heart burdens.

These twelve breastplate jewels, no two alike, borne on the heart of the high priest, represent God's special treasure, "My jewels." Mal. 3:17. They are gathered to the heart of Christ, the Redeemer of the twelve tribes, from every nation and country, some from the depth of the ocean, some from earth's darkest mines.

The Order of the Names. The names in the breastplate were engraved "according to the twelve tribes." Ex. 28:21. Those only were numbered *in the tribes* who were old enough "to go forth to war in Israel," Num. 1:3, mature enough to fight the spiritual battles of the Lord. In their warfare and service for Him, Christ bears these on His heart "continually." They are His "memorial," and He will never forget them. What a comfort this should be to all who labor in His service! The order of these names would naturally be the same as when the tribes were encamped around the sanctuary, and when they marched from place to place. Num. 2:3-13.

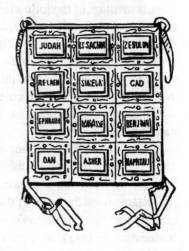

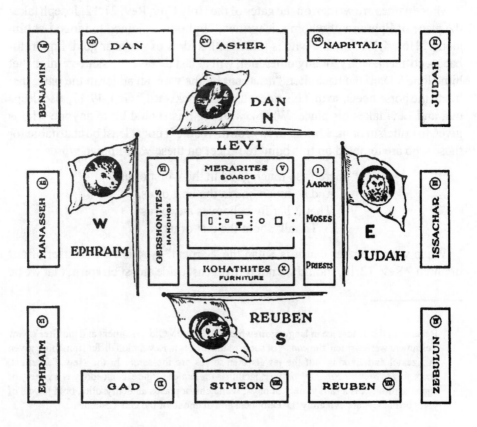

The Urim and the Thummim. Thou shalt put in the breastplate of judgment [justice] the Urim and the Thummim; and they shall be upon Aaron's heart when he goeth in before the Lord; and Aaron shall bear the judgment of the children of Israel upon his heart so to observe that both point back to Eden... In Ezekiel 28:13 there is mention of the following precious stones having been in Eden—the sardius, topaz, and the diamond, the beryl, the onyx and the jasper, the sapphire, the emerald, and the carbuncle. [The Septuagint gives all twelve stones.] It would almost appear as if the breastplate of the high priest pointed back to Eden, promising to God's Israel readmission into its glories, while New Jerusalem speaks of the same, presenting to the redeemed all, and more than all, the glory of Paradise, into which they are introduced by the Lamb—the true High Priest who bears their names on His heart.*

Ezekiel calls these stones the "covering" of Lucifer, king of Tyrus. Eze. 28:12-19. How beautiful is the thought that the breastplate of the high priest spans the gulf between the time when through Lucifer sin entered Eden, tearing its inhabitants from the heart of the Creator, and the time when through Christ sin is entirely and forever blotted out and His children are restored to the heart of their Redeemer, the true High Priest!

Ephraim and Dan "Cut Off"—Why? In the list of tribes given in Revelation 7, whose names are written on the gates of the Holy City, Rev. 21:12, Joseph takes the place of Ephraim of whom it is written, "Ephraim is joined to idols; Let him alone." Hos. 4:17. Anyone who is joined to his idols of silver or gold, liquor, tobacco, coffee, jewelry, or any other idol, will at last receive the same verdict: "let him alone." Dan, the backbiter, "a serpent by the way, an adder in the path, that biteth the horse heels, so that his rider shall fall backward," Gen. 49:17, also drops out, and Levi takes his place. What a warning this should be to anyone who is given to criticism or backbiting in any form! Would it not at least be charitable for those who are tempted on this point to reflect on these well-known words:

> "There is so much good in the worst of us,
> And so much bad in the best of us,
> That it hardly behooves any of us
> To talk about the rest of us."

When we remember that it is Satan the "serpent" who is "the accuser of our brethren," Rev. 12:10, should we not forever cast aside any such spirit, that we be

---

* Because of the difference in language in which the Hebrew Old Testament and the Greek New Testament were written, the *names* of some of the jewels in Revelation differ from those given in Ezekiel and Exodus, but the jewels themselves are the same. In the New Testament, according to *Smith's Bible Dictionary*, jacinth is the same as ligure, chalcedony is a variety of agate, sard-onyx is a sard variety of onyx, while chrysoprasus and chrysolite, both jewels of great brilliancy, are evidently the carbuncle and diamond of the Old Testament.

not classed with him, and finally cast down with him, and lose our place among the redeemed of Israel?

Onyx Stones and Breastplate Bound Together. When the breastplate was finished, a ring of pure gold was set in each of its four corners, two above and two below. To the two upper rings "wreathen chains" of pure gold were fastened with "ouches" or clasps, of gold. These chains reached to rings in the onyx shoulder pieces of the ephod to which they were joined with clasps of gold, thus binding the onyx stones to the breastplate—the army's reserve to the mature and tried warriors. These chains were made double strong, being "wreathen"—twisted and interwoven—veritable cables of pure gold. Ex. 28:13, 14; 39:15-18. So Christ binds His children together, young and old, and according to His Word, no one shall "pluck them out of My Father's hand." John 10:29. How important that these chains were of "wreathen" gold!

In the two lower rings, the breastplate was fastened to gold rings on the two sides of the ephod, next to the curious girdle with a "lace of blue." Ex. 28:28. Think of it! A lace of *blue*, representing obedience to heavenly truth, bound Israel's warriors close to the girdle—that part of the military dress which was connected with the sword, in this case "the sword of the Spirit, which is the Word of God." Eph. 6:17. Thus bound together and thus equipped, Israel's warriors are sure to be victors in their spiritual warfare.

The "Curious Girdle" of the Ephod. "Curious" here means skillful, or expert in workmanship. This girdle was about a hand's breadth wide, wound twice about the upper part of the waist, and fastened in front, the long ends hanging down. Like the ephod, its royal colors were richly embroidered with threads of pure gold, thus fitly representing Christ, who was "girt about the paps with a golden girdle." Rev. 1:13. Such a girdle was a mark of excellent honor, majesty, and royalty, the rich golden girdle of Christ indicating the excellence of His ministration as High Priest.

The Mitre, or Holy Crown. The mitre, like the other garments, was made of fine linen, thus forming a triple crown, "one within another." It was a symbol of the triple crown of Christ. Fastened to the forefront of it with a ribbon of *blue*, was a plate of pure gold on which was engraved the inscription, "HOLINESS TO THE LORD." Because of this, the mitre was called "the holy crown." Ex. 39:30, 31. This plate with its blue ribbon was to be "upon Aaron's forehead," thus symbolizing that as high priest, he understood and was obedient to, the Word of God, a true representative of Christ.

When at the beginning of the one thousands years, the redeemed are associated with Christ as priests, Rev. 20:4, 6, they, too, will wear a holy crown. As their initiation into holy office, Jesus places upon the head of each "the crown of glory...bearing his own 'new name' and the inscription 'Holiness to the Lord.'" GC 646; Isaiah 62:2; Rev. 2:17; 3:12; 22:4. Those who finally wear this holy crown will in their daily lives on earth be that which it represents.

Summary of Priest's Garments. The following comparative summary shows all the garments of priest and high priest:

Common Priests' Garments	High Priest's Garments for the Day of Atonement	The High Priest's "Golden Garments"
Linen under garment	Linen under garment	Linen under garment
Plain linen coat	Plain linen coat	Embroidered coat
Embroidered girdle	Plain linen girdle	Embroidered girdle
"Goodly bonnets"	Plain linen mitre	Mitre with gold plate
Ex. 28:40, 42; 39:27-29; PP 350.	Ex. 39:27, 28; Lev. 16:4.	Ex. 28:4, 8, 36, 39.
		Blue robe of the ephod
		Ephod with onyx stones
		Breastplate
		Curious girdle.

SECTION IV

IN THE HOLY PLACE

CHAPTER 15 PREVIEW

THE HEAVENLY SANCTUARY

- Why We should Understand the Heavenly Sanctuary
- The Earthly Sanctuary a "Figure" of the Heavenly
- No Types in Heaven
- Two Apartments in the Heavenly Sanctuary
- A Safeguard Against Error
- The "Greater and More Perfect Tabernacle"
- The Heavenly Sanctuary Succeeded the Earthly
- The True Tabernacle "Set Up"
- "Heaven Itself"
- The Priesthood of the Heavenly Sanctuary
- Redemption Before Calvary
- The Ministry in the Heavenly Sanctuary Today
- Summary

15

THE HEAVENLY SANCTUARY

Why We Should Understand the Heavenly Sanctuary. The earthly sanctuary is important because it was God's object lesson to illustrate redemption in the heavenly. But the heavenly itself is the *real* sanctuary, "the great original," PP 357, where the work of redemption is actually in progress. Here Jesus is now making His final appeal before the Father in behalf of our salvation. Especially in these closing hours of probation, a serious study of this vital subject can hardly fail to awaken a lively interest in the future life, and be a strong tie that binds the earnest student to heaven.

Moreover, since the plan of salvation is the "grand central theme" of the Bible, an understanding of both the earthly and the heavenly sanctuary is fundamental to a proper understanding of the Bible. Without this, we shall lose the illumination which this subject gives to many parts of the Scriptures, that otherwise seem difficult. Our present study should therefore be to visualize the heavenly, as nearly as possible, as one great unit with Christ as its central figure, and redemption the theme permeating all its parts.

A clear and definite picture of the sanctuary above will enable us to follow Christ where He is now ministering for the salvation of man. This will strengthen our faith in the closing work of the gospel; it will help us to detect and avoid error, and thus be an anchor to the soul. Without it, we shall be unable to do our part in cooperation with Christ; and especially at this time when the Judgment, which decides our eternal destiny, is in session in the courts above. Without it, "it will be impossible…to exercise the faith which is essential at this time." GC 488.

The Earthly Sanctuary a "Figure" of the Heavenly. When God gave Moses directions for making the earthly sanctuary, He repeatedly admonished him to make all things, "according to the pattern [or model] showed [him] in the mount." Ex. 25:9, 10; 26:30; 27:8; Acts 7:44; Heb. 8:5. This sanctuary was to be an exact copy of that which he was shown. There was to be no deviation from the pattern because every detail represented some phase of the redemptive work of Christ. It is important, therefore, that we gain a clear understanding not only of this pattern but also its relation to the heavenly sanctuary.

Because "the holy places" in the earthly sanctuary were "figures of the true" or heavenly sanctuary, Heb. 9:24, some have supposed that the heavenly sanctuary was the pattern shown to Moses. Others have concluded that, since the heavenly sanctuary is "the great original" it must have been the pattern. However, Paul makes it plain that the pattern shown to Moses was but "a shadow" of heavenly things, and *not* the "very image" of those things. Heb. 10:1, 5. Also "the holy places made with hands [the holy and most holy places of the earthly sanctuary] are *the figures* of the true." Heb. 9:11. Thus not only "the things" in the earthly sanctuary, but the "building" itself was a "shadow" or "figure" of the heavenly.

It is true that "God presented before Moses in the mount a view of the heavenly sanctuary," but this was given, not as a pattern, but that he might better understand the relation of the earthly and heavenly sanctuary, and better appreciate the sacredness of his task and the importance of making "all things according to the pattern shown him." PP 349. If it be true that God gave Moses a vision of the heavenly sanctuary *as a pattern*, it would necessarily follow that in heaven there is a court with a brazen altar where sacrifices were offered, for these were part of the pattern shown him. And of the brazen altar, he was specially admonished to make it "as it was shewed [him] in the mount." Ex. 27:8. But, although Moses was shown the court, it is well known that there never was a court in heaven. Rev. 11:2. This earth, where the true Sacrifice was offered on Calvary, is the court of the heavenly sanctuary. "The *patterns* of things in the heavens" were "purified with the blood of calves and of goats," but "the heavenly things themselves with better sacrifices than these." Heb. 9:19, 23.

Just what, then, was this pattern? As already noted [page 24], both Greek and Hebrew translations of the word *pattern* as used in the books of *Hebrews* and *Exodus*, is "model." Accordingly, the pattern God showed Moses was a *model* like the one he was to construct, a *"miniature representation* of the heavenly temple" PP 349,Not only did God give Moses a "miniature representation" of every part of the sanctuary, but He even showed him exactly how these were to be assembled: "And thou shalt rear up the tabernacle according to the fashion thereof which was showed thee in the mount." Ex. 26:30.

No Types in Heaven. From texts stating that John saw the ark, the altar, the golden censer, and the seven-branched candlestick, Rev. 11:19; 8:3; 4:5, in heaven, some have supposed that John saw these articles as they were in the earthly sanctuary. We shall not be confused on this point if we bear in mind that in heaven there are no types—these all belong to the earthly sanctuary. In heaven are the *real* things, their *antitypes*. Everything connected with the earthly was an object lesson to illustrate the heavenly. Thus, when John saw the "seven lamps of fire burning before the throne," antitype of the seven-branched candlestick, he immediately states that they were "the seven Spirits of God." Rev. 4:5. If we have supposed that there is a golden candlestick in the heavenly sanctuary like the type in the earthly, we should consider that the purpose of a candlestick is to give light. Of what use, then, would a candle or candles be in heaven, where the glory of God so illuminates the entire city that even the sun, though shining with sevenfold power, is not visible? Rev. 22:5; 21:23; Isaiah 30:26

The Bible abounds in metaphors, by which some object is employed to illustrate that of which it is a symbol. For example, John declares that he saw four beasts, or living creatures, one on each side of the throne:—a lion, a calf, or ox, a flying eagle, and one having the face of a man. Rev. 4:6, 7. But what were these? He explains later that they were "redeemed from the earth." Rev. 5:8, 9. Therefore, what John really saw were not beasts but redeemed human beings so arranged that to him the groups resembled these creatures. Likewise, he saw the ark, the candlestick, the altar, and the golden censer, not as types but their antitypes.

Two Apartments in the Heavenly Sanctuary. As in the earthly sanctuary there were two distinct places, the holy and the most holy, so in its antitype each division of the work of Christ has its "distinctive place in the heavenly sanctuary." PP 357. When Christ ascended, having offered Himself as a sacrifice here on earth, He went directly within the first vail, "the door into the holy place of the heavenly sanctuary where He was anointed High Priest" to begin His work as Intercessor. When at the end of the 2300 days, he moved within "the second vail" Heb. 9:3, He went into the most holy place, the second apartment of the heavenly sanctuary, where He began His work as Judge. Dan. 7:9, 10, 13. "He still pleaded His blood before the Father in behalf of sinners." GC 429. Thus He becomes our Judge-Advocate and continues His ministry until the close of probation. Then the decree goes forth "He that is unjust, let him be unjust still…he that is righteous, let him be righteous still." Rev. 22:11. At this time the destiny of the entire human race is settled. [See GC 429 referred to in Chapter 23].

A Safeguard Against Error. The safest and surest way to dissipate the darkness of error, is to throw upon it the searchlight of truth—giving a clear and Biblical understanding. This principle applies to the sanctuary. To illustrate, let us examine some of these errors. *First*, there are those who suppose that when Christ as our Forerunner began His work as High Priest in the heavenly sanctuary, He entered directly into the second apartment, the most holy place "within the vail." Heb. 6:19, 20. These apparently overlook the fact that there were two apartments and two vails. The vail at the entrance of the most holy place was "the *second* vail." Heb. 9:3. They also forget that the high priest entered within this vail "alone once every year," at the *close* of his yearly ministry, not at its *beginning*. Heb. 9:1, 7.

Let us examine the texts that have confused some. In Hebrews 9:11, 12, Paul says that Christ at His ascension, "having obtained eternal redemption for us," "entered in once into the holy place." The expression here translated *the holy place*, is literally *the holy places*. It is the same word as is translated "holiest of all" in Hebrews 9:8 and "sanctuary" in Hebrews 8:2, where it plainly refers, not to any one apartment of the heavenly sanctuary, but to "the true tabernacle" in heaven. The earthly sanctuary was holy, the heavenly is the "Holiest of all." The word translated "Holiest of all" in Hebrews 9:3, is another word and refers to the most holy place of the earthly sanctuary. From this study, and remembering that the earthly high priest during the year ministered in the holy place, and not until the close of the year did He enter the most holy place, it seems obvious that Christ, the antitype of the earthly high priest, *began* His ministry as High Priest in the *first apartment* of the heavenly sanctuary, not in the *second*.

Since in the heavenly sanctuary there is not "the very image" of the things in the earthly, others declare that there is no sanctuary in heaven. Such a statement is wholly without Biblical authority, made evidently because of a misunderstanding, or lack of understanding, regarding the *nature* of "the true tabernacle!" A correct understanding of the significance of the earthly sanctuary as a type of the true tabernacle should help us avoid such error. No sanctuary in heaven? Impossible! The sanctuary is indispensable to the work of redemption typified in the earthly sanctuary. But we must always remember that the *true* sanctuary is "a greater and more perfect tabernacle, *not made with hands*, that is to say, *not of this building,*" which *was* "made with hands." Heb. 9:11, 24, italics supplied. Also, the things in the earthly sanctuary were "not the *very image* of the things" in the heavenly sanctuary, Heb. 10:1, but only "miniature representations" of those things. Instead, then, of there being no sanctuary in heaven, the heavenly sanctuary is as much greater than the earthly, as a building is greater than its shadow or its blueprint pattern. Doubtless an understanding of the spiritual significance of the earthly sanctuary and its relation to the *true* tabernacle would have saved the Hebrew nation from rejecting Christ and the truth regarding His work in the true sanctuary, just as it will save God's people today from error and defeat.

The "Greater and More Perfect Tabernacle." Since "the things" in the earthly sanctuary were "not the very image of the things" in the heavenly, and since "the *holy places* made with hands," that is, the "building" itself, was only a "figure" of the true tabernacle, what is the heavenly sanctuary like? Paul describes it as "a greater and more perfect tabernacle, not made with hands." Heb. 9:11. *Not made with hands!* Surely then, its walls were not made of boards carved with cherubim and plated with gold, as in "the holy places *made with hands!*" Heb. 9:24. Nor was this framework covered with badgers' skins, rams' skins, woven goats' hair, and linen embroidered with figures of cherubim. How utterly incongruous!

The "greater and more perfect" tabernacle, which God "pitched," —the true or *real* tabernacle, "the great original," was composed of *real living beings*—angels, not carved, not embroidered, not statues of beaten gold, but real angels pulsating with life. The "pattern" or "shadow" of heavenly things shown to Moses was as different from the "true tabernacle" as the pattern of a garment is different from the garment itself. It was a mere "shadow" of the "true," given to enable man to understand the *real* sanctuary in heaven. That which God showed Moses was merely a "pattern," a "shadow," a "figure," a "miniature representation," a model, of the true, with explicit directions for making all parts *exactly like the model* shown him.

The Heavenly Sanctuary Succeeded the Earthly. The "first tabernacle," Heb. 9:12, was the one made by Moses at Sinai. The temple of Solomon, and later the temple of Zerubbabel and the temple of Herod, were, in their essential features, built after the same pattern. These were all earthly sanctuaries. The earthly sanctuary in all its parts was a type of the heavenly, the "true tabernacle, which the Lord pitched, and not man." Heb. 8:2. The type reached its antitype when at the death of Christ the vail of the temple was rent. This was Heaven's announcement that the work of the earthly sanctuary was ended, and that the service of the heavenly sanctuary was about to take its place. Christ's ministry as High Priest in the heavenly sanctuary did not begin until His sacrificial work was accomplished. When on the cross He uttered the loud cry, "It is finished," John 9:30, all the sacrifices of the court met their antitype in Him, the true Sacrifice. The sacrifice of Christ, made in the court of earth, was an end of all shedding of blood for sin. Heb. 9:12. The typical sacrifices, although continued by the unbelieving Jews for a time, automatically ceased to represent the true Sacrifice. Then was fulfilled the verdict of Christ, uttered with such heartfelt pathos shortly before His betrayal: "O Jerusalem, Jerusalem, Thou that killeth the prophets, and stonest them which are sent unto thee, how often would I have gathered thy children together, even as a hen gathereth her chickens under her wings, and ye would not! Behold, your house is left unto you desolate." Matt. 23:37, 38. Never again was the glory of God manifest in the earthly sanctuary. Never again was it to be the dwelling place of God on earth. The service of the heavenly sanctuary was about to succeed that of the earthly.

The True Tabernacle "Made Manifest." "Before the foundations of the earth were laid, the Father and the Son had united in a covenant to redeem man should he be overcome by Satan." DA 834. It was at that secret council that Christ, the Lamb of God, offered himself as a ransom to redeem him. Zech. 6:13; GC 416, 417. But all will agree that Christ was not actually slain until the cross.

Likewise, in this council of peace every provision was made for man's complete redemption. In His infinite love and foreknowledge the Father *planned* the heavenly sanctuary, in which all Heaven could cooperate, PP 63, 64, and at the time appointed this sanctuary would actually function, or be "made manifest."

While "the first tabernacle was yet standing," "the way into the holiest of all [the heavenly sanctuary] was not yet made manifest." Heb. 9:8. So long as the type [the earthly sanctuary] was fulfilling God's purpose, there was no need of the antitype; the type met its antitype and passed away at the death of Christ and the vail was rent. The Lord piched the true tabernacle in heaven. The "the way into the holiest of all" was made manifest; then the sanctuary on earth gave place to the sanctuary in heaven; then the earthly priesthood was succeeded by the priesthood of Christ, and the ministration was "removed from the earthly to the heavenly temple." DA 166.

Thus while the heavenly sanctuary was conceived in the days of eternity, and in an accommodated sense might be said to have existed from eternity, it could not *actually function* until after the death, resurrection and ascension of Christ when He was anointed High Priest.

On this question, M. L. Andreasen in his book, *The Book of Hebrews*, page 328, states, "Verse 8 [of Heb. 9] means that the way into the true holies [the heavenly sanctuary] was not manifested so long as the service in the Mosaic tabernacle [the earthly sanctuary] was still meeting the mind of God." On page 330 he further states, "the way to the heavenly sanctuary would be open when the earthly sanctuary had fulfilled its appointed mission."

The Heavenly Sanctuary Anointed. The lamb, "a male of the first year" which the priest offered morning and evening as a consecration of Israel to God, represented Christ when at the *beginning* of His earthly life, He entered the court of earth to become the Sacrifice which God gave for "the world." John 3:16. The "ram of consecration," Ex. 29:22, a mature male sheep, which Moses [who represented God] offered when the earthly sanctuary was set up, symbolized Christ as a Sacrifice at the *close* of His life on earth. As the service in the earthly sanctuary could not begin until this sacrifice had been offered and until both the sanctuary and the priests had been anointed, Ex. 40:9-15, 29, so the service in the heavenly sanctuary could not begin until Christ the true Sacrifice had been offered on Calvary, and until at His ascension, He had been anointed High Priest, and "the most Holy," the heavenly sanctuary, had been anointed. Dan. 9:24. This was the last prophetic event before the close of the 70 weeks.

The True Tabernacle Set Up. The Lord Himself "pitched" the true tabernacle. Heb. 8:2. The word here translated "pitched" is better rendered "set up," as by Moffatt. As Moses, who was a type of God, set up the first tabernacle at Sinai, so God "set up" the true tabernacle, which was its antitype. God "set up" the true tabernacle; that is, He organized and arranged all the forces of heaven to cooperate with Christ in the work of redemption, —all heaven was staged for that momentous event. This gives us a very different picture from that of a tent pitched or a building erected. If it were a tent or a structure of some kind, how large would it have to be to enclose all the vast number of angels that surround the throne? And what would be its roof? The earthly sanctuary was but "a faint reflection of its vastness and glory," which "no earthly sanctuary structure could represent." GC 414; PP 357.

This sanctuary into which Christ entered at His ascension is called "heaven itself." Heb. 9:24. "Christ is not entered into the holy places made with hands, which are figures of the true; but into *heaven itself*," into the heavenly sanctuary. And in this sanctuary, "not made with hands" but "set up" by God, Christ began His ministry as our heavenly High Priest.

"Heaven Itself." Let us dwell for a moment on the expression "heaven itself." Heaven is defined by Webster as the abode of God; also, the firmament or sky. When Paul speaks of "heaven itself," Heb. 9:24, he evidently refers to the abode of God. He also called this "the *third* heaven" or "Paradise." II Cor. 12:2, 4. The "firmament with which God surrounded this earth at creation would, then be the *first* heaven [if we may number it], and the space between these two would be the *second* heaven. As the *first* heaven surrounds this earth, so the *third* heaven surrounds Paradise, the dwelling place of God. Just as the first heaven, the firmament, at creation was an inseparable part of the earth itself, so the *third heaven* is an inseparable part of "heaven itself," or Paradise. Paul was caught up "to" the third heaven, "into" Paradise. Paradise which is but another name for the city "which hath foundations, whose builder and maker is God," Heb. 11:10, is the dwelling place of God. Therefore, the heavenly sanctuary [of which the earthly, His dwelling place on earth was a type] is the real dwelling place of God.

By the law of comparison and equality, the heavenly sanctuary therefore is "heaven itself," "into" which Christ entered at His ascension, Heb. 9:24, the Paradise "into" which Paul was caught up. Whether *all* or only *part* of "heaven itself," or Paradise, or the City of God, is devoted to the workin the heavenly sanctuary, we are not told, but we do know that sufficient space is thus occupied to accommodate all the innumerable heavenly beings who assist Christ in the work of redemption.

The Priesthood of the Heavenly Sanctuary. Not only were the "holy places" of the earthly sanctuary and "the things" in it a type of the "true tabernacle," but the earthly high priest was a type of Christ, the heavenly High Priest. Up to the time of His ascension, there had been no actual priest in heaven. Till then the priesthood was confined to the earthly sanctuary. When, at His ascension, Christ began His work as High Priest, a full *representative priesthood* was established. They were the "multitude of captives," Eph. 4:8, margin, who "came out of the graves after His resurrection," Matt. 27:52, 53, and ascended with Him. These are now acting as "priests unto God." Rev. 5:9, 10.

Redemption Before Calvary. Since before Calvary there was no Priest in heaven, and since "without shedding of blood there is no remission" of sin, Heb. 9:22, how did man have redemption before Calvary and before Christ became High Priest? On this point, we should remember that Christ was "the Lamb slain from the foundation of the world," Rev. 13:8,–from the time of that secret "counsel of peace" between the Father and the Son, Zech. 6:13, "before the creation of the earth." PP 63. This, the *promised* Sacrifice, is "the mystery which…now [by his actual sacrifice] is made manifest to His saints," "unto our glory." Col. 1:26; I Cor. 2:7. It was in that secret counsel with the Father "before the foundation of the world" that Christ was "foreordained" as a sacrifice. I Peter 1:18-20. "Before the world began," salvation "was given to redeem man if the need should arise. The need arose in the garden of Eden, when our first parents fell under the dominion of Satan. From that time to the cross, fallen man had forgiveness and redemption through faith in the *promised* blood of Christ; since Calvary, he has forgiveness and redemption through faith in His *shed* blood.

The Ministry in the Heavenly Sanctuary Today. Since there are no types in heaven, it seems evident that when John was given a vision of the heavenly sanctuary, he was shown the living throne of God, antitype of the ark with the mercy seat and the Shekinah; he was shown Jesus as our Intercessor, offering His righteousness as sweet incense before the throne, antitype of the golden altar and the golden censer, both of which had to do with the offering of incense which represented the righteousness of Christ; he was shown the "seven Spirits of God," antitype of the seven-branched golden candlestick "burning before the throne." Thus in the heavenly sanctuary today are united all the persons of the Godhead—Father, Son, and Holy Spirit in His sevenfold power in behalf of our salvation, while angels, obeying the "voices" which like "thunderings" proceed out of the throne, speed like flashes of "lightning," Rev. 4:5, eager to be sent forth "as ministering spirits...for them who shall be heirs of salvation." Heb. 1:14. These angels are the antitype of the cherubim of shining gold engraved in the walls and embroidered in the ceiling and the vails of the earthly sanctuary. As time with rapid pace hastens to its close, the Spirit of God "maketh intercession for us with groanings which cannot be uttered." Rom 8:26. Think of it! Especially at this time, when the destiny of the human race hangs in the balance, so great is the solicitude of the Holy Spirit for your salvation and for mine, that it is beyond words. Only deep groanings can express His soul agony for sinful man. This work of the Father, Son, and Holy Spirit, together with that of the angels, is the work now in progress in the living sanctuary, "the greater and more perfect tabernacle, not made with hands," "the true tabernacle which the Lord pitched, and not man." Heb. 9:11; 8:2.

Summary. To sum up, let us group together in a clear picture the salient features of the heavenly sanctuary as typified in the earthly. *First*, that there is no court in heaven, that this earth where Jesus, the true Sacrifice, suffered and bled and died, is the court of the heavenly sanctuary. *Second*, "vastness and glory" could not be represented in any "earthly structure" or "building" made with hands. *Third*, that the sanctuary above has two "distinctive places," the holy place where Christ began His work as High Priest, and the most holy, where He now officiates as Judge. *Fourth*, that there are no types in heaven, that the earthly building and the things in it are not the very image of the "things" in heaven, but only their "shadow." *Fifth*, that in the heavenly sanctuary all "the things" are *real* and *living*, antitypes of "the things" made with hands. *Sixth*, that the heavenly sanctuary was not made with hands, but was set up by God when the earthly had fulfilled its purpose. *Seventh*, and most important of all, that the final work for man's redemption by the Father, Son, Holy Spirit, and the angels, is now in progress in the heavenly sanctuary, and will soon close. Then, "the harvest," which is "the end of the world," Matt. 13:39, will be past, the wheat, the redeemed, will be gathered into the heavenly garner, and the chaff will be burned up. Matt. 3:12.

CHAPTER 16 PREVIEW

CHRIST ENTERING THE HOLY PLACE OF THE HEAVENLY SANCTUARY

- "Psalms Concerning" Jesus
- Their Fulfillment in A.D. 31
- Why Jesus Observed this Passover One Day Early
- The Lord's Supper Instituted
- Jesus Fulfilling the Types of the Passover Supper
- The Secret of His Victory
- Jesus the True Paschal Lamb
- Ceremonial Sabbaths Abolished
- Jesus the True Wave Sheaf
- The Forty Days After His Resurrection
- Entering the Holy Place of the Heavenly Sanctuary
- At Heaven's Gates
- The Welcome Home Song. *Selah!*
- A Royal Reception
- God's Throne a Moving Throne; A Living Throne;
- •
- A Glorious High Throne
- Christ's Inauguration and Coronation
- The Anointing of the Holy Spirit
- Pentecost the "Conclusion" of the Passover
- The Former Rain and the Latter Rain
- The Holy Spirit in Our Lives Today
- Jesus Our Forerunner

16

CHRIST ENTERING THE HOLY PLACE OF THE HEAVENLY SANCTUARY

"Psalms Concerning" Jesus. Many of the Psalms are prophecies of experiences through which Jesus would pass during His life on earth—"things ... which were written...in the Psalms concerning Me," Christ declared. Luke 24:44. In connection with His entrance into the holy place in heaven, we may look for a moment to Psalms 22, 23, and 24.

The twenty-second Psalm, called "The Calvary, or Golgotha Psalm," begins with the agonizing cry of Jesus, "My God, My God, why hast *Thou* forsaken Me?" Mark 15:34. It ends up with, "He hath done this!" or, as the Hebrew has it, "It is finished!" John 19:30.

The twenty-third Psalm has been called "The Psalm of the Resurrection," because the resurrection follows His "walk through the valley of the shadow of death." It is a prophecy of the unspoken experiences of Jesus as He passed through the "valley." It expresses a marvelous triumph of faith, especially in its closing words:

> I will fear no evil; for Thou art with Me;
> Thy rod and Thy staff, they comfort Me.
> Thou preparest a table before Me
>   in the presence of Mine enemies;
> Thou anointest My head with oil;
> My cup runneth over.
> Surely goodness and loving mercies shall follow me
>   all the days of My life;
> And I shall dwell in the house of Jehovah forever.—R.V.

Following this is the twenty-fourth Psalm, which may be called "The Ascension Psalm." This Psalm of triumph is the climax of the two preceding ones. It foretells some of the wonderful experiences of Christ's ascension from the court of this earth to His entrance into the heavenly sanctuary—into "heaven itself." Heb. 9:24.

Their Fulfillment in A.D. 31. The experiences prophesied in these Psalms were fulfilled at the last divinely recognized Passover and Pentecost, in the crucifixion, resurrection, ascension, and inauguration of Jesus, when the sacred significance of the work of the priests in the earthly sanctuary ended and the ministry of Christ as High Priest in the heavenly sanctuary began.

In A.D. 31 two Passovers were observed—not only the one celebrated by the Jewish people generally, but the one Jesus and His disciples observed one day early. The former was prepared at the regular time, "in the evening" of Abib 14, (See Appendix page 25) and eaten the following night, the beginning of Abib 15. For fifteen long centuries, since the institution of the Passover at the time of the Exodus, this practice had been followed. From this, "some have suggested that the meal Jesus and the Twelve ate together was not the regular Passover repast; but the synoptic record makes clear that it was indeed *the Passover* they ate together. See Mark 14:12, 16, 17; Luke 22:7, 8, 13-15; DA 642, 652." Raymond F. Cottrell, in RH, June 9, 1955, page 18; Emphasis supplied. This statement should remembered, for it is the key to other points sometimes misunderstood.

When was this last true Passover prepared and eaten? "When the feast of unleavened bread drew nigh, which is called the Passover," Jesus told His disciples to "prepare...to eat the Passover." On the first day of the feast, "when they killed the Passover," "they made ready the Passover." Mark 14:12; Luke 22:7, 13. This preparation was made on Thursday, Abib 13, one day before the regular time, the historic time for slaying the paschal lamb being Abib 14. Ex. 12:6. "When the even was come [the beginning of Abib 14], He sat down with the Twelve, and they did eat." Matt: 26:20, 21. This also was one day before the regular time for eating the Passover. "According to the best available astronomical information, Nisan [Abib] 14 fell on Friday, April 27, in A.D. 31, the year of the crucifixion." Raymond F. Cottrell, in RH June 9, 1955.

Why Jesus Observed this Passover One Day Early. Why did Jesus depart from an age-long and well-established custom? Apparently one reason for doing so was that His death might coincide with the slaying of the paschal lamb, and thus perfectly fulfill the type. Another reason: "Jesus knew that His hour was come that He should depart out of this world unto the Father and because "He loved His own ... unto the end." He desired to prepare them for that ordeal. John 13:1, 19. Further, because the death of the paschal lamb symbolized the death of Christ as the Redeemer of the world, it was to be "an ordinance forever" Ex. 12:17, —the work of redemption was never to be forgotten. Now that the Passover type was soon to pass away, it was necessary that another ordinance be provided to take its place, thus perpetuating the memory of redemption. It is obvious, of course, that this be done at once, because when the day ended, He would be lying in the tomb, and in that event, an important link in the plan of salvation would be missing. For all these reasons, it was necessary that Christ eat the Passover one day before the regular time. These reasons are all comprehended in His words, "With desire I have desired to eat this Passover with you before I suffer." Luke 22:15.

The Lord's Supper Instituted. Knowing that the Passover as a sacred ordinance was about to pass away, Jesus now instituted the Lord's Supper "as a memorial of the same event of which the Passover had been a type." PP 539. The paschal lamb had pointed *forward* to His death; the Lord's Supper was to point *back*, commemorative of His broken body and His spilled blood. Luke 22:16-20.

Before the disciples were prepared to partake of the sacred emblems of the Lord's Supper, their hearts must be cleansed from all selfish ambition to be the greatest and from all unholy feelings toward one another. Each one must first "examine himself." I Cor. 11:28. For this a preparatory service was necessary to teach humility and unselfish service. As a "type of the higher cleansing of the soul," DA 646, Jesus proceeded to wash the disciples' feet. The purpose of this humble service on the part of their Lord and Master was to remove from their hearts all evil thoughts, and implant a willingness for any Christian service. Without this cleansing the heart could not "enter into fellowship with Christ" and be "prepared to receive the communion of His body and His blood." DA 650. They would eat and drink "unworthily" and thus "be guilty of the body and blood of the Lord." John 13:4-17; I Cor. 11:26-29. When Jesus finished this service, He instituted feet washing as a sacred ordinance to precede the Lord's Supper, saying, "I have given you an example that ye should do as I have done to you," John 13:15, an ordinance to continue until type reaches antitype, "the higher cleansing: when all the redeemed have been washed in the blood of the Lamb."

Jesus Fulfilling the Types of the Passover Supper. Nisan 14 was a long day of agonizing suffering culminating in His crucifixion. That same night, the chief priests, seeking "how they might take Him by craft, and put Him to death" before the Passover, Mark 14:1, 10, 11, 43-46, bribed Judas to betray Him—Judas, whose feet Jesus had washed only an hour or so before! "For envy they had delivered Him," Matt. 27:18, to a band of officers from the chief priests who, having sought false witnesses against Him, bound Him and led Him to the high priest. John 18:3, 12, 13. From the high priest's palace, as soon as it was day, He was taken before the council where, because He said He was the Son of God, the high priest accused Him of blasphemy and therefore guilty of death. Luke 22:66-71; Matt. 26:63-66.

While it was still early, He was led into the judgment hall, where the priests themselves went not lest they be "defiled" and thus disqualified to participate in the Passover. John 18:28. They seemed not to understand that the things which defile a man come from the heart—evil thoughts, murders, false witness, blasphemies, etc. John 18:28; Matt. 15:18-20. Because they could not enter into the judgment hall, they persuaded the multitude, whom they had influenced, to regard Christ as an impostor, a deceiver, to cry out, "Crucify Him," a cry in which they themselves joined "with loud voices" when He was brought forth. Matt. 27:20-25, 63; John 19:6; Luke 23:18, 23.

During and following His trial, He was scourged, reviled, derided, and railed upon. His persecutors spit on His face and smote Him on the head. They put on Him a crown of thorns and a purple robe, and mockingly cried, "Hail, king of the Jews!" Matt. 26:27; 27:28-31. All this and much more, He calmly endured, and instead of being overwhelmed by such cruelty and injustice, He was not thinking of Himself but for others, one of His last acts being to provide for the care of His mother. John 19:25-27. Even when He was nailed to the cross, His enemies continued their insults and abuse, yet still as He hung there amidst all His agonizing sufferings, He had no unkind feelings toward them, but prayed, "Father, forgive them, for they know not what they do." Luke 23:33, 34. In these bitter afflictions, Jesus completely fulfilled "both as to the event and as to the time," GC 399, the types of the Passover Supper! —the "bread of affliction," Deut. 16:3, 4, and the "bitter herbs," He Himself being the lamb "roast with fire." "Let the imagination grasp each scene. As we thus dwell upon His great sacrifice for us, our confidence in Him will be more constant, our love will be quickened, and we shall be more deeply imbued with His spirit. If we are saved at last, we must learn the lesson of penitence and humiliation at the foot of the cross." DA 83.

It seems almost incredible that the Jews, and especially the leaders of the temple service, should be guilty of having any part in putting to death Him to Whom all the rites of their sacrificial service had for centuries pointed, to show their faith in Him as their Redeemer. But they were "the whole council," or Sanhedrin, Mark 15:1, determined to put Him to death before the Passover, for "if the trial and crucifixion were not brought about at once, there would be a week's delay on account of the celebration." DA 703.

The Secret of His Victory. Under these most trying conditions, how could Jesus be so completely without sin? Was it not because He was familiar with the Scriptures? He knew that His hour was come when He was to be "brought as a lamb to the slaughter," and though "oppressed and afflicted," He was not to open His mouth. Isaiah 53:7. He knew that Judas would betray Him for "thirty pieces of silver" which was "a goodly price." Zech. 11:12, 13. He knew that "for envy" and "by craft" the chief priests would deliver Him to be crucified. Ps. 69:4; Mark 15:10; Matt. 27:18. He knew that in His thirst He would be given vinegar to drink. Ps. 69:21. In fact, from the Scriptures, He understood the whole situation. Therefore, when He was unjustly accused of the chief priests and elders, "He answered nothing...never a word." Matt. 27:12, 14, Mark 15:3, 5.

He knew what death He must die, John 12:32, 33; 18:11, and that the Scriptures must be fulfilled, Matt. 26:52-56; John 13:18, and with a calm faith and steadfast trust in God, He unresistingly submitted Himself to His persecutors. All this He did for your salvation and for mine. It was "for the joy [the joy of seeing souls saved] that was set before Him [that He] endured the cross, despising the shame." Heb. 12:2. He was about to become our "merciful and faithful High Priest" and it was through suffering that He was made perfect. Heb. 2:10, 17. Because He was "in all points tempted like as we are, yet without sin," He is touched with the feeling of our infirmities, and He is able to succor them that are tempted. Heb. 4:14, 15; 2:18. Jesus died, not entirely from crucifixion, for when the soldiers came to hasten the death of the malefactors, He was dead already. John 19:33. He died of a broken heart, for of Him it is written, "Reproach hath broken My heart." Ps. 69:20.

Our time of test and trial is just ahead, and if day by day we follow the example of Jesus, making the Scriptures our safeguard, we shall come off "more than conquerors through Him that loved us." Rom 8:35-39.

Jesus the True Paschal Lamb. Jesus, the true Paschal Lamb, "the Lamb of God, which taketh away the sin of the world," John 1:29, was crucified the sixth hour of Nisan 14, and He died the ninth hour, 3:00 p.m., in the evening, Ex. 12:6; Mark 15:33-37, literally "between the two evenings," a perfect fulfillment "not only as to the event but as to the time," GC 399, of the paschal lamb slain between 3:00 p.m. and sunset. "When the loud cry 'It is finished' came from the lips of Christ, the priests were officiating in the temple. It was the hour of the evening sacrifice. The lamb representing Christ had been brought to be slain....The earth trembles and quakes....With a rending noise the inner vail of the temple is torn from top to bottom by an unseen hand. Matt. 27:50, 51. The most holy place of the earthly sanctuary is no longer sacred.... Type has met antitype in the death of God's Son." DA 756, 757. And yet, even though they, the temple leaders, witnessed all these things, their spiritual eyesight was so blinded that they did not recognized them as the end of the temple service. They were indeed "blind guides." Matt. 23:13-16.

With His blood, Jesus had signed "the emancipation papers of the race." MH 90, and "the death knell of Satan was rung." GC 503. His death was Heaven's announcement that the Passover was now fulfilled in "Christ our Passover." I Cor. 5:7. From that time the Passover "lost its significance," DA 723; PP 539, and its observance henceforth would be but an empty form, a mere farce. The whole system of offerings included in the ceremonial law was done away. The Passover Jesus ate with the Twelve was indeed the last Passover divinely recognized.

Ceremonial Sabbaths Abolished. In this connection it is important that we understand the difference between the "sabbaths" of the yearly ceremonial feasts, and the "sabbath of the Lord thy God" which is part of His eternal law, the Ten Commandments. Of the former there were seven each year. Of the latter there were and still are fifty-two, one each week. Because each of the former came once a year, they are sometimes called "yearly sabbaths." The latter is the "weekly Sabbath" coming the seventh day of every week. The weekly Sabbath is a memorial of creation. Gen. 2:1-3; Ex. 20:8-11. It is not a type pointing to the death of Christ, as were the sacrifices of the ceremonial or yearly Sabbaths. It has no connection whatever with the seven "yearly sabbaths." These latter are "beside the Sabbath of the Lord." Lev. 23:38. They are all listed in Leviticus 23:

Two with the Passover, one on the first day of this feast, the other on the last. Lev. 23:4-8.

One on the Day of Pentecost, the fiftieth day from the morrow after the Passover was eaten. vs.15, 21.

Two connected with the Day of Atonement—the first at the blowing of trumpets on the *first* day of the seventh month to announce its approach, vs. 24, 25; the other on the Day of Atonement, the *tenth* day of the seventh month. vs.27-36.

Two at the Feast of Tabernacles; one on the first, the other on the last day of that feast. vs.34-39.

These days were called "sabbaths" because concerning each the command was, "Ye shall have an holy convocation: ye shall do no servile work therein." "It shall be unto you a sabbath of rest." Lev. 23:7, 8, 32.

From this list it will be seen that while the weekly sabbath day always comes on the seventh day of the week, these yearly "sabbaths" came not on any regular *day of the week*, but on a certain *day of the month*, and, like December 25, or July 4, or one's birthday, the day of the week on which they fell varied from year to year. Whenever a ceremonial "sabbath" fell on the regular weekly "Sabbath," as it would about once in seven years, being a double sabbath, it was called "an high day." John 19:31.

Many sincere but uninformed Christians have been taught that the weekly Sabbath—"the Sabbath of the fourth commandment," Ex. 20:10—was "nailed to the cross" at the death of Christ, and that in honor of His resurrection on the first day of the week, Sunday thereafter became the weekly Sabbath of the New Testament. But nowhere in the Bible is there any authority for this supposed change. Beware of it, for it is one of "the wiles [sly tricks, *Webster*] of the devil," Eph. 6:11, to turn men away from obedience to the eternal law of God.

The "sabbaths" observed in connection with the yearly feasts were part of the ceremonial law which prefigured the sacrifice of Christ on Calvary, and when at His death they met their antitype they automatically came to an end. These are the "sabbaths" that were "nailed to the cross" and abolished. Not so with the Sabbath of the fourth commandment, which being part of God's eternal law will never cease; it will be observed by all who enter in through the gates of the Holy City, and who finally have an eternal home in the new earth. Rev. 22:14; Isaiah 66:23.

Jesus the True Wave Sheaf. As the Sabbath drew on, Luke 23:54, the body of Jesus was tenderly taken down from the cross and laid in Joseph's new tomb. John 19:38-42. Here He quietly rested over the sacred Sabbath. His persecutors and murderers had accomplished their wicked design, and while Jesus lay in the tomb, they were having "an high day" celebrating a Passover that had lost its significance. As Israel had a day of great rejoicing when delivered from Egyptian bondage, singing, "The Lord hath triumphed gloriously," Ex. 15:1, 21, even so, when Christ rested "from the work of redemption," "all Heaven triumphed in the Saviour's victory." DA 758, 769. "A shout of triumph rang through every world." PP 70.

Early Sunday morning, Abib 16 (See Appendix page 25) "while it was yet dark," the women came to the sepulcher with sweet spices to anoint the body of Jesus; but He was not there. "Two angels stood by them in shining garments," Luke 24:4. One of them, the angel Gabriel, who had rolled away the stone, told them that He had risen. Matt. 28:1-6; DA 780. Quickly, they carried the news to the disciples. As soon as the soldiers recovered from the dazzling light of the angels which had caused them to fall as dead men, they went to the chief priests and told them all the things that were done. The priests, trembling, gave them "large money" bribing them to say, "The disciples came by night and stole Him away, while we slept." Matt. 28:11-15; DA 782. Truly, what they had feared, had come to pass, so that their last error was indeed worse than the first. Matt. 27:62-66.

When Jesus by His death fulfilled the type of the paschal lamb, redemption was secured to all who accept the Sacrifice. But, although *secured*, it was not at that time *completed*. It will be completed when the decree goes forth, "He that is righteous, let him be righteous still, and he that is holy, let him be holy still." Rev. 22:11, 12. At His resurrection, Christ fulfilled the type of the wave sheaf of first fruits. Lev. 23:16. He was the true wave sheaf, the "first fruits of them that slept." I Cor. 15:20, and the resurrection of them who die in the Lord was *secured*. It will be *completed* at the first resurrection, Rev. 20:6. Both these types were fulfilled "not only as to the event, but as to the time." GC 399.

The Forty Days After His Resurrection. Early on the morning of His resurrection, Christ ascended to His Father. John 20:16, 17. He had fulfilled His pledge to give His life a ransom for fallen man. The Father accepted the sacrifice, and ratified the covenant He had made with His Son in their "counsel of peace." Zech. 6:13. When this compact was sealed Christ "entered upon His mediatorial work." DA 819. Then He returned to His followers in a world of sin.

For forty days after His resurrection, Christ remained on this earth, "showing Himself alive...by many infallible proofs...and speaking [to the disciples] of the things pertaining to the kingdom of God." Acts 1:3. As this time neared its close, He commanded the disciples "that they should not depart from Jerusalem, but wait until they should be baptized with the Holy Ghost," and receive power for witnessing, vs. 4, 5, 8. This was the fulfillment of the promise He had given them before His death. "It is expedient for you that I go away; for if I go not away, the Comforter will not come unto you; but if I depart, I will send Him unto you." Henceforth the Comforter, the Holy Spirit, was to be Christ's representative on earth. John 16:7, 13, 14. These forty days ended on the 25th day of the second month. (See Appendix page 25).

Entering the Holy Place of the Heavenly Sanctuary. After forty days, He again ascended, this time to enter upon His work "as Priest and Advocate in the heaven of heavens." DA 757; Heb. 4:14; GC 420. In triumph, such as no earthly conqueror ever knew, He ascends. Nor does He go alone. "When He ascended up on high, He led a multitude of captives," Eph. 4:8, margin, —those who came out of their graves "after His resurrection, and went into the holy city, and appeared unto many." Matt. 27:50-53. Christ is "the first begotten of the dead." Rev. 1:5; that is, the first to rise from the dead by his own power, John 10:17, 18, and these redeemed ones are trophies of His triumph whom He presents to His Father. Rev. 5:8-10; DA 829, 834. We do not know who these honored ones were, but we do know that they were raised out of graves in countries where Abel, Noah, Abraham, Isaac, Jacob, Joseph, Isaiah, Jeremiah, Ezekiel, Daniel, Esther, John the Baptist, and other noble worthies were buried before Christ Himself was laid in the tomb. "They were chosen and holy ones of every age, from creation down even to the days of Christ." EW 184. They were redeemed "out of every kindred, and tongue, and people, and nation." Rev. 5:8-10.

As He ascended from the court of earth, "a cloud" [of angels] a living cloud "received Him out of their sight." Acts 1:9. With songs of joy they escorted Him to the Father in heaven. Two angels, "the most exalted of the angel throng," the same two "who had come to the tomb at His resurrection and...had been with Him throughout His life on earth," lingered for a moment to comfort the disciples who were left behind, the assurance that He would come again and receive them unto Himself. John 14:1-3; Acts 1:9-11; DA 831. One of these angels was Gabriel, the "angel of the Lord," Luke 1:11, 19, "he who fills the position from which Satan [Lucifer] fell," "he who on the hills of Bethlehem proclaimed Christ's birth," and who rolled away the stone at His resurrection. DA 779, 780.

At Heaven's Gates. As the procession reaches the gates of the heavenly city, the question is asked, doubtless concerning the accompanying redeemed "multitude:"

> "Who shall ascend into the hill of the Lord?
> Or who shall stand in His holy place?"

Promptly comes back the answer:

> "He only who has clean hands and a heart unstained,
> Who never sets his mind on what is false,
> Who never breaks his word." Ps. 24:4, *Moffatt*.

With this answer, these highly favored ones "receive the blessing of the Lord," vs. 8 —their graduation diplomas and credentials, if you please, preparatory to entering into the City.

The Welcome Home Song. Then begins that wonderful welcome home song. With rapture and confidence the angels sing out to those within, "Lift up your heads, O ye gates; and be ye lift up, ye everlasting doors; and the KING OF GLORY shall come in!"

The angels within joyfully ask, "Who is this KING OF GLORY?" Back comes the answer from those who attend Jesus, "The Lord strong and mighty, the Lord mighty in battle. [The Eternal, conquering from the fight—*Moffatt.*] Lift up your heads, O ye gates; even lift them up, ye everlasting doors; and the KING OF GLORY shall come in!"

Again the angels from within ask, "Who is this KING OF GLORY?" And the answer comes ringing back, "The Lord of hosts, He is the KING OF GLORY. Selah." Ps. 24:7-10. And so, as in antistrophe, they sing back and forth until all heaven echoes and re-echoes with their joyous music.

"Selah!" This wonderful anthem closes with the word *selah*, which, in the musical nomenclature of the Hebrews, is so full of beautiful meaning that it should never be omitted in reading. One authority states that it is an exclamation like *Hallelujah*, and corresponds to the *Amen* which closes many of our modern anthems. Another says it indicates that what has been said deserves to be remembered always, that it is a word of emphasis used to give weight and importance to, and to indicate the truth of, that which is sung or spoken. In this sense it is like *Amen*. Still another states that it indicates a pause in the music when the voices are silent while the instruments or orchestra "burst in more strongly during the silence of the song." Probably all these authorities are correct, depending, to some extent at least, on the setting of the word, the general idea being—here is something of exceptional interest and importance; pause and meditate upon it, and remember it always.

Whichever meaning we choose to accept, its setting in this twenty-fourth Psalm leads us to the conclusion that when the ascending procession reaches the gates of the City, there is a reverent pause and a short period of silence. Then "the portals of the City of God are opened wide, and the angelic throng sweep through the gates amid a burst of rapturous music." DA 835.

As the angels accompanying Jesus join those within the City, they form a united chorus of "ten thousand times ten thousand and thousands of thousands" of voices. Then in a note higher, and with all the pleasing variations of the closing strains of a mighty oratorio, all heaven seems to overflow with joy and praise as they sing their grand finale:

> Se-lah! Se-lah!
> Hal-le-lu-jah! Hal-le-lu-jah!
> A-men and A-men!

With such a display of exultant musical power, we may be sure that this closing burst of vocal and instrumental music gave "weight and emphasis" to this, one of the finest musical compositions ever written.

A Royal Reception. As the "everlasting doors" swing open and the risen Saviour crosses the threshold of the heavenly sanctuary, what a multitude awaits the meek and lowly One! What a reception! Not only the "innumerable company of angels," Heb. 12:22, are assembled to honor their adored Commander, but here also are "the representatives of the unfallen worlds….the heavenly council before which Lucifer had accused God and His Son….and over which Satan had thought to establish his dominion, —all are there to welcome the Redeemer,…eager to celebrate His triumph." DA 833, 834.

Here to the "door" of the heavenly sanctuary, antitype of the door to the holy place of the earthly sanctuary, the very gate of heaven, the Father Himself has come to welcome His only-begotten and well-beloved Son. Seated on His magnificent throne of indescribable glory encircled by the rainbow of promise, and surrounded by cherubim and seraphim, He eagerly awaits the arrival of the Conqueror. In this exalted position, He is the most prominent figure in that vast assembly.

Here Christ "entered in once into the holy place, having obtained eternal redemption for us." He entered not into "the holy places made with hands, which are a figure of the true; but into heaven itself, now to appear in the presence of God for us." Heb. 9:12, 24.

God's Throne a Moving Throne. Do you ask how it is that God's throne at this time appears in the holy place of the heavenly sanctuary instead of in the most holy place, as symbolized in the earthly sanctuary? Being only a type, the earthly could not fully represent the heavenly, because its parts, such as the ark, the golden altar, the candlestick, etc., had no inherent power, while their antitypes in the heavenly sanctuary are full of life and activity. God's throne, the antitype of the ark with the mercy seat, is a living, moving, throne. Sometimes it was seen at the "threshold of the house" —at the door—and again it "stood over the cherubim." Eze. 9:3; 10:18; Rev. 4:1-6. "Whither the Spirit was to go." That is, wherever God desired to go, the throne went. Eze. 1:12, 20. We must therefore conclude that when Christ at His ascension entered the holy place to begin His work as High Priest in the heavenly sanctuary, God with His living throne, moved to "the threshold of the house," that is, to the door of *the holy place*, to welcome His Son.

When Christ began His work of Judgment in the most holy place, God's throne was moved, or placed, "over the cherubim" in *the most holy place*. Dan. 7:9. When Christ comes back to this earth, He is on the Father's throne, "sitting on the right hand of power." Matt. 26:64. And finally, in the redeemed earth, "the throne of God" will be in the City, where Christ will sit down with the Father "in His throne." Rev. 22:3; 3:21. So, from the beginning of Christ's work in the heavenly sanctuary until "the kingdoms of this world are become the kingdoms of our Lord, and of His Christ," Rev. 11:15, the throne of God is not fixed in one place, but changes its location as His work requires. This agrees with the exposition of such reliable authorities as Uriah Smith, S. N. Haskell, and others.

A Living Throne. The throne of God is the center of life and power, from which heavenly messengers speed on divine errands like a "whirlwind" and a "flash of lightning." Eze. 1:4, 14. They are "ministering spirits, sent forth to minister to them who shall be heirs of salvation." Heb. 1:14. They are sent forth from

Him who is on the throne, for "out of the throne proceed" not only "lightings," but also "thunderings and voices" "as of a trumpet." Rev. 4, 5; 1:10.

"In the midst of the throne" —["on each side of the throne, all around it" *Moffatt*] are four living creatures who, like burning coals of fire, and like lamps "ran and returned as the appearance of a flash of lightning." Eze. 1:13, 14. They are full of eyes "before and behind." Eze. 10:12; Rev. 4:6. And "their wings [are] joined one to another." Eze. 1:5, 9. This would indicate that each one is a group of beings. John says the first group was like a lion, king of beasts, representing Him as king, the ox as servant, the man representing His humanity, and the flying eagle His divinity.

These four groups have been redeemed from the earth. Rev. 5:8-10. The only Bible record of a redeemed multitude who are now in heaven are those who "Came out of the graves after His resurrection," Matt. 27:52, 53, and ascended with Christ to associate with Him as priests in the closing work of redemption. Rev. 5:9, 10. Accompanying each was a wheel, *a living wheel*, "for the spirit of the living creature was in them." Eze. 10:9, 17. They were "so high that they were dreadful." Their rims and spokes were "full of eyes all round." Eze. 1:18, *Moffatt*. They "were as if a wheel had been in the midst of a wheel. Their whole body, and their backs, and their hands, and their wings, and the wheels were full of eyes round about, even the wheels that they four had." Eze. 10:10, 12. From this it would seem that the four wheels, like the four living creatures, are groups of celestial beings arranged in the form of wheels, or else a part of the living creatures themselves. However this may be, surely wings and wheels, whirlwinds and lightnings are far from suggesting immobility.

A Glorious High Throne. Describing the throne of God, Jeremiah says, "A glorious high throne from the beginning is the place of our sanctuary." Jer. 17:12, and Isaiah says it was "high and lifted up." Isaiah 6:1. But Ezekiel gives the most complete picture. He says that over the heads of the living creatures with their wheels, was "the likeness of the firmament," and "above the firmament....was the likeness of a throne....and as the appearance of a man above upon it." Eze. 1:22, 26.

This "Man" can be none other than the great Jehovah or the man Christ Jesus who occupies the throne with the Father.

All about the throne is inconceivable brightness and glory, resplendent with brilliant colors, having the appearance of devouring fire, the color of amber, yellow. Eze. 1:4, 26. Moses said it rested on "as it were a paved work of sapphire stone [sky blue], and as it were the body of heaven in his clearness." Ex. 24:10. The "wheels" were the color of beryl, a greenish blue, and "their feet....sparkled like the color of burnished brass." Eze. 1:7-28.

Round about the throne is a rainbow, Rev. 4:3, —a rainbow more glorious and resplendent than any ever seen in earthly sky. When Paul was caught up into Paradise, he said of the things he saw and heard, "it is not lawful for a man to utter," or, as Moffatt puts it, "no human lips can repeat." II Cor. 12:4. And surely a study of Ezekiel, especially chapters one and ten, and Revelation chapter four, will convince anyone that no human language can portray the marvelous intricacy and glory of the throne of God. To us it may seem confusion, but in reality all is perfect order and harmony. Here, before this magnificent throne, the throne of the Father, in the presence of all the angels of heaven and representatives of unfallen worlds, the angel escort presents the Son of God.

Christ's Inauguration and Coronation. At His ascension, Christ's inauguration into holy office began. One of its most outstanding features was His coronation. He "who was made a little lower than the angels for the suffering of death....that He....should taste death for every man," He who only a short time before had worn the shameful crown of thorns, symbol of the curse of sin which He bore for the human race, is now seated on the throne at the "right hand" of the Father of glory. Eph. 1:17, 20. In this exalted position, He is "crowned with glory and honor," Heb. 2:9, and proclaimed "THE KING OF GLORY." Ps. 24:7-10. This was His first coronation.

In the beginning, Adam was made "a little lower than the angels," but not for the suffering of death; he also was "crowned with glory and honor," Ps. 8:5, and was given dominion over all the earth. Through disobedience he lost dominion over all the earth. Through disobedience he lost both his crown of glory and his dominion, and came under the power of death. Then Jesus, "the Lord from heaven," fulfilling His covenant with the Father before the world was, became the second Adam. I Cor. 15:45, 47. When on Calvary the victory was won, and He afterward ascended to the holy place of the heavenly sanctuary, all Heaven welcomed Him as the "KING OF GLORY." At this time, as the second Adam, He was formally made "King over all the earth." Zech. 14:9. When this earth is made new, heaven will be transferred to this planet, and the New Jerusalem where God's throne is, will be its capital, the seat of His universal government. GC 426, 427. Then the lost "dominion" will be fully restored, the second Adam will take possession, and "the government shall be upon His shoulder." Isaiah 9:6. As King of the new earth, He will reign forever and ever.

Amidst the adoration of the assembled multitude, Christ is enthroned with the Father, and from this time He shares His Father's throne. Mark 16:19; Col. 3:1; DA 832. As the Father receives Him and proclaims Him King, His arms "encircle His Son, and the word is given, 'Let all the angels of God worship Him.'" Heb. 1:6; DA 834. At this proclamation that vast host of angels "prostrate themselves before Him, while the glad shout fills all the courts of heaven. 'Worthy is the Lamb that was slain to receive power, and riches, and wisdom, and strength, and honor, and glory, and blessing.' Rev. 5:11, 12. All heaven rings as their voices in lofty strains proclaim, "Blessing, and honor, and glory, and power be unto Him that sitteth upon the throne, and unto the Lamb forever and ever." Rev. 5:13; DA 834, 855. "Being by the right hand of God exalted," Acts 2:33, Christ is indeed glorified with the glory which He had with the Father before the world was. John

17:5. This was Heaven's second celebration of His triumphal work in behalf of man's salvation.

The Anointing of the Holy Spirit. The closing event of Christ's inauguration was His anointing and the anointing of the Most Holy. Dan. 9:24. When this took place, the Holy Ghost descended on the disciples "in rich currents," AA 38, which to them "was Heaven's communication that the Redeemer's inauguration was accomplished." AA 39. This indicated that the work of redemption, typified in the earthly sanctuary, was now fully transferred to the sanctuary above.

The anointing of Christ for holy office in heaven, and the anointing of the church to be co-workers with Him on earth, are correlative events. When the church of believers—"the number of names together were about an hundred and twenty" Acts 1:13-15—when "they were all with one accord in one place," the Holy Spirit overflowed on "the church" AA 38, "the whole congregation" COL 121, and "filled all the house where they were sitting," and "cloven tongues like as of fire...sat upon each of them." Acts 2:1-4. This was the fulfillment of His promise, "Ye shall be baptized with the Holy Ghost not many days hence"—a baptism that would give them power to be "witnesses both in Jerusalem, and in all Judea, and in Samaria, and unto the uttermost part of the earth." Acts 1:5, 8. This baptism took place "when the day of Pentecost was fully come." The night had passed, and it was now "the third hour" of the day, about 9:00 a.m. Acts 2:15. The day had "fully come."

Pentecost the Conclusion of the Passover. "Pentecost was not an insulated day. It stood as an integral part of the Passover. The wave sheaf of the Passover and the two wave loaves at Pentecost tie these two feasts together, making Pentecost the culminating point of the Pentecostal season." *Smith's Bible Dictionary*, 1914, article Pentecost. "The Jews called Pentecost the concluding assembly [the conclusion] of the Passover." *Fausset's Bible Encyclopedia*, 1914. The fact that Christ's entrance into the holy place of the heavenly sanctuary marked the end of divinely recognized service in the earthly sanctuary and the beginning of Christ's ministry in the sanctuary above is one of the high points in the work of redemption. Therefore we do well to study it carefully from various viewpoints.

First, from the Viewpoint of the Regular Prescribed Service for Pentecost as recorded in Leviticus 23:16-20, thus:

"A new meat offering" [two wave loaves]; the first fruits of the harvest (vs. 16, 17).

Seven lambs, one young bullock, and two rams for a burnt offering, with their meat offering and their drink offerings (vs. 18).

One kid of the goats for a sin offering (vs. 19). Two lambs for peace offerings and a wave offering (vs. 19, 20).

This seems a full day's service, and yet the Bible makes not a single mention of it—never a word—in connection with the Pentecost of Acts 2. Instead of these typical offerings, all of which were done away at the cross, the whole day was devoted to the gift and work of the Holy Spirit, events entirely different from the regular Pentecostal service as given in Leviticus.

Second, from the Viewpoint of Consecutive Events. As already noted, the Pentecost of Acts 2 was the conclusion of the Passover Jesus ate with the twelve which "was indeed the last divinely recognized Passover for A.D. 31." Following the events from the Passover Jesus ate on Nisan 14, one day early, to Pentecost of Acts will help to make this clear. On the night of this Passover, Jesus was betrayed. The closing chapters of all the gospels are devoted to a record of His sufferings connected with His trial and crucifixion, also His burial and resurrection. The first chapter of Acts continues with a recital of the forty days after His resurrection, His ascension, and the appointment of Matthias by the church—as they were assembled in "an upper room" "with one accord." Acts 1:3, 9, 13-15, 26. Acts 2 follows with a record of the descent of the Holy Spirit on the day of Pentecost as "they [the church of believers, AA 38] were all with one accord in one place." Acts 2:1. From all these consecutive and closely related events, does it not seem evident that the Pentecost of Acts 2 was indeed the "culminating point" of the Passover Jesus ate?

Third, from the Viewpoint of the Baptism of the Holy Ghost. It is certain that the Holy Spirit did not come on the unbelieving Jews. Had these leaders been thus guided, they would not have bribed Judas at a "goodly price" to betray His Lord; they would not have cried, "Crucify Him" to the officers in charge of His trial; they would not have paid the soldier guards "large money" to lie about His resurrection; nor would they have put the apostles in prison, Acts 4:1-3, because they preached a crucified, risen, and ascended Saviour.

Fourth, from the Historical Viewpoint. The term *historic* as applied to these ordinances, means the regular established dates in Bible history for their observance. Nisan 14 was the historic date for slaying the paschal lamb, Nisan 15 for eating the Passover supper, Nisan 16 for offering the wave sheaf. Fifty days from offering the wave sheaf was counted to Pentecost. Lev. 23:15, 16. While all these dates are Biblically correct, and for fifteen long centuries they have never varied, we must remember that the ordinances governed by them were done away at the cross. The Passover had met its antitype in Christ our Passover, I Cor. 5:7; the wave sheaf of first fruits had met its antitype in His resurrection, I Cor. 15:20; Pentecost met its antitype when, on the fiftieth day from the morrow after Christ ate the last true Passover, He sent His representative, the Holy Spirit, the Comforter, to the early believers, John 16, Acts 2:1-3. At the death of Christ, the whole ceremonial law was abolished, and because of this, none of these ordinances observed by the unbelieving Jews in A.D. 31 are mentioned in the Bible. They had "lost their significance" and were no longer divinely recognized. This fact marked the end of the Hebrew church and the ushering in of the Christian generation of the church.

As we have just seen, the gift of the Holy Spirit to the church of believers locates the Pentecost of Acts 2 as the "culminating point" of the Passover Jesus ate with the Twelve, which Pentecost came on the fiftieth day from Nisan 15, the "morrow after" Jesus ate the Passover. This is the only recorded instance in Bible history when the regular time for observing these ordinances varied. But, as already noted, this change was necessary on account of circumstances surrounding the death of Christ.

As to the day of the week on which the Pentecost of A.D. 31 fell, there are differences of opinion; but instead of entering into these differences, since God wants His people educated to be "thinkers, and not merely reflectors of other men's thoughts" Ed. 17, would it not be better for the reader to decide this question for himself as to which day of the week the Pentecost of A.D. 31 occurred, remembering the promise, "If any of you lack wisdom let him ask of God that giveth to all men liberally, and upbraideth not; and it shall be given him." James 1:5.

It is true that for many years the unbelieving Jews continued the formal routine of these ordinances. This is shown in Acts 20:16 and I Cor. 16:8, the only two places, aside from Acts 2, where the word Pentecost occurs in the Scriptures. Both relate Paul's determination to meet with the Jews on Pentecost. His purpose for so desiring was, not to observe Pentecost which he well knew had been done away as a divine ordinance, but because at this time multitudes of the Jews were assembled, thus offering him a rare opportunity to preach the gospel to large numbers, and if possible win some to Christ. They have no bearing on the question before us.

This last Pentecost was one of the most remarkable in the history of the church, comparable only to the one when God spoke His law in the first Pentecost.

Through this outpouring of the Holy Spirit, the death and resurrection and ascension of Christ were proclaimed with such convincing and convicting power, that "the vail that had prevented them [the Jews] from seeing to the end of that which had been abolished [the types of the ceremonial law] was now removed." "The traditions and superstitions inculcated by the priests were swept away from their minds, and the teachings of the Saviour were accepted." AA 44. As a result, about 3,000 souls were added unto them the same day. And later, "...the number of the disciples multiplied in Jerusalem greatly, and a great company of the priests were obedient to the faith." Acts 2:41, 6:7.

Because of this, and because the apostles preached through Jesus the resurrection from the dead, and because of the miracles they wrought through His name, the rulers of the temple were "grieved" Acts 4:2, they were "greatly enraged" AA 40; therefore, at eventide "they laid hands on them, and put them in hold until the next day," Acts 4:2, 3. This was the end of the day of Pentecost described in Acts 2, the day when the Holy Spirit was poured out on "the church," "the whole congregation" of believers.

The day following, the priests and rulers of the temple were gathered together at Jerusalem. Acts 4:5, 6. Since this was the historic time for them to celebrate Pentecost, did they assemble for that purpose? The Bible does not say, but whether they did or not, since the Pentecost historically due on Sivan 6 (See Appendix page 25) had been abolished, the Bible makes no mention of its celebration.

The Former Rain and the Latter Rain. Before the second coming of Christ, there will be another outpouring of the Holy Spirit, "similar to Pentecost," upon the true believers in the church, "and with greater power." "The outpouring of the Holy Spirit on the day of Pentecost was the former rain, but the latter rain which ripens the harvest will be more abundant." COL 121; Joel 2:23; Hosea 6:3; GC 611, 612.

The latter rain is represented by "another angel come down from heaven, having great power, and the earth was lighted with his glory." Rev. 18:1. This angel will "unite his voice with the third angel [of Rev. 14:9, 10] and give power and force to his message" as it swells into the loud cry. EW 277, 271, when again the church around the circle of the earth will speak with "tongues of fire."

"Notwithstanding the spiritual darkness and alienation from God that exist in the churches which constitute Babylon, the great body of Christ's true followers are still to be found in their communion." GC 390. These, says Jesus, are the "other sheep...which are not of this fold; them also I must bring." John 10:16. When the loud cry of the third angel reaches these sincere Christians who are hungering and thirsting for the truth of God's Word, they will accept the message of the third angel and come into the fold of the Good Shepherd, "and there shall be one fold, and one Shepherd." "Like the stars of heaven, which appear only at night," they are "the firmament of chosen ones" whom "God has in reserve ... that will yet shine forth amidst the darkness, revealing clearly to an apostate world the transforming power of obedience to His law." PK 188, 189.

The Holy Spirit in Our Lives Today. When Christ and the heavenly sanctuary were anointed and the Holy Spirit overflowed on the disciples, the promise to the early Christian believers was, "Repent, and be baptized...and ye shall receive the gift of the Holy Ghost." Acts 2:38. This promise is not alone for these early believers; it is for every truly converted person today who repents and is baptized in the name "of the Holy Ghost." Matt. 28:19.

In Paul's day, "certain disciples" who had been baptized "unto John's baptism" "with the baptism of repentance" confessed, "We have not so much as heard whether there be any Holy Ghost," but when "they were baptized in the name of the Lord Jesus" "they spake with tongues," Acts 19:2-7, and, like the disciples of Acts 2, they were prepared to be ambassadors for Christ.

As Christ as about to ascend, His very last words to His disciples were, "Ye shall receive power after that the Holy Ghost is come upon you: and ye shall be witnesses unto Me both in Jerusalem, and in all Judea, and in Samaria, and unto the uttermost parts of the earth." Acts 1:8. This gift of the Holy Spirit was, and still is, "the promise of the Father" vs. 4, to His disciples, and the commission given by Christ to carry the gospel to all the world was given, not only to the early disciples, but to His followers to the end of time. Would it not be well for each of us to check on our individual Christian experience, remembering that God is more willing to give us the Holy Spirit than parents are to give good gifts unto their children? Luke 11:13.

When the inauguration of Christ was accomplished, and He began His ministry in the holy place of the heavenly sanctuary, He sent His followers the Comforter, the Holy Ghost, to abide with them *forever*. With His abiding presence, we shall bear the fruit of the Spirit: "love, joy, peace, long suffering, gentleness, goodness, faith, meekness, temperance." Gal. 5:22. If this seems too high a standard the Holy Ghost will help our infirmities. John 14:16, 17; Rom. 8:26. He is also the "Spirit of Truth" John 16:13, to teach us all things. On our part, this means faithful, prayerful study of the Bible and cheerful obedience to all its teachings, "for the perfecting of the saints...till we all come in the unity of the faith, and of the knowledge of the Son of God, unto a perfect man....that we henceforth be no more children, tossed to an fro, and carried about with every wind of doctrine.... But speaking the truth in love [we] may grow up into Him in all things." Eph. 4:12-15. Our measuring up to this standard and our sincere devotion in extending "this gospel of the kingdom...in all the world for a witness unto all nations," is the measure of the Holy Spirit in our lives.

Jesus Our Forerunner. When Christ began His work in the heavenly sanctuary He was our "Forerunner"—Heb. 6:20– He "entered for us in advance." *Moffatt*. The purpose of a forerunner is to announce the approach of someone of distinction. He is always hailed with joy, but when he has passed by, the attention of the onlookers is directed toward the one for whom he is the forerunner. So when the inauguration of our Forerunner was accomplished, the attention of all Heaven was directed towards His church on earth. From that time it has been the center of attraction—the object of all Heaven's solicitude and care. Christ "ever liveth" to encourage and strengthen His followers on earth. Heb. 7:25. Redemption now "engaged the attention of our Lord and Saviour." Ed. 136. This fact makes the "hope" of all who have fled for refuge, "sure and steadfast," "an anchor of the soul," Heb. 6:18-20. Since He entered within the first vail as our Forerunner, heaven and earth are closely united. But not until the redeemed stand on the sea of glass will He "see of the travail of His soul, and...be satisfied." Isaiah 53:11.

CHAPTER 17 PREVIEW

THE CHRISTIAN ENTERING THE HOLY PLACE

- Preparation for the Holy Place
- Pressing Toward the Prize
- At the Door
- The Door and Its Pillars as Symbols
- Within the Holy Place
- Three Essentials to Winning the Prize
- Growing Up into Christ
- "The Trysting Place"

17

THE CHRISTIAN ENTERING
THE HOLY PLACE

Preparation for the Holy Place. With Christ we have been crucified at the brazen altar. On the altar we have placed all our evil habits and everything that would tend to draw us away from Him, these to be utterly consumed in the altar fires. Here we have dedicated to His service all our time and talents—all that we have and all that we are, all that we shall ever possess and all that we ever hope to become—all have been consecrated to the service of our Redeemer. At the laver we have been cleansed, our past sins have been buried in the watery grave, and we have risen with Christ to walk in newness of life. As we advance to the holy place of the earthly sanctuary, we must ever look unto Jesus, who is not only the author but the finisher of our faith. As our great Leader, after His resurrection and entrance into the holy place of the heavenly sanctuary, was anointed with the Holy Spirit, so when we, His followers, enter the holy place on earth, the words of Peter to the early Christian believers apply: "Repent, and be baptized…for the remission of sins, and ye shall receive the gift of the Holy Ghost." Acts 2:38. Let us weigh this matter well, lest our experience be like those who had been baptized "unto John's baptism," "the baptism of repentance," but who had "not so much as heard whether there be any Holy Ghost." Acts 19:2-5.

Then, "forgetting those things which are behind, and reaching forth unto those things which are before," we are to "press toward the mark for the prize of the high calling of God in Christ Jesus." Phil. 3:13, 14. This is another forward move on *The Path to the Throne of God*, the Christian's goal. On this path, we do not walk alone, for His promise still holds: "Lo, I am with you alway"[all the time—*Moffatt*]. Matt. 28:20. "I will never leave thee, nor forsake thee." Heb. 13:5. It is our part to deny self, take up the cross, and follow Him. Matt. 16:24. Shall we not from the heart respond:

> Though I meet with tribulations,
> Sorely tempted though I be,
> I remember Thou wast tempted,
> And rejoice to follow thee."
>
> --*James Lawson*.

Pressing Toward the Prize. What does this pressing toward the prize involve? It means that we have now enlisted in God's army; we are His soldiers, volunteers in a lifelong warfare, with Christ and Satan as opposing generals. In this warfare, "we wrestle not against flesh and blood, but against principalities, against powers, against the rulers of the darkness of this world, against spiritual wickedness in high places." Eph. 6:12. To be victorious, we must "put on the whole armor of God, that ye may be able to stand [to hold your ground—*Moffatt*] against the wiles [sly tricks—*Webster*] of the devil." Eph. 6:11.

General weapons are not employed in this warfare. Instead of guns and bombs, the Captain of our salvation has provided every soldier with an armor, complete from head to foot, every part of which is needed if we are to "stand our ground" against the "sly tricks" of our adversary, the devil. "Stand therefore,

> Having your loins girt about with truth,
> And having on the breastplate of righteousness;
> And your feet shod with the preparation ["the
>   stability,"—*Moffatt*], of the gospel of peace;
> Above all, taking the shield of faith, wherewith
>   ye shall be able to quench all the fiery darts of
>   the wicked.
> And take the helmet of salvation,
> And the sword of the Spirit, which is the Word
>   of God;
> Praying always with all prayer and supplication
>   in the Spirit,
> And watching thereunto with all perseverance."
>   Eph. 6:14-18.

Clad in this armor, "let us run with patience the race that is set before us," ever "looking unto Jesus," Heb. 12:1, 2, our Mighty Captain, who has never lost a battle.

Thus equipped, our conversation will be in heaven, Phil. 3:20, because "our citizenship is in heaven" A.R.V. because "we are free citizens of heaven" *Weymouth*; because "we are a colony of heaven" *Moffatt*; because "the empire to which we belong is in heaven." *Twentieth Century*.

Forward, ever forward, is to be our watchword, remembering that "No man, having put his hand to the plough and looking back, is fit for the kingdom of God." Luke 9:62. "After that ye…are known of God, how turn ye again to the weak and beggarly elements, whereunto ye desire again to be in bondage?" Gal. 4:9. Or, as Moffatt has it, "How is it ye are turning back again to the weakness and poverty of the elemental spirits? Why do you want to be enslaved all over again by them?" Having "put off…the old man, which is corrupt," Eph. 4:22, "let your conversation be as it becometh the gospel of Christ." Phil. 1:27. "Having your conversation honest among the Gentiles: that whereas they speak against you as evil doers, they may by your good works…glorify God." I Peter 2:12.

"Therefore leaving the principles of the doctrine of Christ, let us go on unto perfection; not laying again the foundation of repentance from dead works." Heb. 6:1, 2. "And be ye kind one to another, tenderhearted, forgiving one another, even

as God for Christ's sake hath forgiven you." Let us not "give place to the devil...
and grieve not the Holy Spirit of God, whereby ye are sealed unto the day of
redemption." Eph. 4:27-32. With our feet firmly planted on these principles, we
are ready to enter the holy place, which is a type of the holy place of the heavenly
sanctuary into which Jesus has entered.

At the Door. Cleansed and having on the whole armor of God, we advance to the
door, the entrance to the holy place. The door is a fine linen hanging of "blue, and
purple, and scarlet" —all royal colors. On it cherubim are richly embroidered in
shining gold—"figure" or "shadow" of the angels who met Jesus as He approached
the "everlasting doors" of the holy place of the heavenly sanctuary. Ps. 24:7.

The Door and Its Pillars as Symbols. The door hanging was suspended on
five pillars made of shittim wood, completely covered with pure gold. Ex. 26:37.
Jesus says, "I am the door of the sheep." "He that entereth not in by the door into
the sheepfold, but climbeth up some other way, the same is a *thief* and a robber."
John 10:7, 11. As elsewhere, the wood in the pillars represents humanity. Gold is a
symbol of Divinity: "Yea, the Almighty shall be thy gold." Job 22:25, margin. So,
having surrendered all, and being hid in Christ, as the wood is within the gold, we
are to be pillars in His temple. Rev. 3:12.

Why was the door hung on *five* pillars instead of *four* as was the gate, which also
represented Christ? No one symbol can fully represent Him; each symbol represents some special phase of His character or work. The number of its pillars is five,
doubtless for the same reason that the boards of the wall, of which the door was a
part, were held together with *five* bars. One writer has said that these pillars may
represent the name or character of Christ in its five parts: "Wonderful, Counselor,
the mighty God, the everlasting Father, the Prince of Peace." Isaiah 9:6. If so, how
appropriate that they were of gold, a symbol of the Almighty. As brass represents
victory through suffering, another writer suggests that the five brass sockets in
which these pillars were set, symbolize the five wounds which Jesus bears in His
body from Calvary as He entered the holy place above. Ps. 22:16; John 19:34.
These brass sockets are also a fitting symbol of our earthly struggles and our victories, which precede our entrance into the holy place. As all the articles in the court
were of brass, so as we step beyond these sockets of brass at the door, we leave
behind us the last trace of our former experience, our longing after earthly things,
and if we hold to Him who "is able to keep [us] from falling," if we "stand fast...in
the liberty wherewith Christ hath made us free," we need never again be "entangled...with the yoke of bondage" and overcome by worldly lusts, "which war
against the soul." II Tim. 1:12; Gal. 5:1; I Pet. 2:11.

Within the Holy Place Justification, obtained in the court, is our passport into
the holy place. This room is ten cubits wide and twenty long, or at least fifteen by
thirty feet. And what a room! On all sides we see, not brass but pure gold. At the
further end is the vail which separates the holy place from the most holy. Like the
door and the gate, it is of blue, and purple, and scarlet. in it, figures of cherubim are

richly embroidered in gold. The ceiling above is of the same, with cherubim in-wrought with threads of pure gold. All along both sides are boards covered with glittering gold, and having angel figures engraved, or reflected, in their shining surfaces. We are literally encompassed with angel figures, even as Christ was sur-rounded with real angels when He entered the holy place of the *heavenly* sanctu-ary. As before stated, these angel figures represent the "innumerable company" of angels who are connected with the work of the heavenly sanctuary, "ministering spirits sent forth" to this earth "to minister for them who shall be heirs of salva-tion." Heb. 12:22; 1:14; PP 347.

Nearest to the second vail is the golden altar, sending forth the fragrance of its sweet smelling incense. On our right is the golden table, with its twelve loaves of life-giving bread, its flagon and other dishes of gold. On our left "without the vail of the testimony," Lev. 24:3, is the golden candlestick, the soft lights from which add to the sacred atmosphere of the room. The rich colors in the ceiling and in the vails, reflected in the yellow of the golden walls, giving the effect of a rainbow surrounding us, similar to the rainbow around God's throne. Such is the gorgeous place in which we are to develop true Christian character.

Three Essentials to Winning the Prize. The three articles of furniture in this apartment symbolize the three essentials to character perfection, the goal toward which we press. At the golden table with the bread is represented Bible study, at the golden altar with the sweet incense is typified prayer, at the golden candlestick is symbolized service. Because of the feast spread on the table, the holy place has sometimes been called "The Banqueting Room;"—because of the sweet incense offered on the altar with our prayers, it has been called "The Prayer Room."—But in reality it is more than both these; it is "The Sanctification Room"—the room where, as Webster defines this word, we experience "the act or process of God's grace by which the affections are purified, or alienated from sin, and exalted to a supreme love to God and righteousness."

Growing Up Into Christ. The court experience, that of being freed from past sins, —is called the new birth, or the second birth. Then, as "new born babes" I Pe-ter 2:2, —without active sin—we enter into the holy place where we are to spend the rest of our mortal life. Here we are to "grow up into Him in all things." Eph. 4:15. Of what does this growing up process consist?

First, as babes we "desire"—cry out after, hunger and thirst for the sincere milk of the word, illustrated at the golden table that we "may grow thereby." I Peter 2:2. It is through a study of the Word, and obedience to it, that we "grow in grace and in the knowledge of…Christ." II Peter 3:18. Of equal importance to our spiritual growth is prayer, "the breath of the soul," symbolized at the golden altar. As we thus grow, we become fitted to let our light shine in service for others, an experi-ence represented by the golden candlestick. God "worketh in you both to will and *to do* of His good pleasure." Phil. 2:13. The result of this threefold experience in Christian growth is sanctification which follows justification in the court. It is not a theory; it is a life—not a life of idle dreaming, but one of earnest effort to overcome temptation, and bravely meet daily duties and trials.

> Heaven is not reached by a single bound,
> *Christ is* the ladder by which we rise
> From the lowly earth to the vaulted skies,
> And we mount to its summit round by round.

—From Gradatim by J. G. Holland (Variations in Italics).

While justification—the second birth—is the work of a moment; sanctification, this "growing up" process, is the work of a lifetime, the result of battles fought and victories won.

The Trysting Place. Moffatt translates the holy place as the trysting place. Webster defines tryst as engagement for marriage. The Hebrew rendering of the expression tabernacle of the congregation, that is, the holy place or the trysting place, a place where lovers meet to make engagement for marriage; and in some countries, the engagement is regarded just as sacred and binding as the marriage itself. How beautiful is the figure that in the holy place, the place where we spend our entire Christian life, the place where we grow up into Christ,—here, day by day, hour by hour, as life's shuttle goes back and forth, we are weaving the garment of righteousness, the garment of "fine linen [or silk, Eze. 16:10], clean and white," our wedding garment, that we may be ready to be accepted as the bride of Lamb. Rev. 19:7, 8.

With this thought in mind, can we not understand the shamefulness of being untrue to Him to whom we have given our hearts, by going back to the beggarly elements of the world? Now that we have entered the Trysting place, shall we not remain true to the One we have promised, that we be not found without the wedding garment?

> "O Jesus, I have promised to serve Thee to the end;
> Be Thou forever near me, my Master and my Friend:
> I shall not fear the battle if Thou are by my side;
> Nor wander from the pathway if Thou wilt be my Guide."
> —John E. Bode

CHAPTER 18 PREVIEW

THE SANCTUARY WALL AND ITS FLOOR

- Number and Size of the Boards
- The Corner Boards
- Significance of the 48 Boards
- Significance of the Corner Boards
- Shittim Wood
- Carved Boards Covered with Gold
- The Amount of Gold Used
- Gold a Type
- Wood a Type
- The Bars
- The Bars a Symbol
- The Foundation of Silver Sockets
- Value of the Gold and Silver Used
- The Foundation Sockets as Symbols
- God's Protection Over His People

18

THE SANCTUARY WALL
AND ITS FLOOR

Number and Size of the Boards. There were forty-eight boards in the wall of the sanctuary, twenty on each side and eight at the west end. The forty boards on the north and south sides, and six boards on the west [exclusive of the two corner boards], were all of one size,—ten cubits long and one and one-half cubits wide, or not less than twenty-seven inches by fifteen feet. This wall was twice as high as the wall of the court. Ex. 36:20-34.

Reputable Jewish writers state that the boards were one-half a span thick. A span is one-half of a cubit, or at least nine inches. Accordingly the boards were about four and one-half inches thick. Probably this is about correct; at any rate, it was necessary that they be thick enough for the middle bar to "shoot through the boards," reaching "from end to end." Ex. 36:33. Accepting this measure, each board contained a little more than 150 board feet. How much did one board weigh? One square foot of seasoned oak one inch thick weighs about four and one-half pounds. Therefore one board weighed approximately 700 pounds without the gold plating.

The Corner Boards. Whenever the boards at the west end are mentioned, it is always "six boards, and two boards...for the corners," Ex. 26:22, 23, indicating that the corner boards were different from the others. They were the same length as the others; their width, however, was not the same. The Bible nowhere directly gives their width. How, then, may it be determined? The second covering in the roof of the sanctuary was thirty cubits long—just long enough "to cover it." Ex. 26:7, 8, 13. The combined height of two sides of the sanctuary was twenty cubits, thus leaving ten cubits for its width. The total width of the six regular boards for the west wall was nine cubits. This left one cubit for the width of the two corner boards, or one-half cubit for each. Our King James version of Exodus 26:27 reads, "five bars for the *two sides* westward." Moffatt renders this, "five bars for the back or western side." His rendering of verse 24 explains that the two corner boards formed "a double support" so that instead of the west end being double, it was the corner boards that were double.

Significance of the 48 Boards. The number of boards, 48 in all, was divinely dictated to Moses, whom God so frequently admonished to follow the pattern. This cannot be passed by without loss in our spiritual understanding of the sanctuary, "every whit" of which uttereth His glory. Ps. 29:9, margin. As noted on page 53, Solomon speaks of the sixty court pillars of the sanctuary wall as "threescore valiant men...of the valiant of Israel," all holding swords, "being expert in war." These sixty pillars of strong "victorious" brass, bound together with the white linen wall, representing the righteousness of Christ, were like a bodyguard of well-trained loyal soldiers, forming a wall of protection around the sanctuary.

Likewise, the forty-eight boards, standing "upright," with the imprint of heaven upon them and bound together in solid rank by bars and pillars, formed another wall of protection. Why was this protection doubled? Was it not to indicate that, as in the case of Pharaoh's dream which was doubled unto him, because "the thing is established by God?" Gen. 41:32. Like this double protection, so the 144,000, which is a multiple of both 60 and 48, serve as a double protection, so to speak, in the temple eternal. Like the Levites who were the teachers of ancient Israel and who camped close around the earthly sanctuary to do its service and to care for it as it was moved from place to place, so the 144,000 serve in a double capacity. They are not only teachers of *redeemed Israel*, but as they follow the Lamb withersoever He goeth, they witness to *other worlds* of His saving grace.

Significance of the Corner Boards. The corner boards of the sanctuary correspond to the corner stone of the temple built later. Christ is the "precious corner stone," I Peter 2:6; "in whom all the building fitly framed together groweth unto an holy temple in the Lord: in whom ye also are builded together for an habitation of God through the Spirit." Eph. 2:19-22. His children are to be "as corner stones, polished after the similitude of a palace." Ps. 144:12. The special purpose of the corner boards was to "*couple together*" all the boards into one tabernacle, Ex. 26:24; and it is the work of Christ to bind together the members of His household into one body.

Shittim Wood. In his Bible Dictionary, Smith tells us that the shittim wood used in the sanctuary was the wild acacia of the desert—the tree of "the burning bush." In fact, Sinai itself is so called from *Seneh*, or acacia bush. The word *shittim* is the plural form of the word *shittah*, the tree itself being called *the shittah tree*. It was a small thorny tree, one of specially enduring quality, requiring much patient labor to prepare it for use, and therefore of unusual value. These boards were "made boards," Ex. 36:20, and from their size it seems evident that each one was made of many smaller places solidly cemented, or in some way fastened together.

Shittim wood was one of the articles mentioned among the gifts that the people were to bring for the sanctuary: "Every man with whom was found shittim wood for any work of the service, brought it," Ex. 35:24; and without doubt this expensive and beautiful timber was part of the spoils brought out of Egypt, which the Lord foreknew would be needed for the sanctuary.

It is quite likely that some of the Israelites, while slaves in Egypt, were employed in making such boards for Egyptian palaces and temples. Removing the thorns, hewing and smoothing and fitting the pieces together is a fit symbol of the removal of the thorns from our carnal nature, the hewing and polishing that we must undergo before we can be fitted into the heavenly temple. How encouraging to know that God does not consume time on worthless material! He sees the

126

"enduring quality" and "unusual value" of each child of His, and with much patient labor He removes the thorns and does much polishing and fitting until we are ready for our place in His temple.

Carved Boards Covered With Gold. Were the boards carved with figures of angels? The Bible does not say. But Bezaleel was chosen by God to do important work in the construction of the sanctuary because, among other talents, he was gifted "in carving of timber" "to make any manner of cunning work." Besides this natural gift, God filled him with His Spirit "in wisdom, in understanding, and in knowledge, and in all manner of workmanship." Ex. 31:3, 5. If the boards were not carved, there was little left to be carved—merely some parts of the incense altar and the ark. In Solomon's temple "the cedar of the house within was carved." "He carved all the walls of the house round about with carved figures of cherubims." I Kings 6:18, 29. Since Solomon used the wilderness tabernacle as a guide, we may with considerable safety conclude that the boards of the sanctuary were also carved with figures of cherubim. But whether the boards were carved with angel figures and afterward covered with gold, or whether the gold on the boards *reflected* in their resplendent mirrorlike surface the gold angels embroidered on the two vails and the inner covering which formed the ceiling, the lesson is the same—Christ is the gold; we are the wood, I Cor. 3:12, and as the boards were completely covered with gold, so we must be completely covered with His righteousness before we can occupy a place in His temple.

Each of the forty-eight boards was "heavily plated," G.C. 411, on both sides with pure gold. "This was not simply for ornamentation, but to teach us that the temple of God must be the same outside and in. In our lives must be seen what we profess to believe." R. S. Owen in RH, March 26, 1925, pp. 11, 12.

The Amount of Gold Used. The total amount of gold used in the sanctuary was twenty-nine talents and 730 shekels. Ex. 38:24. Suppose we allow five talents and the 730 shekels for the candlestick [made of one talent, Ex. 25:39], the mercy seat with its two cherubim, the covering of the ark, the table and its dishes, the incense altar, the nine pillars—five for the door and four for the vail, the golden censer, the gold embroidery, and the fifty taches used for the inner covering, there would be twenty-four talents left for the forty-eight boards, or one-half talent for each board. A talent of gold weighed about two hundred pounds. Half a talent added to the weight of the wood in one board would make each board weigh about eight hundred pounds. The total weight of the gold used was more than 5800 pounds or nearly 3 tons. Its total value was $877,000.00 which in today's money value would be approximately $87,700,000—an incomprehensible sum!

Gold a Type. Gold always represents special value, and as previously noted, wherever used in the sanctuary it represents the Almighty, Job 22:25, margin. The gold used in the sanctuary was *pure* gold, gold tried in the fire until all the dross had been removed. Only thus could it represent Christ; and only by being thus purified; by becoming partakers of the Divine nature, can we be fitted for our place in His temple. That this may become a reality, God has promised to make the redeemed "more precious than *fine* gold," Isaiah 13:12. This assurance should enable us to accept and appreciate Peter's admonition to "rejoice" in the "fiery trials" of this life, for these are God's workmen to develop the fine gold—gold purified in the fire seven times. I Peter 4:12, 13.

Wood a Type. Shittim wood entered into the construction of every part of the sanctuary where wood was used, and as already noted, wherever used, wood was a type of humanity. Our life accomplishments unless wrought in God are represented as "wood, hay, and stubble." I Cor. 3:12. How thankful we can be that all the wood was completely covered with gold: Only as we are completely "hid with Christ in God" Col. 3:3, can we be safe in the day when "the fire shall try every man's work of what sort it is. If any man's work abide he shall receive a reward. If any man's work shall be burned, he shall suffer loss: but listen, "he himself shall be saved; yet so as by fire." I Cor. 3:13-15. What unbounded mercy toward frail and erring humanity when, in spite of our mistakes, we truly desire to serve God!

The next verse shows that Paul is here speaking of us as the temple of God, for he goes on to say: "Know ye not that ye are the temple of God, and that the Spirit of God dwelleth in you? If any man defile the temple of God, him shall God destroy; for the temple of God is holy, *which temple ye are.*" I Cor. 3:16, 17; 6:19, 20, italics supplied. When we are thus hid in Christ we can truthfully sing:

"Not I, but Christ be honored, loved, exalted;
   Not I, but Christ be seen, be known, be heard;
Not I but Christ in every look and action,
   Not I, but Christ in every thought and word."

"Christ, only Christ, no idle word e'er falling,
   Christ, only Christ, no needless, bustling
      sound,
Christ, only Christ, no self-important bearing,
   Christ, only Christ, no trace of 'I' be found."

The Bars. There were five bars on the north, south, and west walls of the sanctuary, and five pillars on which hung the vail [or door] forming the east wall. Like the boards, these bars and pillars were made of shittim wood, overlaid with gold. The middle bar was made "to shoot through the boards from one end to the other." Ex. 26:28; 36:31-33. The other four bars passed through gold rings—"*four*" on each board. These bars helped to hold the boards in their "upright" position, and the walls, fastened together by the corner boards, kept them in unity as one body, thus forming one temple. The pillars, on which the two vails hung, and their connecting bars also helped to hold the walls firm. PP 347.

The Bars A Symbol. This unity is as important in the spiritual temple as in the temple made with hands. Paul says, "I…beseech you that ye walk worthy of the vocation wherewith ye are called [our *vocation*—not avocation—in life is to become fitted for the heavenly temple], with all lowliness and meekness, with long-suffering, forbearing one another in love; [as brothers standing, like the boards, side by side, and upright] endeavoring to keep the unity of the Spirit in the bond of peace." Eph. 4:1-3. The boards never quarreled among themselves.

What are the five powers that hold the body of Christ in "the unity of the Spirit in the bond of peace," that it may be "one body, and one spirit?" Paul gives us this answer; "One hope … one Lord, one faith, one baptism, one God and Father of all, who is above all, and through all, and in you all." Eph. 4:3-6. The middle bar, running through all the boards from one end to the other, is like the everlasting arms of our heavenly Father, the "Father of all, who is above all, and through all, and in you all." Together with the middle bar, the other four bars and the two corner boards representing Christ, bind all the boards firmly together into "the church of the living God." I Tim. 3:15. "Without controversy great is the mystery of godliness." I Tim. 3:16.

The Foundation of Silver Sockets. "Of the hundred talents of silver were cast the sockets of the sanctuary, and the sockets of the vail; an hundred sockets of the hundred talents, a talent for a socket." Ex. 38:27. Each of the forty-eight boards stood on two tenons, which fitted into two sockets. These sockets were blocks of solid silver, which helped to hold the boards in their upright position. Each weighed one talent, about one hundred pounds. Two hundred pounds, or more, of silver formed the foundation for each board. Counting the four silver sockets under the four pillars that supported the second vail, there were in all one hundred sockets of silver. Thus the total weight of the silver sockets [100 talents] was at least 10,000 pounds, or five tines of solid silver!

How was this great mass of silver provided? As previously noted, all the other gifts brought by the people for the sanctuary were entirely voluntary. Not so with the silver. By the express command of God, a half shekel of silver was brought as redemption money for every man old enough to go to war—every "soldier" of God's army. Ex. 38:25, 26. At 32 cents for one half-shekel the 603,550 men numbered, Num. 1:46, brought $193,136 in silver.

Value of the Gold and Silver used. [At that time, gold was figured at $950.00 per ounce.] Ex. 38:24-28. One talent of silver was equal to 6,000 half shekels. Two talents under each board were therefore equal to 12,000 half shekels. Thus each board rested on the redemption money of 12,000 "soldiers." At $1,920 for a silver talent, the one hundred sockets were worth $192,000 which in today's money value would be about $19,200,000—an enormous sum. Besides this were 1,775 shekels of silver for other parts. Ex. 38:28. Their value at 32 cents per half-shekel, was $1,136. This amount added to the one hundred talents for the sockets [192,000] gives $193,136, the full and exact amount of the redemption money of the 603,550 men numbered. This in today's money value would be about $19,313,600. Adding all this to the $87,700,000 of gold used in the boards, we have $107,013,600—an incomprehensible amount. All this was of the spoils of Egypt, the richest country in the world at that time.

"We might get some idea of the wealth of Egypt at that time were we to visit its great museum in Cairo. In this museum is the mummy of King Tutankhamen, commonly called "King Tut," one of the ancient rulers of Egypt. The inner coffin [there are three] in which is encased this mummy, is of solid gold valued at much more than $1,000,000. Some of the tombs of Egyptian rulers contained more than $20,000,000 of treasures. [See *My Visit to King Tut's Golden Room*, pages 4-9, by H.M.S. Richards. Used by permission.]

Why such tremendous expenditure—not only of gold and silver, but brass, of which there were about 9,000 pounds, Ex. 38:29, margin, and other expensive material?—Only to help us get some faint realization of the infinite cost of our salvation. It cannot be measured. We cannot comprehend it. It will be the science and the song of the redeemed throughout the ceaseless ages of eternity. Even the angels cannot fathom it; but they do "desire to look into" it. I Peter 1:12.

The Foundation Sockets as Symbols. Who is the foundation of the house of God, the dwelling place of the Most High?—"Other foundation can no man lay than that is laid, which is Jesus Christ." I Cor. 3:11. "Thus saith the Lord God, behold I lay in Zion... a sure foundation." Isaiah 28:16. The very habitation of God rests on the redemption effected for each soul by the atoning blood of Christ.

"On Christ the solid Rock, I stand,

All other ground is sinking sand."

Without this solid foundation the tenons would surely sink into the shifting sand, and the building would fall.

God's Protection Over His People. In Solomon's temple "the floor of the house" was "overlaid with gold," I Kings 6:30, but in the portable sanctuary built by Moses, no mention is made of a floor. Evidently, then, its floor was the ground. Num. 5:17. Did the court of the sanctuary and the camp of Israel become a muddy place in time of rain? Each time Israel camped, the location for the sanctuary was selected by Christ Himself in the pillar of cloud, and that spot was holy ground, divinely protected. The cloud protected not only the sanctuary, but "as a canopy" it extended "above the host," by day sheltering them from the heat, and at night "illuminating their encampment." PP 282.

Artists frequently show these coverings in the form of a sloping roof, and some think that at least the two outer coverings were for protection from rain, and that therefore there must have been a ridgepole for proper drainage. But nowhere does the Bible so state. Not human device but God by many coverings Himself was their protection. "On the day that the tabernacle was reared up...so it was alway; the cloud covered it by day, and appearance of fire by night." Num. 9:15, 16. Isaiah puts it this way: "And the Lord will create upon every dwelling place of Mount Zion, and upon her assemblies, a cloud for a shadow in the daytime from the heat, and for a place of refuge, and for a covert from storm and from rain." Isaiah 4:5, 6. With this promise, we have no need to be concerned that the rain would make a muddy place around the tabernacle, or that in the roof there must have been a ridgepole.

As of old the cloud was "a defence," Isaiah 4:5, "constantly assuring them [the people] of the divine Presence," PP 282, so today every true Christian may have the same constant assurance of the presence, protection, and guidance of Him, who, represented in the cloud, led Israel all the way to the promised land.

CHAPTER 19 PREVIEW

THE FOUR COVERINGS

- The Roof of the Sanctuary
- The Covering of Badgers' Skins
- The Covering of Red Rams' Skins
- The Goats' Hair Covering
- The Inner, or Royal Covering
- The Four Coverings Complete
- The Finished Temple a Type

19

THE FOUR COVERINGS

The Roof of the Sanctuary. The roof of the sanctuary was formed of four coverings. The inner covering was "of fine-twined linen, and blue, and purple, and scarlet; with cherubims of cunning work." Over this was a white covering of woven goats' hair. Next was a covering of rams' skins dyed red; and outside of all a covering of badgers' skins. Ex. 36:8-19. The brass "pins of the tabernacle," like tent stakes, held the coverings firmly to the ground. Ex. 38:31. As we shall see, these coverings represent the four phases of the life and work of Christ in the plan of salvation. They also illustrate a deepening experience in the Christian life. Let us trace these experiences from the outer covering downward to the holy places.

The Covering of Badgers' Skins. The badger is supposed by some to be like the seal. It was a marine animal found in the Red Sea. Its dark brown or black skin was tough and durable, and often used for shoe leather and soles. This covering being on the outside would "afford complete protection," PP 347, not protection from rain and storm, for the cloud was that, but being inconspicuous in color, it was well adapted to shield the sanctuary from the evil eye of Arab marauders who roamed in the desert. As in the case of the other materials given by Israel for the sanctuary, these skins were part of the spoils of Egypt, provided in the providence of God.

What an illustration this safe covering is of Christ, who is our protection from the enemy as we journey through life's desert! "Surely He shall deliver thee from the snare of the fowler, and from the noisome pestilence. He shall cover thee with His feathers, and under His wings shalt thou trust...Thou shalt not be afraid for the terror by night; nor for the arrow that flieth by day; nor for the pestilence that walketh in darkness; nor for the destruction that wasteth at noonday....*Because* thou hast made the Lord,...even the Most High, thy habitation," Ps. 91:3-9—thy *sanctuary*! This covering of "shoe leather" fittingly represents Christ's humanity as He walked among men during His life on earth, and as He walks with us in the dust of earth's wilderness, that we may walk with Him on the streets of gold. It is also a symbol of His humility: "Being in the form of God," He "made Himself of no reputation, and took upon Him the form of a servant, and was made in the likeness of men: and being found in fashion as a man, He humbled Himself." Phil. 2:6-8.

As this covering had no outward beauty, so of Christ it is written, "He hath no form or comliness; and when we shall see Him, there is no beauty that we should desire Him." Isaiah 53:2. Christ was a humble man. In His outward appearance, He had no beauty, as men call beauty, but He measured up to God's standard of beauty, for "the Lord seeth not as man seeth; for man looketh on the outward appearance, but the Lord looketh on the heart." I Sam. 16:7. "Beneath the lowly guise of Jesus" was "the presence of Divinity." Thus "His glory [His true beauty] was vailed." DA 43, 63. Passing down through these coverings toward that which represents heaven itself, the badgers' skin covering suggests that we should approach God with sincerity, simplicity, and humility.

The Covering of Red Rams' Skins. The covering of rams' skins dyed red fittingly illustrates the next step in the work of Christ for our salvation, and also in Christian experience. Red being a symbol of sacrifice and suffering, this covering signifies Christ who "became obedient unto death, even the death of the cross." Phil. 2:8. It is the blood of Christ that calls, "Look unto Me, and be ye saved, all the ends of the earth." Isaiah 45:22. In the life of the Christian this covering symbolizes the covenant he makes with God by sacrifice. Ps. 50:5. It indicates that, like Paul, he is crucified with Christ. It represents complete consecration, absolute submission and unquestioning loyalty to his Ruler.

Why were skins of the ram designated for this covering? A ram, a mature male sheep, symbolized Christ's sacrifice, when He is described as "clothed with a vesture dipped in blood." Thus, the covering of rams' skins dyed red is a fit symbol of His sacrifice. The ram was used as:

1. A burnt offering—Lev. 9:2
2. Peace offering—Lev. 9:4
3. Consecration offering—Lev. 8:22, 24
4. Trespass offering—Lev. 5:15-19; Num. 5:6-8
5. Wave offering—Lev. 8:27

The *burnt offering* was of one's "own voluntary will," Lev. 1:3, and indicated complete dedication to the service of God. it secured reconciliation and acceptance with God through the blood of Christ. It was in token of God's acceptance that the Lord provided a *ram* for Abraham to offer in place of his son Isaac. Gen. 22:13. The *peace offering* accompanied the burnt offering as an expression of thanksgiving for peace and oneness with God.

As a *consecration offering*, the ram represented complete dedication to the service of God. It was the offering used in the consecration service of the priests, when ears, hands, and feet were dedicated to God. Workers together with God will be as fully consecrated. Ex. 8:20; Lev. 8:22-24.

As a *trespass offering*, in which restitution was required for sins of "ignorance," sins that were "wist not," the ram represented the full restitution which Christ made for man when He assumed our load of guilt, without which we would have paid the great debt with our lives. Lev. 5:15-19.

The *wave offering* was so called because it was waved to and fro before the Lord, thus offering salvation to the four quarters of the earth. It established communion between God and man, and was an acknowledgment of God's willingness to forgive and of His universal right to rule.

All these were "sweet savor" offerings: Lev. 8:21; that is, they were to God like sweet incense. They represented Christ who gave "Himself for us, an offering and a sacrifice to God for a sweetsmelling savor." Eph. 5:2. How pleasing it would be to Him if all *our* offerings were "sweet savor!" "The sacrifices of God are a broken spirit: a broken and a contrite heart, O God, Thou wilt not despise." Ps. 51:17. Such a sacrifice is to God a "sweet savor." It will be accompanied by the fruit of the Spirit—"love, joy, peace, long-suffering, gentleness, faith, meekness, temperance." Gal. 5:22, 23.

The covering of rams' skins dyed red represents the sacrifice of Christ not only when He poured out His blood on Calvary, but the entire experience of His sacrifice to the very end of His redemptive work. What a picture this gives of the sanctuary covering made of rams' skins dyed red!

The Goats' Hair Covering. Go still deeper, still closer to "heaven itself." What do we find? A pure white covering of woven goats' hair. Inspiration does not mention the color, nor does it mention the color of the badger skin which formed the outer covering. So in deciding this matter we must appeal to some other source of reliable information. On this point a standard encyclopedia says that the hair of the Cashmere goat of Kashmir, India, is white and the hair of the angora goat is long, white, and silky. From the hair of both these goats cloth is woven. When Israel brought their offerings for the construction of the sanctuary, among the gifts listed in Exodus 25:3-8, goats' hair is mentioned. The people had just arrived at Sinai and all these gifts had been brought as spoils from Egypt, a wealthy and powerful nation that traded with the nations of the world. "All the women whose hearts stirred them up in wisdom spun goats' hair." Ex. 35:26.

As white is a symbol of purity and perfection, Rev. 19:8, and as the white goats hair covering follows the covering of rams skins dyed red, it seems safe to conclude that the white goats hair covering fitly illustrates the truth that Christ was made perfect through suffering. It also represents progressive Christian experience, for "though your sins be as scarlet [represented in the red rams' skins] they shall be as white as snow." Isaiah 1:18, 19. "Be ye therefore perfect, even as your Father which is in heaven is perfect" is the Christian's goal. Matt. 5:48.

This covering was composed of eleven curtains, each four cubits wide and thirty cubits long. It was just long enough "to cover" the sanctuary. Ex. 26:13. Five of these curtains were coupled by themselves, and six by themselves, the sixth being "double in the forefront of the tabernacle." On one long edge of all of these large curtains were fastened fifty loops—one hundred loops in all. Into these loops fifty taches, or clasps, coupled the tent together into one large covering. Ex. 26:7-13. These taches were of brass, which as previously noted represent our earthly sufferings, our struggles, and our victories. These brass taches, come just before we reach the inmost covering with its gold embroidered angels. Like the brazen sockets at the entrance of the holy place, they fittingly represent the last race of earthly struggle before we enter the presence of the heavenly angels illustrated by the inner covering.

Why was this covering made of goats' hair? The goat was the animal chiefly used for the sin offering, Lev. 9:3, and was always used in connection with the cleansing of the sins of repentant Israel were in type blotted out. Atonement is at-one-ment, at one with God—perfect peace—peace after a lifelong battle with the enemy. As a flag of surrender is a white flag, so this white covering was an emblem of complete surrender to God. White is also a symbol of purity, of righteousness. And in the new earth where all is righteousness, the redeemed shall be clothed in white garments of light. The goats' hair covering was therefore a type of the righteousness which Christ *imputes* to all who come unto Him, and which He *imparts* to those who continue faithful to the end. In the Lord's goat, the last offering of the typical year, the atonement was completed, and when the antitypical atonement is finished, a people are prepared who "have washed their robes, and made them *white* in the blood of the Lamb." Rev. 7:14.

The Inner, or Royal Covering. Deeper yet. Where are we? We have passed the brass taches, past the last battle with sin, and a royal covering, woven in the loom of heaven, is ours. This covering was made of blue and purple and scarlet [yarn—*Moffatt*], which "wise hearted women did spin." Ex. 35:25. These colored threads were woven in ten curtains or stips the required size by wise—hearted men, each curtain being four cubits wide and twenty-eight cubits long. On them, under the direction of Aholiab, who was not only the master weaver but also the master embroiderer, wise—hearted men embroidered with real gold thread "cherubim of cunning work." Ex. 25:25; 36;8:14. We are not told the size or the number of these embroidered angels, but on ten large curtains each six feet wide and forty-two feet long, or even fifteen feet long if we count only the ceiling, there was room for a number of good sized cherubim. Doubtless the reason the number is not given is because they represented an "innumerable" company. Heb. 12:22.

When these ten curtains were ready, five of them were coupled together, and the other five likewise coupled one to another, thus making two larger curtains, each twenty cubits wide and twenty-eight cubits long, or at least thirty by forty-two feet. On one long selvedge edge of each was fastened fifty loops of blue [blue representing obedience to heavenly truth], so that by means of fifty taches, or couplings, made of pure gold, gold representing the Almighty, these two large curtains were joined together. So it became one covering, and it was called "the tabernacle." Ex. 36:8-13. When placed over the building framework, the taches of this covering were exactly below the brass taches of the goats' hair covering. How significant that under these taches of brass and gold was hung the inner vail, Ex. 26:33, symbol of the flesh [the humanity] of Christ! Heb. 10:20.

This covering woven of royal colored thread must have been very beautiful, similar to changeable silk, the different colors appearing according as the light shown upon it. And when on it figures of angels were embroidered in sparkling gold thread or wires, Ex. 39:3, the effect produced was surely gorgeous. Even the exquisite embroidery of skilled Chinese artists represented in beautiful designs of lively flowers, brilliant birds, and their "sacred" dragon, can in no way compare with this magnificent tapestry with its rich and resplendent embroidery of golden angels on royal colored linen or silk. And well it may thus be, for it represented "the angelic host who are connected with the work of the heavenly sanctuary, and who are ministering spirits to the people of God on earth." PP 347.

The beauty of this covering was surpassed only by that which it symbolized. The blue representing, as elsewhere, obedience to God's eternal truth, woven with the scarlet of sacrifice, made a covering of royal purple, fit for those who enter the companionship of ten thousand times ten thousand and thousands of thousands of angels symbolized by the gold embroidered cherubim. These royal colors are emblems not only of the character of heavenly beings, but they symbolize the qualities of truth and sacrifice which shape the characters of all who become members of the family above.

In these coverings, we recognize the garments with which God desires to clothe Jerusalem. He says: "I clothed thee also with broidered work, and shod thee with badgers' skin, and I girded thee with fine linen, and covered thee with silk. I decked thee also with ornaments, ... and I put a jewel on thy forehead [the Father's name or character, His seal, Rev. 14:1; 7:3], and I put...a beautiful crown [of glory and victory] upon thine head. Thou wast decked with gold and silver; and thy raiment was of fine linen, and silk, and broidered work." Eze. 16:10-13.

This inner covering with its gold-embroidered angels also represents Christ in His exaltation. "Wherefore God also hath highly exalted Him, and given Him a name that is above every name; that at the name of Jesus every knee should bow, of things in heaven, and things in earth, and things under the earth; and that every tongue should confess that Jesus Christ is Lord, to the glory of God the Father." Phil. 2:9, 10.

The Four Coverings Complete. Summing up these four coverings which symbolize Christ in the four division of His redemptive work, we have:

> Badgers' skins—a Lowly Saviour—"He humbled
> Himself" to walk among sinful men. Phil. 2:8
> Rams' skins dyed red—a sacrificial Saviour—He "became
> obedient unto death, even the death of the cross."
> Ibid.
> Goats' Hair, White—a sinless Saviour—He was made
> "perfect through sufferings. Heb. 2:10
> The Royal covering—an exalted Saviour—"Wherefore
> God hath highly exalted Him." Phil. 2:9

These coverings represent true beauty of character, not only of Christ, but of every true Christian: as the gold, the rich embroidery, and the royal colors within, are all beneath the plain outer covering, so "the King's daughter is all glorious within." Ps. 45:13. Outward adorning indicates a lack of inward beauty, of true Christian character. Humility, sacrifice, sinlessness, and royalty—this is the road that leads into the secret chamber of the Most High. It is the road to victory, *The Path to the Throne of God.*

The Finished Temple a Type. From the foregoing, it seems self-evident that the sanctuary as a whole represented Christ, for He was typified in practically every part of it, from the gate of the court to the ark in the most holy place, and from the silver foundation to the coverings which formed the roof. In fact, speaking of the temple at Jerusalem, John says that Christ "spake of the temple of His body." John 2:21.

The church also is represented as the temple building. On this point Paul says: "Ye are...built upon the foundation...Jesus Christ...in whom all the building fitly framed together groweth into an holy temple in the Lord: in whom ye also are builded together for an habitation of God through the Spirit." Eph. 2:19-22. Again Paul says Christ is "Son over His own house, whose house we are, if we hold fast the confidence and rejoicing of the hope firm unto the end." Heb. 3:6. And lastly, this beautiful prophecy from Zechariah 6:13, 15: "He [the Branch] shall build the temple of the Lord ... and *they that are far off* shall come and build in the temple of the Lord." Emphasis supplied.

The temple also symbolizes each individual Christian. "What?" exclaims Paul, "Know ye not that your body is the temple of the Holy Ghost...and ye are not your own?" I Cor. 6:19. And again, "Ye are the temple of the living God, wherefore be ye not unequally yoked together with unbelievers," but "come out from among them...and touch not the unclean thing, and I will...be a Father unto you, and ye shall be my sons and daughters." II Cor. 6:14-18.

Solomon's temple "was built of stone made ready before it was brought thither, so that there was neither hammer nor axe nor any tool of iron heard in the house while it was in building." I Kings 6:7. Likewise, this earth is the quarry where, if we are to occupy a place in the heavenly temple, we must be hewed and polished and all the rough places hammered off before we are ready to be "brought thither." The trials of this life are the tools of iron, God's workmen, with which we are prepared for our place in the temple of the Eternal. Peter says, "Ye also, as lively [living] stones, are built up a spiritual house...to offer up spiritual sacrifices." I Peter 2:5. If we put wood, hay, and stubble into our character temple, it will all be burned, "for the day shall declare it, because it shall be revealed by fire." Only the gold, silver, and precious stones will bear the testing fires. I Cor. 3:12, 13. Day by day each Christian is building his "spiritual house," and his body becomes a "spiritual sacrifice"—"a living sacrifice, holy, acceptable unto God." Rom 12:1.

"We are building in sorrow or joy
　　A temple the world may not see,
Which time cannot mar nor destroy:
　　We build for eternity.

Are you building for God alone?
　　Are you building in faith and love
A temple the Father will own
　　In the city of light above?"
　　　　　　　　　—N.B. Sargent

The golden table had two borders, each mounted with crowns. The shelf enclosed by the lower border provided a place for the golden dishes which were "upon the table"—the bowls, the saucers, the spoons, the flagons or pitchers and the chalices or goblets for the wine. Ex. 25:29; 37:11, 12, 16, *Moffatt*. The Kohathites prepared the bread and brought it every Sabbath to a priest who set it in order at the table and put frankincense on each row. I Chron. 9:32; II Chron. 13:10, 11, Lev. 24:5-8. Christ was the Bread that came down from heaven. The wine represented His blood shed for us. John 6:48-56. Thus, the table was indeed "the pure table before the Lord."

CHAPTER 20 PREVIEW

THE GOLDEN TABLE

- The First Step in Sanctification
  - The Golden Table
- The Two Crowns of the Table
  - Christ the Bread of Life
    - Fine Flour Bread
    - Other Ingredients
  - God's Word Cleanses
  - The Word Sanctifies
- Frankincense on the Bread
  - The "Continual" Bread
  - Earnest Study Essential
- The Scriptures a Safeguard
  - Bread of His Presence

20

THE GOLDEN TABLE

The First Step in Sanctification. We are now fairly within the holy place—the sanctification room of the sanctuary. Before us are wonderful opportunities. With all the resources of Heaven at our command, let us improve every one. As in the court of the sanctuary the work of reconciliation and justification are illustrated at the brazen altar and the laver, so in the holy place, sanctification is symbolized at the golden table, the golden altar, and the golden candlestick. Sanctification is surely a "golden" experience. The table provides our first opportunity for Christian growth for character perfection—for sanctification. It is the real starting point of our growing up "unto a perfect man, unto the measure of the stature of the fulness of Christ." Eph. 4:13.

The Golden Table. Ex. 25:23-30; 37:10-16. The table, located on the north side of the holy place, was made of shittim wood, overlaid with pure gold, thus illustrating humanity and Divinity united. The work of God itself, inspired by God but written by man, shows this union. As already noted, gold, in whatever form it appeared in the earthly sanctuary, was a type of Christ, the Almighty. Job 22:25, margin. Idolatry counterfeits the true, so when Israel apostatized they made gods of "gold." In this they rejected the true God, the Pure Gold, and said, "*These* be thy gods, O Israel, which have brought thee up out of the land of Egypt." Ex. 32:4, 8.

The Table was two cubits long, one cubit wide, and one and one-half cubits high—the same height as the grate in the brazen altar. May this not indicate that reconciliation and sanctification are equally important in Christian experience?

The Two Crowns of the Table. All around the table top was "a crown of gold," Ex. 37:11, called by Moffatt "a moulding." Besides this moulding, there was another; "also he made thereunto a border of an handbreadth [five or six inches] round about, and made a crown of gold for the border thereof round about." Ex. 37:10, 12; 25:25. From this, some understand that this lower border, or moulding, enclosed a shelf located somewhere below the top of the table, such as is found in our modern service tables. This shelf provided a place for the dishes, "which were upon the table." Ex. 37:16. Thus the table was decorated with a double crown of gold—one around the top and another around the shelf which was below the top. Over against this border, in the four feet, were four rings of cast gold for the staves to bear the table. Ex. 37:13, 14; 25:26, 27.

The double border of crowns has a twofold significance. A crown worn by a sovereign indicates authority and power. The Word of God, symbolized by the bread on the table, has dynamic power. Received into the heart, it changes the life. It "is quick, and powerful, and sharper than any two-edged sword, piercing even to the dividing asunder of soul and spirit." Heb. 4:12. It has authority. It brought the world into existence. "By the word of the Lord were the heavens made; and all the host of them by the breath of His mouth." Ps. 33:6. When God speaks, "let all the earth keep silence before Him." Hab. 2:20. It is His to speak; it is ours to obey.

These crowns also fittingly represent the reward that those will receive who "always" eat at the golden table. Anyone who has ever given earnest study to God's Word will agree that it does bring to the soul a double reward.

The Table Dishes of Gold. "And he made the vessels which were upon the table, his dishes, and his spoons, and his bowls, and his cover withal, of pure gold." Ex. 37:16. Moffatt's rendering reads: "The table dishes, the saucers, the flagons, and the chalices, for pouring the libations, were of pure gold." From this, it would seem that the table top was for the bread, and the shelf for the libation of wine, both of which are essential to the table of the Lord—"the pure table before the Lord." Lev. 24:5, 6.

Just how many dishes there were of each kind we are not told, and doubtless the number varied to meet changed conditions. However when the princes brought their gifts, each of the twelve brought, among other gifts, one golden spoon weighing ten shekels—twelve spoons in all. Num. 7:86. The golden "covers to cover withal" were probably used to cover the bread during the week. According to *Clark's Commentary* and also Josephus, the golden saucers were used to hold the frankincense that was placed on each row of loaves, Lev. 24:7, and the spoons, being "full of incense," Nu. 7:14, 20, 26, 32, 44, 50, 62, 68, 74, 80, 86, were evidently for dipping the frankincense into the saucers from the supply provided by the Levites. I Chron. 9:29. The golden flagons, or pitchers, were for the wine, and the golden chalices or goblets, were the individual wine cups.

The Bread on the Table. "Thou shalt take fine flour, and bake twelve cakes thereof: two-tenths deals shall be in one cake. And thou shalt set them in two rows, six on a row, upon the pure table before the Lord." Lev. 24:5-9. Each cake, or loaf, was made of "two-tenths deals" or two-tenths of an ephah of flour. Josephus states that two-tenths of an ephah was equal to 3-1/2 pints. Others give about 3-1/2 quarts. Another says, "These measures must only be accepted as approximately correct, because of the absence of sufficient data, the statement of most writers being doubtful." However, we may safely conclude that these twelve large cakes provided bountifully for the priests, Aaron and his four sons, Ex. 28:1, who represented the twelve tribes. It was eaten in "a holy place," Lev. 24:9, *Moffatt*; that is, "in the court which was a holy place. Lev. 6:26. Nothing was ever eaten in the Holy Place; that is, in the first apartment of the sanctuary, but all eating was in the court. Our King James version of the Bible makes almost no distinction between the court and the first apartment of the sanctuary—both being translated *the holy place*, which is another term for the first apartment. Ex. 40:22, 24, 26. Moffatt's translation is less confusing. He speaks of the court as *a holy place* or *a holy spot*, "the sacred court," Num. 28:7, the first apartment as *the Trysting tent*; and the most holy place as *the sacred place* or *the inner shrine*.

The bread was broken and eaten with the wine by the priests throughout the week. Is not this a beautiful illustration of the truth that if at all our meals throughout the week, after expressing heartfelt thanks for the food, we eat and drink to the glory of God, eating and drinking only that which will nourish the body, and dedicating to God all the strength thus received, "the family board becomes as the table of the Lord, and every meal a sacrament?" DA 660.

Christ the Bread of Life. The bread symbolized Jesus, the Bread of Life. John 6:35. He is the Bread that came down from heaven, the word of God. John 6:32, 33, 38, 63; 1:1. The bread and the wine that were on the table, suggests the Lord's communion table. And let it be noted that this immediately followed the ordinance of feet washing prefigured at the laver. After we are laved, as we partake of the bread and the wine of communion, do we not thus renew our covenant with Jesus to feed daily on the Bread of life and to drink daily from the Fountain of life? John 6:53-56. In these symbols, do we discern His broken body and His spilled blood, and are we willing to continue to partake of His sufferings, which they represent? Let us weigh this well, lest we partake "unworthily." I Cor. 11:28, 29. A spiritual understanding of the sanctuary will help us to discern the Lord's body.

Fine Flour Bread. Not only as a whole, but in each of its "four" ingredients, the bread symbolized Christ. The fine flour of which it was made, was flour ground fine, all unevenness and all coarse particles removed. This represented Christ, who was made perfect through suffering. If we are to be like Him, we too, must pass through the grinding process—we must be refined, all coarseness and roughness removed from our lives. "In Jesus there was no uneveness. He was always even, always the same. In Him one day's walk never contradicted another, one hour's service never clashed with another. In Him every grace was in its perfectness, none in excess, none out of place, none wanting. In Him firmness never degenerated into obstinacy, or calmness into stoical indifference." Andrew Jukes, in *The Law of the Offerings*, P. 75.

Other Ingredients. The shewbread was a true meat offering, besides the fine flour, there was oil, salt, and water, but, like our communion bread, no leaven. Lev. 2:1, 5, 11, 13. *Oil* symbolized Christ working through the Holy Spirit. "We receive Christ through His Word; and the Holy Spirit is given to open the Word of God to our understanding, and bring home its truths to our hearts." MB 164.

Salt is a preservative, a symbol of incorruption. A reverent study of the Word will preserve the Christian Bible student from corrupt doctrines as well as corrupt manners. Salt is sometimes put on icy walks to keep people from slipping and falling, and the Word of God in our hearts will keep us from falling on the slippery paths of life. Salt is not only a preservative, it is also a symbol of perpetuity. "The Lord...gave the kingdom...to David *forever* ... by a covenant of salt." II Chron 13:5. It is also a symbol of wisdom: "Let your speech be alway with grace, seasoned with salt, that ye may know how ye ought to answer every man." Col. 4:6. It is a symbol of friendship and hospitality. Reference to this is made in Ezra 4:14, margin: "Because we are salted with the salt of the palace." And so the

Christian is admonished, "Have salt in your selves, and have peace one with another." Mark 9:50. As we share our faith with others, we must do so with incorruption of mind and sincerity of heart. Our attitude must be one of friendship and hospitality, of peace and good will, and our speech "with grace"—never unkind or critical. It is when we mingle these graces with our efforts to give the Word to others, that we shall become "the salt of the earth." Matt. 5:13.

God's Word Cleanses. The water used in the bread represents the cleansing power of the Word of God. "Wherewithal shall a young man cleanse his way? By taking heed thereto according to Thy Word." Ps. 119:9. Jesus gave Himself for the church, "that He might... cleanse it with the washing of water *by the Word*." Eph. 5:26. "Now ye are clean *through the word* which I have spoken unto you." John 15:3. Obedience to the Word of God cleanses and refines and ennobles our lives, and enables us to be true servants of God.

The Word Sanctifies. To sanctify is to make sacred and to set apart for a sacred use. Obedience to the Word of God, represented by the bread, sanctifies the soul. "Sanctify them through Thy truth: Thy Word is truth." John 17:17. We are born again only of the incorruptible Word of God. I Peter 1:22, 23. It is by the Word that we become "partakers of the divine nature," II Peter 1:4. Its influence upon our lives destroys the carnal life, and imparts a new life—the life of Christ. The Word of God "is able to build up, and to give you an inheritance among all them which are sanctified." Acts 20:32. It is through the Word that we are made perfect. "All scripture...is profitable...for reproof, for correction, for instruction in righteousness: that the man of God may be made perfect." II Tim. 3:16, 17. "Let those who would be truly sanctified search the Word of God with patience, with prayer, and with humble contrition of soul." RH, March 25, 1902.

Unless we eat, digest, and assimilate this bread of life, we can have no life in us, John 6:53, any more than we can live a physical life if we neglect physical food. We may drag along in a semi-starved condition for a time, but sooner or later life becomes extinct. This neglect is the first step toward going back to the beggarly elements of the world. "My people are destroyed for lack of knowledge." Hos. 4:6.

When Jesus said, "I am that Bread of life...if any man eat of this bread, he shall live forever; and the bread that I will give is My flesh, which I will give for the life of the world," the Jews and also the disciples murmured, and said, "How can this Man give us His flesh to eat?" Jesus explained, saying, "It is the Spirit that quickeneth; the flesh profiteth nothing: *the words* that I speak unto you, they are life." John 6:48, 51, 52, 63. The Word of God is the living bread, giving refinement, wisdom, cleansing, spiritual strength and endurance, and finally sanctification and eternal life.

Frankincense on the Bread. "And thou shalt put pure frankincense upon each row, that it may be on the bread for a memorial, even an offering made by fire unto the Lord." Lev. 24:7. This frankincense was the same as that burned daily on the golden altar. At the end of the week, it also was burned on the golden altar, "an offering made by fire unto the Lord." It represented the righteousness of Christ, which, mingled with sincere prayer is given to those who eat the Bread of life "continually." It taught the lesson that "never should the Bible be studied without prayer." When the Bible is studied without prayer, we are told that Satan stands ready to suggest error, or belittle the sacredness of the Word. The frankincense was on the bread "for a memorial," or as Moffatt has it, "a reminder to the Eternal" —a reminder that His righteousness is promised to all who give prayerful study to the Word.

The "Continual" Bread. Of the type, Christ said, the bread was "before Me alway." Ex. 25:30. The table as never without it, therefore it is called the "continual" bread. Num. 4:7. Chosen ones of the Kohathites, a division of the Levites, prepared it every Sabbath, I Chron. 9:32, and at the beginning of each Sabbath, the "newly baked" bread was brought to an incoming priest who "set it in order" on the table "before the Lord." Lev. 24:5-8; PP 348; SB Dict. Then the old bread was taken away, and eaten the following week by the outgoing priests "on behalf of the Israelites, to mark a lasting compact." Lev. 24:8, *Moffatt*. At the end of the week, whatever of the old bread remained, was burned on the brazen altar, "for it is most holy of the offerings of the Lord made by fire." Lev. 24:9. Does this not teach us that our study of the Bible should be constant, a daily partaking of the bread of life? Does it not teach us that during the week we are to *eat* and *digest* the holy bread continually?

This special Sabbath feast, together with daily and prayerfully partaking of the Living Bread, is the first essential to "growing up" into perfection of character. It is essential if we are to be kept from sin—"Thy Word have I hid in my heart, that I might not sin against thee." Ps. 119:11. It is essential to sanctification—it is "most holy" unto the Lord. There is no substitute for earnest study of the Word; it is "fundamental;" it cannot be merely "supplemental," as Christ, the Word, was made flesh, John 1:1, 14, so the Word of God in us must be made flesh. We must not only *know* the word, we must *be* the word.

Earnest Study Essential. Some Christians who have passed through a sincere court experience, know very little of the experience of growing up "unto a perfect man, unto the measure of the stature of the fullness of Christ." Eph. 4:13. They remain "babes," or at least dwarfs, in the Christian life. Why is this? All have equal access to the divine Word, but many neglect or ignore their privileges. Although the banquet is spread before them, they allow the cares of life or the deceitfulness of riches to choke the Word. At times they read the Bible as a Christian duty, but their hearts are on the trivial concerns of everyday life. They hear the word as it is preached from the sacred desk, but it falls on stony ground or among thorns; it does not take root, and soon withers away, or the thorns grow up and choke it, and it yields no fruit. As Paul says, they are "dull of hearing." He further says, although "ye ought to be teachers, ye have need that one teach you again which be the first principles of the oracles of God; and are become such as have need of milk and not of strong meat. For everyone that useth milk is unskilful in the Word...for he is a babe. But strong meat belongeth to them… who by reason of use [of the Word] have their senses exercised to discern both good and evil." Heb. 5:11-14. Should not this be a challenge to all who have entered the holy place? If the Spirit of God discovers to us spiritual malnutrition, the surest remedy is an earnest study of the Word of God, which is our spiritual food.

The Scriptures a Safeguard. If the Bible is truly to be our "safeguard" through times of trouble, we must dig deep into its rich mine of truth, comparing scripture with scripture. In these closing hours of probation, we need to study more earnestly than ever before. Satan knows that the Bible, studied with heart and mind and soul, will be our "safeguard" during the perils of these last days; therefore it is his "constant study to keep the minds of men occupied with those things which will prevent them from obtaining the knowledge of God." 5 T 740; See also GC 593. But if we improve our opportunities to gain a knowledge of the Bible, God will not leave us to the buffetings of the enemy. To those who *hunger* and *thirst* after righteousness the promise is that they shall be filled. Matt. 5:6. This promise, "set in the framework of faith" and "placed in memory's halls," will never fail. 5 T 630. The channel of communication will be unobstructed. "Deep, earnest study of the Word under the guidance of the Holy Spirit, will give fresh manna, and the same Spirit will make its use effectual." 6 T 163. Then let us not depend on others to do our thinking for us, but let us sink the shaft deep into the treasures of His Word.

If our opportunities for education have been limited, how encouraging are these words: "The understanding of Bible truth depends not so much on the power of intellect brought to the search, as on the singleness of purpose, the earnest longing after righteousness." GC 599. "If he [the Christian] would have his powers and capabilities daily improved, he must *study*; he must eat and digest the Word… The soul that is nourished by the bread of life will have every faculty vitalized by the Spirit of God." 6 T 153. If in this spirit we daily feed upon the Word, Jesus will multiply it as He did the five loaves, so that not only shall we ourselves be filled, but through our efforts the multitudes also will eat and be filled. Mark 6:35-44; John 6:9-13.

Bread of His Presence. Shewbread literally means "bread of the face" or "bread of the presence." "The bread of the face," says *Smith's Bible Dictionary*, "is therefore that bread through which God is seen; that is, through the participation of which man attains the sight of God. Whence it follows that we have not to think of bread as such, as the means of nourishing the bodily life, but as spiritual food, as a means of appropriating and retaining that life which consists in seeing the face of God." "The shewbread pointed to Christ, the living Bread, who is ever in the presence of God for us." PP 354. Now, by faith we see His face through His Word, but when type reaches antitype, the promise is we shall see His face and His name shall be in our foreheads. Rev. 22:4

The golden altar or prayer altar had four horns, representing the power of Christ available for all who have learned to pray; also a border of crowns indicating their reward. It was located just before the second vail, nearer to the mercy seat and the shekinah in the most holy place than any other article of furniture. Here, morning and evening, with the prayers of saints, the high priest offered the incense, symbolizing the righteousness of Christ, which makes prayer acceptable and effectual. Ex. 30:6-8. The golden censer was kept with this altar when not used on the day of atonement. EW 251-252.

CHAPTER 21 PREVIEW

THE GOLDEN ALTAR

- The Second Step in Sanctification
- The Golden Altar and Its Significance
- The Incense and Its Significance
- Perpetual Incense
- Who Offered the Incense?
- The Family Altar
- "The Beasts Shall Teach Thee" (a Poem)
- Secret Prayer
- The Prayer Altar Nearest the Throne
- Jesus Our High Priest Presents Our Prayers
- Why Some Prayers Are Not Answered
- Essential to Effectual Prayer
- Assurance of Answered Prayer
- Prayers Lodged by the Throne
- Heaven's Radio (a Poem)

21

THE GOLDEN ALTAR

The Second Step in Sanctification From the table of shewbread, we pass to the golden altar, the altar of incense, the altar of prayer. While the first step in sanctification is symbolized at the table, the altar symbolizes the second step in Christian growth. It is another forward move on *The Path to the Throne of God.* Prayer is as essential to our "growing up" as is partaking of the living bread. In fact, they go hand in hand. The word of God is our spiritual food; prayer is our spiritual breath.

In the sanctuary service, neither the service at the table nor that at the candle-stick was separated from the service at the altar. Incense was put on the bread, and at the time of the lighting the lamps, incense was burned on the altar. The incense of fervent, effectual prayer must be mingled with the eating of the bread of life, and also with our service as light bearers. The Christian who lives in the holy place will live a life of prayer, for only in constant communion with Christ, can he be "Perfected"—only thus can he be "sanctified." Heb. 10:14.

The Golden Altar and Its Significance. Ex. 30:1-10. Like the table, the golden altar was made of shittim wood overlaid with pure gold. It was one cubit long and one cubit wide. The height was two cubits, or about three feet. Like the brazen altar, it was foursquare and it had four horns, one on each corner; but unlike the brazen al-tar, it had a "crown of gold round about." The two staves with which it was carried, were also made of wood overlaid with gold, and the four rings that held the staves were of pure gold. This altar was in the holy place, "in the tent of the congregation before the vail." Ex. 40:26. Nothing but the sacred fire and the prescribed incense was ever placed upon it, except on the day of atonement when the sanctuary was cleansed, the high priest touched its horns with blood. Ex. 30:9, 10.

As gold is a type of the Almighty, Job 31:24, so the golden altar symbolized Christ. As in the table, so in the altar, the wood covered with pure gold represented humanity covered and united with Divinity—Christ and His followers. Being "foursquare" we may indicate that as we approach the prayer altar, we, like Christ, should be foursquare. As on the altar of sacrifice, so on the altar of prayer, the four horns point to Christ. They signify strength, power, victory, and honor. Prayer is the Christian's personal *strength* in overcoming sin. It is his *power* in working for others. Prayer does bring *victory*, and surely it is an *honor* to be invited by the Most High to commune with Him at the place nearest His throne. "Appeals, entreaties, petitions between man and man move men, and act a part in controlling the affairs of nations. But prayer moves heaven." SD 335. Like the crowns around the table, the golden crown around the altar represents not only power, but the reward which the Christian who continues "instant in prayer" will in due time surely receive. Rom. 12:12.

In the brazen altar is represented the sacrifice of Christ in His work on earth for us; in the golden altar we behold Him in His work in heaven, where "He ever liveth to make intercession" for us. Heb. 7:25. "Before the vail of the most holy place was an altar of *perpetual intercession*, before the holy, an altar of *continual atonement*. By blood and by incense God was to be approached,—symbols pointing to the great Mediator, through whom sinners may approach Jehovah, and through whom alone mercy and salvation can be granted to the repentant, believing soul. PP 353.

The Incense and Its Significance. The incense was composed of "four sweet spices; stacte, the finest myrrh; onycha, supposed to be an odoriferous shell; galbannum, a gum resin; and frankinsense, a dry, resinous aromatic gum obtained from a tree that grows in Arabia. Of each of these four fragrant ingredients there was an equal weight, and when "tempered together," they produced a most fragrant perfume, especially when burned. That the incense might always be ready for use, it was kept "before the testimony in the tabernacle of the congregation," a name often applied to the holy place of the sanctuary. Ex. 30:34-36.

In the incense we again find the significant number four. As the four ingredients in the bread represented Christ, the living Bread which came down from heaven, so the four sweet spices of the incense represented His perfect righteousness. As some of the incense was beaten "very small," so Christ was made "perfect through sufferings," that He might be a merciful and faithful High Priest "to make reconciliation for the sins of the people." Heb. 2:10, 17. Likewise our sufferings lead us to the prayer altar, where we may be strengthened and fitted to help others.

Perpetual Incense. The fire upon the golden altar "was kindled by God Himself, and was sacredly cherished. Day and night the holy incense diffused its fragrance throughout the sacred apartments, and without, far around the tabernacle." PP 348. As the bread was "continual," so also the incense offered with the prayers of the people was a "perpetual" incense before the Lord. Ex. 30:8. Prayer is the "breath of the soul," and as we breathe without ceasing, so should we "pray without ceasing," or as Moffatt renders it, "Never give up prayer." I Thess. 5:17.

Who Offered the Incense? God's instruction to Moses was: "Aaron [the high priest] shall burn thereon sweet incense every morning: when he dresseth the lamps, he shall burn incense upon it, and when Aaron lighteth the lamps at even, he shall burn incense upon it." Ex. 30:7, 8. When Aaron offered incense, the divine glory rested upon the mercy seat, indicating that God accepted the offering. Thus our prayers are presented to God, by our heavenly High Priest and Intercessor, who offers His merits continually in our behalf, as sweet incense before God; and God is pledged to answer every request of His Son.

The Family Altar "At the time of Incense," morning and evening, "the whole multitude of the people were praying without." Luke 1:10. It was the sacred hour of worship, when Israel dedicated themselves anew to God, and to His service as symbolized in the lighting of the lamps. "In this custom, Christians have an example for morning and evening prayer. God...looks with great pleasure upon those who love Him, bowing morning and evening to seek pardon for sins committed, and to present their requests for needed blessings." PP 354. To families who observe the hour for daily worship, God has given one of His most precious promises: There "I will meet with thee." Ex. 30:6. This custom in our homes will "diffuse its fragrance" not only in the home itself, but "far around" our tabernacle. It will bring strength, and power, and honor, and victory not only in our own experiences, but in our efforts for others. This is the reward of all who faithfully and sincerely offer the incense of prayer upon the family altar morning and evening.

"The beasts shall teach thee," Job 12:7

The camel, at the close of day,
    Kneels down upon the sandy plain
To have his burden lifted off,
    And rest to gain.

My soul, thou too, should'st to thy knees
    When daylight draweth to a close,
And let thy Master lift thy load,
    And grant repose.

Else how could'st thou tomorrow meet,
    With all tomorrow's work to do,
If thou thy burden all the night
    Dost carry through?

The camel kneels at break of day
    To have his guide replace his load
Then rises up anew to take
    The desert road.

So thou should'st kneel at morning's dawn
    That God may give thee daily care,
Assured that He no load too great
    Will make thee bear.
              —Ann Temple Whitney

Prayer is not necessary in order to tell God our needs; He knows all about our needs before we ask Him. He understands all our perplexities. "Prayer does not bring God down to us, but brings us up to Him," CC 97, thus preparing us to receive Him, to appreciate His gifts and use them to His glory. Regular observance of "*The Morning Watch*" will require steadfast purpose and a sincere love for God that adverse circumstances or wayward moods cannot overthrow. Each morning before the duties and cares of the day have had opportunity to deprive us of this blessed communion with God, to put our lives into His control will bring rich reward all through the day. If we cherish this early hour blessing, we shall come from it exhilarated and reassured for life's problems.

Secret Prayer. "Family prayer and public prayer have their place; but it is secret communion with God that sustains the soul life. It was in the mount alone with God that Moses beheld the pattern of that wonderful building which was to be the abiding place of God's glory. It is in the mount with God—the secret place of communion—that we are to contemplate His glorious ideal for humanity. Thus we shall be enabled so to fashion our character-building that to us may be fulfilled the promise, 'I will dwell in them and walk in them; and I will be their God, and they shall be my people.'" GW 254.

> "In the secret of His presence
>> How my soul delights to hide!
> Oh, how precious are the lessons
>> That I learn at Jesus' side.
>
> Earthly cares can never vex me,
>> Neither trials lay me low;
> For when Satan comes to tempt me,
>> To the secret place I go."
>> *—Ellen Lakshine Goreh*
>> *A converted high class*
>> *woman of India*

The Prayer Altar Nearest the Throne. The altar of incense was nearer to the ark than any other article in the holy place. It was placed "before the vail that is by the ark of the testimony, before the mercy seat that is over the testimony, where I will meet with thee." Ex. 30:6. It was "before the throne." Rev. 8:3. "In the offering of incense the priest was brought more directly into the presence of God than in any other act of the daily ministration.... When the priest offered incense before the Lord, he looked toward the ark; and as the cloud of incense arose, the divine glory descended upon the mercy seat and filled the most holy place, and often so filled both apartments that the priest was obliged to retire to the door of the tabernacle. As in that typical service the priest looked by faith to the mercy seat, which he could not see, so the people of God are now to direct their prayers to Christ, their great High Priest, who, unseen by human vision, is pleading in their behalf in the sanctuary above." PP 353.

Jesus Our High Priest Presents Our Prayers. In Revelation 5:8, certain ones are represented as having golden vials of *odors* [margin, incense] which are *the prayers* of saints; and in Revelation 8:3 the Angel offers incense *with the prayers* of all saints upon the golden altar which is before the throne. Are these "odors" [or incense]—the prayers of saints—the same as the "incense" offered on the golden altar? "The incense, ascending with the prayers of Israel, represents the merits and intercession of Christ, His perfect righteousness." PP 353. "The prayers of God's people passing through the corrupt channels of humanity, unless purified by the righteousness of the great High Priest, are not acceptable to God. To them Christ puts the merits of His spotless righteousness. Thus perfumed, as sweet incense, they rise before God, and gracious answers are returned." E.G.W. in YI, April 16, 1903. Christ's merits are represented by the *incense*, the prayers of saints which rise as "sweet incense" are the *odors*. Therefore David says, "Let my prayer be set forth before Thee as incense." Ps. 141:2.

Why Some Prayers Are Not Answered. It is the very life of our High Priest to receive our request and to present them to the Father. He "ever liveth" to do this, and the Father delights to answer every true prayer. Why, then, are some prayers unanswered? Let us consider some of the reasons:

1. *Unbelief Hinders God*. God has promised: "Him that cometh to Me I will in no wise cast out." John 6:37. Do we believe Him, or do we by our unbelief make Him a liar? I John 5:10. Unless we ask in faith, it is written, "Let not that man think that he shall receive anything of the Lord," James 1:7, for "without faith it is impossible to please Him; for he that cometh to God must believe that He is, and that He is a rewarder of them that diligently seek Him." Heb. 11:6. Let us hang in memory's hall that familiar, yet always inspiring gem; "Prayer is the key in the hand of faith to unlock heaven's storehouse, where are treasured the boundless resources of Omnipotence." SC 98, 99.

2. *Selfishness Hinders God*. That unselfishness is a condition of answered prayer is taught in the sanctuary. "The perfume which thou shalt make, ye shall not make to yourselves according to the composition thereof: It shall be unto thee holy unto the Lord." Because of the pure and holy character of the righteousness of Christ, which the incense represented, the penalty for using it for selfish purposes was "Whosoever shall make like unto that, to smell thereto, shall be cut off from His people." Ex. 30:36-38. Such selfish use of incense seems to represent selfish prayers. "Ye ask, and receive not, because ye ask amiss, that ye may consume it upon your lusts." James 4:3. Such prayers, instead of lifting up to God, cut us off from Him.

   It is said that Raphael used to wear a candle in a pasteboard cap, so that while he was painting, his shadow would not fall upon his work. Many a prayer is spoiled by our own shadow. Too often we pray for what we want rather than that which will be for the glory of God.

3. *Willful Disobedience Hinders God*. When the priest offered incense before the Lord, *he looked toward the ark*, and in the ark was the law of God. Sincere obedience to God's law is a condition of answered prayer, for we are told that "He that turneth away his ear from hearing the law, even his prayer shall be an abomination." Prov. 28:9.

4. *An Evil Heart Hinders God*. "If I regard iniquity in my heart, the Lord will not hear me." Ps. 66:18. The thought in the word regard is not seriously endeavoring to give up. Secret sin cherished in the heart blocks our access to Him. Iniquity must be put away if ever we are truly to pray. We must wear on our

forehead the candle of renunciation—we must be willing and determined to renounce evil attitudes, cherished sins, bad tempers, pride, covetousness, uncleanness, sloth, evil speaking, anger, hatred, and the whole train of vices. We must clear the King's highway, so that Jesus can present our petitions to God with the incense of His righteousness.

5. *Irreverence Hinders God.* Irreverence also is displeasing to God, and it should be offensive to us. The great and all-powerful and holy God should be addressed, not as we would an inferior, or even an equal, not even as we would do a great earthly ruler. As we come into His presence we should remember that He is King of kings, who dwelleth in light unapproachable. Is it any wonder that many of our prayers never reach the throne of God?

6. *An Unforgiving Spirit Hinders God.* "Forgive us our debts as we forgive our debtors" is the prayer Jesus taught His disciples. "If ye forgive not men their trespasses, neither will your Father forgive your trespasses." Matt. 6:12, 15. We must go even further. "If thou bring thy gift to the altar," Christ said, "and there rememberest that thy brother hath ought against thee; leave there thy gift before the altar, and go thy way; first be reconciled to thy brother, and then come and offer thy gift." Matt. 5:23, 24.

Peter was troubled on this point. "Lord," he asked, "how oft shall my brother sin against me, and I forgive him? till seven times?" Jesus answered, "Not...until seven times; but until seventy times seven." Then to explain further, he told the parable of the unmerciful servant whose Lord had forgiven him a debt of 10,000 talents—$300,000,000, or in today's money value, $30,000,000,000, which represented, as nearly as figures can, the debt we owe Christ for our salvation. But when a fellow servant who owed him 100 pence could not pay the debt, he took him by the throat and cast him into prison until he should pay it all. Shame on us who have been forgiven the unspeakable debt, if we from the heart forgive not every one his brother their trespasses. To such Christ says, "Likewise shall My heavenly Father do also to you." Matt. 18:21-35.

7. *Prayer With Thanksgiving Pleases God.* Paul associated prayer with gratitude and right thinking; nor is this accidental. "Be careful for nothing," he says, "but in everything by prayer and supplication with thanksgiving let your requests be made known unto God....Finally, brethren, whatsoever things are true," honest, just, pure, lovely, of good report, "think on these things." Phil. 4:6, 8. Such thoughts will prepare us to pray with assurance. "As we acknowledge before God our appreciation of Christ's merits, fragrance is given to our intercessions...His merits [are] as sweet incense." 8T 178.

When we are tempted to grieve because God has not answered our prayers, we might do well to consider these words from Longfellow's *Table Talk*: "What discord we should bring into the universe if our prayers were all answered! Then *we* should govern the world, and not God. And do you think we should govern it better?...As frightened women grasp at the reins when there is danger, so do we grasp at God's government with our prayers. Thanksgiving with a full heart—and the rest—submission to the Divine will."

ESSENTIALS TO EFFECTUAL PRAYER. 1. *Submission to God's will* is the first essential to effectual prayer. When Christ prayed His thrice-repeated and agonizing prayer, "O My Father, if it be possible, let this cup pass from Me," each time He added "Nevertheless not as I will, but as Thou wilt." Matt. 26:39. Did the Father fail to hear His Son? O no! His prayer was answered "according to His will." I John 5:14. It was for our sakes that the cup was not withheld. The same complete submission on our part is the first condition of answered prayer. God always gives us that which is for our good, and which will be for His glory; therefore, to our requests uttered when we cannot know what is for our good, instead of saying "Yes," He may say "No," or "Wait." But at all times we can trust Him to do just what is best, always remembering, as Philip Brooks has said, that "prayer is not the overcoming of God's reluctance; it is the taking hold of God's willingness."

Paul had a "thorn in the flesh," supposedly his infirmity referred to in Gal. 4:13-15, where he speaks of a serious difficulty with his eyes. He calls this affliction "the messenger of Satan," and three times he besought the Lord that it might depart from him. II Cor. 12:7, 8. Did the Lord take away this affliction? No! Did He hear and answer his petition? Yes! How? "My grace is sufficient for thee," He said, "for My strength is made perfect in weakness." vs. 9. Was Paul satisfied with this answer? He was! "Most gladly therefore will I rather glory in my infirmities," he said, "that the power of Christ may rest upon me. Therefore I take pleasure in infirmities, in reproaches, in necessities, in persecutions in distresses for Christ's sake; for when I am weak, then am I strong." vs. 9, 10. What a beautiful example of Christlike submission! And as a result of this noble, cheerful attitude, what a wonderful work God wrought through this apostle!

The experience of the good king Hezekiah, recorded in II Kings 20, is a sad comment on a petition uttered with an unsubmissive heart. Hezekiah's desire to accomplish more for the kingdom over which he ruled, vs. 20, might have been laudable had it not been prompted by personal pride. Nevertheless, He who sometimes lets us have our own way in order to teach us the wisdom and righteousness of *His* way, reversed His decree, and added fifteen years to the king's life. What was the result? Hezekiah not only took the first step toward betraying the kingdom into the hands of the king of Babylon, but his son Manasseh, who was born during this time, II Kings 21:1, and who came to the throne on the death of Hezekiah, was one of the most wicked kings who had ever ruled over Judah. How much better it would have been had Hezekiah submitted to the will of an all-wise God instead of praying contrary to His will! Since "we know not what to pray for as we ought," if we submit our desires to God's righteous will, the Spirit will make intercession for us "according to the will of God." Rom 8:26, 27.

2. *Asking in His Name*. "Whatsoever ye shall ask in My name, that will I do." John 14:13. "In My name"—that is the secret of prevailing prayer. We came to the

prayer altar with a request. If it is "in My name," Jesus receives it. Then to the Father He presents our request with the incense of His own righteousness, pleading His blood for us. "My blood, Father, My blood, My blood," He pleads. EW 38. "This request is from one for whom I gave my life. He is true and faithful."

"In His name they [the disciples] were to present their petitions to the Father, and they would receive answer…Christ's name was to be their watchword…the source of their success. Nothing was to be recognized in His kingdom that did not bear His name and superscription." AA 28. Every prayer that bears His name and superscription will be presented to the Father who is pledged to answer every petition of His Son.

While our heavenly Father delights to answer every request of His Son, Jesus cannot present to His Father a request that is prompted by wrong motives—He cannot add the incense of His own righteousness to unrighteousness. He cannot endorse such a request with *His name*. To do so would be to offer "strange incense" before God. Ex. 30:9. Our requests must be "in His name"—in harmony with His will and character. Otherwise, they might be compared to a check drawn on a national bank and presented without signature. Of what value would such a check be? With what seriousness, then, should we come before God with the petition, "Lord, teach us to pray." Luke 11:1.

Assurance of Answered Prayer. The Father is more willing to give than we are really concerned to ask. Jesus says to us, "Ask and it shall be given you; seek, and ye shall find; knock, and it shall be opened unto you." Matt. 7:7. This promise is absolute and certain. Sometimes we may not recognize God's answer to prayer. A story is told of a women who prayed for patience, and God sent her a "green cook" which to her was a great trial of faith. Was her prayer answered? Yes; because "the trying of your faith worketh patience." James 1:3. "Every sincere prayer is heard in heaven. It may not be fluently expressed; but if the heart is in it, it will ascend to the sanctuary where Jesus ministers, and He will present it to the Father…as His own desire in that soul's behalf—beautiful and fragrant with the incense of His own perfection." DA 667. "In the future life, the mysteries that here have annoyed and disappointed us will be made plain. We shall see that our seemingly unanswered prayers and disappointed hopes have been among our greatest blessings." MH 474.

Prayers "Lodged by the Throne." "The earnest prayer of contrite souls will be lodged by the throne; and God will answer these prayers in His own time if we cling to His arm by faith." 6T 153. Because of adverse circumstances or for some reason unknown to us, the answer to some prayers may be long delayed, even till probation is about to close; but the prayers of "all saints" are registered on the altar of prayer that is before the throne in heaven. They are not forgotten or ignored. This is clearly taught in the sanctuary. In Revelation 8:3-5 we read that when Christ's work as our Intercessor is about to close, "there was given unto Him much incense, that He should offer it with the prayers of all saints upon the golden altar which was before the throne. And the smoke of the incense, which came with the prayers of the saints, ascended up before God out of the Angel's hand." This Angel is Christ, for He it is, our High Priest in heaven, who presents our prayers to God with the incense of His righteousness.

Thus we are assured that every unselfish prayer, every prayer "in His name," every prayer with the conclusion, "Nevertheless, not my will but Thine be done," will in God's own time receive the sympathetic attention of Him who is our "merciful and faithful High Priest." Heb. 2:17. He is fully able to do this, for He is the "Lamb...having seven horns [complete power] and seven eyes" [perfect discernment] Rev. 5:6. He knows the motive that prompts every prayer, for He is "a discerner of the thoughts and intents of the heart." Heb. 4:12. It is our part not to be over anxious, but to have faith in God's wisdom and goodness, and submit our will to His righteous judgment.

When these prayer have received due attention, the Angel removes the fire from the golden altar, puts it into His golden censer, and casts the censer into the earth, thus indicating that His work of intercession in heaven is ended. The last prayer is answered, and at the end, when we see God's dealings in their true perspective, if we have a prayer lodged by the throne, that prayer will be answered according to His will, and we shall be abundantly satisfied.

Heaven's Radio

There's a radio in heaven,
    Yonder by the great white throne;
The most wonderful invention
    Ever has, or will be, known.
For it catches every whisper
    Uttered on earth's lowly sod,
And broadcasts them without error
    Straight into the heart of God.

The whole wide world's microphone
    Through which we mortals speak;
And we are all broadcasting
    Each hour, each day, each week.
And the radio in heaven
    Is catching every word;
Each Prayer on earth we utter
    By the ear of God is heard.
                —*Mrs. Frank Likens*

The candlestick, made of a talent of pure gold, weighed about 120 pounds, valued at $30,000. It represents Christ, "the light of the world," John 1:9, also His followers, who are to be "the light of the world." Matt. 5:14. Especially did the central shaft to which all the branches are joined, represent Christ who walks in the midst of the seven golden candlesticks. The candlestick had seventy ornaments, and the Lord send out the seventy to preach. Luke 10:1. The Sanhedrin also was composed of seventy of the leaders of Israel. As the gold was beaten, so Christ and His faithful followers "shall suffer persecution." II Tim. 3:12. In the evening the high priest renewed the supply of oil; in the morning he trimmed the lamps with the snuffers, shown here below the lampstand. Ex. 30:7, 8.

CHAPTER 22 PREVIEW

THE CANDLESTICK OF BEATEN GOLD

- The Third Step in Sanctification
- The Parts of the Candlestick
- The Significance of Its Seven Branches
- Almond Ornaments
- Pure Gold
- The Gold Was Beaten
- Pure Olive Oil and Its Significance
- The Oil was Beaten
- The Lamps Burned Continually—the "Daily"
- The "Two Olive Trees"
- Who Lighted the Lamps?
- The Morning and Evening Lightings
- The Candlestick a Light Bearer
- Light Bearing the Fruit of Faith
- God's Broadcasting System
- The Blessing of Service
- The Candlestick a Symbol of the Holy Spirit
- Relation to Sanctification, to Justification
- Righteousness by Faith
- Sanctification Our Passport Into the Most Holy Place

22

THE CANDLESTICK OF BEATEN GOLD

The Third Step in Sanctification. At the golden candlestick is represented the third and crowning step in sanctification, or Christian perfection. If we stop with a study of God's word and prayer, we shall fall short of "the measure of the stature of the fullness of Christ." Eph. 4:13. It is not enough that we have been born again of the incorruptible Word of God, I Peter 1:23, or that as newborn babes we desire the sincere milk of the Word, that we may grow thereby, I Peter 2:2, even though through such an excellent beginning we are "no more children, tossed to and fro, and carried about with every wind of doctrine." Eph. 4:14. It is not enough that our prayers ascend morning and evening with the incense at the altar. We are to be "complete in all the will of God." Col. 4:12. We are to "grow up into Him in all things."

What do we still lack?—It is the candlestick experience. How can we supply this lack? By "speaking the truth in love." Eph. 4:15. We have received the truth into good and honest hearts; we are not now to put our light "under a bushel, but on a candlestick," that it may give "light unto all that are in the house." Matt. 5:14, 15. This light-bearing is the cap sheaf of Christian growth, of sanctification.

The Parts of the Candlestick. Ex. 25:31-40. The candlestick, or lampstand, had one main shaft, with three branches projecting from each side. These six branches were alike, each having "three bowls made after the fashion of al-monds...a knop and a flower," "resembling lilies" PP 348—nine ornaments in each branch. The main shaft had *four* bowls made like almonds, his knops, and his flowers—twelve ornaments. Thus, the shaft and the six branches had sixty-six or-naments. Under each of the three pairs of branches was a knop—three more orna-ments. Including the ornamental base, the candlestick had, therefore, a total of seventy ornaments.

What a detailed description! Yet, even though this inspired description is so minute, the caution is added: "Look that thou make them after their pattern, which was showed thee in the mount." Ex. 25:40. Why all this detail, re-enforced by special words of caution? Doubtless, because as already noted, any variation from God's exact plan would destroy or mar the meaning, and thus fail of teaching important spiritual truth pertaining to the plan of salvation.

The Significance of Its Seven Branches. In its entirety, the candlestick repre-sents Christ, "the Light of the world." John 8:12. Especially does the main shaft, with its significant number *four*, represent Christ. He it is—"One like unto the Son of man" —who walks "in the midst of the seven candlesticks," Rev. 1:12, 13, which "are the seven churches," the entire church of God. Rev. 1:20. As seven rep-resents not only completeness but perfection, so the church of God is to be perfect, a church "holy and without blemish." Eph. 5:27. Jesus also said to His disciples, "Ye are the light of the world," a "city set on a hill cannot be hid." Matt. 5:14.

Almond Ornaments. In the breastplate, God's workers are represented as His jewels; in the candlestick, as His ornaments. Why were the ornaments to be made "like unto almonds?" The Hebrew word for almond means *to hasten*, for the almond tree blossoms very early in the season—it *hastens* to put forth blossoms. It was regarded by the Jews as a welcome indication that the new life of another spring had come, a striking picture of the resurrection. Thus the almond ornaments are an emblem of Christ who is "the resurrection and the life," John 11:25, and also of the new life that will come to all who witness for Him. The candlestick throughout bore this symbol of the *resurrection* of Christ which Christians are to "hasten" to proclaim to the world. "The King's business requires haste." I Sam. 21:8. Jeremiah 1:11, 12 gives the same thought: "The word of the Lord came unto me, saying, Jeremiah, what seest thou? And I said, I see a rod of an almond tree. Then said the Lord unto me, Thou hast well seen: for I will *hasten* My word to perform it."

The word for almond also means wakeful. This beautifully illustrates the work of Christ for us: "He that keepeth Israel shall neither slumber nor sleep." Ps. 121:4. The "seven eyes" of the Lamb go "forth into all the earth." Rev. 5:6. Why is Jesus thus searching the earth? "The eyes of the Lord run to and fro throughout the whole earth, to show Himself strong [the Lamb had "seven horns" as well as seven eyes] in the behalf of them whose spirit is perfect toward Him." II Chron. 16:9.

The thought of zeal is also in the root of the word almond—to be zealous; to watch eagerly as a leopard; to be intent upon something; to be awake and vigilant. Jer. 5:6. The seven lamps which were before the throne were "lamps of fire" —Rev. 4:5, His church which the Holy Spirit fires with zeal.

Seventy Ornaments. Why were there seventy ornaments? What do they represent? The Lord gave His commission not only to the twelve to go into all the world and preach the gospel, but He "appointed other seventy also, and sent them two and two before His face into every city and place, whither He Himself would come." What was the result of their efforts? They returned with joy, saying, "Lord, even the devils are subject unto us through Thy name." Luke 10:1, 17. They were connected with the Source of power, the true Light of the world, and success attended their efforts. Like the apostles, they "received supernatural endowments as a seal of their mission." MH 94. It has been said that these seventy ornaments represent the consecrated trusty laymen whose hearts burn with zeal to hold aloft the torch of truth that someone's feet may be led to walk in the *Path to the Throne of God*. And why not? Does not the candlestick represent the *entire* church in faithful service?

The first seventy elders were appointed when the covenant of God was ratified at Sinai. Ex. 24:1, 9. They were the chief representatives in the respective tribes, the most conspicuous for integrity and sincerity as well as for rank and influence. Later they became special assistants to Moses in his arduous and perplexing duties. When they were appointed, "the Lord came down in a cloud....and took the spirit that was upon him [Moses], and gave it unto the seventy." Num. 11:14, 16, 17, 25. Their authority extended to all matters concerning the public welfare. They were a sort of governing body, a parliament. To them was entrusted the spirit of prophecy—extraordinary penetration in discovering hidden evil and in settling difficulties. Num. 11:24-30. Jewish writers say that this was the origin of the Sanhedrin, the supreme court of their nation.

Pure Gold. Unlike the table and the altar, which were made of wood covered with gold, the candlestick "was made of one solid piece of gold," PP 348, "his shaft, and his branches, his bowls, his knops, and his flowers." Also, "his snuffers or tongs, and his snuff-dishes." "Of a talent of pure gold made he it, and all the vessels thereof." Ex. 25:38; 37:23. Of the church whom Jesus is purifying, it is written "He shall sit as a refiner and purifier of...the sons of Levi, and purge them as gold and silver, that they may offer unto the Lord an offering in righteousness." Mal. 3:3. As the refiner of gold works with the precious metal until his own image is reflected in the molten mass, so "Christ is sitting for His portrait in every disciple. Everyone God has predestinated to be conformed to the image of His Son." Rom. 8:29; DA 827. When we reflect His image in our lives, our light will shine for Jesus.

Gold also represents value. A talent of gold, which weighed about 120 pounds, was used in the candlestick. Its value was approximately $30,000. Since in the time of Christ day's wage was fifteen cents, the value of the candlestick in our day would be about $3,000,000. The candlestick was the most costly as well as the most elaborate of the sacred vessels. By this immense amount of gold used in it, the inspired Artificer would convey the extreme importance of, and the high value that Jesus places on, true soul service. It is a symbol of the motto, "share your faith." "Let your light so shine before men, that they may see your good works, and glorify your Father which is in heaven." Matt. 5:16.

The Gold Was Beaten. The candlestick was not only pure gold, it was "beaten" gold. Ex. 25:31, 36. It required many a skillful blow to shape all the details of its ornaments. So Christ was "wounded for our transgressions; He was bruised for our iniquities; the chastisement of our peace was upon Him." Isaiah 53:3-10. "Yea, and all that will live godly in Christ Jesus shall suffer persecution." II Tim. 3:12. It is trial that purifies the church and fits it to be the light of the world. This has been demonstrated in the sufferings of the thousands of martyrs of the Dark Ages and during the Reformation, but "the blood of the martyrs was the seed of the church." Also in our own day, many a worker for God has suffered stripes and imprisonment for the truth's sake. God permits the fires of affliction, that the dross may be consumed, and the worthless separated from the valuable, so that the pure metal may shine forth. "He passes us from one fire to another, testing our true worth.... If prosperity or adversity discover falseness, pride, or selfishness, in our hearts, what shall we do when God tries every man's work as by fire, and lays bare the secrets of all hearts?" 4T 85. For this reason the candlestick, representing both Christ and His co-laborers, was made of *beaten* gold.

Pure Olive Oil and Its Significance. "Command the children of Israel, that they bring unto thee pure oil olive beaten for the light, to cause the lamps to burn continually." Lev. 24:2; Ex. 27:20. Several words in this text stand out prominently—the oil was *pure*, it was *beaten*, and the lamps were to burn *continually*. What does the pure oil signify? —The vision of the candlestick which God gave Zechariah explains: "And the angel...said unto me, What seeset thou? And I said, I...behold a candlestick all of pure gold, with a bowl upon the top of it, and his seven lamps thereon...And two olive trees by it, one upon the right side of the bowl, and the other upon the left side thereof. So I answered and spake to the angel that talked with me, saying, What are these, my Lord? The angel...answered,...Knowest thou not what these be? And I said, No, my Lord. Then he answered,... This is the word of the Lord unto Zerubbabel, saying, Not by might, nor by power, but by My Spirit, saith the Lord of Hosts." Zech. 4:1-6. The oil, then, is the Spirit of God, that causes the lamps to send forth light. And Christ is the "bowl" from which the oil flows into the seven lamps, for He it is who sends the Holy Spirit to the seven churches. Without this "pure oil" of the Spirit it is impossible for the followers of Jesus to let their light shine to the world in its full brightness.

The oil was used in coronation services, thus being associated with sovereignty. Its use also is indicative of divine joy: "Thou anointest my head with oil; my cup runneth over." Ps. 23:5. It is associated with prayer for healing: "Is any sick among you? Let him call for the elders of the church; and let them pray over him, anointing him with oil in the name of the Lord." James 5:14.

The Oil Was Beaten. Even as the candlestick itself was of "beaten" gold, so also the oil was beaten, indicating that the Holy Spirit has shared the suffering that our salvation has cost. This oil was beaten "to cause the lamps to burn always." Ex. 27:20. What a responsibility this places upon those who are light bearers for God! The more fully we, as sons of God, sense the suffering that our salvation has cost all Heaven, the more earnestly we shall long to let our lamps "burn always," not more fitfully but constantly. "In season" and "out of season" we are to let shine forth His own heavenly light "in the midst of a crooked and perverse nation." II Tim. 4:2; Phil. 2:15.

The Lamps Burned "Continually." As the bread on the table was "continual," Nu. 4:7, and the incense on the altar was "perpetual," Ex. 30:8, so the lamps burned "continually." Lev. 24:2. They "shed their light by day and by night." PP 348. Just so the light of the church should shine around the circle of the earth by day and by night. "In the morning sow thy seed, and in the evening withhold not thine hand." Eccl. 11:6. No matter what our occupation in life, every service should be definitely directed to advance God's work. Thus day by day all may be true light bearers, "ambassadors for Christ." II Cor. 5:20.

In this connection, it is both interesting and important to observe that the words *continual* and *perpetual* used to describe the services at the table, the altar, and the candlestick, as well as at the brazen altar where the "continual burnt offering" was sacrificed morning and evening—these words in the original are the same as the word *daily*—used in Daniel 8:11-13, where the blasphemous work of "the little horn" is brought to view. We do well to keep this in mind, for it will come up later. Meanwhile, let us beware, lest "through the wiles [sly tricks] of the devil," we neglect our "continual" and "daily" opportunities for sanctification. The time of these continual services "came to be observed as the set time for worship throughout the Jewish nation" when the whole multitude of the people bowed in prayer with their faces toward Jerusalem. PP 353, 354; Luke 1:10.

The "Two Olive Trees." Again Zechariach asked the angel, "What are these two olive trees upon the right side of the candlestick and upon the left side thereof,…these two olive branches which through the two golden pipes empty the golden oil out of themselves?" The angel answering said, "These are the two anointed ones, that stand by the Lord of the whole earth." Zech. 4:11-14.

What is represented by these two "anointed ones," these two olive trees that supply the oil to the lamps? In Revelation 11:3, 4, Jesus said: "I will give power unto My two witnesses,… *These* are the two olive trees…standing before the God of the earth." What are these two witnesses? Are they not the Scriptures that "witness" to the power of God? Of the Old Testament scriptures Jesus said, "They…testify of Me," John 5:39; and concerning the New Testament He declared, "This gospel of the kingdom shall be preached…for a witness." Matt. 24:14. The Old Testament and the New Testament are therefore Christ's "two witnesses," the "two anointed ones" symbolized by the two olive trees that empty the golden oil out of themselves through the two golden pipes. They fill the lamps, His light-bearers, with the oil, thus causing the lamps to give light. "The entrance of Thy Words giveth light." "Thy Word is a lamp unto my feet, and a light unto my path." Ps. 119:130, 105. God has given "power" unto these "two witnesses," and they are the source of our power, as they were the source of Christ's power when He met the enemy with the challenge, "It is written." Matt. 4:4, 7, 10.

Through the Word of God, the Holy Spirit supplies the oil to the lamps so the lamps burn "continually." Only through a "continual" study of both the Old and the New Testament, is it possible for the Christian to receive the full supply of oil for his lamp that he may witness for Christ. Without this constant flow of oil into his life, his lamp, like those of the five foolish virgins, will surely go out. There are those who discredit some parts of the Bible, particularly the Old Testament and the book of Revelation. What will be the result of thus "hurting" these two olive trees, so that they cannot supply the oil?—"If any man will hurt them, fire proceedeth out of their mouth, and devoureth their enemies: and…he must in this manner be killed." Rev. 11:5.

The olive tree grows slowly, and lives to an immense age, thus being emblematic of strength and longevity. "I am like a green olive tree in the house of God: I trust in the mercy of God forever." Ps. 52:8. It is also an emblem of divine blessing in our homes: Thy children are "like olive plants round about thy table." Ps. 128:3.

Who Lighted the Lamps? Aaron, the high priest, lighted the lamps. Num. 8:3. So Christ, our High Priest, must light our lamps before we can shine for Him. He, the central shaft, sends oil to all the branches, and that without measure—its measure being "the measure of the fullness of Christ." Eph. 4:13. This contact with the source of light may be compared to the electric power in the wires. Only as we are connected with this power can we truly shine. A broken circuit cannot pass the current to the lamps, but a perfect circuit brings power and victory to the human worker. The Holy Spirit brought victory to Gideon. It caused Philip to "run," and the Ethiopian was converted. It worked with Peter, and Cornelius accepted salvation.

The Morning and Evening Lightings. When Aaron burned the incense on the altar in the morning, he trimmed the lamps. "Every morning ... he dresseth the lamps; at even he lighteth the lamps [margin, "causeth to ascend"] Ex. 30:7, 8. In the evening a fresh supply of oil was put into the lamps, in the morning the dressing, or trimming, of the lamps caused them to shine in their fullness. The burning of the incense and the care of the lamps were closely associated. So, as we kneel at our altar of prayer morning and evening, our High Priest will give us a fresh supply of His Holy Spirit as a new fitting up for service.

The Candlestick a Light Bearer. As the purpose of the candlestick was to give light, so the sole purpose of the church is to give light. A lamp that gives no light, or that shines with a dim, uncertain light, is of little value; and a church that does not shine, has only a *form* of godliness, "denying the power thereof." II Tim. 3:5. Service is the only reason for the existence of a church. Unless it shines, the world is left in darkness, and many will lose their way on the *Path to the Throne of God*. Every true member of the church will let his light shine, and shine "continually" no matter where he is. So Jesus says to His church, "Ye are the light of the world...Let your light so shine." Matt. 5:14, 15.

> His lamps are we
> To shine where He shall say;
> And lamps are not for sunny rooms,
> Nor for the light of day,
> But for dark places of the earth
> Where shame and wrong and crime have birth,
> Or for the murky twilight gray,
> Where wandering sheep have gone astray;
> Or where the lamp of faith grows dim,
> And souls are groping after Him,
> And so sometimes a flame we find,
> Clear shining through the night
> So dark we cannot see the lamp,
> But only see the light.
> So may we shine, His love the flame,
> That men may glorify His name.
>
> —*R.J. Flint*

Light-Bearing the Fruit of Faith. Service that truly shines has been called "second mile willingness." "Whosoever shall compel thee to go a mile, go with him twain... Whosoever shall smite thee on thy right cheek, turn to him the other also. If any man will sue thee at the law, and take away thy coat, let him have thy cloak also." Matt. 5:39-41. This is really loving our enemies. It is such service that entitles us to be "children of [our] Father which is in heaven." Such service is the fruit of all who will be "perfect, even as [their] Father which is in heaven is perfect." Matt. 5:44, 45, 48. Such service before men will lead them to "glorify God." Matt. 5:16.

Without this "second mile willingness" there can be no true faith. "Show me thy faith without thy works, and I will show thee my faith by my works;" or, as Moffatt renders it, "You show me your faith without any deeds, and I will show you by my deeds what faith is." James 2:17, 18. This "labor of love" is the "work of faith" [*Moffatt*], a "faith which worketh by love," Gal. 5:6, faith that is counted for righteousness,—right-*doing*—a faith that results in sanctification. Service without faith and love has been well called "dull gray servitude."

We are all servants, servants either "of sin unto death, or of obedience unto righteousness." Rom. 6:16. How can we be servants of obedience? There is but one way: "As many as received Him, to them gave He power." John 1:12. This power is the birthright of everyone who has experienced the second birth, everyone who has been reconciled and justified in the court and who has entered the holy place to be sanctified. This is forcefully expressed by H. J. Tippett in his inspiring book *My Lord and I*, p. 51: "God intends each of us to be a spiritual masterpiece, His building. The great tragedy of human life is that we so often choose our own plans instead of what is heaven's destiny for us." "The tragedy of life in spiritual things is to see hundredfold power producing thirty-fold accomplishment" Ibid. 31. "God reaches down through our scrap pile of broken resolutions, faded ideals, crushed hopes, seared consciences, untempered wills, for the buried talents of nobility and service to make us 'servants of righteousness'" Ibid. 46. Then let us keep our lamps on a candlestick, not under a bushel, ever remembering that "Not more surely is the place prepared for us in the heavenly mansions than is the special place designated on earth where we are to work for God." COL 327.

God's Broadcasting System. In Revelation 4:5, the "lightnings and thunderings and voices" that proceeded out of the throne, before which "seven lamps of fire" were burning may be called God's broadcasting system. From this central station through "the seven Spirits of God," the full manifestation of the Spirit through His entire church—the seven-branched candlestick—He sends out streams of light to all the world.

"God is a constant worker." "The angels are workers, ministers of God to the children of men," and God designs that all whose hearts have been lighted shall be workers, "fishers of men." "The toiling beast of burden answers the purpose of its creation better than does the indolent man.... Those who look forward to a heaven of inactivity will be disappointed; for the economy of heaven provides no place for the gratification of indolence…. It is the faithful servant who will be welcomed from his labors to the joy of the Lord." MYP 216; CT 280.

> "Down by the sea
> Of blue Galilee
> The Saviour passed time and again;
> From the shore of the sea
> He called 'Follow Me,
> And I'll make you fishers of men.'
>
> He is calling today
> In the same earnest way.
> He is calling for fishers again;
> And the brightest names known
> Up around God's throne
> Will be those who were fishers of men."
> —*Author Unknown*

The Blessing of Service. Our efforts to help others and point them to the way of life, will not only benefit them but it will "react in blessings upon ourselves. This was the purpose of God in giving us a part to act in the plan of redemption. He has granted men the privilege of becoming partakers of the divine nature, and in their turn, of diffusing blessings to their fellowmen. This is the highest honor, the greatest joy, that it is possible for God to bestow upon men." SC 83. Such light-bearing is not stinted or meager. It is thus described by Luke: "Give, and it shall be given unto you; good measure, pressed down, and shaken together, and running over, shall men give into your bosom. For with the same measure that ye mete withal it shall be measured to you again." Luke 6:38. Acceptable service for God is prompted by the Spirit of Christ. Of those who serve from selfish motives, no matter how good that service may appear on the surface,—of them it is written, "There is none that doeth good, no, not one." Rom. 3:12; Ps. 14:3.

The Candlestick a Symbol of the Holy Spirit. As already noted, the antitype of the seven-branched candlestick is the "seven lamps of fire burning before the throne, which are the seven Spirits of God." Rev. 4:5. These seven Spirits of God are "sent forth into all the earth" by the Lamb, Rev. 5:6, in fulfillment of His last promise to the disciples, "I will send .. unto you the Comforter, which is the Holy Ghost;" "He shall teach you all things." John 16:7; 14:26. To those who seek, He will reveal spiritual truth and bestow spiritual power.

As in the earthly sanctuary the candlestick* represented letting our light shine in service for God, so in the heavenly sanctuary, in all the fullness of His complete sevenfold power, the Holy Spirit is searching all the dark corners of the earth and all the dark corners of our "deceitful" and "desperately wicked" hearts, to win lost souls to obedience to the living Word of God. Jer. 17:9. The Suffering of the Holy Spirit, as with unutterable agony, Rom. 8:26, He pleads with sinful men, is represented by the fact that not only the gold but the oil used in the candlestick was "beaten." Through neglect of the Word, of prayer, and of service, we "neglect so great salvation." Heb. 2:3. Let us beware that we thus "grieve not the Holy Spirit of God," for through this agency alone can we be "sealed unto the day of redemption." Eph. 4:30; 1:13.

Sanctification, Its Relation to Justification. The terms justification and sanctification are usually feebly comprehended and too often entirely misunderstood. Frequently, justification is confused with sanctification, one being regarded as a synonym of the other, while in reality they are quite different. As before noted, reconciliation and justification, illustrated in the court, result in the second birth, at which time, the righteousness of Christ is *imputed* to the repentant sinner, covering all his past sins. This righteousness is not obtained by the works of the law, Rom. 3:20, 24, it is a free gift from Jesus Christ, received by faith. Rom. 5:16, 18. The bestowal of this gift is but the work of a moment.

On the contrary, sanctification is the work of a lifetime, during which we are to *work out* our own salvation with fear and trembling. Phil. 2:12. This is an active dynamic Christian experience in daily *obedience* to the law of God. Here, through Christ, *the works of the law* are manifest *in the deeds of the life*, without which our faith is dead. James 2:16, 17. During this lifelong experience, the righteousness of Christ is *imparted* to the Christian; that is, it becomes a *part* of him,—he becomes a partaker of the divine nature. This righteousness *imputed* in the court and *imparted* in the holy place, is beautiful and full of meaning because in the sanctuary it is seen in its true perspective. The first experience, justification, is our "title to heaven," the second, sanctification, is our "fitness for heaven." RH, June 4, 1895. The Spirit of God received into the heart by faith, is the beginning of the life eternal. John 17:3; 6:54.

Sanctification is a three fold—experience, symbolized in the holy place at the table, the altar, and the candlestick, is thus forcefully expressed by H. M. Tippett: "In the waiting time, those are being most blessed who are standing on tiptoe,

---

*   In 70 A.D. when Jerusalem was destroyed by the Roman army, the candlestick was carried to Rome by the Roman general Titus, as a trophy of his victory. Doubtless all the rest of the gold in the sanctuary was also taken as spoil, except the ark of which we shall study later. As a memorial of his triumphal celebration, the arch of Titus was constructed, on which was placed a large plaque of the candlestick. This remained until Rome itself was destroyed, leaving the arch in ruins.

reaching out for God's best things,—on tiptoe in faithful reading [studying] of the Word, on tiptoe in prayer, on tiptoe in service." *My Lord and I*, p. 311. These are the three essentials to "growing up" into Christian manhood and womanhood. Through these agencies the mind is focused on Christ, and thus we "abide" in Him. This is sanctification, which, in the light of the sanctuary, is clear and tangible, and rich in spiritual experience.

Righteousness by Faith. This includes both justification and sanctification. The first is wholly an act of faith without the deeds of the law, accepting the righteousness of Christ as a free gift; the second is "God working in you" not only "to will" [justification] but also "to do" of His good pleasure [sanctification]. Phil. 2:12, 13. While justification is the first step in righteousness by faith, sanctification is its completion. Both come through faith in Christ. From the time we enter the gate of the court until mortal life ends in the holy place, the entire Christian experience is righteousness by faith. Only thus can anyone be either justified or sanctified, that Christ may be all in all. Col. 3:11. In the words of Peter, this is gained by "giving all diligence, add to your faith [to your justification] virtue,... knowledge,... temperance,... patience,... godliness,... brotherly kindness,... charity." "He that lacketh these things...hath forgotten that he was purged from his old sins" [his justification], but "if ye *do* these things...an entrance shall be ministered unto you abundantly into the everlasting kingdom of our Lord and Saviour Jesus Christ." II Peter 1:5-11.

Sanctification Our Passport into the Most Holy Place. While imputed righteousness frees us from the *penalty* of our *past* sins, imparted righteousness frees us day by day from the *power* of sin, and gives us "power to become the sons of God." John 1:12. It is this that keeps us from falling, and presents us "faultless before the presence of His glory with exceeding joy." Jude 24. God has "condemned sin in the flesh" by "sending His own Son in the likeness of sinful flesh." He did this that His righteousness "might be fulfilled *in us*." Rom. 8:3, 4. By thus condemning sin in the flesh of His Son, He challenges its right to exist in our lives. "These things write I unto you, *that ye sin not*." I John 2:1. "All who consecrate soul, body, and spirit to God, will be constantly receiving a new endowment of physical and mental power. The inexhaustible supplies of heaven are at their command." DA 827.

In the holy place—"the Trysting place"—if we have remained true to our baptismal vows—true in studying and obeying God's Word, instant in prayerful dependence upon our Redeemer, and in doing our part as ambassadors for Christ, beseeching others to be reconciled to God, —if this has been our experience, at the end of life's journey we are clothed in our wedding garment of "fine linen, clean and white," Rev. 19:8, which is the righteousness of Christ, ready to be accepted as the bridge of the Lamb. Rev. 19:7, 8. When we have thus finished our course in "the Trysting place," we can say with Paul, "Henceforth there is laid up for me a crown of righteousness, which the Lord, the righteous Judge, shall give me at that day." II Tim. 4:8. Then we shall have the Father's name—His character—in our forehead. Rev. 22:4. This is sanctification; it is our passport into the most holy place, into "the presence of His glory" for glorification. Jude 24.

SECTION V

IN THE MOST HOLY PLACE

CHAPTER 23 PREVIEW

CHRIST ENTERING THE MOST HOLY PLACE OF THE HEAVENLY SANCTUARY

- The "Time Appointed"
- The Last "Time" Prophecy
- Two Divisions of the Heavenly Ministration
- Intercession Continues During the Judgment
- Daniel's View of the Court Room in Heaven
- John's View of the Court Room
- Waiting for the Advocate
- Christ's Third Triumphal Celebration
- Isaiah's View of the Scene
- The Father Welcomes His Son
- Who Is The Judge?

23

CHRIST ENTERING THE MOST HOLY PLACE OF THE HEAVENLY SANCTUARY

"The Time Appointed." Prophecy foretold the time when Jesus passed within *the first vail* into the holy place of the heavenly sanctuary and was anointed High Priest. Dan 9:24, 27. The time was also foretold when He passed within *the second vail* into the most holy place to act as Judge. Dan. 8:14; 7:10, 13, 14. This judgment work of Christ, our heavenly High Priest, was symbolized in the work of the earthly high priest on the day of atonement—the day of judgment for ancient Israel. In the earthly it was called the cleansing of the earthly sanctuary; in the heavenly, the cleansing of the heavenly sanctuary. Dan. 8:14.

The cleansing of the earthly sanctuary was, in type, the cleansing of ancient Israel from the sins which, by confession and reformation, had been transferred to the sanctuary. The cleansing of the heavenly sanctuary is, not in type but in reality, the blotting out of the forgiven sins of redeemed Israel which during this life have been recorded in the books of the sanctuary above, and have gone before to judgment. I Tim. 5:24.

By Divine appointment, the day of atonement came "in the seventh month, on the tenth day of the month." Lev. 16:29, 30. This date never varied; it was "a statute forever," "an everlasting statute." vs. 29, 34. Likewise, the antitypical day of atonement, the real day of Judgment in the heavenly sanctuary, had a Divinely appointed date, and this date cannot be changed. Referring to this, Paul says, "He hath appointed a day in the which He will judge the world in righteousness by that Man whom He hath ordained." Acts 17:31. As the day of atonement came at the end of the yearly round of service, so this "time appointed" came when "the end shall be;" "at the time of the end shall be the vision." Dan. 8:19, 17. The "time appointed" for the service in the most Holy Place of the heavenly sanctuary is as definite as was the day of atonement in the earthly sanctuary. It is revealed in Daniel 8:13, 14, "Then I heard one Saint speaking, and another saint said unto that certain Saint which spake, How long shall be the vision? ... to give both the sanctuary and the host to be trodden under foot? And He said unto me [Daniel], Unto two thousand and three hundred days; then shall the sanctuary be cleansed," or "restored" as Moffatt and some other authorities have it. "That part of his prophecy which related to the last days, Daniel was bidden to close up and seal 'to the time of the end.' Dan. 12:4. Not till we reach this time could a message concerning the Judgment be proclaimed, based on a fulfillment of these prophecies." GC 356.

The Hebrew name of "that certain Saint which spake" is "Palmoni, the Wonderful numberer." Dan. 8:13, margin. This evidently refers to Christ, Dan. 10:21, who knows and numbers every "time appointed." The other "saint," was Gabriel, vs. 16. The unusual importance of this prophecy concerning the restoring and cleansing of the heavenly sanctuary—the Judgment of Daniel 7:10—which began at the close of the 2300 days, is indicated by the fact that Michael [Christ] came with Gabriel to give Daniel "skill and understanding" concerning the "vision" Dan. 9:21, 22; also from the words of Gabriel, "There is none that holdeth with me in these things, but Michael your Prince." Dan. 10:21.

The Last "Time" Prophecy. In several respects, this prophecy is one of the most outstanding in the Bible. No other contains so many definite dates, making it pre-eminently a *time* prophecy:

1. It began when the commandment was given "to restore and build Jerusalem," in 457 B.C., Dan. 9:25; Ezra 7, margin.

2. During the 70 weeks allotted to the Jews, Dan. 9:24, at the end of seven weeks [49 years] after "the commandment," the building of the wall of Jerusalem was completed. Dan. 9:25.

3. The time of the baptism of Christ as "the Messiah" [the Anointed One] was 62 weeks after the rebuilding of the wall or 69 weeks after "the commandment," 27 A.D., Dan. 9:26

4. The Jewish nation was rejected at the end of that week; 34 A.D.

5. The cleansing of the heavenly sanctuary, the Judgment of the "house of God," began at the end of the 2300 days, 1810 years after 34 A.D. or 1844 A.D., Dan. 8:14.

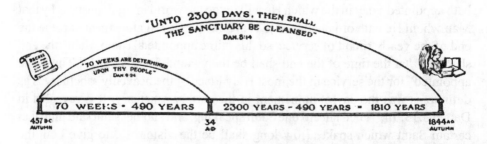

There can be no doubt that the 2300 days, which began in 457 B.C. reached to the year 1844, "the time of the end," "the time appointed" when "the end shall be." Dan. 8:17, 19. According to the best information now available, the tenth day of the seventh month of the year 1844 fell on October 22, Jewish reckoning. Every event from the beginning to the close of this prophecy has been fulfilled on time, a time definitely foretold.

172

This prophecy is not only the longest, but the *last* "time" prophecy given by Inspiration. Of it the angel declared to John, "there shall be time no longer;" Rev. 10:6; that is, after its expiration, there should be no other definite *time* prophecy, not even one giving the hour of Christ's second coming, for Jesus said, "Of that day and that hour knoweth [maketh known] no man, no, not the angels which are in heaven, neither the Son, but the Father." Mark 13:32. The Father has reserved to Himself the rightful privilege of announcing to the universe the day and the hour when His Son shall appear in the clouds of heaven. EW 15, 34; 285. Therefore, after the close of the 2300 days in 1844, anyone who sets a *time* for the second coming of Christ is assuming a prerogative of Jehovah.

Another feature that makes this prophecy remarkable is that it reveals the exact time of two of the most important events in the plan of redemption; namely the time when Christ would give His life a ransom for the world, and the time when He would begin the Judgment of the "house of God." Was it any wonder that Christ, the "Wonderful Numberer," He who had numbered the vision, should come in person to answer the question, "How long shall be the vision," and say to Daniel, "Unto two thousand three hundred days; then shall the sanctuary be cleansed?" Dan. 8:13, 14.

Two other correlative events in this prophecy stand out in bold relief. At its *beginning*, in 457 B.C., when the commandment went forth "to restore and to build Jerusalem," Dan. 9:25, "a very great congregation of men and women and children" Ezra 10:1; 2:64, 65; 8:3-14, 18-20, left the land of their captivity, and returned to Zion. These made up the citizenship of the *earthly* Jerusalem. At the *end* of the 2300 days, the Judgment call was sounded, "Prepare to meet thy God, O Israel," Amos 4:12, —prepare to leave the land of your captivity and move to the *heavenly* Zion. Those who respond to this call will be numbered with the citizenship of the *heavenly* Jerusalem. It was then, in 1844, in the heavenly sanctuary, that the citizenship of the heavenly Jerusalem began to be made up—those of the "house of God" who pass the test of the Judgment.

Two Divisions of the Heavenly Ministration. As the earthly ministration consisted of two divisions, the daily and the yearly, each occupying a period of time, so the heavenly ministration consists of two distinct divisions, the first which began when Christ ascended to act as High Priest, the second when He began His work as Judge. The first in the holy place of the heavenly sanctuary, continued *until 1844*, the second in the most holy place, has been in progress *since 1844*. The whole period of time from 1844 to the close of probation is the antitype of the ancient day of atonement, Israel's day of Judgment.

Intercession Continues During the Judgment. On the day of atonement, the high priest performed not only the special service in the most holy place but in the court was also offered the regular daily sacrifice—"the continual burnt offering," which represented the continual atonement of Christ. Num. 28:3, 4. Also in the holy place on the golden altar, the high priest burned the daily incense, symbol of the merits of Christ's righteousness, Lev. 16:12, to which all had access. Thus as the earthly priest on the *typical* day of Judgment officiated, in the court and in the holy place, as intercessor as well as in the most holy as judge, so Christ, our heavenly High Priest, during the *real* Judgment, acts not only as Judge but also as Intercessor, continuing to "plead His own blood" and the merits of His own righteousness "in behalf of sinners." See GC 428, 429. How grateful we can be that so long as probation lingers, there is hope for all. We may still come to the throne of grace and find help.

Daniel's View of the Court Room in Heaven. When the great clock of time struck the hour for the end of the 2300 days, the beginning of the antitypical tenth day of the seventh month, the Father, who up to this time had been seated with Christ in the holy place of the heavenly sanctuary, moved His throne into the holy of holies, preparatory to the beginning of the Judgment. EW 55.

The scene in the heavenly holy of holies at this time is, without doubt, one of the most awe-inspiring of any since the giving of the law at Sinai. Describing it, Daniel says: "I beheld till the thrones were cast down and the Ancient of Days did sit, whose garment was white as snow, and the hair of His head like the pure wool: His throne as like the fiery flame, and His wheels as burning fire. A fiery stream issued and came forth from before Him: thousand thousands ministered unto Him, and ten thousand times ten thousand stood before Him: the Judgment was set, and the books were opened" Dan. 7:9, 10—opened before the law of liberty which had been transgressed, and by which every dead will be judged. James 2:12. Moffatt gives this rendering: "I watched until an assize was held;" that is, a court of justice for the trial by jury of civil or criminal cases.

John's View of the Court Room. John also described this same scene. "Behold," he says, "a door [the second vail] was opened in heaven…[not *into*, but *in*: the *first* vail represented the entrance *into* heaven] and, behold, a throne was set in heaven, and One [the Father] sat on the throne. And He that sat was to look upon like a jasper and a sardine stone; and there was a rainbow round about the throne, in sight like unto an emerald. And round about the throne were four and twenty seats [the Greek rendering is *"thrones"*]; and upon the seats [or thrones] I saw four and twenty elders sitting, clothed in white raiment; and they had on their heads crowns of gold [indicative of victory and reward] … and in the midst of the throne, and round about the throne, were four living creatures." Rev. 4:1-6, margin. The four living creatures and the four and twenty elders were not in the scene presented to Daniel, probably because it was after Daniel's day that they were "redeemed" from the earth and made "priests" unto God. Rev. 5:8-10. "And I beheld…many angels round about the throne." Rev. 5:11.

The Greek rendering of Revelation 4:1 is: "A door [the second vail] was *open* in heaven." Since this door was "open," John continuing his description of the work going forward in the court room above, saw not only the throne of God, antitype of the ark in the most holy place of the earthly sanctuary, but he also saw "seven lamps of fire burning *before the throne*," antitype of the seven-branched candlestick which was in the first apartment of the earthly sanctuary. Rev. 4:5; Ex. 40:24.

At another time he saw "the golden altar which was *before the throne*" antitype of the altar of incense in the first apartment of the earthly sanctuary. Rev. 8:3. Do not these scriptures indicate that, the door between the two apartments being "open," John was privileged to look into both the holy and the most holy place in the heavenly sanctuary?

Waiting for The Advocate. In the most holy place in "His great and calm eternity," MH 417, the Father waits; here the two covering cherubim, wait, one at His right, and the other at His left, honored guards of God's throne. PP 357. The four living creatures and the four and twenty elders wait. The vast multitude of angels wait; "in the presence-chamber of the King of kings, they wait—'angels that excel in strength, ministers of His, that do His pleasure.' 'hearkening unto the voice of His word.' ten thousand times ten thousand and thousands of thousands." GC 511. All are waiting in earnest expectation.

Why are they waiting? The Ancient of Days is on His throne; the assistant priests are on their thrones; angel witnesses are in their places; the Judgment is set, the books containing the life records of those who are to be judged; are opened, ready for examination. What is lacking? Still they wait; eagerly they wait. They wait for the arrival of the Advocate, Jesus Christ the righteous. I John 2:1. The Judgment cannot proceed until He comes—He who is to plead the merits of His blood for repentant sinners that their sins may be blotted out.

Christ's Third Triumphal Celebration. Now He comes! He comes! "I saw in the night visions, and, behold, one like the Son of Man came with the clouds of heaven [clouds of angels, 'the chariots of God,' Ps. 68:17], and came to the Ancient of Days [the Father], and they [the angels] brought Him [the Son of Man] near before Him [the Father]." Dan. 7:13. In a flaming chariot, He [Jesus] passed within the second vail, whence the Father had gone and was now seated on His glorious throne. EW 251. "The Lord will come with fire, and with His chariots like a whirlwind." Isaiah 66:15.

What an imposing scene! As a mighty conqueror, borne by His admiring associates in battle, is brought victoriously to be honored, so clouds of heavenly angels escort their victorious General in heavenly state within "the second vail" to the scene of His final work for the salvation of the human family. No other event so important and so solemn had ever before taken place in the universe of God. The King of heaven on His way to the Judgment of the household of God, there to confess before the Father those who have confessed Him before men. Matt. 10:32.

Christ "comes to the Ancient of Days in heaven to receive dominion, and glory, and a kingdom, Dan. 7:14, which will be given Him at the close of His work as Mediator... Our great High Priest enters the holy of holies to begin the work of the Investigative Judgment." GC 480.

Isaiah's View of the Scene. As the angels who accompanied Jesus when He ascended to begin His work in the holy place of the heavenly sanctuary, were met with the joyous exclamation, "Who is this King of glory?" so now He is again greeted by the heavenly choir, "Who is this?" They never tire of honoring Him because of His unselfish sacrifice and the wonderful salvation that He has wrought for the human family.

> "Who is this that cometh...with dyed
> garments, (AV)
> His robes redder than the vintage?
> they ask,
> "Who is it, arrayed in splendor,
> Striding in His strength,
> Radiant with victory,
> A mighty Champion?" *Moffatt.*

The answer comes back from Him who leads the approaching retinue,

> "I that speak in righteousness,
> Mighty to save." (AV)

The waiting angels seem not to be satisfied with so simple an answer; they want their loved Commander to receive the honor due Him because of His sacrifice to save man, so they ask again:

> "Wherefore art Thou red in Thine
> apparel,
> And Thy garments like him that treadeth
> in the winefat?" (AV)

Then comes back the answer:

> "I have trodden the winepress alone;
> And of the people there was none with
> Me: (AV)
> "I looked, but there was none to help;
> I was amazed that there was none to aid;
> "So My own power gained Me the victory,
> It was My passion bore Me on.
> I resolved upon a day of vengeance;"
> *Moffatt*
> "And the year of My redeemed is come."
> (AV)
> "The time to free my folk has come,
> The hour of His Judgment is come."
> Rev. 14:7
> "So I trod the foe in My anger;

'Twas their blood spashed My robes,
Till all my clothes are stained.'" *Moffatt*

In these words Isaiah pictures the fierceness of the lifelong battle between Christ and Satan, from the command of Herod to slay all the children "from two years old and under" Matt. 2:16, in his effort to destroy Jesus, to the final conflict. Then turning away from this picture of His own sufferings and struggles, to extol the goodness of God, He continues:

> "I will mention the loving kindness of the
>   Lord," (AV)
> "Praising His acts of love,
> After all the Eternal has done for us,"
>   *Moffatt*
> "And the great goodness toward the
>   house of Israel,
> Which He hath bestowed on them
>   according to His mercies,
> And according to the multitude of His
>   loving kindnesses," (AV)
> "When He said, 'Surely they are My own
>   people,
> Sons that will never play me false;
> And so He proved Himself their Saviour."
> Isaiah 63:1-8; (AV and *Moffatt*)

With this song of adoration and praise, the angels accompanying Christ bring Him before the Ancient of Days. This was Christ's third triumphal celebration—fit introduction to that most important event, when He takes up "the golden censer" Rev. 8:3, 4, and begins His final work of intercession for fallen man.

The Father Welcomes His Son. As Jesus, in His flaming chariot of angels, accompanied with thousands of other angel chariots, approaches the Father, there proceed out of the throne "lightnings and thunderings and voices." Rev. 4:1, 5. What were the lightnings and thunderings and voices? The four living creatures that were "in the midst of the throne, and round about the throne," Rev. 4:6, "ran and returned as the appearance of a flash of lightning," Eze. 1:14, as they execute the commands of Him that sits on the throne, whose voice is as "the voice of a great thunder." Rev. 14:2; Ps. 104:7. As the Judgment begins, the Father welcomes His only begotten Son to sit with Him in His throne, Rev. 3:21, "on the right hand of God." Col. 3:1. Thus again Jesus shares His Father's throne. DA 832.

Who Is the Judge? "The Ancient of Days is God the Father.... It is He...that is to preside in the Judgment." The holy angels, as ministers and witnesses, "attend the great tribunal." GC 479. But "Christ has been made Judge. The Father is not the Judge. The angels are not. He who took humanity upon Himself, and in this world lived a perfect life, is to judge us." Heb. 2:17, 18; 9T 185. Only He who has taken humanity upon Himself and "was in all points tempted like as we are, yet without sin, "only He who has been "touched with the feeling of our infirmities," is really qualified to be our High Priest or our Judge. Heb. 4:15. "The Father judgeth no man, but hath committed all judgment unto the Son... And hath given Him authority to execute judgment also, because He is the Son of man." John 5:22, 27. "Christ Himself will decide who are worthy to dwell with the family of heaven. He will judge every man according to his words and his works." COL 74.

CHAPTER 24 PREVIEW

THE CHRISTIAN
ENTERING THE MOST HOLY PLACE

- Sanctification Our Passport Into the
  Most Holy Place
- The Second vail and Its Significance
- The vail His Flesh
- The vail a Record
- The vail "Renewed Yearly"
- Within the vail
- In the Most Holy Place
- The Cleansing Room
- The Glory Room
- Sanctified Wholly
- The Reward Room

24

THE CHRISTIAN ENTERING THE MOST HOLY PLACE

Sanctification, Our Passport into the Most Holy Place. As justification, obtained in the court, is the Christian's passport into the Holy place, so sanctification accomplished in the holy place, is his passport into the Most Holy place. But since sanctification is not completed until life on earth ends, or probation closes, the Christian who has finished his life work, enters the Most Holy place for judgment, not in person, but through his life record that has been written in the books of heaven. Since the beginning of the Judgment in 1844, all, both living and dead, whose names have been written in the Book of Life, have been in *the time* of the Judgment—the judgment of the house of God.

The Second vail and Its Significance. At the entrance of the Most Holy place, there was hung a "second vail." Heb. 9:3. This was similar to the first vail, which hung at the entrance to the holy place. God told Moses, "Thou shalt make a vail of blue, and purple, and scarlet, and fine twined linen of cunning work: with cherubim shall it be made. And thou shalt hang it upon four pillars of shittim wood overlaid with gold: their hooks shall be of gold, upon the four sockets of silver. And thou shalt hang up the vail under the taches." Ex. 26:31-33, 6, 11.

That this vail with its pillars represented Christ is shown by several details: the royal colors—blue and purple and scarlet, and fine twined linen, the "four" pillars and their sockets, the wood, the gold, and the silver, —all as previously explained, represent our Redeemer in various phases of His redemptive work.

The vail His Flesh. Paul definitely states that the vail represented the flesh of Christ. He says, "Having therefore, brethren, boldness to enter into the holiest by the blood of Jesus, by a new and living way, which He hath consecrated for us, through the vail, that is to say, His flesh;...let us draw near with a true heart" —a heart "sprinkled from an evil conscience." Heb. 10:19-22. The vail represented Christ in the flesh, made sin for us. That it was hung on "four" pillars also indicates that it represented Christ, even as the four gospels describe and support the four phases of the earthly life of Jesus when in the flesh He lived among men.

As the vail separated the priest from the most holy place, where the presence of God was manifest in the Shekinah above the mercy seat, so sin has separated us from God. But Christ in human flesh took our sins upon Himself. He took our place of separation, that we might be restored to the presence of God. vailing His divinity with humanity, He became the Mediator between God and sinful man to make it possible for us at last to see His face. When redemption is finished, "the people of God...hold open communion with the Father and the Son," "without a dimming vail between." GC 676, 677. Then shall be realized the long-looked-for fulfillment of the prophecy, "The tabernacle of God is with men, and He will dwell with them, and they shall be His people, and God Himself shall be with them, and be their God." Rev. 21:3.

When Jesus died on the cross, the vail was rent "from the top to the bottom," Matt. 27:51, by the hand of God. The rent vail represented Christ's torn flesh. It was the sign given by the prophet Daniel to show when "the sacrifice and the oblation" would cease. Dan. 9:27; Matt. 27:50, 51. Then the Holy of Holies, no longer a sacred place, was exposed to human view. The Shekinah was no longer there. By divine appointment, the holy services in the earthly sanctuary were at an end. Henceforth, Christ Himself in heaven above was to be our sanctuary. Then, all that remains of the vail, the symbol of His bruised and bleeding flesh, are the glorified scars in His feet, His hands, and His side—scars that will forever shine like "bright beams," Hab. 3:4, margin, [like "a lightning blaze."—*Moffatt*].

The vail a Record. In the type all confessed sin was in some way transferred to the sanctuary, but not always in the same way. When the anointed priest sinned and when the whole congregation of Israel sinned, in both cases the priest dipped his finger in the blood of the sin offering, and sprinkled it seven times [complete reconciliation] "before the vail." Lev. 4:6, 17. Strong's Hebrew Dictionary translates the expression "before the vail," on *the face of vail*, on *the forefront of the vail*, showing that the vail was actually touched with the blood of the sin offering; it bore the "finger print" of the high priest. This illustrates the fact that Jesus, "His own self, bore our sins in His own body on the tree." I Peter 2:24.

These "finger prints" of the high priest made the vail a preserver of records, showing that sin had been confessed and forgiven, and had gone beforehand to judgment. I Tim. 5:24. "He that covereth his sins shall not prosper; but whoso confesseth and forsaketh them shall have mercy." Prov. 28:13. These records of confessed sins remained on the vail until the day of atonement when the sanctuary was cleansed, and all confessed sin was in type blotted out.

Shrinking from the thought, someone may exclaim, "Surely that beautiful tapestry could not have been spotted with blood!" But was not the sinless life of Jesus more, much more, than a royal colored linen vail richly embroidered with gold? Yet, the iniquity of us all was laid on Him, that with His stripes we might be healed. Isaiah 53:5, 6. As the high priest sprinkled the face of the vail with the blood of the sacrifice made for "the whole congregation of Israel," Lev. 4:13, 17, so Christ taking our sins in His own body, "has opened the way to the Father's throne, and through His mediation the sincere desire of all who come to Him in faith may be presented before God." GC 489.

The vail "Renewed Yearly." We are told that the vail was "renewed yearly," 3SP 3:166, 167. This expression evidently does not mean that the vail was taken down at the end of each year and replaced by a new one. The vail was never taken down except when the camp was moved from place to place, at which time it was most sacredly handled. If a new vail were hung up at the end of each yearly round of service, about 500 new vails, 40 of them during the wilderness wandering, were made before a permanent temple was built in Jerusalem, and more than 1500 before the vail was rent at the death of Christ. Anything, a house, a garment or anything else, can be "renewed" without being *replaced* by another. In fact, *renewing* does not mean *replacing*. According to Webster it means to restore, to renovate. Moreover, to replace the vail each year would certainly spoil the sense of the type that the vail represented the flesh of Christ, for then would Christ often have died, or another have taken His place. Heb. 9:25.

How, then, was the vail "renewed?" This is a proper question, and demands a clear and satisfactory answer. With equal propriety we may also ask, How were the blood stains removed from the mercy seat, the golden altar and other places where sin had, in figure, been transferred by blood?

Someone may suggest that since the Levites had charge of the sanctuary, Num. 1:53, would it not be their duty at the close of the year's service, to remove these stains? It is true that the Levites were specially set apart by God to assist the priests. Num. 8:5-24. But the only time they were allowed within either apartment of the sanctuary was when the camp was moved from place to place. Even then, not until the furniture was covered by the priests, did they enter the sanctuary "to do the work of the tabernacle of the congregation." Num. 4:15, 20; 18:3. Do not these scriptures preclude the Levites from having any part in cleansing the sanctuary from these blood stains? The inspired word of Jeremiah states that sin cannot be removed by washing even "with nitre" and "much soap." Jer. 2:22. The removal of sin is a miracle of God's grace. Would it not therefore seem that the answer given by F. C. Gilbert, an authority on the Jewish economy, is Biblical and correct; namely, that on the day of atonement, this rich drapery, like other parts of the sanctuary where blood had been placed, was "miraculously restored" to its original purity? The blood of the Lord's goat which the high priest used in all parts of the sanctuary on the day of atonement "was used to cleanse the sanctuary from the sins of the people. Lev. 16:19. "Thus typifying the blood of Christ which alone can cleanse from sin." E.G. White in *Sons and Daughters of God*, p. 225.

Within the vail. As already noted, while Christ lived on this earth, He never entered either the Holy or the Most Holy apartment of the earthly sanctuary. Heb. 9:24. As an Israelite, He remained in the court, to which alone Israel had access. Not until His ascension when He was anointed for the priesthood, did He go beyond the court. At that time He entered upon His priestly ministry in the Holy place of the *heavenly* sanctuary. When the Judgment began in 1844, He passed into the Most Holy place of the heavenly sanctuary. Through faith in our High Priest who is passed into the heavens, we too may come within "the second vail" into "the Holiest of all." Heb. 9:3.

What does it mean to us to enter within the vail? What difference does it make whether by faith we follow Christ into the Most Holy place or remain outside? The answer is found in another question: What difference did it make to the Jews who through unbelief refused to follow Christ when He left the court of earth and entered upon His work in the holy place of the heavenly sanctuary? We know the answer. It meant their rejection by the Redeemer. So with us, we must follow Christ where He leads the way or we cannot be benefited by His atonement, and finally we shall be cut off from His people.

To enter within the second vail means to accept the judgment message of Revelation 14:7-12, and to walk in all the light. If we don't, we shall be like the unbelieving Jews. There can be no halfhearted work now, for we are facing eternity with all that is involved. Since 1844, the judgment message continues to be preached all over the world, and tens of thousands of earnest, consecrated Christians have responded and by faith have followed Christ within the second vail for salvation.

In the Most Holy Place. The holy of holies represents the audience chamber of the Most High. It is the most sacred place in the sanctuary, containing the sacred ark, glittering with gold, enshrined within which and guarded by two golden cherubim, are the tables of stone containing the ten commandments, the "law of liberty" by which all "shall be judged." James 2:12; EW 252. Covering the ark is the golden mercy seat with its two golden cherubim, stretching their overshadowing wings on high. Between and above these cherubim is the Shekinah, the visible manifestation of the glory of God. Resting on the mercy seat between the angels is the golden censer, Heb. 9:3, 4; EW 32, 252, placed there by the high priest as he entered, but at other times kept in the holy place with the golden altar, both of which were for burning incense. EW 251, 252. From it rises the smoke from the incense, which like a veil dims the glory of the Shekinah, and fills the room with fragrance.

On the golden walls surrounding the ark are forms of angels while the vail and the inner covering of the ceiling, are covered with cherubim richly embroidered in sparkling gold thread. These shining angels on every side, represent the "innumerable" company of angels that surround the throne of God, while the blue, and purple, and scarlet colors of the ceiling and the vail, reflected in the yellow gold, suggests the rainbow around the throne. The entire room is made dazzlingly brilliant by the presence of the Shekinah, whose glory is everywhere reflected from the surrounding gold. All this is "but a dim reflection of the glories of the temple of God in heaven, the great center of the work of man's redemption." PP 349. No wonder we are told that no language can describe the glory of the heavenly scene.

The Cleansing Room. An appropriate name for the Most Holy place is the *cleansing room*, because here on the day of atonement all confessed sin was in figure blotted out, and the sanctuary cleansed. The Bible recognizes three cleansing agencies—water, fire, and blood. Water is used at baptism; fire at last will destroy every trace of sin from the universe; blood makes effective both water and fire. "The blood of Jesus Christ...cleanseth us from all sin." I John 1:7. Since 1844, now more than a century, the inhabitants of earth have been living in the great antitypical day of atonement. Today, the Judgment is set, and the books are opened. Today, the cases of the dead who have professed to love and serve God, and whose names have at some time been written in the Book of Life, are coming in review before the great Judge. Small and great stand before Him, and are being "judged out of those things which were written in the books, according to their works." Rev. 20:12.

We are nearing the end of the journey. We are in the time when "there shall be a great shaking in the land of Israel." Eze. 38:19. For many, probation is now closing. Only those who are sanctified can be accepted. All others will be shaken out and finally destroyed, cut off from among God's people. "Cut off" or "cleansed" —which shall it be for me? Which shall it be for you?

The Glory Room. The most holy place, filled with the Shekinah glory, has also been called *the glory room*. What does this mean in our own individual experience? Christ's last prayer for His disciples before His crucifixion was, "Now, O Father, glorify thou Me with Thine own self with the glory which I had with Thee before the world was...And the glory which Thou gavest Me, I have given them." John 17:5, 22. How may we obtain this glory? —Only through a personal and enduring Christian experience. If, through the court experience, the righteousness of Christ has been *imputed* to us, covering all our *past* sins, and giving us reconciliation and justification; if, in the holy place, His righteousness is now being *imparted* to us, freeing us day by day from the *power* of sin which leads to sanctification, and if we remain true and faithful to the end of life, then, and only then, shall we be prepared for glorification, typified in the Most Holy place.

Justification, the work of a moment, and sanctification, the work of a lifetime, prepare us for glorification, which also is the work of a moment. It is bestowed at the second coming of Christ, "in a moment, in the twinkling of an eye, at the last trump." Then, we who "have borne the image of the earthly"..."shall bear the image of the heavenly," I Cor. 15:51, 52, 49, for the image of God in which man was created will be fully restored. then we shall be like Him, incorruptible and immortal. This is the experience typified in the Most Holy place of the earthly sanctuary.

The life experience of every victorious child of God is symbolized in the three parts of the sanctuary, and is well expressed by F. E. Belden, an eminent hymn writer:

> "Reconciled by His death for my sin,
> Justified by His life, pure and clean;
> Sanctified by obeying His word,
> Glorified when returneth my Lord."

Sanctified Wholly. We who are now living are to take a definite forward step in Christian experience; we are to be sanctified "wholly." Our whole attention is to be centered on preparation for the second coming of Christ. Toward this event the full blaze of Bible truth is focused. More now is expected of us than of those who have gone before. And, why not? "For unto whomsoever much is given, of him shall be much required." Luke 12:48.

At this time, the words of Paul especially apply: "The very God of peace sanctify you wholly; and I pray God your whole spirit and soul and body be preserved blameless unto the coming of our Lord Jesus Christ." I Thes. 5:23. Goodspeed's translation of this verse reads: "May God Himself...consecrate you through and through, spirit, soul, and body; may you be kept sound, and be found irreprovable when our Lord Jesus Christ comes."

"Your Whole Spirit." What is the "spirit" of a person? It is his disposition, whether good or bad, —that which lies back of and influences all his words and actions. It concerns the secret thoughts and motives, even the tone of his voice. What is a wholly consecrated spirit? It is a spirit of Christlike love that in all its manifestations is "very patient, very kind... knows no jealousy...makes no parade, gives itself no airs, is never rude, never selfish, never irritated, never resentful;... never glad when others go wrong...always slow to expose, always eager to believe the best, always hopeful, always patient." I Cor. 13:4-7, *Moffatt*. David prayed, "create in me a clean heart, O God; and renew a right spirit within me." Ps. 51:10. If we have a right *spirit*, our words and actions will be right.

"Your Whole Soul." What is the "soul" of a person? It is his *life*. When God created man He "breathed into his nostrils the breath of *life*; and man became a living *soul*." Gen. 2:7. A wholly consecrated soul is a truly consecrated life, a life whose every energy is fully dedicated to God, every unholy ambition laid aside, every plan and purpose that will not advance the kingdom of God given up.

"Your Whole Body." What is a wholly consecrated body? It is a body under obedience to clean and healthful living habits—so that every physical power will be in the best possible condition to work for God. Such a life—spirit, soul, and body, —will bring us "blameless" and "without fault before the throne of God." Rev. 14:5. Is this too high a standard? Yes, it is, for human achievement, but the next verse tells how it may be reached: "He who called you can be relied on, and *He will do this*." I Thes. 5:24, *Goodspeed*.

The Reward Room. The most holy place is also the reward room. When all the sins of the righteous are forever blotted out and Christ comes, He says, "My reward is with Me, to give every man according as his work shall be." Rev. 22:12. This is symbolized by the "crown of gold" round about the ark in which is embosomed God's law by which all shall be judged. There is a crown for every overcomer, Rev. 2:10—for everyone who has obeyed God's law. "When the Lord makes up His jewels, the true, the frank, the honest, will be looked upon with pleasure. Angels are employed in making crowns for such ones." 5 T 96. "Behold, I come quickly; hold that fast which thou hast, that no man take thy crown." Rev. 3:11. The faithful are now preparing to be glorified at the second coming of Christ. "Whom He justified, them He also glorified." Rom. 8:30. Justification, sanctification, glorification,—these are the three steps from the altar of sacrifice, where God called, "Come unto Me," to the throne, where He calls again, saying, "Come, ye blessed of My Father, inherit the kingdom prepared for you from the foundation of the world." Matt. 25:34.

Christ is the gate, "the way" to the court; He is "the door" to the Holy place: He is "the vail" where we may enter into the Most Holy place. The gate, the door, the vail, is a threefold revelation of His grace and glory to all who "enter in," John 10:9, and who "come boldly" all the way unto the throne of grace. Heb. 4:16. It is His thrice repeated call to "grow in grace, and in the knowledge of our Lord and Saviour Jesus Christ." II Peter 3:18. It is *"The Path to the Throne of God."*

With humility the high priest, dressed in his plain white linen garments, entered the most holy place on the day of atonement. On the mercy seat he placed the golden censer, the smoke from which dimmed the glory of the Shekinah, Within the ark, symbol of God's throne, are the tables of stone on which God engraved the Ten Commandments, the law by which all shall be judged. The overshadowing wings of the cherubim "touch each other," EW 252, and "covered the mercy seat." Ex. 37:9. Their heads bowed toward the ark, show their reverence for God's eternal law of love.

CHAPTER 25 PREVIEW

THE ARK AND ITS CONTENTS

- The Ark of the Covenant
- An Ark a Place of Safety
- The Ark, God's "Treasure Chest"
- The Golden Crown
- The Staves
- The "Tables of Testimony"
- The Tables of Stone Written on Both Sides
- The Significance of Duplicating the Law
- The Pot of Manna and Aaron's Rod
- Where is the Ark Now?
- Where are the Tables of Stone?
- The Special Work of All Who Enter the Most Holy Place

25

THE ARK AND ITS CONTENTS

The Ark of the Covenant. In the most holy place of the sanctuary was the ark with its cover, the mercy seat. Because the ark contained "the words of the covenant, the Ten Commandments," Ex. 34:28, it is frequently called "the ark of the covenant," and Christ Himself, who spoke the law from Sinai, is called "the Angel of the covenant." Heb. 9:4; PP 252.

The instructions for making the ark were very specific: Thou shalt "make an ark of shittim wood: two cubits and a half shall be the length thereof, and a half the breadth thereof, and a cubit and a half the height thereof. And thou shalt overlay it with pure gold, within and without...and shalt make upon it a crown of gold round about. And thou shalt cast four rings of gold for it, and put them in the four corners...and thou shalt make staves of shittim wood, and overlay them with gold. And thou shalt put the staves into the rings...they shall not be taken from it. And thou shalt put into the ark the testimony which I shall give thee." Ex. 25:10-16. These instructions were accompanied by the oft repeated command, "After the pattern [the model]...even so shall ye make." Ex. 25:9. To Bezaleel, the master workman in gold and other metal, was committed the sacred and exalted task of making the ark. Ex. 37:1.

An Ark, a Place of Safety. Webster defines the word *ark* as a place of safety or refuge. Besides the ark of the covenant, the Bible mentions two other arks, both of which were designed as places of safety. First, Noah's ark in which all the righteous people of his day found refuge; second, the ark that Jochebed made for the safety of her baby Moses. Likewise, the ark of the covenant was a place of safety—safety for the law of Jehovah embosomed within it.

The law was put into the ark and covered with the mercy seat, a symbol of the seat, or throne, of the Ruler of all. This was the safest place in all the universe, and shows how supremely sacred Heaven regards the law of God, His fundamental law, the constitution of His universal government.

The Ark, God's "Treasure Chest." The ark has been called God's treasure chest, because within its heart rested His law, His special treasure. As in all the other places where wood was used in the construction of the sanctuary, the ark also was made of shittim wood—the thorny acacia of the wilderness. Fausset's *Bible Encyclopedia* gives us this beautiful thought: "In the thorn of man's curse appeared the Angel of the covenant to Moses in the burning bush at Horeb, to bless man, and out of this wood was formed the ark of the covenant, the typical source of his blessing." And the source of *our* blessing and *our* eternal safety is in obedience to the law that was enclosed within it.

Noah's ark and Moses' ark were made water tight by a coating of pitch "within and without," Gen. 6:14; Ex. 2:3, but the sacred ark of God's covenant was overlaid "within and without" with pure gold. Ex. 37:2. As gold represents Divinity, so this double covering of gold represented God's double protection of His law. Being made of gold and wood, the ark was a symbol of the divine-human character of Christ, who said, "I delight to do Thy will, O My God: yea, Thy law is within My heart." Ps. 40:8. O, precious ark of safety! God could place His law in *that* heart for He knew that there it was safe. It would never be betrayed; it would never be forsaken; it would never be misrepresented. And what God did for His only begotten Son, He will do for every other son within whose heart His law abides.

The Golden Crown. The border of crowns of pure gold encircling the ark fittingly typified not only the "many crowns" which the Saviour will wear, Rev. 19:12,—but it also represents the crowns which He will place upon the heads of all the redeemed, whose "delight is in the law of the Lord" and upon which they "meditate day and night," Ps. 1:2,—those in whose lives God has written His law "not with ink, but with the Spirit of the living God; not in tables of stone, but in fleshy tables of the heart." II Cor. 3:3. As in the table and the golden altar, this border of crowns also represents authority and power—power over sin, which is the transgression of the law. I John 3:4. There is no promise of a crown for those who willfully disregard any of its sacred teachings, or who attempt to change or destroy even "one jot or one tittle" of the law of God. This, even Christ Himself could not do. Matt. 5:17, 18.

The Staves. The staves also were made of shittim wood and covered with pure gold. They were put into rings of cast gold, "that the ark may be borne with them," and at no time were they to be taken from it. Ex. 25:12, 14, 15. This was a very definite command of God, a command not mentioned in connection with any other article of sanctuary furniture. Why? There can be but one answer: because this "treasure chest" of God, containing His choicest treasure, must never be touched by human hands—hands that have known sin. In moving from place to place, the ark, covered with the vail, Num. 4:5, "His flesh," was borne with its staves resting on the shoulders of chosen Levites, divinely appointed for this responsible task.

The penalty for disobedience on this point is shown when David undertook to bring the ark to Jerusalem. "When they came unto the threshing floor of Chidon, Uzzah put forth his hand to hold the ark; for the oxen stumbled. And the anger of the Lord was kindled against Uzzah, and He smote him, because he put his hand to the ark; and there he died before the Lord." I Chron 13:9, 10. This deeply grieved David, but it certainly teaches us that we should regard the holy law of God with the utmost reverence, never treat it with indifference, or knowingly disregard any of its precepts.

"Tables of Testimony." The tables of stone on which God wrote the Ten Commandments are called "tables of testimony," and the ark is called the "ark of the testimony." Ex. 32:15; 30:6. The Hebrew meaning of the word testimony is *wit-*

ness, evidence, proof. Thus the Ten Commandments are a "witness" of God's authority; they are the "evidence" or "proof" that the great Creator is the only true God. This witness, evidence, proof centers especially in the fourth or Sabbath commandment, which Satan has so cunningly endeavored to abolish. Let us beware of his satanic deceptions, lest we aid him in his nefarious work. The law of God within the heart of Christ, Ps. 40:8, that "precious ark of safety," made His life an "evidence," a "proof," a "witness" to the world "that they might know the only true God," and have "life eternal." John 17:3.

The Tables Written on Both Sides. "Thou shalt put into the ark the testimony which I shall give thee." Ex. 25:16. "And He gave unto Moses, when He had made an end of communing with him upon Mount Sinai, two tables of testimony, tables of stone, written with the finger of God." Ex. 31:18. "The writing was the writing of God, graven upon the tables." Ex. 32:16. Unlike the writing of man, the writing of God, "graven," carved in stone in sunken pattern as with a cutting tool used by engravers and sculptors, an indelible writing that could never be erased or changed. [See Webster].

"The tables were written on both their sides." Ex. 32;15. We sometimes think of these tables of stone as written on one side only. Is this correct, or are we to take Exodus 32:15 as it reads? If we are to take the Bible as it reads, it seems plain that the ten commandments are duplicated, being written on both sides of the tables. This is stated in another way in Deuteronomy 4:13, which reads: "He wrote *them* [the Ten Commandments] upon *two* tables of stone;" that is, all the ten were written on each table. Thus when the tables were "folded together like a book," EW 32, the first four commandments would be on the left table and the last six on the right, Matt. 22:37-40, no matter which way the tables were folded, and each table would contain the entire Ten Commandments.

Moffatt's translation of Exodus 32:15 reads: "tablets written on both sides, on this side and that." Another authority comes in a personal letter from the Hebrew Union College of Cincinnati, Ohio: "Rabbi Abraham Ibin Ezra (1092-1167) interprets the words literally; viz., that the writing was duplicated on both sides. This seems to be the connotation of the verse." Then the rabbi adds that Deuteronomy 4:13 "is used to support the view that each table contained all the ten commandments." While even rabbinical interpretations differ on some points, they agree that the writing was duplicated, written on both sides of the tables.

The Significance of Duplicating the Law. Since it appears clear that the law of God was duplicated on the tables of stone, we may ask, Why is this? Why was the law written twice? Doubtless for the same reason that Pharaoh's dream was doubled unto him twice—"because the thing is established by God." Gen. 41:32. Anciently, valuable documents as scrolls were sometimes written within and without and then sealed. Their accuracy and validity were ascertained if, when the seal was broken, the writing within corresponded to that without. Thus, God would make his law unquestionably accurate and valid—"established by God."

An illustration of this custom is given in Ezekiel 2:9, 10 and also in Revelation 5:1. Of the former, *Jameson, Faussett, and Brown's Commentary* says: "Within and without' —on the face and on the back. Usually the parchment was written only on the inside when rolled up; but so full was God's message of impending woes in Ezekiel 2:9, 10, that it was written also on the back." The same authority, commenting on the scroll of Revelation 5:1, described by Moffatt as "a scroll with the writing on the back as well as inside," says, "The writing on the back implies fullness and completeness, so that nothing more needs to be added." The roll, or book, appears from the context to be "the title deed of man's inheritance," D.E. Burgh, "redeemed by Christ, and contains the successive steps by which he shall recover it from the usurper, and obtain actual possession of the kingdom already purchased for Himself and His elect saints."

So God's law written on both front and back of the tables of stone, indicates their unusual importance, also their "fullness and completeness, so nothing more needs to be added." They express "the whole duty of man." Eccl. 12:13.

There is no place in the Bible where the character of the law of God, its sacredness, its validity, its immutability, its perpetuity, and its relation to our salvation is so naturally, so plainly, and so forcefully presented as in the most holy place of the sanctuary. Satan, whose enmity against God's law resulted in his being cast out of Heaven, would have men believe that God's law is a yoke of bondage, but James, inspired by the Spirit of God, calls it "the perfect law of liberty." James 1:25. Paul tells us that sin, "the transgression of the law," I John 3:4, is our bondage—"the bondage of corruption," Rom. 8:21, from which those who obey God shall be delivered. And John says, "His commandments are not grievous." In fact, in keeping His commandments we show that we love God and that we know Him. I John 5:3; 2:3, 4. God's law of love is not a "new commandment ... but an old commandment which ye had from the beginning." Deut. 5:6-22. The "new commandment," I John 2:7, 8, which Christ came to give to the world, was the "old commandment" stripped of all its manmade regulations, See Matt. 5-7, —regulations that were indeed a yoke of bondage.

The Pot of Manna and Aaron's Rod. In addition to the tables of the covenant, the ark contained "the golden pot that had manna, and Aaron's rod that budded." Heb. 9:4. When were these added? At the time when, contrary to God's direction, some of the people went out to gather manna on the Sabbath, the Lord said to Moses, "Take a pot [a golden pot], and put an omer [.4428 gal. or nearly two quarts] full of manna therein, and lay it up before the Lord, to be kept for your generations.... So Aaron laid it up before the testimony, to be kept." Ex. 16:33, 34. God's purpose in preserving for many years a sample of this food, which otherwise spoiled overnight, was not only to give His people an evidence of His constant care over them, but to remove from all minds any groundless speculations by future generations as to how the vast multitude of Israel were fed during their forty years' wandering in the wilderness, where no other food of any kind and no water [except from the rock] could be obtained. Num. 20:5.

Aaron's rod was placed "before the testimony" at the time of the rebellion of Korah, Dathan, and Abiram against Moses and Aaron, Num. 16:3, God's chosen leaders. Although occupying important positions as Levites, these men sought "the priesthood also." Num. 16:10. This spirit of self-exaltation was the same spirit that Lucifer had, and it was very displeasing to the Lord. God recognized Aaron as high priest by the miracle of Aaron's rod that overnight "brought forth buds, and bloomed blossoms, and yielded almonds." Num. 17:8. Then the Lord said unto Moses, "Bring Aaron's rod again before the testimony, to be kept for a token against the rebels; and thou shalt quite take away their murmurings from Me." Num. 17:10.

It seems that both the pot of manna and Aaron's rod were kept in the ark during the forty years' wanderings of Israel. But when the ark was put into Solomon's temple at the time of the dedication of the temple, nearly 500 years later, we are told that "there was nothing in the ark save the two tables of stone, which Moses put there at Horeb, when…the children of Israel…came out of the land of Egypt." I Kings 8:9.

Where Is the Ark Now? From the time of Solomon until the capture of Jerusalem by the Babylonians in B.C. 606, the ark with its sacred treasure was unmolested. At that time righteous men, under the faithful witness of Jeremiah, "determined to place beyond the reach of ruthless hands the sacred ark containing the tables of stone…. With mourning and sadness they secreted the ark in a cave, where it was to be hidden from the people of Israel and Judah because of their sins, and was to be no more restored to them." PK 453. After the return of the Jews from the Babylonian captivity, the temple was restored. But at its dedication "no cloud of glory was seen to fill the newly erected sanctuary. The Shekinah no longer abode between the cherubim in the most holy place; the ark, the mercy seat, and the tables of the testimony were not to be found therein. No voice sounded from heaven to make known to the inquiring priest the will of Jehovah." GC 24. No wonder that many of the "ancient men that had seen the first house,…wept with a loud voice." Ezra 3:12.

Where are the Tables of Stone? God's law, written with His own finger is the standard by which all men, good and bad, shall be judged. James 2:12. Therefore, when in 1844 the Judgment of "the house of God" began in the most Holy place of the heavenly sanctuary, the tables of stone with which the ark had been secreted in a cave, evidently had at some time later been rescued and divinely transported to the most holy place in heaven, there to be God's law book, by which every case shall be decided for eternal life or eternal destruction. "The tables of stone are hidden by God, to be produced in the great Judgment day, just as He wrote them." RH March 26, 1908. "In the temple in heaven, the dwelling place of God,…in the most holy place, is His law, the tables of stone," EW 33, the great rule of right by which all mankind are tested. GC 415. Here it must remain as the standard by which the wicked will be judged during the thousand years.

At the end of the thousand years, when the New Jerusalem comes down to be located on the new earth, the hosts of Satan surround the City planning to capture it. In it is a throne, "high and lifted up," upon which sits the Son of God. To the astonishment of the surrounding hosts, "there appears against the sky a hand holding two *tables of stone* folded together like a book." EW 32; GC 668. "The hand opens the tables, and there are seen the precepts of the Decalogue, traced as with a pen of fire." GC 639. The wicked see "the tables of the divine law, the statutes which they have despised and transgressed." GC 668. "They are in the hands of Christ their Author who gave His life, not 'to destroy the law...but to fulfil' it, Matt. 5:17, and thus demonstrate that God's law, 'holy, and just, and good,' is eternal, Rom. 7:12, as enduring as its Author Eternal. Such a law, being an expression of the mind and will of God, must be as enduring as its Author." 4T 257. This is the last mention we have of the tables of stone. From the hands of Christ, they will undoubtedly be returned to their place in God's eternal throne, "close by Jehovah." EW 255. Here, as long as God rules, they will remain as evidence that God's law, that great law of divine love, engraved on these tables by His own hand and embosomed in His treasure chest, is the eternal foundation of His throne, the fundamental law of His universal and eternal government. To destroy this law would be to undermine His throne and overthrow His government.

The Special Work of All Who Enter the Most Holy Place. In this connection it is important to note that when the Judgment was set in 1844, when "the time of the dead that they should be judged" arrived, Rev. 11:18, at this time a knowledge of the law of God, which for centuries had been buried under the rubbish of error, was restored to His people. Rev. 11:19. This was under the sounding of the seventh angel, Rev. 11:15, the last angel to give a message to the human race, for "in the days of the voice of the seventh angel, when he should begin to sound, the mystery of God should be finished." Rev. 10:7. Then "the kingdoms of this world are become the kingdoms of our Lord, and of His Christ." Rev. 11:15. From these texts it seems self-evident that the special work of all who enter the most holy place, is to unite with the seventh angel in proclaiming the everlasting obligation of obedience to the law of God as found in the ark. God's last message, which is now being preached in all parts of the world, is to develop a people who "keep the commandments of God and the faith of Jesus." Rev. 14:12. When this is accomplished, "the mystery of God" shall be finished.

CHAPTER 26 PREVIEW

THE MERCY SEAT AND THE SHEKINAH

- The Mercy Seat
- The Mercy Seat a Symbol of God's Throne
- The Cherubim of Beaten Gold
- Who Are Represented by These Cherubim?
- The Angel of the Covenant
- The Shekinah a Symbol of Jehovah
- God's Will Revealed from the Shekinah
- God's Law the Foundation of His Throne

26

THE MERCY SEAT AND THE SHEKINAH

The Mercy Seat. "And thou shalt make a mercy seat of pure gold; two cubits and a half shall be the length thereof, and a cubit and a half the breadth thereof." "And he made two cherubims of gold, beaten out of one piece made he them, on the two ends of the mercy seat." "And the cherubims shall stretch forth their wings on high covering the mercy seat with their wings, and their faces shall look one to another; toward the mercy seat shall the faces of the cherubims be. And thou shalt put the mercy seat above upon the ark." Ex. 25:17-21; 37:7-9.

The mercy seat was so called because it symbolized the place where mercy was dispensed to man over the law that he had transgressed. It also represented Christ, for Paul says that God hath set Him forth to be a "propitiation," Rom. 3:25; I John 2:2, or "mercy seat," as the same word is translated in Hebrews 9:5. Through Him only do we have "remission of sins"—He is our propitiation or atonement, our mercy seat.

The Mercy Seat A Symbol of God's Throne. Unlike the ark which was made of wood covered with gold, the mercy seat was made "of pure gold." John locates God's throne in the most holy place when he says: "The golden altar...was before the throne." Rev. 8:3. The golden altar was in the holy place directly before the mercy seat, which was in the most holy place. Between the cherubim was the Shekinah, representing the visible presence of God. David says, "He [God] sitteth between the cherubim;" "Thou...dwelleth between the cherubim." Ps. 99:1; 80:1; II Kings 19:15. Here, "between the cherubim" which were upon the mercy seat covering the ark of the testimony, "God gave commandment unto the children of Israel." Ex. 25:22.

God's throne is a seat, or throne, of mercy—a mercy seat. "Mercy is compassionate treatment of an enemy, with a disposition to forgive," says Webster. Whose seat then did the mercy seat represent? The only answer is that it represented the seat, or throne, of Him who is "merciful and gracious, slow to anger, and plenteous in mercy." Ps. 103:8. "The Lord God, merciful and gracious, long-suffering,...keeping mercy for thousands [to a thousand generations, Deut. 7:9], forgiving iniquity and transgression and sin." Ex. 34:6, 7; 20:5, 6.

The ark was made expressly to be the innermost shrine of the tables of stone on which were engraved God's ten-commandment law. The transgression of this fundamental law of the universe is sin, I John 3:4, and all have sinned; Rom. 3:23; all are enemies by wicked works. Col. 1:21. But on God's throne or seat, a seat of mercy, sits our Father, who treats an enemy with compassion and a disposition to forgive.

"God's love for the fallen race is a peculiar manifestation of love—*a love born of mercy*... Mercy implies imperfection of the object toward which it is shown. It is because of sin that mercy was brought into active exercise." 7T 264. When all the enemies of righteousness are no more forever, when there are no more sinners, there will be no more opportunity for the "active exercise" of mercy. When sin is done away, God's eternal love still lives, though it is manifest not in mercy, for this quality of love can be exercised only toward enemies and sinners. The *disposition* to forgive and the *disposition* to show mercy, being qualities of the eternal One, are eternal. These qualities of God belong to the eternal "throne of God and the Lamb." Were God's throne anything but a mercy seat, we would be utterly without hope. "His throne is upholden by mercy." Prov. 20:28. Were this not true, what would be the result to the throne itself?

The Cherubim of Beaten Gold. On each end of the mercy seat was a magnificent angel form made of solid gold. The two wings stretched forth on high "touched each other." EW 252. The angels faced each other, and, expressive of reverence, bowed their heads toward the holy law of God within the ark below.

These cherubim were not only of solid gold but of *beaten* gold. As already noted, the candlestick, representing Christ the light of the world, was also of beaten gold, the oil used for the lights, symbolizing the Holy Spirit, was beaten, and the gold thread with which the angel forms were embroidered was cut from beaten gold. Ex. 39:3. That the gold was beaten represented the sorrow and suffering that Heaven has endured because of sin. "Few give thought to the suffering that sin has caused our Creator. All Heaven suffered in Christ's agony; but that suffering did not begin or end with His manifestation in humanity. The cross is a revelation to our dull senses of the pain that, from its very inception, sin has brought to the heart of God." Ed. 263. Not only the Father, the Son and the Holy Spirit, but all the angels of heaven were involved in the infinite Sacrifice required to redeem man. At the news of man's transgression, every angel harp was hushed. In disappointment and sorrow, the angels cast their crowns from their heads. How could they give up their beloved Commander to a life of humiliation and suffering? And from that time, all through the working out of the plan of salvation, for every temptation suffered, for every trial and persecution endured for Christ's sake, there has been a responsive suffering in heaven. Isa 63:9.

Who Are Represented by These Cherubim? These two cherubim of matchless splendor, one standing at the right, the other at the left of the Shekinah glory, represent two special angels who are the "shining guardians" of the law of God and of His "eternal throne," "the abiding place of the King of kings." PP 357; GC 414. They represent the "most exalted of the angel throng." These were with Christ throughout His life on earth, and they came to the tomb at His resurrection. John 20:12; DA 780, 830. They are the two who at His ascension waited in sympathy and love to comfort the disciples with the assurance: "This same Jesus, which is taken up from you into heaven, shall so come in like manner as ye have seen Him go into heaven." Acts 1:11; DA 780, 831, 832.

What are the names of these two angels? The Bible tells us the name of only one of them. Before sin entered the universe, Lucifer, the light bearer, was "the anointed cherub that covereth." It was he who was "upon the holy mountain of God;" Eze. 28:14; he stood next in honor to the Son of God. When Lucifer was cast out of heaven, Gabriel was appointed to take his place. DA 693, 780. This same

197

Gabriel, who is called "an angel of the Lord," foretelling the birth of John as the forerunner of Christ, declared, "I am Gabriel, that stand in the presence of God." Luke 1:11, 16, 19; DA 98. It was Gabriel who was sent by God to Mary to tell her of the birth of Christ. Luke 1:26-28; DA 780. It was Gabriel who was honored in that "awful crisis, when everything was at stake, when the mysterious cup trembled in the hand of the Sufferer," who came to the side of Christ in Gethsemane to strengthen Him and speak words of encouragement. DA 693.

Not only in behalf of Christ, but on other occasions, Gabriel has been sent on special errands of honor and trust. It was Gabriel, "His angel," whom Christ sent to John on the Isle of Patmos to signify [that is, to show by *signs*, or symbols] "things which must shortly come to pass." Rev. 1:1; DA 99, 234. It was Gabriel who gave Daniel understanding regarding the 2300 days and the cleansing of the sanctuary, Dan. 8:14, 16; 9:21, and who said, "There is none that holdeth with me in these things, but Michael [Christ] your Prince." Dan. 10:21. "Wonderful thought—that the angel who stands next in honor to the Son of God is the one chosen to open the purposes of God to sinful men!" DA 99.

How utterly incomprehensible that the evil ambitions of Lucifer, whose place at the throne of God was taken by Gabriel, could blind his eyes to his marvelous privileges and opportunities! And equally incomprehensible is it that human beings can throw away their prospects of the future immortal life in the glorious and sinless home of eternal peace and joy for a few paltry and fleeting pleasures of sin!

The Angel of the Covenant. The ark is called "the ark of the covenant," Num. 10:33; Heb. 9:4, because in it was placed the covenant, the "tables of stone" that God gave to Moses. Ex. 25:16; 31:18. Christ is called "the Messenger of the covenant," Mal. 3:1, or "the Angel of the covenant" PP 252, because when He gave the law at Sinai, He was God's messenger, doing the will of the Father. From the fact that Christ is called "the Angel of the covenant," some have concluded that Christ was one of the covering cherubim. But this cannot be, for Christ occupies the position of King on the throne with the Father. "The Angel of the covenant, even our Lord Jesus Christ, is the Mediator who secures the acceptance of the prayers of His believing ones." 8T 179. He is not an angel in the ordinary acceptation of that word. When He is called "Angel" the term is used in the sense of messenger.

The Shekinah a Symbol of Jehovah. Between the mystic cherubim on the mercy seat was the Shekinah glory. The brilliancy of this dazzling light, reflected from the overshadowing cherubim, was too bright for human eyes to look upon. The word Shekinah is not found in the Bible. It is used by both Jews and Christians to express the visible majesty of Jehovah, especially when dwelling between the cherubim on the mercy seat in the first sanctuary and in the temple of Solomon, but not in the second temple, because in that temple there was no ark and no mercy seat. The idea that the different accounts in the Scriptures convey is that of a most brilliant and glorious light, enveloped in a cloud, so that for the most part the cloud alone was visible; but on particular occasions the glory appeared. There are frequent allusions to it in the Bible, such as "Thou that dwellest between the cherubim, *shine forth*;" Ps. 80:1; "Who are Israelites; to whom pertaineth the adoption, *and the glory*;" Rom. 9:4; "To see Thy power and *Thy glory*, so as I have seen Thee in the sanctuary." Ps. 63:2.

Literally, the word Shekinah means *dwelling place*. Its root is also found in the word *tabernacled*. Light is thrown on this thought in the literal rendering of Genesis 3:24. "So He drove out the man, and He tabernacled [He shekinahed] at the east of the garden with cherubims; and a glittering, flickering flame turned every way to keep the way about the tree of life."

God's Will Revealed from the Shekinah. Through the inquiring priest, the will of Jehovah was made known not only by Urim and Thummim, but above the mercy seat from the Shekinah, the manifestation of the Divine presence. "There I will meet with thee, and I will commune with thee from above the mercy seat, from between the two cherubims which are upon the ark of the testimony, of all things which I will give thee in commandment unto the children of Israel." Ex. 25:22; Nu. 7:89. How was this done? "Divine messages were sometimes communicated to the high priest by a voice from the cloud. Sometimes a light fell upon the angel at the right, to signify approval or acceptance, or a shadow or cloud rested upon the one at the left to reveal disapproval or rejection." PP 349.

Thus it seems plain that while the mercy seat was a symbol of the seat or throne of God in heaven, the Shekinah represented the glorious presence of Jehovah Himself. As the angel forms represented on the walls, the vail, and the ceiling, filled the most holy place, so, in a vision of the heavenly sanctuary, Isaiah saw "the Lord sitting upon a throne,...and His train [of angels] filled the temple." Isaiah 6:1. As a shadow portrays but a mere outline of an object or a person, not revealing the life and character, so the mercy seat with the Shekinah, unspeakably magnificent though their glory, can be but a dim reflection of that of which it was a mere shadow.

God's Law the Foundation of His Throne. As the ark upheld the mercy seat, so the law within the ark represents the foundation of God's throne or government. "Righteousness and justice are the foundation of His throne." Ps. 97:2; ARV. Here again it is illustrated that "Mercy and truth [love and law] are met together; righteousness and peace have kissed each other." Ps. 85:10. To destroy the fundamental law of God's government would be to undermine His throne and overthrow His government. The tables of the law embosomed in the ark, together with the mercy seat, before which Christ pleads His blood for those who have transgressed the law, represent "the union of justice and mercy in the plan of human redemption. This union infinite wisdom alone could devise, and infinite power accomplish; it is a union that fills all Heaven with wonder and adoration.... This is the mystery of mercy into which the angels desire to look—that God can be just while He justifies the repenting sinner." GC 415; I Peter 1:12.

CHAPTER 27 PREVIEW

ISRAEL'S DAY OF ATONEMENT
AND ITS ANTITYPE

- The Silver Trumpets
- Antitype of the Blowing of Trumpets
- The Cleansing of the Earthly Sanctuary
- The Cleansing of the Heavenly Sanctuary
- Christ Our Great Sin Bearer
- The Time of the Day of Atonement
- The Services
- "An Holy Convocation"
- "Ye Shall Afflict Your Souls"
- "An Offering Made by Fire"
- "A Sabbath of Rest"
- Our Part in the Cleansing of the Sanctuary
- The High Priest's Blessing at the Close of the Day
- The Feast of Tabernacles, a Time of Rejoicing

27

ISRAEL'S DAY OF ATONEMENT
AND ITS ANTITYPE

The Silver Trumpets. God said to Moses, "Make thee two trumpets of silver; of a whole piece shalt thou make them, that thou mayest use them for the calling of the assembly, and for the journeying of the camp. Also in the day of your gladness, and in your solemn days, and in the beginning of your months...that they may be to you for a memorial before your God" —for a memorial, or reminder, of His leadership and of their deliverance. Num. 10:2, 8-10. When in the wilderness all the people were together in one large camp, two trumpets were sufficient to make any necessary proclamation, but when settled throughout the land of Canaan, it would seem that more would be needed, especially when the proclamation was to be given all over the land of Israel in one day.

Why did God instruct that these trumpets be made of silver? And why was the silver to be "of a whole piece?" Silver was a symbol of redemption, especially prefigured on the day of atonement. As the priests' garments woven in one piece represented that his life was to be riveted to one great purpose, so these trumpets "of a whole piece" were to remind the people that especially at this solemn time, their thoughts were to be centered on preparation for the day of atonement. Therefore the day when the trumpets were blown was to be "a sabbath...an holy convocation," when every family was to "offer an offering made by fire unto the Lord" —an offering of consecration and thanksgiving. Lev. 23:23-25.

The most solemn of the "solemn days" when the trumpets were blown was to proclaim the approach of the day of atonement. "In the seventh month, in the *first* day of the month," there was to be "a memorial of blowing of trumpets." Lev. 23:24. This was ten days before the day of atonement, which came on the *tenth* day of the seventh month. Lev. 23:27.

This blowing of the trumpets by the priests notified the people that the day of atonement was near, and that they must hasten to confess every sin and make every wrong right. It gave everyone time to make the necessary preparation and present himself in Jerusalem at the time of the cleansing of the sanctuary, for "in that same day," Lev. 23:28-30, every case in Israel was decided. This was in type the final separation of the sinner from his sin, if that sin had been confessed; of it not, it was in type the final separation of the sinner from the house of Israel.

Antitype of the Blowing of the Trumpets. The day of God's Judgment for the human race, when every individual will either be separated from his sins or cut off from the heavenly family, is the antitype of the day of atonement. According to the prophecy of Daniel 8:14, this real day of Judgment began at the end of the 2300 days, in 1844.

As in the type, ten days before "the tenth day of the seventh month," the priests blew the silver trumpets warning everyone to get ready, so in the antitype, the judgment message began to be proclaimed about *ten years*, "each day for a year" Num. 14:34, preceding 1844. [See *Our Firm Foundation*, Vol. I, p. 345]. During this period of time, every Christian nation on earth heard in trumpet tones the announcement of the message of Revelation 14:6, 7: "The hour of His Judgment *is come!*" This was a fulfillment of the prophecy of Joel: "Blow ye the trumpet in Zion, and sound an alarm in My holy mountain…for the day of the Lord cometh, for it is nigh at hand." Joel 2:1.

The Cleansing of the Earthly Sanctuary. In the earthly sanctuary, one year's round of service symbolized the entire plan of salvation. On the last day of this yearly service, the day of atonement, the high priest first offered a bullock, the largest and most costly of the sacrifices, as a sin offering to make atonement "for himself and for his house." Lev. 16:11-14. Dressed in his plain white linen garments which were worn only in the most holy place on the day of atonement, he went alone into the sanctuary. Lev. 16:4, 7; Heb. 9:7. Here he sprinkled the blood of the sacrifice on the mercy seat in the most holy place, then in the holy place, and finally on the altar in the court. This atonement for his own sins and for his house, qualified him to act as mediator for the people.

Following this, Aaron cast lots on the two goats, one lot for the Lord, and the other for the scapegoat. Lev. 16:5-8. He then killed the Lord's goat, "the sin offering for the people" vs. 15, which symbolized Christ who died for their sins, and brought the blood into the sanctuary. By this act, as Christ's representative, he in type took upon himself the sins of repentant Israel. He then sprinkled the blood "seven times," [complete reconciliation] upon the mercy seat over the law that had been transgressed, also in the holy place, and "on the altar that is before the Lord" in the court, thus making atonement for "all the congregation." This was "an end of reconciling." vs. 14-20. The services of the day were now about to close, and while the sun was sinking in the western sky, anyone who still had unconfessed sin was cut off from Israel. The destiny of every Israelite had been decided.

The last event of the day now took place. The goat on which the lot fell to be the scapegoat, was presented alive before the Lord. vs. 7-10. The high priest, laying both his hands on the head of the goat, confessed over him all the sins of repentant Israel, thus in figure transferring the sins from himself to the goat. The goat was then sent away "into the wilderness;…unto a land not inhabited," vs. 21, 22, where he finally perished, never to return to the camp of Israel. Thus in type every true Israelite had been cleansed from all sin, and the sanctuary where his sins had been recorded in blood was cleansed. Because the events of this day determined the future of every Israelite, the day of atonement was the most seriously solemn day of their lives. See GC 420.

The Cleansing of the Heavenly Sanctuary. As in the earthly, so in the heavenly sanctuary, the work of Christ, our heavenly High Priest, on the great day of final judgment for the true Israel, the household of God, is the antitype of the work of the earthly high priest on the day of atonement for Israel of old. When this final work of Judgment began, at the end of the 2300 days of Daniel 8:14, in 1844, Jesus passed from the holy place, of the heavenly sanctuary into "the Holiest of all," Heb. 9:3—the most holy place, to begin the cleansing of the *heavenly* sanctuary. Since "Judgment must begin at the house of God," I Peter 4:17, the cases of those only who at some time in their lives have become members of the family of God on earth, and whose names have been written in the Book of Life, are considered, or investigated, at this time. This investigation is to determine who have endured to the end, and it is therefore called the *Investigative Judgment*. Matt. 10:22. Those who have never accepted Christ as their personal Saviour, who have never become members of the true Israel, Gal. 3:20, are not considered at this time. Their cases need no such investigation—their Judgments will be executive.

In the earthly sanctuary, "while the sin offering [the Lord's goat] pointed to Christ as a sacrifice, and the high priest represented Christ as a mediator, the scapegoat typified Satan." GC 422. As the high priest, by virtue of slaying the sin offering, the Lord's goat, and receiving this blood, took the sins of Israel upon himself, and coming out of the sanctuary placed them upon the scapegoat, so Christ, at the close of His ministration for sinners, by virtue of His own blood, removes the sins of the truly repentant from the record books in the heavenly sanctuary, and places them upon Satan the originator and instigator of sin, who will bear their punishment. See GC 673; EW 178, 281. As the scapegoat, bearing the sins of repentant and forgiven Israel, was sent away "into a land not inhabited" where he finally perished, never again to return to the camp of Israel, so Satan who is responsible for all sin, will during a thousand years spend his last days in this earth which will then be desolate and without inhabitant. Here, when the earth is burned up, he will be eternally destroyed, never again to afflict God's people. Nahum 1:9.

When the Investigative Judgment closes, all the *sins* of Israel will have been forever blotted out, not in type but in reality, and all the *names* of *unrepentant* Israel will be forever blotted out from God's family record book—"cut off" from Israel. At this time the eternal destiny not only of the "house of God" the true Israel, but of the entire human family, is forever decided. This blotting out of the sins of repentant Israel recorded in the books above, constitutes the cleansing of the *heavenly* sanctuary. Thus, "the holy of holies [in the earthly sanctuary] … forms the connecting link between heaven and earth." PP 348.

Christ Our Great Sin Bearer. Because the high priest transferred the sins of repentant Israel to the scapegoat which represented Satan, some have concluded that his makes Satan, instead of Christ, the sin bearer. These apparently overlook the fact that the scapegoat had no part in the atonement of Israel; his blood was not taken into the sanctuary at all. On the contrary, the atonement for sin was effected by the blood of the Lord's goat, which represented Christ the true Sin-offering, the great Sin-bearer whose blood cleanses from all sin. I John 1:7. Unlike Christ, though, Satan will finally perish. He dies, not to *redeem* man, but because of the sins he has caused to be committed.

It is important that we be not confused on this point. Christ, the heavenly High Priest, voluntarily gave His life for the sins of the whole world. John 3:16. Those who accept His sacrifice—those who have placed their sins on the great Sin-bearer—are thus freed from the penalty of their sins. But, since the inevitable consequence of sin is death, someone must pay the final penalty. Who? In justice, he who is responsible for these sins. Therefore, when the real Judgment closes, Christ, the antitypical High Priest, places them on Satan, the antitypical scape-goat, who in Justice "must suffer for all the evil that he has done, and be punished for the sins that he has caused to be committed." GC 660. Again in justice, those whose names have not been retained in the Book of Life as well as all whose names have never been written there will, with Satan, be cast into the lake of fire where they will be punished for their share of their own sins, and finally be eternally destroyed. Rev. 20:10, 15. Thus, from first to last, God's justice is fully vindicated.

The Time of the Day of Atonement. The day of atonement, the *typical* day of Judgment, began exactly on time: "In the ninth day of the month at even," and continued "from even unto even." Lev. 23:32. The "even" is God's appointed time for the beginning and close of every day; therefore, the ninth day at even at the setting of the sun, marked the beginning of the tenth day. At that time every Israelite was to be in his place in Jerusalem, having been forewarned by the blowing of trumpets ten days previously. Likewise, the time of the beginning of the *real* day of Judgment, when the heavenly sanctuary is to be cleansed, is divinely appointed; "Unto 2300 days, then shall the sanctuary be cleansed." Dan. 8:14. According to reliable information, the tenth day of the seventh month in 1844 fell on October 22. At that time the Investigative Judgment *began* in the heavenly sanctuary. Dan. 8:14. It will *close* when probation ends. As on the day of atonement when Israel, in type, had been cleansed from all sin, the high priest pronounced his blessing on the people so when the *real* Judgment day closes and the sins of redeemed Israel have been blotted out, then Christ the heavenly High Priest will pronounce His blessing, saying, "He that is righteous, let him be righteous still, and he that is holy let him be holy still." Rev. 22:11; also GC 613. Thus like all the other ordinances of the Jewish year, the Day of Atonement will be fulfilled "not only as to the event but as to the time." GC 399-400.

The Services. The services on the day of atonement were as definite as was the time. These also were divinely appointed. Aside from the duties of the high priest, there were four definite assignments for the people: "It shall be an holy convocation unto you; and ye shall afflict your souls, and offer an offering made by fire unto the Lord. And ye shall do no work—no service work—in that same day; for it is a day of atonement." Lev. 23:27, 28. These are the words that the Lord spoke unto Moses to deliver unto Israel. Every requirement must be met on penalty of separation from Israel.

"An Holy Convocation." The day of atonement connected with the earthly sanctuary was an all-day service—an holy convocation at Jerusalem from which no Israelite was to absent himself. Nor was it a time for idle, careless, trifling associations. It was a day of deep heart searching and earnest prayer, that as the high priest officiated at the mercy seat, every confessed sin might be put away. No one could afford to let the day close with one known sin resting upon his heart. If this was neglected, the sinner was no longer counted among Israel.

Since the day of atonement was of such importance to ancient Israel, how infinitely more important to us is its antitype, the real and final day of Judgment! How much more should we who have entered "into the holiest by the blood of Jesus,…through the vail,…draw near with a true heart in full assurance of faith!" How much more should *we* "hold fast the profession of our faith without wavering!" How much more should *we* "consider one another to provoke unto love and good works; not forsaking the assembling of ourselves together,…but exhorting one another: *and so much the more*, as ye see the day approaching!" Heb. 10:19-25.

"Ye Shall Afflict Your Souls." What is it to "afflict" the soul? Moffatt translates it "abstain and fast." During the antitype of the day of atonement, unbelievers are "eating and drinking," feasting and making merry, "as it was in the days of Noah." Matt. 24:37-39. They express their merriment in boisterous laughter and trifling song, disregarding the Scripture, "Is any merry? let him sing psalms." James 5:13. They are restless and unhappy unless they are being entertained by amusements that drown the conscience and unfit the mind for sober study of God's Word. They do not realize the seriousness of the times. Like the rich man in the parable, they "pull down their barns, and build greater;" and to their souls they say, "Soul, thou hast much goods laid up for many years; take thine ease, eat, drink, and be merry." Poor souls! Their riches cannot save them, for they are "not rich toward God." Luke 12:18, 19, 21.

Satan exerts every conceivable effort to sway them away from the path of right. Their only safety is to be of those of whom Paul wrote: "But ye, brethren, are not in darkness, that that day should overtake you as a thief… Therefore,…let us watch and be sober,… putting on the breastplate of faith and love; and for an helmet, the hope of salvation." I Thess 5:4-8. "For whatsoever soul it be that shall not be afflicted in that same day, he shall be cut off from among his people." Lev. 23:29.

"An Offering Made by Fire." The regular morning and evening burnt offerings, which symbolized "the daily consecration of the nation to Jehovah, and their constant dependence upon the atoning blood of Christ," PP 352, formed a part of the service on the day of atonement. Burnt offerings were called "sweet savor" offerings because, being expressive of complete consecration of body, soul, and spirit, they were to God as sweet smelling incense. They were also expressive of thanksgiving and gratitude to Him who gave Himself as a whole burnt offering.

They were burned on the brazen altar type of the place where first we gave our hearts to God, and where every idol of the heart and evil thing was placed to be completely consumed. Now, in the evening of the Judgment day, at the time of the evening sacrifice, the time when "the fire shall try every man's work of what sort it is," I Cor. 3;13-15, shall we not return to our first love, once more dedicating to God all that we have and are for the *finishing* of His work?

"A Sabbath of Rest." Another requirement for the observance of the day of atonement was: "Ye shall do no work ['no servile work,' Lev. 23:25] in that same day," "whether it be one of your own country, or a stranger that sojourneth among you." Lev. 16:29. "Ye shall do no manner of work...it shall be unto you a sabbath of rest." Lev. 23:28-32. This requirement was as important as it was emphatic, for "Whatsoever soul it be that doeth any work in that same day, the same soul will I destroy from among his people." The entire thought and time of every true Israelite was to be centered on the services of the day. There was to be no divided heart, —the day of atonement demanded complete and wholehearted consecration of every power.

During this, our antitypical day of atonement, the actual day of Judgment, are we then to be idle? By no means. Nevertheless, we are told that "those who do not cleanse the soul temple, but who engage in some enterprise not in harmony with His work, those who engage in side issues to satisfy their own selfish purposes, are joining with the enemy of God and man." RH, Jan. 21, 1890. Again, "When the professed people of God engage in side issues to gratify their own selfish purposes, they do so at the risk of losing eternal life." Manuscript EGW. Is not this the "servile work" which at this time God forbids? If while Jesus in the heavenly sanctuary is examining the cases of those who have identified themselves as His children, we are indifferent to, or halfhearted in, the task of carrying the judgment message to those who have never heard, can *we* expect a less serious pronouncement than that given to Israel in the type? Is God less concerned and less particular in this, the *real* day of Judgment, than He was in its type or "shadow?" To do "no servile work," Lev. 23:25, but to observe the day as "a sabbath of rest" —does this not mean that in this antitypical day of atonement, all our time, all our income, all our energy of body, mind, and soul, all our labors of whatsoever nature, should be devoted to the sole purpose of advancing and finishing the work of God on earth? With such a complete consecration to God, with our all on the altar, our offering will indeed be a sweet savor to God.

Paul, the tent maker, who gave his life so unreservedly to the service of God, labored with his hands, not to gain earthly wealth, but that he might be "chargeable to no man." II Cor. 11:9. Another noble example is found in the life of William Carey, the cobbler, who said that his business was to serve the Lord: he cobbled shoes to pay expenses. Is not such labor in perfect harmony with the "sabbath of rest" of the antitypical day of atonement? We catch glimpses of the fruitage of such a consecrated life in the fact that when Carey went to India, his first convert from high class Brahamnism was a man by the name of Mockergee. This was in the year 1800. His grant grandson, N. G. Mockergee, accepted God's last message in 1897, and is now a missionary to his own people in India. Also, a young man, Brian Carey, great, great, great grandson of William Carey, later a theological major at Pacific Union College, Angwin, California, has his heart set on carrying the gospel of Christ's soon coming to the native people of Kenya Colony, East Africa, where he was born and reared.

Our Part in the Cleansing of the Sanctuary. "Now, while Christ is cleansing the temple in heaven from the sins of the people, shall we not work in harmony with Him upon the earth, cleansing the soul temple from every moral defilement?" RH, Feb. 11, 1890. Not only must the soul temple be cleansed, but our bodies must be cleansed from everything that weakens physical power and unfits us to do our part in finishing the work of God on earth. That we may be prepared to "stand before Him a perfect people," "God demands that the appetites be cleansed." 9T 153, 154. "The indulgence of appetite" brings "physical debility, and so deadens the perceptive organs that sacred and eternal things [may] not be discerned... The struggle of the temptation to indulge perverted appetite can be measured only by the inexpressible anguish of Christ in that long fast in the wilderness. Adam fell in the indulgence of appetite [and] Christ began the work of redeeming man just where the ruin began... The declension of virtue and degeneracy of the race are chiefly attributable to the indulgence of perverted appetite." 3T 486. "Those who are slaves to appetite will fail in perfecting Christian character." 3T 492.

"God hath made man upright; but they have sought out many inventions," Eccl. 7:29—inventions that please but often pervert and deprave the appetite. For their own well being, God appointed our first parents simple, unprocessed food. Gen. 1:29. Anyone who is "given to appetite" says the wise man, is putting a knife to his throat, Prov. 23:2. In this, our day of atonement, God's instruction is "Whether therefore ye eat or drink, or whatsoever ye do, do all to the glory of God." I Cor. 10:31. If we persistently refuse to obey this instruction, continuing to practice those habits which tend to weaken the system or to create disease, how can we claim God's protection from the plagues which are soon to spread over the earth? As we place our offerings on the "foursquare" golden altar, shall we not be foursquare with our Creator and Redeemer? In this age of degenerate physical power, and especially with the abundance of reliable and instructive literature on healthful living now available, is it not the duty of every true Christian to become informed and to give conscientious obedience to all God's laws of health as well as to His moral law? Is not the transgression of the laws that God had established for our physical well being, as verily sin as is the transgression of His moral law? If we cannot give up all "fleshly lusts, which war against the soul," I Peter 2:11, what will God say of us, when our names come up for judgment? What did He say to Ephraim who did not give up *his* idols? Hosea 4:17.

The High Priest's Blessing at the Close of the Day. As "in the typical service the high priest, having made the atonement for Israel, came forth and blessed the congregation, so Christ at the close of His work as Mediator, will appear...to bless

His waiting people with eternal life." GC 485. Then will be fulfilled the promise: "Blessed are they that do His commandments, that they may have right to the tree of life, and may enter in through the gates into the City." Rev. 22:14.

> "Some one will enter the pearly gate,
> By and by, by and by,
> Taste of the glories that there await;
> Shall you, Shall I, Shall *you*? Shall *I*?
> Someone will travel the streets of gold,
> Beautiful visions will there behold,
> Feast on the pleasures so long foretold;
> Shall you? Shall I, Shall *you*? Shall *I*?

The Feast of Tabernacles, a Time of Rejoicing. The day of atonement had ended; the sins of repentant Israel had, in type, been blotted out. It had been a solemn day, but now with glad hearts, the people returned at the setting of the sun to their homes. The next five days were spent "ingathering" the "fruit of the land." On the fifteenth day of the seventh month, corresponding to our October, when the harvest was past, they assembled again to keep "a feast unto the Lord." This feast was called the feast of tabernacles, a word meaning "tents" because the Israelites kept it under booths of branches in memory of their dwelling in tents in their passage through the wilderness. It was one of the three great yearly feasts, the others being Passover and Pentecost. Because it came at the time of the final ingathering of the harvest, it is sometimes called the "Feast of Ingathering." Ex. 23:16. This was a time of great rejoicing and freedom—freedom from sin and from daily toil. For seven days they lived, or tabernacled, in booths made of the branches of "goodly trees, branches of palm trees, and the boughs of thick trees, and willows of the brook," "Olive branches and pine branches, and myrtle branches." Lev. 23:40; Neh. 8:14, 15. For this reason this feast is also called the "Feast of Tabernacles."

The Feast of Tabernacles was not only commemorative of their "dwelling in booths when the Lord brought them out of Egypt," Lev. 23:43, but it was also typical. It pointed forward to the time when redeemed Israel, with all sin forever blotted out at the close of the real Judgment, their labors ended, and their "ingathering" of souls completed, shall "come to Zion with songs and everlasting joy upon their heads," bringing their "Sheaves with them," Isaiah 35:10; Ps. 126:6, as a thank offering, to keep a feast unto the Lord. See PP 540-542.

As Israel, after the short interval of five days following the day of atonement, built booths in which they lived for seven days—seven, indicating a complete number—so redeemed Israel, after the short interval of one thousand years—short in comparison with eternity—shall in the new earth build houses of all kinds of goodly trees, patterned after the garden of Eden, Gen. 2:9. These they inhabit, Isaiah 65:21, not for seven days only, but "forever and ever." Rev. 22:5. What a time of rejoicing will be this, *our* Feast of Tabernacles!

This was the last typical feast of the Jewish year, two of which, Passover with its concluding Pentecost, came in the spring; the other two, Day of Atonement with its conclusion, Feast of Tabernacles, in the fall. All of these feasts have been or will be fulfilled "not only as to the event, but as to the time." GC 399-400. The Feast of Tabernacles is the only one yet to be fulfilled but in God's own appointed time, it also will be fulfilled.

Am I ready, at the close of my earthly career with all my sins blotted out, to do my final work before the Lord comes?

CHAPTER 28 PREVIEW

THE JUDGMENT AND THE SABBATH

- The Sabbath from the Beginning
- The Sabbath and God's Name
- The Sabbath and God's Seal
- The Sabbath God's "Ensign"
- The Ensign of the Enemy
- The Sabbath a "Sign" of Sanctification
- God's Law a Law of Love
- His Law Eternal and Universal
- God's Law Perfect
- God's Law Unchangeable
- Sabbath Reform Among Sabbath Keepers
- The Sabbath and the Judgment

28

THE JUDGMENT AND THE SABBATH

The Sabbath from the Beginning. From the creation of the world, through the entire four thousand years of Old Testament times, the seventh day of the week was recognized by all worshipers of the true God, the Creator, as His holy day. Christ, "as His custom was," faithfully observed the Sabbath, Luke 4:16; the disciples also kept the Sabbath day "according to the commandment." Luke 23:56. During the centuries that followed, there came "a falling away," and that "man of sin," "the son of perdition," began his deceptive work. II Thess 2:3, 4. During the dark period of his supremacy, from 538 to 1517 known in history as the Dark Ages, among many other deceptive errors introduced into Christendom by this antichristian power, was the observance of Sunday as the Sabbath, and, as the Bible was not allowed in the hands of the common people, many were led astray.

Following the Dark Ages, during the great Reformation of the sixteenth century, printing came into use, and the Bible, which up to that time had been only in *written* form, was printed and finally made available to the common people in their own tongue. But in spite of this tremendous advantage, many of the errors introduced by Antichrist still survived in the hearts of the people.

In 1844, when the Judgment began in the heavenly sanctuary, those who by faith went with Christ into the most holy place, within the second vail, were divinely directed to a study of the sanctuary. God's message to them at this time was "Rise and measure the temple of God." Rev. 11:1. Eagerly they responded, giving special study to the temple, or sanctuary. As a result, "the temple of God was opened in heaven, and there was seen in His temple the ark of His testament." Rev. 11:19. In the ark was the law of God, the Ten Commandments engraved in tables of stone, which revealed the Sabbath "according to the commandment." As time went on, further study has revealed more and more light on the sanctuary and the law of God, especially regarding the Sabbath commandment, which from the beginning of sin has been Satan's special point of attack. We are now to consider some of these truths.

The Sabbath and God's Name. "The Sabbath was set apart to be kept in honor of God's holy name." EW 33. In Bible times a name expressed character. Lucifer, which means light-bearer, was so named because he lived in and reflected the glorious light of the throne of God; when he sinned, his name was changed to Satan, the adversary, the destroyer. I Peter 5:8; Rev. 12:9. When Jacob, the supplanter, repented and prayed all night for his brother who hated him, his name was changed to Israel, one who prevails with God. Gen. 32:28. After Abram's test of faith and his victory, his name was changed to Abraham, the father of the faithful, a father of nations; Sarai's name to Sarah, a princess and mother of nations. Gen. 17:3-5; 17:15, 16. Jesus, meaning Saviour, was so named because "He shall save His people from their sins." Matt. 1:21.

Likewise, the name Jehovah is an expression of His character and power. That is why from the beginning Satan has attacked the fourth commandment, the only one of the ten that defines the name of God as the Creator. In dong so, he has attacked God's character and denies His right to rule this earth. From the time of his fall in heaven, it has been his lifelong ambition to defame the name, or character, of God by attempting to eliminate the Sabbath commandment from the heart of God's law. And this will continue to be His point of attack until at last he is cast into the lake of fire with those who have been his agents in this nefarious work. Rev. 20:10.

The Sabbath and God's Seal. A seal imparts authority and validity to a document. It contains the name of the ruling power and the territory over which he rules. In the very heart of the law of God, in the Sabbath commandment, is enshrined the name of God, expressive of His authority, and the territory over which He reigns—His name, "the Lord thy God," the Creator; His kingdom, "Heaven and earth, the sea, and all that in them is." Ex. 20:10, 11. This is God's seal with which He seals His law among His disciples. Isa 8:16.

God commemorated His work of Creation by resting on the seventh day. This made it "the Sabbath [the rest day] of the Lord thy God." "Wherefore [because of His own act of resting on this day], He blessed the Sabbath day [a special blessing given to no other day], and hallowed it [made it a holy day]." Ex. 20:9-11. Then He "sanctified it;" Gen. 2:3, that is, He set it apart from all the other days to be used for sacred purposes. No other day received this honor, God had *made* it holy and sacred; He made it not for the Jews only, nor any one class of men, but "for man," for all mankind. Mark 2:27. Then to man He said, "Remember the Sabbath day to *keep* it holy." Ex. 20:8. Every precept of God's holy law is a divine requirement for which there is no substitute, for the Holy Spirit through James says: "Whosoever shall...offend in one point; he is guilty of all...he is a transgressor of the law...the law by which all shall be judged." James 2:8-12.

The Sabbath commandment as God's seal makes the law of God "a perpetual covenant" between God and man "forever," Ex. 31:16, 17, having the authority of the Creator of heaven and earth and sea. As a seal ratifies a document, so the Creator's seal ratifies His law. Without this, none of His law would have any divine authority. Without the fourth commandment the law being without God's seal, would lose its validity.

The Holy Spirit is the instrument that stamps the seal of God on the heart. Eph. 4:30. Without this, the Sabbath loses its sacredness and becomes merely a day of physical rest and recreation—not a holy day. If we keep the Sabbath "holy," the Holy Spirit will place the seal of God upon us, and we shall have "the earnest of the Spirit in our hearts." II Cor. 1:22. The Holy Spirit is the "earnest," the pledge or the assurance, whereby we obtain our divine inheritance. No one can truly keep the Sabbath "holy" without the Holy Spirit in his heart.

The Sabbath, God's "Ensign." The Sabbath is also called God's *ensign*. Isaiah 11:10-12. An ensign is a banner, a standard, a flag, "the colors," indicating nationality. When one nation is victorious over another, the conquering nation sets up its ensign, its "colors" in the conquered territory, as evidence of its victory. If one should tear down this flag, or ensign, would the deed be passed by as of little consequence? We all know that the offender would be considered a rebel, and be severely punished, perhaps even put to death. Instead of thus disregarding the nation's banner, every loyal citizen will honor his country's flag. He will also protect it, and display it on every proper occasion. Because the Sabbath of the Decalogue points out the true God and His dominion, it is His ensign, which "He will lift up...to the nations from far." Isaiah 5:26. Shall human beings treat it without due respect and reverence?

The Ensign of the Enemy. "Thine enemies...set up their ensign for signs." Ps. 74:4. Satan, the arch enemy in the conflict between right and wrong, has set up his ensign. He would like to destroy God's seal, and thus make His law of none effect. He would like to have *his* name in the law that governs the world, thus expressing his authority to rule. Through Antichrist, that "man of sin... the son of perdition," he has trampled under foot God's holy day, he has thought to change God's law, Dan. 7:25, by substituting the first day of the week to take the place of the seventh day instituted at creation as "the Sabbath of the Lord." "And," says the prophet, "the whole earth went after the beast in wonder, worshiping the dragon [Satan, Rev. 20:2] for having given authority to the beast." Rev. 13:3, 4, *Moffatt*. Nevertheless, God's holy day still stands as a memorial of His creative power. Beware! Beware! lest *we* trample underfoot God's banner, and thus enlist under "the colors" of that great adversary, the devil!

The Sabbath, a "Sign" of Sanctification. At creation God "sanctified" the seventh day. Gen. 2:1-3. At that time, says Goodspeed, a well-known Bible translator, the Sabbath, which is the heart and strength of God's law, "was wrought into the very fabric of the universe." At Sinai, in awful grandeur, God proclaimed the Sabbath a "sign"—a sign of sanctification, saying, "Verily My Sabbaths ye shall keep: for it is a sign between Me and you throughout your generations; that ye may know that I am the Lord that doth sanctify you." Ex. 31:12-17.

How is the Sabbath a sign, a signboard, pointing to sanctification? We have already learned that sanctification is the result of three distinct experiences obtained in the holy place—study of, and obedience to, God's Word, prayer, and service for God. Anyone who has ever experienced the transition from disobedience to God's law—whether ignorant or willful—to keeping the Sabbath of the Lord, knows full well that he at once begins a more earnest study of the Scriptures, often studying far into the night to learn the truth more fully. His prayers also become more definite and earnest; and having accepted the truth into his own heart, his first thought is to serve God by helping someone else—a relative, a neighbor, or a friend—to understand that which to him has become so precious. Anyone who has never known this experience has missed one of the greatest blessings that can come into his life. And if he is to have a living, growing experience in sanctification, he will continue to study God's word more diligently, to pray more fervently, to let his light shine more faithfully. A true Sabbath keeper then, will be a thorough Bible student, a person of effectual prayer, and an untiring worker for God, one having a real soul burden for those who do not know God's truth. Thus the Sabbath becomes a *sign*, a real *signboard*, pointing to sanctification, the end of the Christian's earthly life experience, as typified in the holy place of the sanctuary.

God's Law, a Law of Love. A certain lawyer, a pharisee, designing to catch Christ in His words, once asked Him, saying, "Master, which is the great commandment of the law?" Jesus answered, "Thou shalt love the Lord thy God with all thy heart, and with all thy soul, and with all thy mind. This is the first and great commandment. And the second is like unto it, Thou shalt love thy neighbor as thyself. On these two commandments hang all the law and the prophets." Matt. 22:35-40, 46. At this the lawyer was silenced, and durst not ask Him any more questions.

God is love, and His law is embodied in the one word—LOVE. "The *first* and great commandment" of this law of supreme love to God is expressed in the first four commandments on the first table of the law, and the *second*, a "like" love to "thy neighbor," is expressed in the last six on the second table. As a result of sin, it was drawn out into ten commandments, "worded to meet the case of fallen intelligences...in consequence of the minds of men being blinded by transgression." *Signs of the Times*, April 15, 1875. "It was added because of transgression." Gal. 3:19.

How was God's law preserved and taught? "The antediluvians... had no written records; but with their great physical and mental vigor, they had strong memories, able to grasp and retain that which was committed to them, and in turn to transmit it unimpaired to their posterity." PP 83. In this way, through nine generations, covering nearly one thousand years, Adam taught his descendants the law of God. It "was preserved by Noah...[who] taught his descendants the Ten Commandments... When the Lord brought [Israel] forth from Egypt, He came down upon Sinai...and in awful majesty spoke His law in the hearing of all His people. Then, for the benefit of future generations, He engraved it in tables of stone, that it might never be forgotten. PP 363, 364. At that time, it was enshrined in the ark, the foundation of the mercy seat, a symbol of God's throne on which were two golden cherubim representing the two most exalted angels of heaven who are honored guards of His throne and His law. Later, this law of love was more fully made known through His dealings with man as recorded in the complete Bible. In fact, the Decalogue has been called "an abridged edition of the Bible," because it expresses "the whole duty of man." Eccl. 12:13.

His Law Eternal and Universal. In the eternity of the past, before this world was created, God's law of supreme love was written not in stone, but in the hearts of unfallen beings. Until sin entered the universe, these unfallen beings had no sense of the restrictions of law, for God's law is a "law of liberty." James 2:12. Those who obey law have perfect freedom, and are unconscious of its existence. "Against such there is no law," declares Paul. Only when one disobeys law does he realize its authority. So "when Satan rebelled against the law of Jehovah, the thought that there *was* a law came to the angels almost as an awakening to something unthought of." MB 109. When they discovered that sin, "the transgression of the law" I John 3:4, means death, they began to realize how terrible is transgression, and how unchangeable is God's law. The two great commandments of LOVE, on which "hang all the law and the prophets," the same law that existed in the eternity of the past, and was written in the hearts of unfallen beings, will continue to exist as the fundamental law of God's entire universe in the eternity to come. This is the law of which Christ said, "I delight to do Thy will, O My God: yea, Thy law is within My heart." Ps. 40:8. And of the redeemed, God says, "I will put My law in their inward parts, and write it in their hearts." Jer. 31:33. Paul says that even now are we to be the epistles of Christ, "written not with ink, but with the Spirit of the living God, not in tables of stone, but in fleshy tables of the heart." II Cor. 3:3. From this is it not clear that as in the eternity of the past, so in the eternity to come, the Ten Commandments in their entirety, embosomed in God's "treasure chest," His "jewel casket," is the law for God's entire universe, eternal and universal, His law for all His created intelligences throughout all ages?

God's Law Perfect. Of God's law, Paul says it is "holy, and just, and good." Rom. 7:12. It is a transcript of the character of Him who made it. David declares:

> "The law of Jehovah is perfect, converting the soul;
> The testimony of Jehovah is sure, making wise the
> simple.
>
> The statues of Jehovah are right, rejoicing the heart:
> The commandment of Jehovah is pure, enlightning
> the eyes.
>
> The fear of Jehovah is clean, enduring forever:
> The judgments of Jehovah are true and righteous
> altogether.
>
> More to be desired are they than gold, yea, than much
> fine gold:
> Sweeter also than honey and the honeycomb.
>
> Moreover by them is thy servant warned:
> And in keeping of them there is great reward."
> Ps. 19:7-11.

This inspired commentary on the law of the infinite Jehovah should forever settle its immutability in the mind of finite man.

God's Law Unchangeable. Whatever God does is perfect, and therefore cannot be changed. To change that which is perfect, would make it imperfect. An able writer has convincingly shown that the law of God is unchangeable. He says: "Consider the glory and majesty attending the broadcast of that law from the flaming mountain top! A vast retinue of holy angels was present. Millions of men and women stood at attention. Lightnings flashed; the earth trembled; and amid this signal display of infinite power, the divine Lawgiver announced the precepts that embrace the whole duty of man. Eccl. 12:13. If that law were to be changed, would a faithful allwise God alter or annul it in less impressive and conspicuous manner than when proclaimed from Sinai? Would it be done so secretly and inconspicuously that the church would be left in ignorance and uncertainty? If Christ designed to substitute Sunday for the Sabbath, would He do it so unannounced that even the chosen apostles would not hear of it until many years later? A thousand times, *no!"* Roy R. Cottrell, in *Our Times*, Dec. 1947.

Another noted writer puts it this way: "And do you think any being can change that law? —Not till he can break through the bodyguard of angels into the inner temple, dethrone Jehovah, wrench from its position the world's mercy seat of pardon and salvation, and with his would-be omnipotent finger, mutilate the records of the imperishable tables."—Uriah Smith, in *Looking Unto Jesus*, p. 321. "The law of God, being a revelation of His will, a transcript of His character, must forever endure," as a faithful witness in heaven. GC 434.

Sabbath Reform Among Sabbath Keepers. The enemy has made a "breach" in the law of God. Knowing that his time is short, he centers his attack on the Sabbath commandment, the commandment which is "the foundation of many generations." Isaiah 58:12. This same prophecy of Isaiah tells us that before Jesus comes, there is to be a reform in the matter of Sabbath observance. Nor does this apply wholly to those who do not understand, and therefore disregard, the Sabbath of the Lord. It is addressed to "My people," "the house of Jacob," those who "seek Me daily, and delight to know My ways," those who "take delight in approaching to God." To those who are looking for His soon coming, He sends a cry of alarm, saying, "Cry aloud, spare not,…show my people their transgression." Isaiah 58:1, 2. What is their transgression? They, "My people," have trampled the Sabbath underfoot. To whom does this refer? Let us check with God's standard of Sabbath keeping, and see under whose ensign we really stand.

First. "Turn away thy foot from the Sabbath, from doing thy pleasure on My holy day." Isaiah 58:13. Do we look forward to the Sabbath as a day of freedom from the ordinary cares of the week, when we may have a social time with our friends, when we may take a pleasure ride, or a hike, or an outing, or indulge in some other personal pleasure which the manifold duties of the week crowd out? Can we call such a day "the holy of the Lord?"

Second. "Turn away thy foot from the Sabbath," not "speaking thine own words." vs. 13. It is on this point that we find our greatest test. How do we line up to this test? Is our Sabbath conversation "in heaven; from whence also we look for the Saviour?" Phil. 3:20. Do we meet to exchange ideas on our week's Bible study, or some special good received from the services of the day? Do we talk about the progress of God's work in the earth? Do we review evidences of His soon coming in current events that are a fulfillment of prophecy? Or is our conversation on common, everyday, secular topics? It is easy to forego some "pleasure" on the Sabbath, but to control the tongue is a closer test of our Sabbath keeping. "Speaking thine own words!" The tongue is our unruly member. "If any man offend not in word, the same is a perfect man." James 3:2-8

How, then, can a true Sabbath keeper honor God's holy name on the Sabbath? In this same prophecy God tells us how. He says: "Undo the heavy burdens… Deal thy bread to the hungry,…bring the poor that are cast out to thy house,"…"when thou sees the naked…cover him." Isaiah 58:6, 7. "Then shalt thou call, and the Lord shall answer,"…"and the Lord shall guide thee continually."…Then "thou shalt be called the repairer of the breach, the restorer of paths to dwell in." Isaiah 58:9, 11, 12.

The Sabbath and the Judgment. We have seen that a Sabbath revival and true Sabbath reform in this hour of the Judgment is a matter of prophecy. This reform is to prepare us "to ride upon the high places of the earth," and to partake of "the heritage of Jacob." Isaiah 58:13, 14. Among Sabbath keeping Christians who are looking for the second coming of Christ in this generation there are two companies: "the church and the world." The one is "deeply interested" in spiritual things, the other is "uninterested and careless." EW 54. They say, "My Lord delayeth His coming," or, "We are rich, and increased in goods, and have need of nothing;" knowing not that they are "wretched, and miserable, and poor, and blind, and naked." Rev. 3:17. To which group do we belong?

We are now in the last hour of the Judgment. It is the hour when Isaiah's prophecy, "Seal the law among My disciples," Isaiah 8:16, is being fulfilled. It is the time when 144,000 who will be living on the earth when Jesus comes, will be sealed, "having the Father's name [His sign or signature] written in their foreheads," Rev. 14:1—reflecting His righteous character in their very countenances. No mere nominal profession will answer now. The Sabbath of the Lord is a special test,—a test of loyalty to God,—even to those who profess to be Sabbath keepers. Are we meeting the test? Or are we grieving the Holy Spirit of God "whereby" we are "sealed unto the day of redemption?" Eph. 4:30.

Israel of old failed, but now in this final Judgment hour, the Lord has "set His hand again the second time to recover the *remnant* of His people." Isaiah 11:11, 12. As the loud cry of the third angel goes forth, proclaiming the Sabbath more fully, then will be fulfilled the prophecy: "He will lift up an ensign to the nations from far," calling them to the decisive battle between truth and error, between Christ and Satan, and "they shall come with speed swiftly," Isaiah 5:26, "and build in the temple of the Lord." Zech. 6:15. Is not this the time for every true child of God to gather within the second vail, and take his stand under the ensign of Christ? Those who do this will receive the promised blessing: "Blessed are they that do His commandments, that they may have right to the tree of life, and may enter in through the gates into the City." Rev. 22:14.

CHAPTER 29 PREVIEW

BEFORE THE THRONE

- Heaven's Record Books
- Type and Antitype
- "The Judgment Is Set"
- "The Books Are Opened"
- The Judgment Seat, a Mercy Seat
- Sins, or Names, Blotted Out - Which?
- The Angel With the Golden Censer
- The Man With a Writer's Inkhorn
- The Men With Slaughter Weapons
- Christ, the Deliverer
- Duration of the Judgment
- "Get Ready!"

29

BEFORE THE THRONE

Heaven's Record Books. The Bible mentions three books, or sets of books, that are kept in the archives of the heavenly sanctuary, and were opened when the Judgment began. One of these books is called *"The Book of Life* of the Lamb slain from the foundation of the world." Rev. 13:8. This book has to do only with those who have availed themselves of the great sacrifice of the Lamb of God, and have identified themselves with "the house of God." I Peter 4:17. It is different from the other books that "were opened," which Daniel and John mention. Dan. 7:10; Rev. 20:12. John calls it "another book," and Moses called it *"Thy* book which *Thou* [God] hast written ." Ex. 32:31, 32. It is God's family record book. In it God Himself has written the names of all who from the foundation of the world, beginning with Adam, have been adopted into His family, and have entered His service. Phil. 4:3; Rev. 21:27; GC 480.

Another book, or set of books, is called the *Book of Remembrance*. This book contains a record of the good deeds of "them that feared the Lord, and that thought upon His name," those who "spake often one to another." Mal. 3:16; GC 481. This book is so called because God delights to remember every good deed. These deeds never die, therefore the book in which they are recorded has sometimes been called the Book of Life, in contrast with the Book of Death. EW 52. Each one whose name has been registered in the Book of Life has a page or pages in this book written by his guardian angel.

Another record book which our guardian angel has been compelled to write for each one, has fittingly been called the *Book of Sins* or the "Book of Death." In this book evil deeds are recorded. "Thine iniquity is marked before Me, saith the Lord God." Jer. 2:22. "Behold, it is written before Me: I…will recompense … your iniquities, and the iniquities of your fathers together, saith the Lord." Isaiah 65:6,7. "The portion which the wicked must suffer is meted out according to their works, and it is recorded against their names in the Book of Death." GC 661.

Not only the wicked but the righteous have their evil deeds recorded in their Book of Death, for "all have sinned, and come short of the glory of God," Rom. 3:23, the difference being that the righteous have repented. Their sins have gone before to judgment, I Tim. 5:24, and forgiveness has been written after each one. It is in the holy of holies, the most holy place of the heavenly sanctuary, that these books are now open—opened for examination in the court room of the universe. When the judgment of the house of God closes, every evil deed of the righteous will be blotted out, and their Book of Death will doubtless be destroyed, their evil deeds never again to be "remembered, nor come into mind." Rev. 20:12; Isaiah 65:17.

Type and Antitype. In the type, the earthly sanctuary, from day to day throughout the year sins were confessed and forgiven. "The repentant sinner brought his offering to the door of the tabernacle, and placing his hand upon the victim's head, confessed his sins, thus in figure transferring them to the innocent sacrifice. By his own hand, the animal was then slain, and the blood was carried by the priest into the holy place and sprinkled before the vail, behind which was the ark containing the law which had been transgressed." PP 354. Thus the sin was in type transferred to the sanctuary. And what was done *in type* in the ministration of the earthly sanctuary, is done *in reality* in the ministration of the heavenly sanctuary. Here, "the sins of the repentant are by faith placed upon Christ, our Sin Offering and Sin Bearer, and transferred in *fact* to the heavenly sanctuary," where they are recorded in the Book of Sins—the Book of Death. GC 420, 421.

"The Judgment Is Set." When our life in the holy place is ended, when our guardian angel has made the last entry in our Book of Remembrance and in our Book of Sins, through these life records, we approach the throne and appear before the great Judge of all the earth. Let us hope all our sins have, by repentance and reformation, gone "before to judgment," I Tim. 5:24, that our passport, sanctification, secured in the holy place, will be accepted. Neither parents nor friends can help us now. "Though Moses and Samuel stood before Me;" Jer. 15:1; "though...Noah, Daniel, and Job" are there, "they shall deliver neither son or daughter; they shall but deliver their own souls by their righteousness." Eze. 14:14, 16. We stand alone before the throne. Jesus, our Advocate, is there to plead His shed blood for all who have endured to the end. The angel witnesses are present with our life record books open, and we are "judged out of those things which are written in the books, according to [our] works." Rev. 20:12. Everyone has a case at court, and court is set. Just as truly as Christ would have given His life had there been but one soul to redeem, just so surely will He "examine the case of each individual with as close and searching scrutiny as if there were not another being upon the earth. Everyone must be tested, and found without spot or wrinkle or any such thing." GC 490.

"The Books Are Opened." From the Book of Life, "Thy book which Thou hast written," the Father, who "presides" in the Judgment, calls a name. Is it my name? Is it your name? The record of your life that has been written in the Book of Remembrance is read by the guardian angel before the Father, Christ the Judge, and the angel witnesses. Here every generous and thoughtful deed, every kind word, every tender, loving thought prompted by God and done in His name, has been faithfully registered. Every prayer offered, "every temptation resisted, every evil overcome, every word of tender pity expressed, is faithfully chronicled." GC 481. Every little act of self-sacrifice made for Jesus' sake, every trial endured for Him—every one has been written, and all will come up in remembrance before the Father when our name is called.

Also, before the angel witnesses, is opened the Book of Sins, the book of death, containing the record of all our wrong doings. In this book has been entered with terrible exactness every wrong and idle word, Matt. 12:36, 37, every selfish act, every unfulfilled duty, every secret sin, and every attempt to deceive. Unheeded warnings, neglected reproofs, wasted moments, unimproved opportunities, the influence of our example with its far-reaching results, all have been written by our recording angel. See GC 482. Are repentance and reformation written after each sin? Prov. 28:13.

The Judgment Seat, a Mercy Seat. How thankful we may be that Jesus, our Advocate, "was in all points tempted like as we are, yet without sin," Heb. 4:15. How thankful that our Father's throne is a mercy seat; that "as the heaven is high above the earth, so great is His mercy toward them that fear Him!" Ps. 103:13. He is our Father, and "like a father pitieth his children, so the Lord pitieth them that fear Him." Ps. 103:13. How our Father longs to cast all our sins behind His back, and "into the depth of the sea." Isaiah 38:17; Micah 7:19. Such are the "loving kindness and tender mercies" with which our Father crowns His own. Ps. 103:4. With this assurance, we may be certain that the Judge of all the earth will do right. Gen. 18:25.

God will take into consideration even the conditions of each one's birth. "The Lord shall count, when He writeth up the people, that this man was born there. Selah!" Ps. 87:6. Whether a follower of His was born in Egypt, Babylon, Philistia, Tyre, or Ethiopia, if he has experienced the *second* birth and has endured to the end, the Eternal writes him "in His census" as belonging to Zion "*by birth*." Ps. 87:4-6, *Moffatt*. Among the faithful, some were born in "Babylon," a synonym of rebellion against God; others were born "in Egypt," a synonym of idolatry and spiritual darkness; still others were born "in Zion," having light and truth and every spiritual advantage. Our Judge understands all this, and will act accordingly. He "seeth not as a man seeth; for man looketh on the outward appearance, but God looketh on the heart." I Sam. 16:7.

But "be not deceived; God is not mocked," Gal. 6:7, for although the Lord is "merciful and gracious, long-suffering, and abundant in goodness and truth, keeping mercy for thousands, forgiving iniquity and transgression and sin," yet He "will by no means clear the guilty." Ex. 34:6, 7. This He *cannot* do. If He should "acquit the guilty" *Moffatt*, the sacrifice of Christ would have been of no avail; everything would be lost; the whole universe would be plunged down to ruin. No, No! This can never be, for our God is just and righteous. "He will make an utter end [of sin and sorrow, of pain and death]; Affliction shall not rise up the second time." Nahum 1:9.

To backsliding Israel, God says, "I am weary of repenting." He calls not only for repentance but for a change of life. Some day His mercy will end. Then He will say, "O Jerusalem...thou art gone backward; therefore will I stretch out Mine hand against thee, and destroy thee." Jer. 15:5, 6.

Sins or Names Blotted Out—Which? David prayed, "Blot out my Transgressions," "blot out all mine iniquities." Ps. 51:1, 9. To those who denied Christ before Pilate, Peter urged, "Repent ye therefore, and be converted, that your sins may be blotted out." When? "When…He shall send Jesus Christ, which before was preached unto you." Acts 3:13, 19, 20. In his passionate soul yearning for sinful Israel, Moses prayed, "If Thou wilt forgive their sins—; and if not, blot me, I pray Thee, out of Thy book which Thou hast written." Ex. 32:32. And Jesus says "He that overcometh…I will not blot out his name out of the Book of Life, but I will confess his name before My Father, and before His angels." Rev. 3:5. "When any have sins remaining upon the books of record, unrepented of and unforgiven, their names will be blotted out of the Book of Life, and the record of their good deeds will be erased from the book of God's remembrance." GC 483.

Sins "crucify…the Son of God afresh, and put Him to an open shame." Heb. 6:6. This is a fearful fact! Nevertheless, when I sincerely repent of and confess my sin, making proper restitution, Jesus assumes the guilt and grants me forgiveness. Every sin thus confessed has gone "before to judgment." I Tim. 5:24, and is marked *forgiven* in my book of death. But the sin is not then blotted out. Like the blood record on the vail in the type, its record remains in the book in the heavenly sanctuary. After this life is ended, or my probation closes, when my name comes up in the Judgment, if I have been faithful, Jesus confirms His forgiveness, and I am granted complete and eternal absolution from sin. Then, but not till then, my sins are forever blotted out, never again to come into mind. How wonderful!

"Who is a God like unto Thee that pardoneth iniquity, and passeth by the transgression of the remnant of His heritage? Because He delighteth in mercy…He will have compassion upon us…He will cast all our sins into the depths of the sea." Micah 7:18, 19. "Into the depths of the sea" is a striking figure. As one writer says its *average* depth is about two and one half miles, while its greatest depth, near the Island of Guam, is nearly seven miles where no light ever enters. Thus our sins will not only be forgiven but forgotten, for God Himself says, "I will remember their sin no more." Jer. 31:34. Wonderful! Wonderful!

The Judgment of the dead of the house of God is now in progress, but so far as we know it has not begun on us who are living. The command to us now is not "Get ready" but "Be ready." "Be ye also ready; for in such an hour as ye think not the Son of man cometh." Matt. 24:44. Therefore it is important that day by day, before we go to sleep at night, every sin has been confessed and has gone before to judgment, and so much the more as we see the day approaching; for we know not what hour our life may be snuffed out and our probation closed.

My name or my sins—which shall be blotted out? Which shall it be for me? Which shall it be for you? A few more short years will decide. Only those enter the City of God whose names at that time "are written in the Lamb's Book of Life." Rev. 21:27. In this, our antitypical day of atonement, let us be sure that every day our sins "go before to judgment."

The saddest of all sad things in the Judgment is that some names once recorded in the Book of Life must be blotted out, an act typified by the "cutting off" from

Israel on the earthly day of atonement. The Father keeps a personal watch over every one whose name has been written in "His Book," and over whom all heaven rejoiced when as a sinner he repented. Luke 15:10. After all His years of watchfulness and loving solicitude, what grief it must cause Him when a name once recorded must be blotted out!

Some enter the Christian life, but do not endure to the end. Matt:. 10:22. Of such Ezekiel gives us this faithful picture: "When a righteous man turneth away from his righteousness, and comitteth iniquity, and dieth in them...all his righteousness that he hath done shall not be mentioned ... in his sin that he hath sinned, in them shall he die." "Again, when the wicked man turneth away from his wickedness...and doeth that which is lawful and right, he shall ... surely live, he shall not die." "Therefore...repent, and turn yourselves from all your transgressions; so iniquity shall not be your ruin. For I have no pleasure in the death of him that dieth, saith the Lord God; wherefore turn yourselves, and live ye." Eze. 18:26, 24,27,28,30,32; 33:12-20. What an appeal from the heart of the Almighty!

The Angel With the Golden Censer. There were many brazen censers, used by Israel on different occasions, Nu. 16:39, but only one golden censer. The golden censer was used only by the high priest on the day of atonement, at "the ark of the covenant," "After the second vail." Heb. 9:4, 3. On that day, after burning incense on the golden altar in the holy place, the high priest filled the golden censer with live coals from the altar. He then sprinkled incense on the coals and carried the censer into the most holy place, putting it on the mercy seat between the two golden cherubim. Lev. 16:12, 13, EW 32, 252.

When the high priest began his service in the most holy place, his ministration in the first apartment ceased—"There was no man in the tabernacle of the congregation;" that is, in the first apartment. Lev. 16:17. Likewise when Christ entered the holy of holies to perform the closing work of the atonement, "He ceased His ministration in the first apartment, but when the ministration in the first apartment ended, the ministration in the second apartment began...and He still pleaded His blood before the Father in behalf of sinners." GC 428, 429. This will continue until His ministry as Intercessor is over.

As the work of Christ the heavenly High Priest, is closing, John saw an Angel, "having a golden censer," who came to the golden altar and offered much incense with the prayers of all saints [those who afflict their souls during the Judgment hour] upon the golden altar which was before the throne. And the smoke of the incense, which came with the prayers of the saints, ascended up before God out of the Angel's hand. Rev. 8:3, 4.

What act of Christ immediately follows this His last offering of incense? "And the Angel took the censer, and filled it with fire of the altar, and cast it into the earth [where Satan bears sway]; and there were voices, and thunderings and lightnings, and an earthquake." Rev. 8:3-5. By this act, Christ declares His work as Intercessor ended. The antitypical day of atonement is past, and probation for the human family is forever closed. Mercy is no longer extended to the impenitent, and the decree goes forth, "He that is unjust, let him be unjust still; and he which is filthy, let him be filthy still; and he that is righteous, let him be righteous still; and he that is holy, let him be holy still." Rev. 22:11, 12. Then the confessed sins of *all* the righteous as well as those "which had been confessed while He [Christ] was in the most holy place, were placed upon Satan, the originator of sin, who must suffer their punishment." GC 422. Here in this earth, which he himself has made a wilderness, he will be left to roam about until at last he is destroyed. Rev. 20:1-3, 7-10. This was symbolized in the earthly sanctuary in the closing service of the day of atonement, when the high priest having finished his mediatorial work for the year, came out of the sanctuary, confessed the forgiven sins of Israel on the head of the scapegoat, and sent him into the wilderness to perish. EW 280, 281; Also GC 422.

The Man with A Writer's Inkhorn. When Christ throws down His censer, His people are left without a Mediator. EW 280. Then a man "clothed with linen, with a writer's inkhorn by his side," Eze. 9:2, is commanded to go through Jerusalem and set "a mark upon the foreheads" of those who with heart and soul have devoted their all to the service of the day of final Judgment. Eze. 9:4. What is this mark? Is it not the Father's name, Rev. 14:1, which seals His loyal children as His own? Finally the man in linen reports that done. vs. 11.

The Six Men With Slaughter Weapons. Those who have not participated in the services of the antitypical day of atonement do not receive the mark, and are cut off from Israel—subjects for the work of the angels with slaughter weapons in their hands. Eze. 9:2, 5-7. So terrible and so extensive is this work that Ezekiel fell upon his face, crying, "Ah, Lord God! wilt Thou destroy all the residue [the remnant] of Israel in Thy pouring out of Thy fury upon Jerusalem? vs. 8.

Christ, the Deliverer. When the work of intercession is over and probation has closed, at that time shall "Michael stand up, the great Prince which standeth for the children of Thy people: and there shall be a time of trouble, such as never was since there was a nation even to that same time." Dan. 12:1; GC 613. "And after these things"—after the close of the sixth seal, Rev. 6:12-17, the sealing of the 144,000 is finished. Rev. 7:1-8. "And many of them that sleep in the dust of the earth shall awake, some to everlasting life, and some to shame and everlasting contempt." Dan. 12:2. "All who have died in the faith of the third angel's message come forth from the tomb glorified, to hear God's covenant of peace with those who have kept His law." GC 637. Then the seventh seal is opened—that seal which is characterized by "silence in heaven," Rev. 8:1, because all the inhabitants of heaven have left and are accompanying Christ at His second coming to claim His redeemed. "And at that time Thy people shall be delivered, every one that shall be found written in the book"—the Book of Life. Dan. 12:1.

Duration of the Judgment. According to the prophecy of Daniel 8:14, this work of Judgment began more than one hundred years ago. Does one hundred years seem a long time? Certainly God *could* do it in less time, but let us remember that He is dealing now, not with material things as at creation—water, and earth, and air—but with the souls of those who were created in His own image and whom His Son died to redeem. Moreover, Satan must have no excuse to say that God was partial or that He acted unjustly. O no! Beginning with the patriarchs, all whose names have ever been written in the Book of Life are called, one by one. "Every name is mentioned, every case closely investigated." GC 483. Have all their sins been confessed? Have their sins gone before to judgment? Have they "endured unto the end" of their lives? If so, Jesus confesses their names before the Father, Matt. 10:32; Luke 11:8, all their mistakes and failures are forever blotted out, and their names are retained in the Lamb's Book of Life. Rev. 3:5.

For such a work is one hundred years a long time? In one hundred years there are 876,600 hours. If an average of half an hour is allowed for each case, only 1,753,200 cases could be considered, sins blotted out, and names confessed by Christ before the Father, or names and good deeds blotted out, and sins retained. A much longer time, one thousand years, will be given to the judgment of the wicked. Rev. 20:4, 6.

"Get Ready!" The Sands of time are now nearly run out. When the cases of the righteous dead have all been considered, Judgment will begin on the living. Then your case and mine will come in review before Jehovah, the Ancient of Days. How thankful we can be that Jesus is now pleading for His people, "not as a petitioner to move the Father to compassion, but as a conqueror who claims the trophies of His victory." GW 154. When the Judgment of the righteous living is completed, the blotting out of sin will be finished, the "household of God" will be made up, Eph. 2:19, and Jesus will come to take His children to their eternal home. John 14:3. "The great day of the Lord is near, it is near, and hasteth greatly." Zeph. 1:14. Am I ready? Are you ready? "Get ready! Get ready! Get ready!" is Heaven's appeal to us today. EW 64-67; 119.

The Judgment is set, the books have been opened,
How shall we stand in that great day,
When every thought, and word, and action,
God, the righteous Judge, shall weigh?

How shall we stand in that great day?
How shall we stand in that great day?
Shall we be found before Him wanting?
Or with our sins all washed away?
—*F. E. Belden*

CHAPTER 30 PREVIEW

THE TABERNACLE SET UP AND ANOINTED

- The Camp at Sinai
- The Tabernacle Finished
- An Awe-Inspiring Procession
- Moses Inspects the Work
- Setting Up the Tabernacle
- Placing the Furniture
- The Holy Anointing Oil
- The Tabernacle and the Priests Anointed
- The Antitype of this Anointing
- God Dwells Among His People

30

THE TABERNACLE SET UP AND ANOINTED

The Camp at Sinai. "The order so strikingly displayed in all the works of God was manifest in the Hebrew economy." "Even before they left Egypt... the people were arranged in companies, under appointed leaders. At Sinai the arrangements for organization were completed." Ed. 37. Here, the people were grouped according to their tribes around an open space in which Moses and Aaron camped. On the east side of this court were the three tribes of Judah, on the south the three tribes of Reuben, on the west the three tribes of Ephraim, and on the north the three tribes of Dan. Num. 2:3, 10, 18, 25. To Moses in this open space the people brought their gifts for building the sanctuary, and here, under his supervision and the instruction of teachers chosen by God, all its parts were constructed. Thus located, the tribes could follow the progress of the work.

The Tabernacle Finished. From careful consideration of the events that occurred after Israel left Egypt several months elapsed from the time they began to build until the work was finished. This was truly a great accomplishment, impossible without God, for "Except the Lord build the house, they labor in vain that build it." Ps. 127:1. During the next few months the laws that were to govern the nation, including those concerning offerings and sacrifices as recorded in the book of Leviticus, were carefully explained. At last, one year from the time the people left Egypt, Ex. 12:2, and about ten months after they came "into the wilderness of Sinai," on the first day of the first month, Ex. 40:2; the tabernacle was set up. Ex. 40:17. In the mount God had showed Moses not only all the parts of the sanctuary, but also just where they were to be placed "Thou shalt rear up the tabernacle according to the fashion thereof which was showed thee in the mount." Ex. 26:30.

An Awe-Inspiring Procession. "And they brought the tabernacle unto Moses." Ex. 39:33. Bezaleel of the tribe of Judah with his assistants in gold and silver and brass, in cutting of stones, and in carving of timber, brought their work which they had faithfully and skillfully and accurately done. And Aholiab of the tribe of Dan with his assistants which did the engraving, the embroidering and the weaving for all the hangings, the coverings, and the priests' garments, came with the finished products of their labors. This surely must have made a most awe-inspiring procession. Let us endeavor to get a mental picture of the scene.

Following somewhat the order as given for the line of march when the people left Sinai, Bezaleel with his helpers come first carrying the sacred ark glittering with gold. Ex. 40:3. Next comes the mercy seat with its two cherubim of solid gold, their wings reaching above the heads of its carriers. Others bring the forty-eight boards, carved with cherubim and "heavily plated" with pure gold, each massive plank weighing about eight hundred pounds, and requiring the service of a number of men. Next are the fifteen golden bars, and one hundred solid silver sockets each weighing a talent, 200 pounds. Then come the nine golden pillars for the vail and the door. With these are the sixty shining brass pillars for the court, each crowned with silver and requiring a number of carriers. Others come with the sixty-five brass sockets for the court wall and the door, the brass pins, the cords, and the gold and brass vessels for the service of the sanctuary.

Aholiab with his helpers follow, bringing the blue and purple and scarlet vail, door, gate, and the inner covering of the tabernacle with its hundred gold taches, each resplendent with rich embroidery in pure gold thread. Others bring the white goats' hair covering, measuring at least 45 by 66 feet, with its one hundred brass taches, the covering of red rams' skins, and the covering of brown badgers' skins; also the four hundred twenty feet of white linen court hangings.

Others of Aholiab's trusty workers bring the white linen garments of the priests and the gorgeous garments of Aaron—the white linen coat with its exquisite tessellated embroidery, the sky blue robe with its border of tinkling gold bells and bright colored pomegranates, the wonderfully gold embroidered ephod with its shoulder clasps of engraved onyx stones and its elaborately embroidered girdle. Another carries the breastplate, its twelve precious stones glistening like diamonds and magnifying the names of the twelve tribes engraved upon it, EW 251, while another carries the holy crown with its plate of pure gold bearing the inscription, "HOLINESS TO THE LORD."

Following these are the golden altar of incense, the golden table, the candlestick of solid beaten gold, each borne by consecrated, trusty workmen. And lastly a number of Bezaleel's faithful carriers, bringing the shining brazen altar at least seven and one-half feet square and four and one-half feet high, and the laver with his foot, both of polished brass, which like mirrors reflect everything around them. This was indeed a most brilliant and colorful procession.

Moses Inspects the Work. "Moses did look upon all the work, and behold, they had done it as the Lord had commanded." Ex. 39:43. "A formal inspection was made to ascertain whether it was made 'according to the pattern.' The result of a careful and minute survey showed that every plank, curtain, and article of furniture had been most accurately made as designed by the Divine Architect." JF&B Com. "And Moses blessed them," Ex. 39:43,—perhaps the same blessing, or a similar one, that the Lord later commanded Aaron to pronounce upon Israel:

> "The Lord bless thee, and keep thee,
> The Lord make His face shine upon thee;
> And be gracious unto thee;
> The Lord lift up His countenance upon thee,
> And give thee peace." Num. 6:22-27.

Setting Up the Tabernacle. "On the first day of the first month," Ex. 40:2, 17, Moses, following the explicit directions of the Lord, set up the tabernacle. First, the boards were raised up, set in their sockets, the bars put in them, and the pillars for the vail and the door erected. Thus the walls, securely fastened to the two corner boards, were "held firm." PP 347. Next the four coverings were spread above this framework, Ex. 40:18, 19; first, the richly embroidered royal covering, then the white goats' hair covering, the taches of both these coverings being directly above the second vail. Next above these were the red ram's skins and the brown badger skin coverings.

Placing the Furniture. When the structure was ready for the furniture, Moses reverently put the tables of the testimony into the ark—the same tables that God had given him when he was in the mount; the staves, which were never to be removed, he placed in their rings, covered it with the mercy seat, and it was brought into the tabernacle. Then the second, or inner vail, was hung on its four golden pillars. It was hung "under the taches" which divided "between the holy place and the most holy." Ex. 26:33. Following this, he set the golden table on the north side of the holy place, and arranged the bread and the dishes in order upon it. On the south side, "without the vail of the testimony, in the tabernacle of the congregation," Lev. 24:3, he put the candlestick and supplied the lamps with oil. Ex. 40:25. Before the inner vail he placed the golden altar, and put incense upon it, vs. 27. Then the door—the outer vail—was hung on its five pillars, thus completing the furnishing of the sanctuary proper. Ex. 40:22-28.

In the center of the court before the sanctuary, was placed the brazen altar, and between the altar and the door of the tabernacle, the laver and his foot. Into the laver water was poured, and Moses, Aaron, and his sons washed their hands and their feet thereat. Lastly, the brazen court pillars were raised up, on which were hung the court hangings and the gate. "So Moses finished the work," and it was done "as the Lord had commanded." Ex. 40:29-33.

The Holy Anointing Oil. As the shewbread and the sweet incense each containing *four* ingredients, represented Christ, so also the holy anointing oil consisted of *four* sweet spices pointed to Christ. These spices were pure myrrh, an odorous resin or liquid which exudes from a tree that grows in Arabia; sweet cinnamon, the aromatic substance produced from the inner bark of the sweet gum imported chiefly from Ceylon; sweet calamus, a reed-like plant, a native of India, and of remarkable fragrance; cassia, a sweet spicy herbaceious plant grown in Arabia and India. These spices weighing about 48 pounds [*Moffatt*] were compounded in an hin [1-1/2 gal., *Moffatt*] of olive oil. Ex. 30:23-25, thus making sufficient for anointing the priests and the sanctuary. The olive oil representing the Holy Spirit, and the *four* fragrant spices symbolizing Christ, being "compounded" indicates the close cooperation of Christ and His representative, the Holy Spirit. This accounts for the warning given against compounding any like it or using it for any common purpose, under penalty of being cut off from Israel. Ex. 30:31-33.

The Tabernacle and the Priests Anointed. "And thou shalt take the anointing oil, and anoint the tabernacle of the congregation; [that is, the holy place], and all that is therein," "and the ark of the testimony," "and the altar of burnt offering with all his vessels, and the laver and his foot." Aaron and his sons were also anointed. Ex. 30:26-30. Aaron, dressed in his holy garments, was anointed high priest. Upon his head the oil was "poured," so that it ran down his beard and his garments. His sons and their garments were "sprinkled" with the holy oil. Ps. 133:2; Ex. 29:4-9, 21.

In connection with their anointing another service formed part of the consecration of the priests. As God in the Garden of Eden offered the first sacrifice, foreshadowing the Sacrifice that later was made on Calvary, so Moses, who by Divine appointment was as God to Aaron, Ex. 4:16, offered the first sacrifice, the "ram of consecration." Ex. 29:15, 22. When he killed the ram, he took "of his blood and put it upon the tip of the right ear of Aaron, and upon the tip of the right ear of his sons and upon the thumb of their right hand, and upon the great toe of their right foot." Ex. 29:20; Lev. 8:22-24. This signified complete consecration of ears, hands, and feet. Moses then placed the "whole ram upon the altar: it was a burnt sacrifice for a sweet savour." Lev. 8:21. As it was placed on the brazen altar there "came a fire out from before the Lord, and consumed the sacrifice…which when all the people saw, they shouted, and fell upon their faces." Lev. 9:24. Thus God expressed His acceptance of the work and the consecration of Israel. This fire kindled by God, was never to go out. Lev. 6:13. Likewise, God will accept the service of every ambassador who is fully consecrated, and the influence of such service will never die—their works will follow them. Rev. 14:13.

To complete the service of this inauguration day, Moses carried coals from the brazen altar to the altar of incense and burned incense upon it, and with this fire he lighted the lamps of the candlestick. Ex. 40:25-27.

The Antitype of This Anointing. The setting up and anointing of the earthly sanctuary was a type of the setting up and anointing of the heavenly sanctuary, "the most holy," which took place at the ascension of Christ, and which Gabriel explained to Daniel. Dan. 9:21, 24. The anointing of Aaron as high priest and of his sons as associate priests was their inauguration for holy office. It was a type of the anointing of Christ as heavenly High Priest at His inauguration and of His followers, Acts 2, and of all the redeemed—those who have "part in the first resurrection" and who "shall be priests of God and of Christ." Rev. 20:6. As the service in the earthly sanctuary could not begin until it was anointed and until the "ram of consecration" had been offered, so the service in the heavenly sanctuary did not begin until "the most holy" was anointed, Dan. 9:24, and Christ had been sacrificed on Calvary and received the anointing of the Holy Spirit at His inauguration. Then, and not till then, "the way into the holiest of all was made manifest." Heb. 9:6.

When the tabernacle had been erected and the consecration service was completed, all that God commanded Moses had been done. What next?

God Dwells Among His People. On this inauguration day, while the people—a vast assembly—were drawn up in calm and orderly arrangement around the newly erected tabernacle, "contemplating the scene with reverent satisfaction," all eyes were suddenly directed toward the summit of Mount Sinai. Here "a cloud," Ex. 40:34—literally "the" cloud—the familiar cloud which had guided them from Egypt to Sinai and which was to them a symbol of the divine presence, appeared to be in motion. "If many among them had a secret misgiving about the issue, how would the fainting heart revive, the interest of the moment intensely increase and the tide of joy swell in every bosom, when the symbolic cloud was seen slowly and majestically descending toward the plain below, and enveloping the tabernacle!" Ex. 40:34, and in majestic splendor it passed into the interior of the most holy place, and rested between the cherubim of the mercy seat. From that moment the ark was sacredly hidden from common view within the most holy place. Even Moses, in overwhelming awe, stood aloof and was not able to enter the tabernacle. See JF&B Com. on Ex. 40:34, 35; PP 349.

Inauguration day, a day never to be forgotten, was drawing to a close, and Israel quietly and reverently retired to their camp. The Father's heartlonging, "Let them make me a sanctuary; that I may dwell among them," Ex. 25:8, was realized.

SECTION VI

THE CHURCH IN THE SANCTUARY

CHAPTER 31 PREVIEW

THE CHURCH OF THE COURT—
THE HEBREW CHURCH

- The Four Generations of the Church
- The Hebrew Church Organized
- The First Pentecost the Birthday of the Hebrew Church
- The Oracles of God
- The Mission of the Hebrew Church
- Their Failure
- God's Plan Finally to Be Carried Out

31

THE CHURCH OF THE COURT—
THE HEBREW CHURCH

The Four Generations of the Church. In preceding sections it has been shown that Christ in the various phases of His redemptive work is symbolized in the sanctuary. It has also been shown that the sanctuary illustrates individual Christian experience. The present section is to consider how it represents the church as a whole. God calls His church "a chosen generation." I Peter 2:9. This title applies to the church in all ages, during which time it has four successive "generations" or divisions—the Hebrew generation of the church, the Christian generation, the Remnant generation, and the church of the Firstborn. How are these generations illustrated in the sanctuary?

First, the Hebrew generation of the church, whose sacrifices in the court symbolized Christ. But although for centuries these sacrifices were offered day after day, yet because they were "not...mixed with faith" Heb. 4:2, their significance was finally lost. As a result, when Christ came to this earth, the church did not recognize Him as the true Sacrifice, and consequently when He ascended, they refused to follow Him by faith into the holy place of the sanctuary above. They continued to offer their now meaningless sacrifices in the court. This church, then, is the *church of the court*.

Second, the Christian church. After the death of Christ, this church accepted Him, not only as the true Sacrifice but as their crucified, risen, and ascended Lord. By faith, they left the court and entered with Him into the holy place of the heavenly sanctuary where He was anointed heavenly High Priest. This church may therefore be called *the church of the holy place*.

Third, the Remnant church, the last generation of the church on earth, not only accept Christ as their Sacrifice and their High Priest in the holy place above, but by faith they enter with Him into the most holy place of the heavenly sanctuary, where He now acts as Judge. This church may therefore be called *the church of the most holy place*.

Fourth, the church of the firstborn, the church of the finally redeemed. This church by faith follow their Lord all the way from His sacrificial life in the court of earth, through His work as High Priest in the holy place above, and as Judge in the most holy place, till they "come...unto the city of the living God, the heavenly Jerusalem, and to an innumerable company of angels, to the general assembly and church of the Firstborn." Heb. 12:22, 23. This church, having its place of worship forever in the temple eternal in the New Jerusalem, may be called *the church of the temple eternal*.

These four generations of the church should not be confused with the seven churches of Revelation, symbolized by the seven-branched candlestick. These seven divisions of the church cover only the Christian era, while the four generations now to be considered extend from the time God organized the first church at Sinai to the last church—the church of the Firstborn—the finally redeemed in heaven.

Let us now look at each of these four generations of the church, noticing their beginning, their special mission, their peculiar experiences, and how a correct and spiritual understanding of the sanctuary could have saved them from error, and guided them forward and upward.

The Hebrew Church Organized. When God called Abram away from his kindred, who were idolatrous descendants of the builders of the tower of Babel, His promise was, "I will make of thee a great nation, and I will bless thee, and make thy name great; and thou shalt be a blessing." Gen. 12:1, 2. In this blessing was wrapped up the promise of the Saviour—the same promise that had first been given to Adam in Eden. Gen. 3:15. About 1500 B.C., this "great nation" was divinely led out of Egypt to Sinai, where, under the personal direction of God Himself, the Hebrew church was organized. It was the first regularly organized church on this earth. Previous to this time, the worship of God had been conducted by each patriarch for his own household. The descendants of the patriarchs, to whom the promise of redemption had first been given, comprised the membership of this church.

The first step in the organization of the Hebrew church was the giving of a "constitution," a fundamental law which expressed "the whole duty of man," and by which all should be guided. From the top of Mount Sinai, amid most awe-inspiring scenes and in the hearing of all the people assembled in the plain below, God with His own voice proclaimed the *constitution* for His church. This was the very same law that throughout the eternity of the past had guided the universe, and which would continue to be a guide for all the future. The constitution of an earthly government may be amended because finite human beings cannot see the end from the beginning, and their work may therefore be defective. But the "constitution" of God's government cannot be amended because, being infinite, "whatsoever God doeth, it shall be forever. Nothing can be put to it, nor anything taken from it: and God doeth it, that men should fear before Him." Eccl. 3:14.

The First Pentecost the Birthday of the Hebrew Church. God spoke His law from Sinai on the fiftieth day from the "morrow after" Israel ate the first Passover, Lev. 23:15, 16, when they were delivered from Egypt. The day was then named *Pentecost*, a word meaning *fiftieth*. This first Pentecost was the birthday of the Hebrew church.

The Oracles of God. God gave the Hebrew church every "advantage"—"Much every way," but "chiefly, because that unto them were committed the oracles of God." Rom. 3:1,2. An oracle is defined as a revelation of the will of a deity. To the Hebrew church the Divine Deity gave a revelation of *His* will when He spoke His law from Sinai, and anyone desiring to know the will of this Deity will find it only by consulting His law—His oracle. That this oracle might not be lost sight of, God Himself with His own finger engraved it in tables of stone. That its sacredness might be most deeply impressed on His people, it was enshrined in the ark in the most holy place of the sanctuary, directly beneath the Shekinah, the visible symbol of the presence of the Deity, and overshadowed by two angels of beaten gold, representing the "shining guardians"—guards of honor—for His throne and His holy law. PP 357. This law together with divine revelations from the Shekinah and from the urim and the thummim in the breastplate worn by the high priest, composed the "oracles" of God.

The Hebrew church was the only organization on earth that had a knowledge of the true God or of His divine law which, in the fourth or Sabbath commandment, distinguishes Him above all gods, as the Creator of "heaven and earth, the sea, and all that in them is." Ex. 20:10, 11. It was this knowledge of the true deity and His law that gave the Jew the "advantage" over every other nation. Rom. 3:2, 1. All others, because they knew not the Creator, because they knew not His oracle, were idol worshipers "having no hope, and without God in the world." Eph. 2:12. With a heart observance of the Sabbath of God's law—an institution commemorative of the Creator and His creative work—there never could have been an idol worshiper.

The Mission of the Hebrew Church. To each generation of the church, God has given a special assignment toward carrying the everlasting gospel to the world. The task, the high and holy privilege, of the Hebrew church was to teach the idolatrous nations around them of the true and living God that inhabiteth eternity, and of the holy and just and eternal character of His law, His oracle.

In their deliverance from Egypt, God executed judgment not against the people, but "against all the gods of Egypt," Ex. 12:12, and thus the Israelites had seen the utter helplessness of false gods; they had experienced the mighty power of the true God, the One who had delivered them in time of need. At Sinai they had witnessed His glory in the proclamation of His law, the fourth commandment of which identifies Him as the true God, the Creator. All this was intended to help them realize the importance and the seriousness of their mission.

That they might have still further "advantage," they were given as their home the land of Canaan, the cross roads of the nations, where they would be constantly in touch with those whom they were to help. All through the twenty-five hundred years of the supremacy of the Hebrew church, special emphasis was placed upon the Sabbath of God's law, as evidence that He who created the world is the only true God, and that therefore heart obedience to His law is a necessary passport to heaven. The same eternal passport will be required of every succeeding generation of the church, for only "they that do His commandments...may have right to the tree of life, and may enter in through the gates into the City." Rev. 22:14.

Their Failure. Instead of living up to their privileges, and teaching the idolatrous nations of the Creator and His law, the Hebrew church gradually mingled unlawfully with them, and as a result, many themselves disregarded the Sabbath, the sign of the true God and the seal of His law. In doing this they rejected the Creator and became an easy prey to the worship of idols. They lost sight of the truths which the sanctuary represented, and its services finally became to them an empty form. To such an extent was this true that instead of looking for a Deliverer from sin as represented in the sanctuary, their desire and hope was for a mighty conqueror who would deliver them from the oppression of surrounding nations. Therefore, when the true Deliverer came, not as a powerful earthly king, but as a helpless Babe of Bethlehem, they did not recognize Him as the One to whom the sanctuary and its services pointed. "He came unto His own, and His own received Him not." John 1:11.

Having rejected Christ when He entered the court of earth, they at last crucified Him, the very One who alone could have been their Deliverer. Even when, at the moment of His death, the inner vail of the temple was rent from the top to the bottom by an unseen hand, their hearts were so hardened that they saw no connection between the rent vail and His torn and bleeding "flesh." The rent vail indicated that the work of the earthly sanctuary was ended. In the death of Christ the earthly sanctuary with its services had met its antitype, and the heavenly sanctuary was about to take its place. Having rejected Christ in His humanity, when He rose from the dead and ascended to begin His work as High Priest in the holy place above, they refused to accept Him as their High Priest and Mediator. Although for a time the earthly priests continued to offer their now useless sacrifices in the court, their worship was meaningless and vain. A spiritual understanding of the sanctuary would have saved them from their errors and consequent defeat, but having lost that, the Hebrew church, as the organized representative of God on earth, was at an end.

God's Plan Finally To Be Carried Out. To the Hebrew church God had given the promise, "If ye…hallow the Sabbath day, to do no work therein; then shall there enter into the gates of this city [Jerusalem] kings and princes sitting upon the throne of David… and this city shall remain forever." Jer. 17:24, 25; II Chron 33:4. But because Israel desecrated the Sabbath and went into idolatry with the nations around them, another prophecy was fulfilled: "But if ye will not hearken unto Me to hallow the Sabbath day, then will I kindle a fire in the gates thereof, and it shall devour the palaces of Jerusalem, and it shall not be quenched." Jer. 17:27. Nevertheless, God's plan that Jerusalem shall stand forever, will be carried out, not on this sinful earth, but in the heavenly Jerusalem where the seventh day, "the Sabbath of the Lord," Ex. 20:10, will be reverenced and observed throughout eternity by those who "enter in through the gates into the city" of God. Isaiah 66:23; Rev. 22:14.

THE CHURCH OF THE HOLY PLACE—
THE CHRISTIAN CHURCH

- Organization of the Christian Church
- The Last Pentecost of the Birthday
  of the Christian Church
- The Mission of the Christian Church
- The Call to Come Out of the Hebrew Church
- The Price of Loyal Obedience and Service
- "A Falling Away"
- The Work of Antichrist—"the Daily"
- The Power of Antichrist Broken
- The Third Generation of the Church Due

32

THE CHURCH OF THE HOLY PLACE—
THE CHRISTIAN CHURCH

Organization of the Christian Church. The church of the court was gone, but at the last Passover, while Christ was still on earth, He Himself laid the foundation of the Christian church; the church of the holy place. "It was God who gave to them the name of Christian. This is a royal name, a 'worthy name' [James 2:7], given to all who join themselves to Christ." "The disciples were called Christians first at Antioch." Acts 11:26. The first step in the organization of the Christian church was taken when Christ ordained the Twelve, "that they should be with Him, and that He might send them forth to preach." Mark 3:14; AA 18. It was continued when at the last—the Passover eaten by Jesus with the twelve—He instituted the Lord's Supper to take the place of the Passover. It was completed at the last Pentecost when, as the church "were all with one accord in one place," Christ sent His representative, the Holy Spirit, to "the whole congregation," of believers, the number of whom at the time being "about an hundred and twenty." Acts 1:15. These may therefore be called the charter members of the Christian church.

The Last Pentecost, the Birthday of the Christian Church. This pentecostal experience showed the disciples that although the heavenly sanctuary and the ministration of our High Priest are invisible to us, yet "while Jesus ministers in the sanctuary above, He is still by His Spirit [His representative] the minister of the church on earth." DA 166. Therefore, the disciples did not at once enter upon their mission, because Jesus had told them to "wait" for the Spirit. Acts 1:4; John 14:16, 17. Fifty days after the Passover Jesus ate, and about ten days after the ascension, as they were assembled in "the house" [an upper room] in Jerusalem on the day of Pentecost, Acts 2:2; 1:13, 14, they received the gift of the Holy Spirit, Christ's representative, and were thus set apart to carry forward the work of God.

As the manifestation of the power of God when He through Christ spoke His law from Sinai on the *first* Pentecost—fifty days after the first Passover—marked the birthday of the Christian church. This Pentecostal experience pointed the disciples from the earthly sanctuary to the heavenly where Jesus had gone, and they understood that the heavenly sanctuary had succeeded the earthly.

It was because the Jews rejected the Messiah that they did not understand the change in the sanctuary service from earth to heaven, and therefore they could not receive the pentecostal blessing, nor could they be benefited by the mediation of Christ in the holy place of the sanctuary above. Only those who by faith followed Him from the earthly to the heavenly sanctuary, could be benefited by His work of atonement for man.

The Mission of the Christian Church. The same commission that Christ had given to the Hebrew church, He now gave to His disciples—the Christian church; "Go ye…and teach all nations…to observe all things whatsoever I have commanded you," "beginning at Jerusalem." Matt. 28:19; Luke 24:47; Mark 16:15. The Christian church was built upon the same foundation as was the Hebrew church. Though the Hebrew had failed, God had not changed. His eternal law remained, Christ Himself declaring: "I am not come to destroy [the law], but to fulfil… Till heaven and earth pass, one jot or one tittle shall in no wise pass from the law, till all be fulfilled." Matt. 5:17, 18. Christ was "a perfect fulfillment of God's law." MH 456. The early Christian church accepted this without question, as all must do who truly believe in God as the Creator. They picked up the golden chain of truth where the Hebrew church had lost it, and went a step further proclaiming faith in Christ as their crucified, risen, and ascended Lord.

Paul made clear the relation of these two generations of the church when he said, "Do we then make void the law through faith? God forbid: Yea, we establish the law." Rom. 3:31. In this Paul recognized the truth that "faith without obedience is presumption." As long as God is Creator, His law cannot fail. Should one jot or one tittle be done away, all true worship of the Creator would automatically cease, and all the world would revert to the worship of idols. This truth is axiomatic. No need for the Christian church to emphasize the obligation of the law, for that was at once self-evident and obvious. Their special mission was to proclaim faith in a crucified, risen, and ascended Saviour.

The Call to Come Out of the Hebrew Church. The preaching of the gospel of a crucified, risen, and ascended Lord was to begin at Jerusalem. Luke 24:47. On the day of Pentecost the apostles had been given "tongues like as of fire," Acts 2:3, and through this zeal of the Spirit-filled apostles thousands of the honest in heart responded to the call to come out of the new fallen Hebrew church. Among others, the great and learned apostle Paul left the Hebrew church and threw all his talents and power into preaching the gospel of a crucified, risen, and ascended Lord. "I determined," he said, "not to know anything among you, save Jesus Christ, and Him crucified." I Cor. 2:2.

Although the divine presence had left the earthly sanctuary, God in His tender mercy gave the Jews three and one-half years longer, till the end of the seventy weeks in A.D. 34, Dan. 9:27, to turn to Christ, their ascended Lord and Redeemer. Even then, though the Hebrew church as the divinely organized representative of God on earth was at an end, God continued to plead with the people. One of the longest epistles of Paul is his epistle to the Hebrews, in which with all the eloquence of the learned man that he was, and with the power of the Holy Spirit resting upon him, he explained the work of the heavenly sanctuary and of Christ as High Priest.

The Price of Loyal Obedience and Service. Did all this labor and loyalty cost anything? Listen again to the words of Paul: "Are they Hebrews? So am I. Are they ministers of Christ (I speak as a fool) I am more; in labors more abundant, in stripes above measure, in prisons more frequent, in deaths oft. Of the Jews five times received I forty stripes save one. Thrice was I beaten with rods, once was I stoned, thrice I suffered shipwreck, a night and a day I have been in the deep; in journeyings often, in perils of waters, in perils of robbers, in perils by mine own countrymen, in perils by the heathen, in perils in the city, in perils in the wilderness, in perils in the sea, in perils among false brethren; in weariness and painfulness, in watchings often, in hunger and thirst, in fastings often, in cold and nakedness. Beside those things that are without, that which cometh upon me daily, the care of all the churches." II Cor. 11:22-28. Did these things discourage Paul? Listen again to that mighty champion of the Christian faith: "None of these things move me, neither count I my life dear unto myself, so that I might finish my course with joy,…to testify the gospel of the grace of God." Acts 20:24.

Not only Paul, but many a faithful witness for Christ met a martyr's death. John the Baptist was beheaded in a loathsome dungeon. James was killed with the sword, Stephen was stoned, Peter was crucified head downward. John the apostle and revelator was exiled to the lonely Isle of Patmos. But none of them faltered in their labors of love, or proved untrue to their sacred trust.

"A Falling Away." History repeats itself. As the Hebrew church lost their vision of the divine meaning of the sanctuary and its services, and formed alliances with the heathen world around them, so in the Christian church there came "a falling away," and "that man of sin" was revealed, "the son of perdition." II Thess. 2:3. Paul, even in his day, says, this "mystery of iniquity doth already work." II Thess 2:7.

For centuries after the early apostles had done their mighty work for God, the church continued to teach the obligation of God's law. Even today the creeds of practically all Christian sects express absolute confidence in the binding claims of the Ten Commandments as given to Israel.

Faith in Christ as the Son of God, the Saviour of the world, was the great burden of the preaching of the apostles. But as time went on even this fundamental truth degenerated into the blind teaching: "Faith, only have faith." To such an unbalanced and meaningless extent was this carried, that obedience to the eternal law of God was well nigh lost sight of. The Hebrew generation of the church failed because their sacrifices were "not mixed with faith," Heb, 4:2; on the tombstone of the fallen Christian generation of the church is written, "Faith, if it hath not works, is dead." James 2:17.

Foreseeing the dangers of the church, God through John left the warning, "Love not the world, neither the things that are in the world. If any man love the world, the love of the Father is not in him. For … the lust of the flesh, and the lust of the eyes, and the pride of life…is of the world…. As ye have heard that antichrist shall come, even now are there many antichrists." I John 2:15-18. "Many deceivers are entered into the world, who confess not that Jesus Christ is come in the flesh. This is…antichrist." II John 7.

The Work of Antichrist — "the Daily." In Daniel 7:8 and 8:9, this power is called "the little horn." It is a development of the "dreadful and terrible" beast of Daniel 7:7, which was revealed to the prophet in vision and which Protestants agree symbolizes the papacy. Because "Satan...the arch deceiver, hates the great truths that bring to view an atoning Sacrifice and an all-powerful Mediator," GC 488—truths symbolized in the sanctuary, — power described in Daniel 8:9-13 directed his wrath against the sanctuary. "By him the daily was taken away, and the place of his sanctuary was cast down." vs. 11.

As already noted, the Hebrew word here translated "daily" is the same word as is translated "continual," "perpetual," and "continually" in Numbers 4:7; Exodus 30:8, and Leviticus 24:2, where the services at the golden table, the altar of incense, and the candlestick are set forth, each of which points to Christ; Also the "continual burnt offering" of the lamb morning and evening on the brazen altar, represented Christ.

This little horn "swelled high" [*Moffatt*] and "cast down some...of the stars to the ground, and stamped upon them." [AV] vs. 10. Moffatt continuing, says: "It even magnified itself to match the Prince of the starry host, and deprived Him of the daily sacrifice [in the court, and of the daily in the holy place], demolishing the place of His sanctuary [that great object lesson of salvation through Christ, which is "the key to the whole treasure-house of God's Word." Ed. 126]. Thus was the daily profanely treated, the true religion was beaten down, and the horn practiced and prospered in his career." Dan. 8:10-12. How long was this blasphemous work to continue? The prophecy declares, "Unto 2300 days [which ended in 1844], then shall the sanctuary be cleansed;" [Hebrew, restored to its rightful position]. Dan. 8:14. Is it any wonder that when Daniel, with his sacred regard for the sanctuary, understood the vision and learned that this work against high Heaven and against the people of God on earth would continue for nearly 2500 years from his day,—is it any wonder that he "fainted, and was sick certain days?" Dan. 8:27.

How is it that this "man of sin...the son of perdition," II Thess 2:3, practiced and prospered in his career? It was because a study and understanding of the sanctuary had been neglected or lost sight of. Let us beware lest the "sly tricks" of the devil deprive *us* of the blessings which a study of the sanctuary invitingly holds out.

This same little horn has not only "profanely treated" the daily sacrifice *in the court*, and the daily services *in the holy place* of the sanctuary, with the intent to "cast down the truth," to "demolish" the true religion symbolized in the sanctuary, but he has even entered the *most holy place*, where no one but the high priest was ever allowed, and boldly declared that the law of God [located in the ark] is subject to *his* authority, that the Sabbath of the Lord containing the seal which validates His law is done away, and his own seal, the observance of Sun-day [the first day of the week] has taken its place. By this act, he has turned the attention of the church away from the Creator memorialized in the Sabbath commandment, to that base idol—the god of the sun, "and" says John, "all the world wondered after the beast." Rev. 13:3—"went after the beast in wonder…worshiping the beast." *Moffatt*.

The horn not only "thought to change the times and the law," RSV, of the Most High, Dan. 7:25, but he treacherously introduced other errors into the Christian church. He substituted sprinkling or pouring for baptism by immersion, a symbol of the death, burial, and resurrection of Christ, which John the Baptist administered and which Christ Himself experienced "to fulfill all righteousness." Matt. 3:15. Contrary to the Word of God, this "man of sin" has even counterfeited the priesthood of Christ, declaring that *he* has power to forgive sin and that confession should be made to *him*. He taught the people that man is immortal, and that therefore all sinners must suffer eternal torment as a punishment for sin. He taught them that the living might hold communion with the dead. These and many other doctrines, entirely contrary to the pure teachings of the Word of God, were slyly introduced into the Christian church. Thus the pure teachings of Christ and the early apostles were hidden beneath the rubbish of error, and the church knew it not.

The church knew it not because for centuries this same power had deprived them of the Scriptures, "teaching for doctrines the commandments of men." Mark 7:7. In fact, so fully was the work of our great High Priest in the heavenly sanctuary misrepresented and distorted that Inspiration declares that this "man of sin" "opposeth and exalteth himself above all that is called God, or that is worshipped; so that *he* as God sitteth in the temple [sanctuary] of God, showing himself that *he* is God." II Thess. 2:4. Almost the entire Christian church now follows the dictates of that "wicked one," "the son of perdition," some of its members even ready to fight for the claims of this anti-Christian power.

But this cannot always continue, as James Russell Lowell has so well expressed:

> "Truth forever on the scaffold;
> Wrong forever on the throne;
> But that scaffold sways the future,
> And beyond the dim unknown
> Standeth God within the shadow,
> Keeping watch above His own."

The Power of Antichrist Broken. Not until the Great Reformation of the sixteenth century exposed some of the deceptive errors of the little horn, and broke his power; not until about that time, when printing from movable type came into use and the Bible was translated into modern language, was the Word of God in its purity made accessible to the common people.

The Third Generation of the Church Due. In spite of the Great Reformation which did so much to break the power of the little horn, and to restore the Bible to the Christian church, in spite of the noble work of the missionaries of "the Carey

Epoch" in giving the Bible to the *heathen* world, many deceptive and destructive errors still survived, causing confusion and unbelief, and dividing the Christian church into many different sects. The time was at hand when all the false teachings of Antichrist were to be exposed, and a knowledge of the pure Word of God was to be given to "whosoever will." Rev. 22:17.

Just at this time, the church was awakened by "a loud voice" "having the everlasting gospel to preach," and proclaiming: "the hour of His Judgment is come," Rev. 14:6, 7; "Prepare to meet thy God, O Israel." Amos 4:12. God gave the Hebrew church three and one-half years in which to accept the message of a crucified, risen, and ascended Lord: He gave the Christian generation of the church ten years in which to accept the Judgment message. During these ten years, this message shook the religious world, but comparatively few responded. It was on this decisive issue that the Christian generation of the church finally closed its career. The end of the 2300 days, when the heavenly sanctuary was to be cleansed, Dan. 8:14, had arrived. Then Christ closed His ministry in the holy place of the heavenly sanctuary, and entered upon His work as Judge in the most holy place. As the Hebrew church had refused to follow Him within the *first* vail into the *holy place* of the heavenly sanctuary, so now the Christian church as a whole refused to follow their Lord within the *second* vail into the *most holy place*. A correct understanding of the sanctuary would have lighted their way and saved them from disaster. A more complete knowledge of the sanctuary was about to give birth to the third generation of the church, called the Remnant church, the church of the most holy place. Rev. 12:17.

CHAPTER 33 PREVIEW

THE CHURCH OF THE MOST HOLY
PLACE—THE REMNANT CHURCH

THE CHURCH OF THE MOST HOLY PLACE—THE REMNANT CHURCH

The "Remnant." Webster says a remnant is "that which is left after a part has been removed;" also "a small number of people." The church of the most holy place is called the *Remnant church* not only because it is the last part of the church on this earth, but in comparison with the millions of professed Christians who now live on the earth, it gathers in but few, a mere remnant, who choose at all hazards to remain true to the pure Word of God. This is the church that John saw, with whom "the dragon was wroth"—"the great dragon...that old serpent, called the devil, and Satan"—who "went to make war with the *remnant of her seed* [the seed of the woman, the church], which keep the commandments of God, and have the testimony of Jesus Christ." Rev. 12:9, 17.

As the Hebrew church, the church of the court, lost its way in what had become a lifeless round of meaningless ceremonies and dead formalism, likewise the Christian church, the church of the holy place, so victoriously begun by the early apostles, so courageously continued by the mighty leaders of the Reformation who gave the pure Word of God to the people in *modern languages* of the civilized world, and so nobly followed by the early missionaries of "The Carey Epoch," whose great contribution to the gospel was the translation of the Bible into *heathen tongues*—this generation of the church lost its way in the blinding fogs of error that Antichrist, "the dragon," introduced. From the time that the Hebrew church was finally rejected in A.D. 34, and the Christian church had taken its place, 1810 years, the last division of the 2300 days, had passed, then, according to the time records of Christ, "Palmoni, the Wonderful Numberer," Dan. 8:14, margin, the fulfillment of the prophecy—"unto two thousand and three hundred says, then shall the sanctuary be cleansed"—was due. Dan. 8:14.

The end of the 2300 days, 1810 years after A.D. 34, pointed unmistakably to the year 1844, when the cleansing of the heavenly sanctuary began.

This was not only a cleansing of the house of God from all the sins that had gone before to Judgment, but from all the deceptive errors of the little horn, that "the true religion," *Moffatt*, Dan. 8:12, which the sanctuary symbolized and which the little horn had "cast down...to the ground" might be "restored to its rightful position." [Hebrew rendering of vs. 14]. Thus the gospel would be proclaimed in its original purity, and the church prepared to meet Christ at His coming.

At this time the two Judgment prophecies: the prophecy of Daniel 7:10 "the Judgment was set, and the books were opened," and John's prophecy of Revelation 14:6-12: "The hour of His Judgment is come" began to be proclaimed to the world. The whole period of time covered by these prophecies, reaching from 1844 to the last day of probation, is the antitype of the Hebrew day of atonement, the last day of the yearly round of service. The Remnant generation of the church is now living in this "last day" of probation.

Organization of the Remnant Church. At the organization of the Hebrew Church, the church of the court, the power of God shook Mount Sinai. At the organization of the Christian church, the church of the holy place, the power of God was mightily manifest in Jerusalem at the time of Pentecost. During the approximately ten years immediately preceding the ushering in of the Remnant church, the warning "The hour of His Judgment is come;" "Prepare to meet thy God, O Israel," Amos 4:12, was proclaimed simultaneously by godly men in practically all parts of the civilized world. This warning stirred all Christendom as it had not been stirred since the days of the apostles.

He who organized the first two generations of the church is still the same; He is "the same yesterday, and today, and forever." Heb. 13:8. His plans, being perfect, cannot change. Therefore the church of the most holy place, the Remnant church, is built upon the same foundation as were the two preceding generations of the church,—the same eternal law of God that the Hebrew church was to proclaim, and faith in a crucified, risen, and ascended Lord, which was the special message of the Christian church. Though both these generations of the church had fulfilled the time allotted to them, the work to be accomplished for God had not been completed, and another must take their place and finish the task.

The Sanctuary the Corner Stone of the Church. The sanctuary truth has always been the real heart of God's message for His church, because it so fully and so clearly reveals the redemptive work of Christ. The enemy, knowing this, centers his determined effort to keep the church in ignorance and indifference regarding it. The Hebrew church, although having at its organization such marvelous light on the sanctuary, finally lost its spiritual significance, and therefore fell short of fulfilling God's plan. The Christian church, although in the days of the apostles discerning the mission of Christ as revealed in the sanctuary, having lost the illumination which the sanctuary gives to all Scripture, at last fell a prey to the errors of Antichrist.

Had the Hebrew church preserved a spiritual understanding of the sanctuary, it would not have rejected Christ when at His birth, He entered the court, not at His ascension when He entered the holy place of the sanctuary above. Had the Christian church kept the faith as revealed in the sanctuary, it would not have rejected the Judgment message. But, at that time, Christian churches generally thought that *this earth* was the sanctuary, they had little or no idea of the existence of a sanctuary *in heaven* where at his ascension Christ began His high priestly work. Because of this general lack of understanding, the Remnant church stumbled on this very same point. Therefore, as the end of the 2300 days approached about the middle of the nineteenth century when the cleansing of the sanctuary prophesied in Daniel 8:14 began to be preached, the only logical conclusion was that *this earth* was to be cleansed—cleansed by fire, which of course meant the second coming of Christ and the end of the world. Then, when the date, October 22, 1844, pointed out in the prophecy for the event, passed and Jesus did not come, the believers were perplexed and greatly disappointed. This has since been known as the Great Disappointment of 1844. With many, this error caused unbelief in the message itself.

God works in a mysterious way His wonders to perform, and through this Disappointment He was able to lead His people to special light on the sanctuary, which is really the corner stone of every generation of the church. The very next morning after the Disappointment, which according to Bible reckoning was still October 22, while some who had preached the judgment message were praying for light, the Holy Spirit flashed into their minds the familiar text, "The temple [or sanctuary] of God was opened *in heaven*," Rev. 11:19. This revealed the truth that *this earth* was not the sanctuary to be cleansed, but that the true tabernacle is *in heaven*. Heb. 9:24; 8:2. When they rose from prayer, one of them exclaimed, "I suppose I have read that text a hundred times, but I never saw in it what I see now."

The Sanctuary and God's Law. As these earnest Bible students looked again into the text which the Holy Spirit had illuminated with such great light, they read, "there was seen in His temple the ark of His Testament," in which was God's eternal law. This verse continues with the remarkable words, "and there were lightnings, and voices, and thunderings, and an earthquake," which seems to indicate that the special power of God would accompany the proclamation of this message, till it would shake the whole earth.

The light on this text led to a prayerful and earnest study of God's law, the Ten Commandments, which revealed to them the astounding fact that "the seventh day" of the week is "the Sabbath of the Lord," Ex. 20:10, and not the first day as all their lives they had been taught. They learned that instead of the Sabbath being a type that met its antitype at the cross and was then done away, it was a foretaste of their eternal rest, Heb. 4:1-5, and that in the future life it would continue to be observed forever and ever. Isaiah 66:23. This was the very same Sabbath that both the Hebrew church and the Christian church when organized by Christ, had observed and honored. God was leading His people back to His eternal law, which the little horn *thought* to change. Dan. 7:25. So great was the joy of the people who discovered the divine truth, that as one, greeting another asked, "What's the news?" the joyful answer was, "Saturday is the Sabbath!" It was this correct understanding of the sanctuary and the Sabbath of God's law that gave birth to the Remnant church. They are the two pillars of the Judgment message.

Referring to this experience later, Uriah Smith in his terse style wrote:

> "The temple is opened, and no man can shut it;
> The ark is seen, and no man can obscure it;
> The corresponding movement on earth is in
> progress; and no man can stop it." LJ 231.

A Prophetic Command. As these earnest seekers for truth continued their study of the Bible, the Spirit of the Lord shed light on the prophecy recorded in Revelation 10 to 11:1, 2. This revealed the fact that their failure to understand the sanctuary, and their consequent Disappointment were in themselves matters of prophecy. From the tenth chapter of Revelation, they learned that a study of "the little book" of Daniel, although in the mouth "sweet as honey" would, after it was eaten, be bitter. Rev. 10:2, 8-10. They had experienced both the sweetness of its study and in their disappointment they had tasted its bitterness.

But this disappointment was not to discourage them, said the angel: "Thou must prophecy again before many peoples, and nations, and tongues, and kings." Rev. 10:10, 11. How were they to be prepared to give this worldwide message? The angel continued: "Rise, and measure the temple of God." Rev. 11:1, 2. What did he mean by measuring the temple of God? Uriah Smith gives this exegesis: "To measure any object requires that special attention be given to that object. The call to rise and measure the temple of God is a prophetic command to the church to give the subject of the temple, or sanctuary, a special examination." DR 532, 1944 edition.

"Rise, and measure the temple of God." This led to an earnest study of the heavenly temple, which disclosed the fact that at the end of the 2300 days of Daniel 8:14, instead of Christ's coming to this earth to cleanse it by fire, He then entered the most holy place of the heavenly sanctuary, where as Judge He began His work of *cleansing the church* preparatory to His coming in glory, instead of coming to execute Judgment on the wicked. He then began His Investigative Judgment of *the Righteous*. The discovery of these truths explained their Disappointment, and enabled them to understand why Christ had not come to this earth as they had expected and proclaimed. It revived their hope so that they could "rise [from their disappointment] and measure the temple of God."

As Satan saw this message developing, his wrath was aroused, for he knew that his kingdom was threatened. To his followers he said, "We must watch those who are calling the attention of the people to the Sabbath of Jehovah,.... Hold the minds of the people in darkness till that work [the ministration of Christ in the heavenly sanctuary] is ended and we shall secure the world and the church also." TM 472. This shows that it is Satan's plan to nullify the message of Revelation 11:19, so let us beware lest by neglecting to gain a spiritual understanding of the sanctuary, which points out the true Sabbath, we are ensnared in "the wiles [sly tricks] of the devil." Only by having on "the whole armor of God" are we safe from the great deceiver. Eph. 6:11.

The Special Mission of the Remnant Church. The charter members of this church were the few who at its beginning accepted and proclaimed the judgment message. Compared with the two preceding generations of the church, it has always been few in number. Yet to them God has committed a mighty task. Since this church parallels the entire time of the Investigative Judgment, which extends from 1844 to the second coming of Christ, the special features of this worldwide message is the proclamation of the prophecies concerning the Judgment and Christ's second coming, together with an understanding of the sanctuary and its relation to the law of God—subjects which are definite contributions of the Remnant church to Christendom.

The mission of this church includes even more than preaching these special truths, important as they are. During the preceding generations of the church, when for many centuries the little horn dominated the church, many other gospel truths had been buried beneath the rubbish of error, and even salvation through Christ was almost lost sight of. It is the task of the Remnant church through Christ to rescue these truths from their companionship with error, and reset them in the framework of truth. This last generation of the church on earth—"they that shall be of thee," and "raise up the foundations of many generations." They are to be "the repairer of the breach, the restorer of paths to dwell in"—especially restoring "the Sabbath…the holy of the Lord." Isaiah 58:1, 2, 12, 13. As the sanctuary is understood and preached, it will dismantle many of the errors and evils that have crept into the church, and the gospel will shine forth in all its original purity and luster—a gospel which is to prepare a people for the kingdom. "And this gospel of the kingdom shall be preached in all the world for a witness unto all nations." When this is accomplished, "then [and not till then] shall the end come." Matt. 24:14.

To this Remnant generation of the church, has also been unfolded the signs of Christ's second coming just as He gave them to His disciples:—deceptions regarding the manner of His coming: wars and rumors of wars; famines, and pestilences, and earthquakes in divers places; persecutions; "signs in the sun, and in the moon, and in the stars; and upon the earth distress of nations, with perplexity, [dismay—*Moffatt*; bewilderment; no way out—*Wymouth*] Luke 21:25; false christs and false prophets showing great signs and wonders to deceive, if possible, the very elect; riotous living and drunkenness as in the days of Noah; even some of His own 'servants' eating and drinking with the drunken, while saying in their hearts, 'My Lord delayeth His coming.'" Matt. 24:48. This generation of the church—the Remnant church—is to proclaim these signs to the world; and of it Christ declared, "This generation shall not pass, till all these things be fulfilled." Matt. 24:34.

Some claim that, like the two preceding generations of the church, the Remnant also has failed, and another must take its place and finish the work. But the Bible declares, and the sanctuary clearly shows, that the Remnant church, the church of the most holy place, which began its work in 1844, with the Judgment hour, is the last generation of the church to live on this earth, and it will finish the work. Surely this generation has a great and important task, but in the hand of the Omnipotent One it will be accomplished. When Isaiah was shown the sanctuary, and responded to God's call to go and tell the people, he asked the Lord, "How long?" And the answer was, "until the cities be wasted without inhabitant… and the land be utterly desolate." Isaiah 6:1, 9, 11. Such consecration and untiring faithfulness are needed by the church today.

The First Angel's Message. John presents the mission of the Remnant church under the figure of three angels flying "in the midst of heaven." The first angel has "the everlasting gospel to preach unto them that dwell on the earth…saying with a loud voice…Fear God…for the hour of His Judgment is come." Rev. 14:6, 7.

The second part of this message is, "Worship Him that made heaven and earth, and the sea, and the fountains of waters." Comparing this with Exodus 20:8-11, there is a striking similarity between the first angel's message and the Sabbath commandment. In fact, the proclamation of the Sabbath of the Lord as an integral part of this Judgment message was a prewarning against the then rising teaching of evolution by Charles Darwin, whose book "*The Origin of Species*" was published in 1859. This was Satan's plot to undermine faith in the Sabbath of the fourth commandment—the day that commemorates the creation of this world and points out its true origin. This doctrine would also undermine faith in Christ and in the Judgment message itself, for if man can develop, or evolve, by a power inherent within himself, he would in time be fit for heaven, and there would be no need of a Judgment or of a Saviour.

Second Angel's Message. The first angel's message was quickly accompanied by a second. So blinding and so universal was the confusion in the church, caused by the deceptions of Antichrist, that God calls this condition in the church Babylon, a word that means confusion. To rid the church of all this confusion and error, the second angel came "down from heaven" proclaiming "mightily with a strong voice…Babylon the great is fallen…Come out of her, My people." Rev. 14:8; 18:1, 2, 4. Come out of Babylon; come away from all her errors and deceptions; come out of all this confusion which has split the church into almost numberless sects. Follow the example of the noble Bereans who in Paul's day "searched the Scriptures daily," Acts 17:11, that they might know the truth. Study, *study* until, instead of confusion in the church, "we all come in the unity of the faith," Eph. 4:13, and until we can present to others the pure Word of God. Come within the second vail into the most holy place of the sanctuary, where others are studying to learn the truth of the everlasting gospel, and where Christ now intercedes for His people.

Third Angel's Message. In close connection with the first and the second came the third angel's message. This message is a most solemn warning not to worship the beast and his image, nor receive his mark or his name, but to become identified with those who "keep the commandments of God, and the faith of Jesus." Rev. 14:9-12.

"All heaven watched with the deepest interest" the reception by the church of this threefold message. EW 260. How was it revived? The Christian church repeated the experience of the Hebrew church. When the rending of the temple vail indicated that they should cease their worship in *the* earthly sanctuary, and follow Christ into *the holy place* of the heavenly sanctuary within the *first* vail, only a few at first responded, "about an hundred and twenty." Acts 1:15. Likewise, in 1844 when the Judgment message came to the Christian church to follow Christ by faith into *the most holy place* within the *second* vail, whither He had gone to act as Judge, only a small number from the various sects of the church responded.

What will be the fate of all who persistently refuse to follow their Lord? Even as the Jews, who refused to follow Jesus into *the holy place* of the heavenly sanctuary, so to those who now deliberately refuse to follow Him into *the most holy place*, He will say as He said to them, "Your house is left unto you desolate." Luke 13:34, 35; "Having a form of godliness, but denying the power thereof." II Tim. 3:5. We, too, unless we follow where Christ leads, will grope along in darkness not realizing that the work of Christ as Judge and Redeemer is fast closing, and that His coming "is near, even at the doors." Matt. 24:33.

The Worship of the Beast. The warning of the third angel is against the "worship" of the beast and his image. What is *worship*? Webster defines it as divine honor paid to God; an act of homage as a religious service. The threefold message of Revelation 14 calls the followers of Christ to *worship God* the Creator, and warns against the worship of the beast and the receiving of his mark. God has made the Sabbath His "seal;" the beast has given a spurious sabbath as *his* "mark" or seal. In this the beast demands that homage as a religious service be given to him by worshiping him on his spurious sabbath instead of worshiping God on *His* Sabbath—"the Sabbath of the Lord thy God." He demands that the honor due alone to God as the Creator be given to *him*. He demands that we receive his "mark" or seal, thus indicating that we belong to God. Thus he "opposeth and exalteth himself above all that is called God, or that is worshiped, so that he as God sitteth in the temple of God, showing himself that *he* is God." II Thess. 2:4. The observance of the true Sabbath, therefore, is not merely cessation from all secular occupations, it is worshipful honor paid to God the Creator, disregarding the demands of the beast who *pretends* that *he* is God.

The terrible seriousness of following the beast instead of God is shown in the warning: "If any man worship the beast and his image, and receive his mark in his forehead, or in his hand, the same shall drink of the wine of the wrath of God, which is poured out without mixture into the cup of His indignation." Rev. 14:9,10.

Immediately following this fearful denunciation against those who worship the beast, a special blessing is pronounced on those who "die in the Lord from henceforth;" Rev. 14:13; that is, from the time when these messages began to be preached. Why "from henceforth?" Because, although they "rest from their labors," "their works do follow them." Is it not also because as a special reward for their faithfulness unto death, those dying in the faith of the three angels message, will have part in the special resurrection of Daniel 12:2, to see Jesus come, and to hear His "covenant of peace?" GC 637; EW 285. They also escape many of the trials and persecutions of the last days. Therefore, "Blessed are the dead who die in the Lord from *henceforth*."

The Spirit of Prophecy in the Church. Various "gifts" have been placed in the church, Eph. 4:8-14; I Cor. 12:1, 4, 8-10, but no more precious gift has ever been bestowed on it during the entire period of its probation than the gift of the Spirit of prophecy. The Hebrew church—the church of the court—had its prophets; Moses, Isaiah, Jeremiah, Ezekiel, Daniel, and others. The Christian church—the church after 31 A.D., within the first vail, had its prophets: Paul, Peter, John, and others. The Remnant church—the church after 1844, within the second vail—must also have the Spirit of prophecy, "so that ye come behind in no gift; waiting for the second coming of our Lord Jesus Christ." I Cor. 1:7, 8. Therefore, when Christ passed within the second vail to engage in the work of the Judgment, God gave the Spirit of prophecy to the Remnant church.

How to Identify a True Prophet. The Remnant church has two especially distinguishing characteristics: they "keep the commandments of God, and the faith of Jesus" Rev. 14:12, or "the testimony" of Jesus Christ. Rev. 12:17. What is the "faith" or "testimony" of Jesus? "The testimony of Jesus is the Spirit of prophecy." Rev. 19:10. It is the instruction, encouragement, and warning that Jesus sends to His church through a divinely appointed messenger called a prophet. A true prophet of the Remnant church must speak from within the second vail; that is, the testimony must be in harmony with the truths that God gives to the church within the second vail. Therefore, the testimony of a true prophet of God for the Remnant church will emphasize the truths of the Judgment, the sanctuary, the Sabbath "according to the commandments," the signs of Christ's second coming, and the everlasting gospel in its original purity. It will be in harmony with the law of God located in the ark. "To the law and to the testimony: if they speak not according this word, it is because there is no light in them." Isaiah 8:20. Thus, a true perspective and a spiritual understanding of the sanctuary will enable the church to identify the true from the false. And surely, amid the perils and deceptions that confront the church today, divine guidance and instruction are needed fully as much as in preceding generations of the church.

The Work of a Prophet. Without the Spirit of prophecy, especially in these last days, when the dragon is wroth with the woman and has gone to make war with the remnant of her seed, the church would be left to the merciless buffetings of the enemy, "tossed to and fro, and carried about with every wind of doctrine," Eph. 4:14, so that while "ever learning," it would never be able "to come to the knowledge of the truth." II Tim. 3:7. The Spirit of prophecy is to protect the church from these evils. With other gifts of the Spirit, it is "for the perfecting of the saints, for the work of the ministry, for the edifying of the body of Christ: till we all come in the unity of the faith, and of the knowledge of the Son of God, unto a perfect man, unto the measure of the stature of the fulness of Christ." Eph. 4:12, 13. To disregard the testimony of the Spirit of prophecy would be like trying to explore the glories of the heavens without a telescope, or understand the beauty and wonders of the invisible things of creation without a microscope. Surely no real student would deprive himself of such valuable help. The "testimonies" of God's Spirit are even more needed to a deeper and more complete understanding of His Word.

The Spirit of Prophecy a Life-giving Power. A church guided by God through the Spirit of prophecy will be a living, growing church with a steadily deepening experience, one that imparts life to all around it. Ezekiel illustrates this experience under the figure of a river which grows deeper and deeper from its source until it goes "into the sea." The waters of this river "issued out of the sanctuary," which was the secret of its life and growth. Eze. 47:1-12. The man with the measuring line in his hand measured the depth of the water at *four* different places. As the prophet passed through the water at these points, they were first "to the ankles," next "to the knees," then "to the loins," and finally "waters to swim in, a river that could not be passed over." Too high to be forded, *Moffatt*. vs.3-5.

The prophet here represents the church, and from the fact that the waters issued eastward out of the sanctuary, Eze. 47:1, 12, it seems evident that the four increasing depths of the waters through which it passes, represent the ever deepening experience of the church in its four generations. As illustrated in the sanctuary, the Hebrew church, the church of the court, had an ankle-deep experience; the Christian church of the holy place had a knee-deep experience; the Remnant church of the most holy place must advance again to a still deeper experience, for here "the waters were to the loins."

The fourth period of the church, the church of the Firstborn—the church of the temple eternal, has the deepest experience, for "the waters were risen, waters to swim in, a river that could not be forded." Eze. 47:5. This church is no longer called to pass through the deep waters, but it is caught up to meet the Lord in the air. I Thess. 4:17. The church militant has finished its course and has become the church triumphant.

The Remnant a Life-Giving Church. Of this growing river the prophet further says, "Everything...shall live...whither the river cometh...and by the river upon the bank thereof, on this side and on that side, shall grow all trees for meat, whose leaf shall not fade, neither shall the fruit thereof be consumed: it shall bring forth new fruit according to his months, because their waters they issued out of the sanctuary; and the fruit thereof shall be for meat, the leaf thereof for medicine." Eze. 47:9, 12. We at once recognize this river as the river of life, and the "very many trees on the one side and on the other" as the tree of life. Rev. 22:1, 2.

This river of life "issued out of the sanctuary," or as John says, proceeded "out of the throne of God and of the Lamb." Rev. 22:1. In it there were "a very great multitude of fish," and "because these waters shall come thither...they [the fish] shall be healed; and everything shall live whither the river cometh." And "the fishers shall...spread forth nets." Even so, the church with a living and ever deepening experience will become "fishers of men," bringing the healing water of life to "a very great multitude," "exceeding many." Eze. 47:8, 9. It is God's purpose that His church in all its generations should bring life and healing to a sin sick world.

As a church and as individual Christians, it is our privilege to have this life-giving experience. If we respond to the invitation, "Follow Me," going with Jesus all the way from the altar in the court to the ark in the most holy place, we shall become like the waters of the river of life. Then those whom we contact from day to day will realize a life-giving healing influence, because "the waters they issue out of the sanctuary."

What is our depth of experience? Is it only ankle deep, only a court experience? If so, there is but one remedy: it is found in the holy place at the *table*, at the *golden altar*, and at the *candlestick*. Are we daily *studying* the Word of life—not merely reading, but purposefully studying, comparing scripture with scripture, digging deep into its treasures? Are our prayers earnest, unselfish requests that reach the throne of God, not formal repetitions of customary words and phrases? Are we carrying a real burden for some sick sick soul? Are our lamps like those of the wise virgins, filled with the oil of the Holy Spirit as we wait for the Bridegroom? If so, we are growing in sanctification, we are approaching the loin-deep experience. And the Spirit of prophecy is given to help us gain this experience in Christian growth.

The Latter Rain for the Remnant Church. Under the figure of "the rain, the former rain, and the latter rain," the prophet Joel points out the work of the Spirit of God in the church. Joel 2:23. The *rain* accompanied the work of the Hebrew church: the *former rain* was given to the Christian church on the day of Pentecost following Christ's ascension; the *latter rain* is an experience for the Remnant church. It ripens the grape for the harvest just before Christ's second coming, which is the end of the world. Matt. 13:39.

The latter rain can never fall upon anyone who is not with Christ within the second vail. And so the call to the Christian generation of the church is, "Come out of her, My people," gather with the Remnant church within the second vail where Christ now officiates. Do not delay, for at this time "He will finish the work, and cut it short in righteousness: because a short work will the Lord make upon the earth." Rom. 9:28. Although the work of the Remnant church, the church since 1844, has now been in progress for more than one hundred years, yet when compared with the twenty-five hundred years of the Hebrew church, and the eighteen hundred ten years allotted to the Christian church, this is indeed a "short" time in which to finish His work in the earth.

A Sifting in the Church. During the work of Christ in the most holy place of the heavenly sanctuary, and especially as it draws to a close and the church nears the end of its pilgrimage on earth, it passes through a special and final sifting time—a time when some will be sifted out. In every generation of the church there have been those who have proven untrue. Among others in the Hebrew church where Korah, Dathen, and Abiram; in the Christian church, Annias and Sapphira,

Demas and others were dropped out, and from its beginning the Remnant church has suffered from similar influences. As the church nears the end, this sifting will be more and more pronounced. The prophet Amos says of it, "I will sift the house of Israel among all nations, like as corn is sifted in a sieve." Amos 9:9. Ezekiel calls it "a great shaking in the land of Israel." Eze. 38:19. Nor do these prophecies apply only to ancient Israel, for referring to our own time, we read that it is a "mighty shaking," "when everything that can be shaken will be shaken." EW 50; 6 T 352.

The ancient day of atonement was the time when all who were indifferent or careless among Israel were "cut off" from God's people—sifted out from Israel. We are now living in the antitypical day of atonement, when the Judgment of the house of God is about to close. It is a time when as in the type every true Israelite was to "afflict his soul" in order to detect any hidden sin in his life. The danger of the Remnant church is expressed in these words: "Mammon is the idol of many. The love of money, the desire for wealth...reputation and worldly honor...a life of selfish ease and freedom from responsibility is the idol of others." GC 48, 49. Jesus says, "The cares of this world and the deceitfulness of riches, and the lust of other things entering in, choke the Word." Mark 4:19. Let us beware, lest these things crowd our time and our thoughts until little remains for earnest study of the Word and it becomes choked. Of this condition of the church, God through the prophet says, "there are 'sinners' among 'My people.'" What will be the result of this sifting?—"All the sinners of My people shall die...which say, The evil shall not overtake nor prevent [go before] us." Amos 9:10.

In this sifting process, "chaff like a cloud will be borne away on the wind, even from places where we see only floors of rich wheat," "yet shall not the least grain fall upon the earth." Amos 9:9. In this chaff will be "many a star that we have admired for its brilliancy," which "will then go out in darkness," because though "assuming the ornaments of the sanctuary... they are not clothed with Christ's righteousness." 5 T 81. In the Judgment these will say, "Lord, Lord,...have we not .. in Thy name done many wonderful works?" The answer will come back, "I never knew you, depart from Me." Matt. 7:22, 23. What a sad picture this presents!

Sanctuary Study a Keeping Power. As already noted, God has repeatedly urged upon the Remnant church the necessity of thorough and earnest study of the sanctuary. Why is this? Is it not because the sanctuary represents the ground work of the plan of redemption which holds the church in the narrow path and keeps it moving steadily forward? It keeps out deceptive and destructive error. When the truths of the sanctuary are lost sight of, the church slips from its moorings and loses its way.

When the Hebrew church began their work for God, it was the sanctuary that gave it its power. When the Christian church was organized, Paul and other apostles, working for both Jew and Gentile, drew convincing and converting power from the sanctuary as a type of the work of Christ for their salvation. When these generations of the church lost the spiritual significance of the sanctuary, they lost their power, and the next generation—the Remnant church—was called to pick up the lost truth, and finish His work.

A Revival of Sanctuary Study Now Due. At the very beginning of the Remnant church, a study of the "temple," or sanctuary, threw a flood of light on the Judgment message to be given the world at that time, and gave power to the preaching of this timely truth. During the years that have followed, a continued study of the sanctuary has been more or less neglected. But before the end, the sanctuary is to be "restored to its rightful position." Dan. 8:14. The time allotted for this restoration is about to close, and of that time the prophet says: "In *that day* will I raise up the tabernacle of David that is fallen, and close up the breaches thereof; and I will raise up his ruins, and I will build it as in the days of old." Amos 9:11.

This prophecy was referred by James in his appeal before the Jerusalem Council saying, "I...will build again the tabernacle of David, which is fallen down, and I will build again the ruins thereof... that the residue [the remnant] of man might seek after the Lord." Acts 15:16, 17. Is not this a challenge to the Remnant church who are looking for the soon coming of Him whom the sanctuary typifies? Does it not indicate that before the end there will be a revival of sanctuary study among the people of God? The final fulfillment of this prophecy is now due. There can be no doubt about this, because the time has fully come when the work of redemption is being finished, and a knowledge of the sanctuary is needed to give us more distinct views of the work of our High Priest, and a broader comprehension of the value of eternal realities.

In the light of the sanctuary, we more fully comprehend the plan of redemption, and because this is "the key that will unlock... the whole treasure house of God's word," Ed. 126, through its study all Scripture takes on new beauty and fullness of meaning, until the Bible becomes a new and fascinating Book. Then the desire for wealth, reputation, honor, selfish ease, and other lusts will gradually lose their hold upon us and we shall find the necessary time so that the Word shall no longer be choked. Then these worldly lusts, rather than we ourselves, will be sifted out—the chaff will be separated from the wheat. Such a study of the sanctuary will not only vitalize and establish Christian experience, but it will strengthen faith in the closing work of the gospel.

How will this revival of sanctuary study affect the progress of God's work in the earth? "That they may possess...all the heathen which are called by My name." Amos 9:12. In this final harvest of souls, "the plowman shall overtake the reaper, and the treader of grapes him that soweth seed;" Amos 9:13; that is, those who have only begun the work in the Lord's vineyard will overtake those who have toiled through the heat of the day, and with their combined efforts, the harvest will be quickly gathered; "The final movements will be rapid ones." 9 T 11.

What reward is promised these faithful workers?—"I will bring again the captivity of My people Israel, and they shall build the waste cities, and inhabit them; and they shall plant vineyards, and drink the wine thereof; they shall also make gardens, and eat the fruit of them. And I will plant them upon their land, and they shall no more be pulled up out of their land which I have given them, saith the Lord God." Amos 9:14, 15.

Be Ye Also Ready. We are now living, not in the Hebrew generation of the church, nor yet in the Babylon condition of the Christian church, we are in the Judgment hour of the Remnant church! This is to be the hour, not of an ankle-deep experience, nor of a knee-deep experience; a loin-deep experience is for this final hour of probation.

God is in earnest with the Remnant church. He is not willing that any should perish; but we must remember that this is the *last generation* of the church to live on this present earth—a church that He is now preparing for translation at His soon coming, a church that is to be "a glorious church, not having spot, or wrinkle, or any such thing...holy and without blemish." Eph. 5:27. Therefore, while He is now cleansing the sanctuary in heaven, His church on earth must be cleansed from all evil.

We are nearing the midnight hour, the hour for the Bridegroom to come, the hour when the call is not "*Get* ready," but "Be ready:" "Be ye also ready: for in such an hour as ye think not the Son of man cometh." Matt. 24:44. Are we ready for the Bridegroom? Are we prepared to join "the church of the Firstborn," the church of "the temple eternal in the heavenly Jerusalem" with its innumerable company of angels? Heb. 12:22, 23.

> "Are you ready for the Bridegroom
>   When He comes, when He comes?
> Are you ready for the Bridegroom
>   When He comes, when He comes?
> Behold, He cometh! Behold, He cometh!
>   O Soul, be ready when the Bridegroom
> comes!"

CHAPTER 34 PREVIEW

**THE CHURCH OF THE TEMPLE
ETERNAL—THE CHURCH OF THE FIRSTBORN**

- The Church After Redemption
- Christ the Firstborn—Its Divine Head
- The "Household of God"
- The Membership of the Church of the Firstborn
- The Final Addition to This Church
- Its Mission Governed by Changed Conditions
- The First One Thousand Years
- Varied Occupations of the Redeemed
- Students in "The School of the Hereafter"

34

THE CHURCH OF THE TEMPLE ETERNAL—
THE CHURCH OF THE FIRSTBORN

The Church After Redemption. When the work of the Remnant church, the church of the most holy place, is completed, the Investigative Judgment, the Judgment of the house of God, closes. Then all whose names have not been blotted out of the Book of Life—those who have passed the Judgment test—will be removed from this earth to "the city of the living God, the heavenly Jerusalem," and become "the general assembly and church of the Firstborn." Heb. 12:22, 23.

When the Son of God left heaven and entered upon His mission in the court of earth, the prophecy of Micah 5:2 met its fulfillment. When at His ascension He left the court and entered the holy place of the heavenly sanctuary, the prophecy of Daniel 9:24 was fulfilled. When in 1844 He left the holy place, and passed within the second vail into the most holy place, the prophecy of the 2300 days of Daniel 8:14 was fulfilled. When His ministry in the most holy place closes, and His mediatorial work is finished, the prophecy of Revelation 8:3-5 will be fulfilled. These prophecies mark epochal events in the work of redemption. When all are fulfilled, the redeemed in the New Jerusalem "shall be priests of God and of Christ,…a thousand years," Rev. 20:6, during which time they are associated with Him in the judgment of the wicked. I Cor. 6:2, 3.

Christ "The Firstborn." Christ, the only begotten Son of God, is also the Son of man. He is "the firstborn" of those who, though human, have become "partakers of the divine nature," "conformed to the image of His Son." II Peter 1:3,4; Rom. 8:29. He is "the firstborn of every creature." Col. 1:15. He is "the first begotten of the dead;" Rev. 1:5; that is, the first who rose from the dead by His own power, for concerning His life He said, "I have power to lay it down, and I have power to take it again." John 10:17, 18. He thus becomes "the first-fruits of them that slept." I Cor. 15:20. By virtue of this double relationship—being Song of God and Son of man—and by virtue of the fact that like the earthly high priest who was the firstborn who inherited his office because he was the firstborn, so Christ the Firstborn becomes, by inheritance, the heavenly High Priest, the divine-human Head of the church of the Firstborn.

The "Household of God." Christ is declared to be "the Firstborn of a great brotherhood," Rom. 8:29, *Moffatt*, "Christ the first fruits; afterward they that are Christ's at His coming." I Cor. 15:23. He is the "Elder Brother," the redeemed are His brethren. In the household of God there will be no divided families. "Both He that sanctifieth and they that are sanctified are all of one; for which cause He is not ashamed to call them brethren." Heb. 2:11; Matt. 12:50. Having been "born again," born into the family of God, Christ's brethren, like Himself, are "the sons of God." I John 3:2. At His coming the "household of God," Eph. 2:19, so long separated from Him, will be united, and then Christ's prayer "that they also may be one in Us," John 17:21, will be fully answered.

The Membership of the Church of the Firstborn. "They that depart from Me shall be written in the earth," Jer. 17:13, but the names of "the general assembly and church of the Firstborn" are "written in heaven," Heb. 12:22, 23,—written by the Father Himself in His book, Ex. 32:32, the Book of Life. These compose the membership of the church of the heavenly Jerusalem. They are "a great multitude, which no man could number." Rev. 7:9. They have been gathered from every nation, kindred, tongue, and people, from the days of Adam to the close of probation. All these have been redeemed by the blood of Christ. They are graven upon the palms of His hands, Isaiah 49:16, and are pre-eminently His—His church, the church of the Firstborn.

The Final Addition To This Church. The last group added to the church of the Firstborn is spoken of in the Bible as the 144,000. Rev. 7:4. Because they have stoutly refused to worship the beast and his image, but have kept "the commandments of God, and the faith of Jesus," Rev. 14:9, 12, the wrath of Satan is aroused, Rev. 12:17, and he is allowed to bring upon them every imaginable distress to test their faith and sway them, if possible, from their allegiance to God. As a result, it is written of them, "These are they which came out of great tribulation;" Rev. 7:14; that last fearful conflict with the beast and his image. The redeemed of all ages have had to battle with the beast, but in this last great struggle, the 144,000 meet him under the most adverse conditions, when he is more furious than ever before against those who obey God. Unlike any other group of the redeemed, they live through the time of trouble such as never was since there was a nation. Dan. 12:1. "They have endured the anguish of the time of Jacob's trouble; they have stood without an Intercessor through the final outpouring of God's judgments;…they have seen the earth wasted with famine and pestilence, the sun having power to scorch men with great heat, and they themselves have endured suffering, hunger, and thirst," GC 649. At times, it has almost seemed that God has forsaken them. This enables them better to understand that last agonizing prayer of Christ, "My God, My God, why hast Thou forsaken Me?" Matt. 27:46. These extreme circumstances require unprecedented endurance and patience, therefore of them it is written, "Here is the patience of the saints." Rev. 14:12.

While this has been a severe test of their faith, yet they have remained loyal to God and His Word. His truth has been their "shield and buckler." Ps. 91:4. Finally they have been delivered, and to them is fulfilled the precious promise, "They shall hunger no more; neither thirst any more; neither shall the sun light on them, nor any heat; for the Lamb which is in the midst of the throne shall feed them, and shall lead them unto living fountains of waters; and God shall wipe away all tears from their eyes." Rev. 7:16, 17.

Victory under these unfavorable and distressing conditions, brings a special reward. As in the type the Levites in the earthly sanctuary were honored with the care of the sanctuary because they stood true in a crisis hour, so the 144,000 who have stood true in *their* crisis hour, are honored by serving God day and night in His temple, a "token of highest honor." Ed. 148. The 144,000 have this special reward, not so much because they have reached a higher state of character perfection than others of the redeemed, for *all* who inherit the earth, will be meek, *all* who obtain mercy will be merciful, *all* who see God, will be peacemakers. Matt. 5:5-9. *All* the redeemed will be free from guile, *all* will be partakers of the divine nature. To *all* are addressed the words, "Be ye therefore perfect, even as your Father which is in heaven is perfect." Matt. 5:48. *All* will be without fault before the throne of God. *All* will be like Him, for they shall see Him as He is. I John 3:2. Of *all* it is written, "They... have washed their robes, and made them white in the blood of the Lamb." All the "spots" have been washed away, all the "wrinkles" ironed out, all the "blemishes" removed. Eph. 5:27.

Its Mission Governed by Changed Conditions. While the foundation of every generation of the church is the same, being laid by Him with whom there is "no variableness, neither shadow of turning," James 1:17, yet to each generation has been committed a work specially needed in, and suited to, its time. As already noted, the special responsibility of the Hebrew church, the church of the court was presenting to idol worshipers a knowledge of the true God, the Creator, as memorialized in the Sabbath of His law; the Christian church, the church of the holy place was to emphasize faith in a crucified, risen, and ascended Lord; the special assignment given to the Remnant church, the church of the most holy place may be summed up thus: proclaiming the judgment message as revealed in prophecies, giving to the world a correct understanding of the sanctuary and of the law of God, preaching the gospel of the kingdom in its original purity, and proclaiming the signs of Christ's second coming.

What will be the special mission of the church of the Firstborn, the church of the temple eternal? It will certainly be vastly different from that of any preceding generation of the church, because its environment and conditions will be entirely different. Loyalty to God's unchangeable law needs no emphasis now, because His law is in the mind, and written in the heart of everyone who has been redeemed. Heb. 8:10. There will be no need to urge faith in Christ as the Sacrifice for sin, for faith is now lost in sight—He bears in His own glorious body the marks of His sacrifice. No need now to warn men of a Judgment to come and to urge them to prepare for the second coming of Christ; all this is past.

In this church there will be no need for missionaries to leave their homes and face dangers and hardships that those in darkness may know of the love of God. O, no! "They shall not teach every man his neighbor, and every man his brother, saying, Know the Lord; for all shall know Me, from the least to the greatest." Heb. 8:11. There will be no need for doctors or nurses, for there "the inhabitant shall not say, I am sick." Isaiah 33:24. No need there for carpenters, plumbers, electricians, mechanics, bakers, tailors, lawyers, and those of other occupations by which men now earn a livelihood, for "my God shall supply all your need according to His riches in glory by Christ Jesus." Phil 4:19. "All things are yours...and ye are Christ's and Christ is God's." I Cor. 3:21, 23.

The First One Thousand Years. During the first one thousand years following their arrival in heaven, the redeemed, those who had "part in the first resurrection...shall be priests of God and of Christ." Rev. 20:6; Dan. 7:22. "The saints shall judge the world," I Cor. 6:2—the wicked who still await their judgment. They shall also "judge angels," I Cor. 6:3; Jude 6—"the third part" of the angels who with Satan were "cast out into the earth." Rev. 12:4, 9; GC 600, 601.

As nothing else could do, this experience will make clear to the redeemed that in the final and complete destruction of the wicked, root and branch, Mal. 4:1, God is just and righteous. Even in the case of relatives and friends who have refused or neglected salvation, Heb. 2:1-3, they will be satisfied that He has done everything that a God of love and justice could do and at the same time keep His promise that "affliction shall not rise up the second time." Nahum 1:9. To many of the redeemed this will be a time of mourning and weeping, but when it is past, when the new heaven and the new earth are created, God "shall wipe away all tears from their eyes," and "there shall be no more death, neither sorrow, nor crying, neither shall there be any more pain; for the former things are passed away." Rev. 21:4. This participation in the work of the Judgment will be a sort of postgraduate course in that science of all sciences—the science of redemption.

Varied Occupations of the Redeemed. When the one thousand years are past, what shall the redeemed do? Surely, merely to sit idly by the river of life and eat of the tree of life, or to play a harp of gold and sing a lively song throughout eternity—this would not be heaven for those who have the immortal vigor of eternal youth. There will be earnest, but joyful work for all, but not all will necessarily have the same occupation. Some will "build houses," but not as we build here; some will "plant vineyards," Isaiah 65:21, though under vastly difference conditions of soil and climate; they shall not labor in vain, vs. 23, and they "shall long enjoy the work of their hands." vs. 22. Others will serve God "day and night in His temple;" Rev. 7:15; and "follow the Lamb whithersoever He goeth."

Students in the School of the Hereafter. The entire church of the Firstborn will be students in "The school of the hereafter," and Christ Himself will be the Master Teacher. Besides this school, which meets for instruction during the week, outside the New Jerusalem, we are told that in the City "from one Sabbath to another, shall all flesh come to worship before...the Lord." Isaiah 66:23. This will be the weekly Sabbath-school and divine service for the church of the Firstborn. Here also, all the angels will be present, thus making up God's "whole family;" Eph. 3:15; no one will be absent, no one tardy.

In the earthly sanctuary the Shekinah, representing the glory of God, was hidden by the vail. But in the New Jerusalem the redeemed may look upon His glory "without a dimming vail between." GC 677. "The people of God are privileged to hold open communion with the Father and the Son." "And they shall see His face." Rev. 22:4. They "shall stand in His presence, and behold the glory of His countenance." GC 676. "Thine eyes shall see the King in His beauty." Isaiah 33:17. As if this were not enough to satisfy every soul desire, we are told that the redeemed, unfettered by mortality will have the wonderful privilege of visiting the unfallen worlds, and sharing with them the joys of redeeming love. What a glad occasion this will be both for the redeemed and for the "worlds afar!" GC 677.

Will it not be abundantly worthwhile to be a member of the church of the First-born? We may, if at the close of our probation we can say with Paul, "I have fought a good fight, I have finished my course, I have kept the faith: henceforth there is laid up for me a crown of righteousness, which the Lord, the righteous Judge, shall give me at that day: and not to me only, but unto all them also that love His appearing." II Tim. 4:7, 8.

SUMMARY
The Four Generations of the Church

Sinai	Calvary	End of the 2300 Days	Close of Probation
Hebrew Church of the Court	Christian Church of the Holy Place	Remnant Church of the Most Holy Place	Firstborn Church of the Temple Eternal
Christ Rejected and Crucified	Faith in a Risen Saviour	Judgment of the House of God	Christ as Priest King Forever

Every Generation of the Church Sealed with the Sabbath. The Sabbath is God's seal with which He seals His disciples, His church. Isaiah 8:16. It is "a sign between Me and you [God and His church] throughout your generations." Ex. 31:13-17. This sign, His signature, is His name which He writes in the foreheads of those who are sealed. Rev. 7:3; 22:4. As a seal validates a document, so God's seal, the Sabbath, validates His church. At the very beginning of each generation of His church, God put on it His seal, the Sabbath, "the foundation of many generations." Isaiah 58:12.

1. The Hebrew generation of the church was founded on God's law, the seal of which is the Sabbath. About 1500 B.C. when the Father through the Son spoke His law from Sinai with power and great glory. This was the birthday of the Hebrew church.

2. The Christian generation of the church was established when Christ's representative, the Holy Spirit, was sent to the church of believers. Acts 2:1-4. This was on the last divinely recognized Pentecost which in A.D. 31 fell on the Sabbath. It was the birthday of the Christian church.

3. At the very beginning of the Remnant generation of the church, October 22, 1844, the Sabbath, God's seal, which "the little horn" had buried beneath the rubbish of error, was divinely revealed and restored to the people of God. Rev. 11:19. This was the birthday of the Remnant Church.

4. The church of the Firstborn which will begin at the second coming of Christ, will continue to observe the divine command, "Remember the Sabbath day to keep it holy," as throughout eternity it will meet for worship "from one Sabbath to another." Isaiah 66:23. Thus on every generation of the church God has placed His sign or signature. His name. His seal the Sabbath. And those who obey, cooperate with Him who came to this earth to "magnify the law and make it honorable." Isaiah 42:21.

SECTION VII

THE SANCTUARY AFTER REDEMPTION

CHAPTER 35 PREVIEW

CHRIST COMING FOR HIS BRIDE

- Waiting for the Bridegroom
  - The Lamb's Bride
  - The Wedding "Guests"
  - The Homeward Journey
  - The Joyous Home Coming
    of the Redeemed
  - On the "Sea of Glass"
  - Before the Jasper Wall
  - At the Gates of Pearl
  - On the Streets of Gold
  - Welcome Home
- "Nearing Home" (A Poem)

35

CHRIST COMING FOR HIS BRIDE

Waiting for the Bridegroom. The Judgment of the righteous is over. Their redemption is accomplished. That "great multitude, which no man could number, of all nations, and kindreds, and people and tongues," Rev. 7:9, is waiting for the Bridegroom. There is "silence in heaven about the space of half an hour," Rev. 8:1, about seven literal days, for all its inhabitants are coming with Christ, the Bridegroom, to receive His bride. "With power and great glory" "the Son of man shall come in the glory of His Father," Matt. 16:27, in His own glory, Matt. 24:30, and in the glory of all the holy angels. Matt. 25:31. This is "the glorious appearing of the great God and our Saviour Jesus Christ." Titus 2:13.

Groups of loyal believers have fled from their homes because of the death decree issued by their persecutors, Rev. 13:15, and have found refuge in secluded places. Here with prayerful hearts they wait. "Soon they hear the voice of God...which gave...the day and hour of Jesus' coming." "The wicked could not understand the words," which to them "rolled through the earth like peals of loudest thunder," but to the waiting saints, His voice "sounded like many musical instruments." EW 15, 34, 35; 1 T 181. Soon after this, they see "the sign of the Son of man in heaven"—a small black cloud which, as it comes nearer, becomes a great white cloud. Matt. 24:30; GC 640. Looking up, they exclaim, "Lo, this is our God; we have waited for Him, and He will save us:...we will be glad and rejoice in His salvation." Isaiah 25:9.

About this time, the general resurrection of the righteous takes place. Rev. 20:6. Then "we which are alive and remain unto the coming of the Lord...shall be caught up together with them, to meet the Lord in the air." I Thess. 4:15-17. Christ sends "His angels ... and they shall gather the elect from the four winds, from one end of heaven to the other." Matt. 24:31. Wonderful deliverance!

The Lamb's Bride. Throughout the Scriptures, the relation of Christ and His Church is described as that of husband and wife. A few texts will suffice to show this:

Isaiah 54:5—Thy Maker is thine Husband;
    the Lord of Hosts is His name.
Jer. 31:32—I was an Husband unto them, saith the Lord.
II Cor. 11:2—I have espoused you to one Husband.
Eph. 5:23-32—After speaking somewhat at length of this
    relationship, Paul concludes by saying, "I speak
    concerning Christ and the Church."

When John saw the holy city, New Jerusalem, decorated as it is with gold and precious stones, and shining with the glorious light of heaven, he said it was "prepared *as a bride* adorned for her husband." Later, by a metaphorical figure of speech, in which the Bible abounds, the angel who talked with John said, "Come hither, I will show thee the bride, the Lamb's wife." And he showed him "the holy Jerusalem, descending out of heaven from God." Rev. 21:2, 9, 10. Again, speaking of the Lamb's wife, John says, "And to her was granted that she should be arrayed in fine linen, clean and white: for the fine linen is the righteousness of saints...which are called unto the marriage supper of the Lamb." Rev. 19:7-9.

What, then, is the Lamb's bride or wife? Is it the city, the New Jerusalem, or is it the redeemed saints, or both? Commenting on these texts, Uriah Smith says, "By the figure of personification, which attributes life and action to inanimate objects," the City is called the bride, the Lamb's wife. "But," continues, "a city without inhabitants would be but a dreary and cheerless place.... The goodly apparel of this city, so to speak, consists of the hosts of the redeemed" in their shining garments. DR 733, Revised Edition. Thus, speaking nonfiguratively, the redeemed, arrayed in fine linen, clean and white, are the Lamb's wife. Thus arrayed they are called to the marriage supper of the Lamb in the New Jerusalem. When the Bridegroom comes for His bride—the redeemed—He will take them to the New Jerusalem, where the wedded celebration follows. Would it not seem therefore, that strictly speaking, the redeemed are the bride, while the city adorned "as a bride" is called the bride only in an accommodated sense?

The Wedding "Guests." The parable of the marriage of the king's son, Matt. 22:2-13, represents the church during the time of the Judgment. The invitations are sent out but many slight them, and are pronounced "not worthy." Among those who accept the invitation there are "both bad and good." At that time all are called "guests." During the examination of the guests, which represents the Investigative Judgment, the bad who do not have on the wedding garment are cast out, because though invited guests who have accepted the invitation, they have not made the necessary preparation. The others, having made the required preparation, are accounted worthy. They are no longer invited "guests"—they are now the redeemed, the Lamb's bride. Thus, the "guests... cannot be represented also as the bride." GC 427. The bride, the church of the Firstborn, has on the "wedding garment;" she is arrayed in fine linen, clean and white. Thus arrayed she is the "ornament" of Zion, Isaiah 49:18. Her beauty is not beauty of form or of complexion, but true beauty, the beauty of holiness, the beauty that adorns the New Jerusalem.

The Homeward Journey. All are now ready for the seven-day journey "unto the city of the living God, the heavenly Jerusalem," Heb. 12:22—unto the city toward which they have looked and longed, "which hath foundations, whose builder and maker is God." Heb. 11:10. The Father and the Son are in Their chariot, "even thousands of angels." Ps. 68:17. "On each side of the cloudy chariot are wings, and beneath it are living wheels; and as the chariot rolls upward, the wheels cry,

'Holy,' and the wings as they move cry, 'Holy,' and the retinue of angels cry, 'Holy! holy! holy! Lord God Almighty!' And the redeemed shout 'Alleluia! as the chariot moves onward toward the New Jerusalem.'" GC 645.

Speaking of this grand journey, Uriah Smith says, "From our little world we pass out to our sun 93,000,000 miles away; on to its nearest neighboring sun, twenty-five million million miles away; on to the great double pole star, from which it takes light four hundred years to reach our world; on past systems, groups, constellations, till we reach the great star Rigel, in Orion, shining with the power of fifteen thousand suns like ours!" DR 683; Revised Edition. Is it any wonder that after such a journey, the great company of the redeemed break forth in that song of victory, saying, "Great and marvelous are Thy works, Lord God Almighty?" Rev. 15:3.

In this constellation of Orion, is a nebula or open space, which for centuries has fascinated the best astronomers. One astronomer said, "The creative power which made the universe lavished its richest gifts in and around Orion." Through this open space in the heavens is seen a brilliantly-lighted avenue of indescribable glory.

While astronomers have puzzled and wondered and studied this vast concealed mystery, they do not understand and cannot explain the existence of this aperture in the heavens. Herschel, the founder of modern astronomy, gave much study to this problem, which to astronomers still remains unsolved. But they have figured that this opening has a diameter of more than 16 trillion miles, its depth cannot be measured. Why not? This is abundantly large enough to permit Christ with all the inhabitants of heaven to descend to this earth at His second coming, Matt. 25:31, and also at His third coming to permit the descent of the Holy City to this earth, Rev. 21:2, where it will be permanently located as the capitol of the universe. Down through this brilliantly lighted corridor the voice of Jehovah is heard proclaiming the day and hour of Christ's coming. Mark 13:32.

The constellation Orion appears about midnight in November in the southeasterly heavens. And the Son of Man appears in the east at midnight. Matt. 24:27; 25:6. See EW 41; also *Astronomy and the Bible*, by L. A. Reed, chapter 23.

The Joyous Homecoming of the Redeemed. "The open space in Orion," EW 41, the avenue through which the Holy City will at last come down to this earth, and the avenue which Christ, with the Father and all the inhabitants of heaven, come for the redeemed, is doubtless the avenue through which the bridal party moves onward and upward toward the City of God. This is the time of that wonderful homecoming, the reunion of God's "whole family in heaven and earth," Eph. 3:15, the "general assembly and church of the Firstborn, which are written in heaven." Heb. 12:23. And such a homecoming! As a sort of telescopic side light, we are told on good authority that as the victorious procession of the redeemed, accompanied by all the inhabitants of heaven, journeys forward, "representatives from all over God's universe will line the way on either side of the procession, eager to catch glimpses of the triumphant throng."

On at least two other special occasions, representatives from unfallen worlds have been present or have taken part: *first*, when the foundation of this earth was laid, "the morning stars sang together, and all the sons of God shouted for joy," Job 38:6, 7; again, when Christ broke the fetters of the tomb, and came forth a victorious Conqueror, and ascended on high to begin His work in the holy place of the sanctuary above, "the sons of God, the representatives of the unfallen worlds" assembled with the angel hosts to honor the King of glory. "The heavenly council before which Lucifer had accused God and His Son, the representatives of those sinless realms…all are there to welcome the Redeemer. They are eager to celebrate His triumph and to glorify their King." DA 833, 834.

Ever since sin marred this fair creation, and the work of redemption began, its inhabitants have been "a spectacle [a theatre, margin] to the world [the inhabited universe], the angels [who live in heaven], and to men" [those who live on this earth]. I Cor. 4:9. During the centuries, these unfallen worlds, the "sons of God," have watched with unabated interest the working out of man's salvation. They have rejoiced over victories won and grieved over every defeat. Luke 15:7, 10; GC 677. And now as the grand climax of redemption is about to be enacted, will they be less interested to join in the final celebration of the Redeemer? How could they? "The whole universe is looking with inexpressible interest to see the closing work of the great controversy between Christ and Satan." 6 T 145.

On the "Sea of Glass." At last, the bridal party reaches the heavenly City, the New Jerusalem, having observed one Sabbath during the week's journey. Surrounding the city is a vast area like transparent glass. This area is evidently the "foundations" of the City, Heb. 11:10, extending far beyond the city walls. EW 17. Of this transparent platform, Uriah Smith says: "It may extend under and be the foundation…the City itself." DR on Rev. 4:6, p. 411, 1944 edition. This is probably correct, as it corresponds with John's description of the City street, which is "as it were transparent glass." Rev. 21:21. These foundations, twelve in number, are "garnished [brilliantly lighted up] with all manner of precious stone," stones that emit flashes of light of different colors making, "as it were, a sea of glass [Greek: a glassy sea; i.e. transparent] mingled with fire." Rev. 21:14, 19, 21; 15:2. Here in these precious stones are portrayed "the names of the twelve apostles of the Lamb." Rev. 21:14. On this magnificent broad expanse, which surrounds on all sides the city foursquare, Rev. 21:16, stands the innumerable multitude of the redeemed. Over this platform they march to the twelve gates [three on each side] of the city. EW 16, 17, 12. Here they pause. As in the type, the twelve tribes, arranged in four groups of three tribes each, formed a hollow square around the earthly sanctuary, so in the antitype, the redeemed stand on the sea of glass in "a hollow square" around the City. GC 645, 646.

Before the Jasper Wall. Before the redeemed rises the magnificent wall of the city. It is built of jasper, "a stone most precious." Rev. 21:11, 18. This precious stone is said to be wavy with the various colors of the rainbow, having a watery crystalline brightness: Being "clear as crystal," vs. 11, the beauties of the city are not entirely hidden from the eyes of the redeemed.

The wall is "great and high," "huge and high," [*Moffatt*] *huge* probably indicating its thickness. The angel who measured it said it was 144 cubits, or about 216 feet. This may indicate its thickness as well as its height. Its length measured 12,000 furlongs, Rev. 21:12, 16, 17, or 1500 miles. Some commentators claim that this is the measure *all around* the city, 375 miles on each side; others understand that *each side* is 1500 miles. Which is correct? We shall know when we reach our city home.

Let us compare this wall with the great wall of China, which, without question, is the most famous wall ever built by man. This wall varies in height from fifteen to thirty feet [about one-tenth the height of the City wall], with a thickness of twenty-five feet at its base and fifteen feet at its top. It is made of brick and mortar and filled in with common rock. After two thousand years, most of it still stands, while other famous walls have crumbled to the ground. Yet, though one of the greatest human achievements, how utterly inferior is it to the wall of the City made by God! As the redeemed stand before this magnificent wall of precious stone with its gates of shining pearl, how their hearts must thrill at the prospect of soon passing beyond it into the City!

At the Gates of Pearl. Each of the three massive gates on each side of the City wall is made of one immense pearl. Rev. 21:12, 13, 21. In Psalms 24:7, 9, where these gates are called doors, seems to indicate that they are two-leaved gates. Why are the gates made of pearl? The pearl is the result of pain and suffering caused by some foreign substance, perhaps only a tiny grain of sand, getting within the shell of the oyster. The oyster cannot expel the substance; if it should try to do so, its tender body would become torn and lacerated in the vain effort. So it quietly submits, and the cruel substance is covered with a secretion from its own body. This secretion gradually develops into the beautiful, polished, costly gem. Likewise, the redeemed have passed through trials, disappointments, suffering, and sorrow, caused by the grain of sin, but they have "fought a good fight," II Tim. 4:7, not with carnal weapons of warfare, but through the mighty power of God. II Cor. 10:4. Having submitted themselves to God, He has transformed the sin within them into the "pearl of great price." Matt. 13:46. Through Christ their "warfare is accomplished;" Isaiah 40:2; and at last they have reached the gates of pearl, which are wide open to receive them. "The gates...shall not be shut at all by day: for there shall be no night there." Rev. 21:25.

"Before entering the City the Saviour bestows upon His followers the emblem of victory, and invests them with the insignia of their royal state...." For each there is a crown, bearing his own 'new name' Rev. 2:17, and like the inscription on the crown of the earthly high priest, *Holiness to the Lord*. In every hand is placed the *victor's palm* and the shining harp." GC 645, 646; Rev. 7:9; 15:2.

On the Streets of Gold. The City foursquare corresponds to the most holy place of the earthly sanctuary, which was a perfect square. In its center is the throne of God, antitype of the ark in the center of the most holy place of the earthly sanctuary. From the four sides of the City, in perfect order, the redeemed pass over the brilliantly lighted sea of glass, past the jasper wall, through the pearly gates, each long line passing through the gate on which is written the names of the tribes to which it belongs. Rev. 21:12. As these triumphant processions, twelve in number, enter the pearly portals, they are welcomed by the angel at the gate. Clothed with white robes of light, and waving the "palms [of victory] in their hands," Rev. 7:9, with their glittering crowns and shining harps enhanced by the glory streaming from the throne, this mighty, and glorious, and victorious procession moves forward. As they pass along the streets of transparent gold to the four sides of the throne, they make a sight wholly beyond human language to describe or even the most vivid imagination to picture—a sight that "eye hath not seen,…neither have entered into the heart of man." I Cor. 2:9.

As they approach the four sides of the throne, the redeemed "behold the Paradise of God, the home of Adam in his innocency." GC 646. Here the two Adams meet—the first Adam who through transgression lost his dominion, and the last Adam, "The Lord from heaven," I Cor. 15:45, 47, who through infinite sacrifice redeemed it. GC 647. Then shall be fulfilled the prophecy of Isaiah: "In that day shall this song be sung in the land of Judah: We have a strong city; salvation will God appoint for walls and bulwarks. Open ye the gates, that the righteous nation which keepeth the truth may enter in." Isaiah 26:1, 2.

> "In a little while we're going home.
> In a little while, in a little while,
> We shall cross the billow's foam;
> We shall meet at last,
> When the stormy winds are past,—
> In a little while we're going home."

Welcome Home. As the earthly high priest at the close of the day of atonement came out of the sanctuary, and with his hands lifted to heaven pronounced a blessing on the forgiven children of Israel, so Jesus our heavenly High Priest, the "Alpha and Omega the beginning and the end, the first and the last," Rev. 22:13, His mediatorial work being now closed, standing "in majesty high above saint and angel," His countenance beaming upon them "full of benignant love," GC 646, lifts His hands in blessing over the redeemed multitude, saying, "Blessed are they that do His commandments, that they may have right to the tree of life, and may enter in through the gates into the City." Rev. 22:13, 14. "That voice, richer than any music that ever fell on mortal ear, is heard saying, 'Your conflict is ended.' 'Come, ye blessed of My Father, inherit the kingdom prepared for you from the foundation of the world.'" Matt. 25:34; GC 646. Never until we ourselves actually hear the voice of Jesus giving this blessed welcome home, never until we actually enter the gates of pearl, can we realize the wondrous thrill of this experience. "O brother, be faithful, soon Jesus will come."

Nearing Home

Where the tree of life is growing
And the river softly flowing,
That's the place where we are going;
    And it fills our soul with song.

For it keeps the heart warm glowing,
As the gospel seed we're sowing
For the debt of love we're owing
    To the One who bore our wrong.

Though the world is bent on killing,
Man his brother's blood is spilling,
Hearts with dreadful fear instilling,
    There is peace within our soul.

They are prophecies fulfilling—
Wonderous signs, momentous, thrilling—
When God's people shall be willing
    As we press toward the goal.

Where the tree is blooming fragrant,
Winds life's river gently vagrant;
There with love forever fragrant,
    We shall find our home, sweet home.

—Arthur Mountain
(Used by permission)

CHAPTER 36 PREVIEW

"THE MARRIAGE of the LAMB"

- The Four Celebrations of Redemption
- The Setting of the Fourth Celebration
- The Rainbow About the Throne
- Significance of the Rainbow
- Assembling around the Throne
- The Celebration; a Seven-part Oratorio
- The Anthem of the Four Living Creatures
- The Song of the Four and Twenty Elders
- The Song of the 144,000
- The Song of the "Great Multitude"
- The Hallelujah Chorus
- The "Amen" sung by the Angels
- The Father's Solo
- The Response of the Universe
- Jesus, Wonderful Saviour
- The Marriage Ceremony: Christ Crowned
- "KING OF KINGS AND LORD OF LORDS"
- "The Marriage Supper of the Lamb"

36

"THE MARRIAGE OF THE LAMB"

The Four Celebrations of Redemption. Four times in the work of Christ, Heaven celebrates the four outstanding events in the progress of redemption; *first*, when as the Babe of Bethlehem He entered the court of earth to become our Sacrifice; Luke 2:3-20; *Second*, when He entered the holy place of the heavenly sanctuary to be our High Priest, Ps. 24:7-10; *third*, when He entered the most holy place within the second vail to act as Judge. Dan. 7:9-14; Isaiah 63:6. Every one of these celebrations was indeed a splendid expression of Heaven's approval of the work of the Lamb of God. The *fourth*, given after the close of probation, will be more magnificent than any that has preceded it, because at this time "the marriage of the Lamb" takes place, fulfilling the prophecy: "Let us be glad and rejoice, and give honor to Him: for the marriage of the Lamb is come, and His wife hath made herself ready." Rev. 19:7.

The Setting of the Fourth Celebration. For this occasion all the redeemed from the twelve tribes have now gathered at the four sides of the throne, each group having entered the City through the gate that bears his own family name. It is, of course, utterly impossible to give anything like an adequate picture of this scene, and yet we shall lose much unless we can, in our human way, visualize something of the surroundings and their indescribable glory.

As in the earthly sanctuary the ark was located in the center of the most holy place, so in the heavenly sanctuary, God's throne its antitype, "In the midst of the Paradise of God," occupies the center of the New Jerusalem. Rev. 2:7; 22:1, 2. "Far above the city, upon a foundation of burnished gold, is a throne high and lifted up." Isaiah 6:1; GC 664. It is located on Mt. Zion. Ps. 48:2; Heb. 12:22. How high up is the throne? The Bible does not tell us, but we know that it is high enough to be seen by Satan and his host when at a later time they surround the city designing to capture it. With this in mind, reliable mathematicians figure that, in order to see over the wall, which is 216 feet high, to the center of the city, at least 187-1/2 miles distant, the throne must be a number of miles high, not less than the height of Mt. Everest. At any rate, it is very "high and lifted up," *"far above* the City."

The throne itself is "a glorious throne." "His train [of glorified beings] fills the temple," Isaiah 6:1, even as the angel symbols of the earthly sanctuary completely surrounded the ark and formed a glittering canopy overhead, at either side of the throne stand seraphim, antitype of the two angel forms of solid gold that stood on the mercy seat over the ark. These, the two most exalted of the angel throng, stand as *honored guards* of God's "throne" and of His holy law. PP 357.

On the throne, occupying the center of the picture, in all their indescribable glory, sits God the Father in "His great and calm eternity," MH 417, and at His right the Son. So great is the glory radiating from them that "the City had no need of the sun,…to shine in it: for the glory of God did lighten it, and the Lamb is the light thereof." Rev. 21:23. As the stars are not visible by day because of the greater light of the sun, so the sun in the New Jerusalem, although shining "sevenfold" as bright as here on earth, Isaiah 30:26, is invisible because of the overpowering light shining from the throne of God to the City's remotest bounds.

The Rainbow About the Throne. "And there was a rainbow round about the throne." Rev. 4:3. The light reflected and radiating from the throne is not just plain dazzling light; it is broken into all its beautiful colors, revealing the intrinsic beauties resident in light, only these radiant colors round about the throne of God are as much more gorgeous than those of an earthly rainbow as heaven is more beautiful than earth. If you have ever seen a double rainbow where the first bow is so bright that a second is reflected from it, you have been captivated by the sight. But what about the rainbow surrounding the throne of God? How many reflections do you think it has?

The rainbow in heaven is "round about" the throne, not arching above it. In this life we never see a complete rainbow.

> "Our lives are broken circles here,
> The glory doth not yet appear,
> As only half of God's fair bow
> Is visible to man below.
>
> Behind the clouds the colors meet
> Full-orbed; hereafter shall be shown
> The covenant of love complete,—
> A Rainbow 'round about the throne."
> —*Author Unknown*

Significance of the Rainbow. As the first rainbow was a token of God's covenant with the human family that never again would there be a flood to destroy the earth, Gen. 9:8-17, even so the rainbow about His throne is the emblem of His everlasting covenant of peace with the redeemed. "My kindness shall not depart from thee, neither shall the covenant of My peace be removed." Isaiah 54:8-10. It is "an assurance that God is true; that in Him is no variableness, neither shadow of turning…. The honor of His throne is staked for the fulfillment of His word to us." 8 T 23. It is a pledge that God will keep all His promises of salvation to those who have put their trust in Him. It is His assurance that "affliction shall not rise up the second time," Nahum 1:9, and that even as He kept His promise to Noah, so never again should the earth be destroyed by fire. "The rainbow of promise encircling the throne on high is an everlasting testimony that 'God so loved the world, that He gave His only begotten Son, that whosoever believeth in Him should not perish, but have everlasting life.' It testifies to the universe that God will never forsake

His people in their struggle with evil. It is an assurance to us of strength and protection as long as the throne itself shall endure." DA 493.

"The rainbow spanning the heavens with its arch of light is a token of the everlasting covenant between God and every living creature. Gen. 9:16.... As the bow in the cloud results from the union of sunshine and shower, so the bow above God's throne represents the union of His mercy and His justice." Ed. 115.

Assembling around the Throne. "In the midst of the throne and round about the throne" are the four living creatures, Rev. 4:6, 7, "and they sparkled like the color of burnished brass." Eze. 1:7. As symbolized on the four standards of Israel, Num. 2:3-21, and as located by Ezekiel, the group "like a lion" is on the south a group having "the face of a man," and on the north is the group "like a flying eagle." Eze. 1:10. These groups are the most closely associated with the throne.

Next to the four living creatures, round about the throne, are "four and twenty thrones" on which are seated "four and twenty elders." Rev. 4:4. In the earthly sanctuary, these were represented by the twenty-four courses of priests, each serving twice a year, one week at a time. II Chron 31:2. Both these groups are clothed in "white raiment," and have on their heads "crowns of gold." Rev. 4:4. And everyone of them have harps. They have been "redeemed ... out of every kindred, and tongue, and people, and nation." Rev. 5:8-10. They are "the multitude of captives set free at His resurrection," Matt. 27:50-53; Eph. 4:8, "representatives of that great multitude who shall come forth from the grave at His second coming." DA 833, 834.

As "representatives," others will be added to these "at His second coming." To the first group, "nearest the throne" will be added "those who were once zealous in the cause of Satan, but who, plucked as brands from the burning, have followed their Saviour with deep, intense devotion." GC 665. Paul the persecutor, who became the great apostle, and Mary Magdalene out of whom Jesus cast seven devils, could fittingly illustrate this group.

To the second group, the twenty-four elders, will be added "at His second coming," "those who perfected Christian characters in the midst of falsehood and infidelity," GC 665, and have finally become great leaders in the cause of God. Men like Luther and other leaders in the Reformation who stood so nobly for Bible truth amidst the false teachings of the papal power could well illustrate this group. Others added to those around the throne are "those who [like the 144,000] honored the law of God when the Christian world declared it void, and the millions of all ages who were martyred for their faith." And beyond is "the great multitude which no man could number, of all nations, and kindreds, and people, and tongues ... clothed with white robes [emblem of the spotless righteousness of Christ which now is theirs] and palms in their hands," [symbol of their triumph]. Rev. 7:9; GC 665.

Surrounding the redeemed are "all the angels," Rev. 7:11, "ten thousand times ten thousand, and thousands of thousands," Rev. 5:11. There they are, a glittering phalanx, as if on guard about the redeemed. And beyond are the representatives of the unfallen worlds who from all over God's universe joined the triumphant throng as Jesus led the redeemed to the City. No earthly procession to celebrate the crowning of any king or queen, can in any way compare, either in numbers, in worldwide representation, or in dazzling splendor, with this one that has assembled to celebrate the second coronation of King Jesus and the marriage of the Lamb. No such company ever before graced the courts of heaven. It is a sight that beggars all description.

The Celebration; a Seven-part Oratorio. Everything is now ready for this magnificent celebration, an oratorio consisting of seven parts. "The keynote of every anthem is salvation to our God, and unto the Lamb." GC 665. It is one vast, continuous outburst of joyous song and adoring praise. Twice it is called "a new song;" Rev. 5:9; 14:3, so called probably because "it was never before sung in Heaven." TM 433. While it cannot adequately be described, we can bring together some of the anthems that are sung by different groups, and perhaps get some faint foretaste of its wonderful inspiration. Our only hope of ever really knowing what it will be like is to be among the redeemed when this celebration of the marriage of the Lamb actually takes place.

The Anthem of the Four Living Creatures. This group of redeemed being in the very midst of the throne, seems to take the lead. Every one of them have harps. Rev. 5:8. They "give glory and honor and thanks to Him that sat on the throne," and they "rest not day and night, saying, Holy, holy, holy, Lord God Almighty, which was, and is, and is to come." Rev. 4:6-9. Since their song goes on continuously, it would seem like a murmured accompaniment to those that follow.

The Song of the Four and Twenty Elders. These are closely associated with the first group. They also have harps. Casting their crowns before the throne, they sang a new song, saying, "Thou art worthy, O Lord, to receive glory and honor and power; for Thou has created all things, and for Thy pleasure they are and were created." "Thou art worthy…for Thou was slain, and has redeemed us to God by Thy blood out of every kindred, and tongue, and people, and nation; and hast made us unto our God kings and priests; and we shall reign on the earth." Rev. 4:10, 11; 5:8-10.

The Song of the 144,000. This group "having the harps of God" next takes up the strain. Having "gotten the victory over the beast, and over his image, and over his mark, and over the number of his name," "they sung as it were a new song before the throne, and before the four living creatures, and the elders: and no man could learn that song but the 144,000, which were redeemed from the earth." Rev. 15:2; 14:1-3. It is the song of their deliverance from the beast and his image, the song of their experience, saying, "Great and marvelous are Thy works, Lord God Almighty; just and true are Thy ways, Thou King of saints. Who shall not fear thee, O Lord, and glorify Thy name? For thou only art holy: for all nations shall come and worship before Thee; for Thy judgments are made manifest." GC 649; Rev. 15:2-4. This anthem, called "the song of Moses… and the song of the Lamb," Rev. 15:3, honors a more glorious triumph and deliverance than "the song of Moses" which honored Israel's deliverance from Pharaoh's mighty armies at the Red Sea, where "the Lord triumphed gloriously." Ex. 15:21.

The Song of the "Great Multitude." "After this I beheld, and lo, a great multitude, which no man could number, of all nations, and kindreds, and people, and tongues, stood before the throne, and before the Lamb,…and cried with a loud voice, saying, Salvation to our God which sitteth upon the throne, and unto the Lamb." Rev. 7:9, 10. "With a loud voice"—such surely would a chorus consisting of an innumerable company of singers. And as they repeat and repeat the words of their anthem, they make all Heaven ring.

The Hallelujah Chorus. As a fitting closing to this greatest of all oratorios comes the hallelujah chorus. "And after these things," says John, "I heard a great voice of much people in Heaven, saying, Alleluia; salvation, and glory, and honor and power, unto the Lord our God: for true and righteous are His judgments: for He hath judged the great whore, which did corrupt the earth with her fornication, and hath avenged the blood of His servants at her hand. And again they said, Alleluia!…And the four and twenty elders and the four living creatures fell down and worshiped God that sat on the throne, saying, Amen! Alleluia!" Then followed "the voice of a great multitude" "like the shout of a great host and the sound of many waves, and the roar of heavy thunder," *Moffatt*, saying,

> Alleluia, for the Lord God omnipotent reigneth.
> Let us be glad and rejoice, and give honor to Him:
> For the marriage of the Lamb is come,
> And His wife hath made herself ready." Rev. 19:1-7.

The "Amen" Sung by the Angels. "And I heard the voice of many angels round about the throne and the beasts and elders,… saying with a loud voice, Worthy is the Lamb that was slain to receive power, and riches, and wisdom, and strength, and honor, and glory, and blessing." Rev. 5:11, 12. "And all the angels … fell before the throne on their faces, and worshipped God, saying *Amen*: Blessing, and glory, and wisdom, and thanksgiving, and honor and power, and might, be unto our God forever and ever. Amen." Rev. 7:11, 12.

How fitting that the "Amen" is left for the angels to sing! They have never fallen, so they know not the experience of redemption, but with all their melodious might they can sing "Amen" to all that the other groups have sung. "Amen"—a word defined as meaning *true* or *truth*, a term used as a strong and positive assertion, fixing, as it were, the stamp of truth upon the assertion which it accompanies, and making it binding *as an oath*. And so the angels sing the grand "*Amen and Amen*."

The Father's Solo. Then comes the climax of this unspeakable marvelous oratorio. It is a solo. "A voice came out of the throne." Rev. 19:5. Every other voice is hushed. Now a harp string is touched. Listen! Powerful, melodious, clear, expressive of infinite love, a voice that reaches to the very ends of the universe. He can no longer keep silent. Like the other parts of this oratorio, the Father's solo first expresses praise to His own Son:

> "Praise our God, all ye His servants, And ye that fear Him,
> both small and great." Rev. 19:5

Zephaniah has given us a more complete description of this song of the Father. He says:

> "The Eternal has routed your foes,
> He has driven off your enemies;
> Israel's King is in your midst,
> You shall have no more trouble....
> Fear not, droop not your hands, O Zion."
> "The Eternal your God is in your midst
> A Warrior to the rescue;
> He thrills with joy over you,"
> He renews His love,
> He "exults with festal song."
>
> Zeph. 3:15-17, *Moffatt*

Or, as the authorized Version renders it;

> "In that day shall it be said to Jerusalem
> The Lord thy God will save,
> He will rejoice over thee with joy;
> He will rest in His love.
> He will joy over thee with singing."

The Response of the Universe. Answering the challenge of the Father:

> "Praise our God, all ye His servants,
> And ye that fear Him, both small and great,"

not only the representatives of unfallen worlds who have come to honor the Redeemer, but "every creature which is in heaven, and on the earth, and under the earth, and such as are in the sea, and all that are in them, heard I saying, Blessing and honor, and glory, and power, be unto Him that sitteth upon the throne, and unto the Lamb forever and ever." Rev. 5:13. The unfallen worlds in every part of God's great dominion are happy to be thus represented in this oratorio of the universe, for they know that if Jesus had not gained the victory over Satan, not only this earth, but all other worlds have come under his dominion.

Jesus, Wonderful Saviour. What is Jesus doing during this celebration? The only mention made of Him is that He sits on the throne with the Father. Surrounded with those whom He has redeemed, His lovely countenance beaming with joy and radiating happiness, His last prayer for His loved ones is now answered, "Father, I will that they also, whom Thou has given Me, be with Me where I am; that they may behold My glory," John 17:24. He sees the travail of His soul and He is satisfied. Isaiah 53:11. He rests in His love, love and joy too deep for utterance in word or song. Precious Saviour! Wonderful, wonderful Redeemer!

The Marriage Ceremony, Christ Crowned "KING OF KINGS AND LORD OF LORDS." John calls this fourth celebration of redemption "the marriage of the Lamb." Rev. 19:7. Christ, the Bridegroom, has brought the redeemed to their beautiful home, the New Jerusalem. They are His bride, "His wife [who] hath made herself ready…. She is arrayed in fine linen, clean and white…[which is] the righteousness of saints." vs. 7, 8. This is the garment of sanctification, the wedding garment, woven on earth during a life-long experience in the Trysting place. The wedding is celebrated in that most holy place of the heavenly sanctuary, where Christ receives His kingdom, the New Jerusalem, His bride. EW 251. As a bride at her marriage receives a new name, the name of the bridegroom, so Christ's bride, the redeemed, "Him that overcometh," is given "a new name," a *character* name, "which no man knoweth saving he that receiveth it." Rev. 2:17. It is also called "the Father's name," Rev. 14:1; 22:4, because through the second birth the redeemed are partakers of His nature; they are His "off-spring," His sons and daughters. Acts 17:28.

The first coronation of Christ, in the holy place of the heavenly sanctuary took place at the beginning of His mediatorial work in Heaven; His second in the most holy place will come at its close. At that time, "On His vesture and on His thigh a name [is] written, KING OF KINGS AND LORD OF LORDS". He is literally covered with royal honors. On His crown, "He has a name written, that no man knew, but He Himself." Rev. 19:13, 16. As a name given by Heaven represents character—the result of struggle and victory over the enemy, so in this name, given to Christ at the close of His mediatorial work, is wrapped up all the victorious sufferings that redemption has cost—sufferings that no man can ever comprehend. The most that we can understand is that this name means "Faithful and True," "The Word of God." vs. 11, 13. This name on the crown of Christ corresponds to the inscription "HOLINESS TO THE LORD" which was on the golden plate of the mitre, "the holy crown," Ex. 29:6, worn by the earthly high priest.

This nineteenth chapter of Revelation seems to indicate that the coronation of Christ as KING OF KINGS AND LORD OF LORDS, takes place at the marriage of the Lamb. Rev. 19:7, 16. When the crown, the seal of the marriage, is bestowed on the Bridegroom, "A great voice of much people in Heaven" bursts forth in a mighty and prolonged "HALLELUJAH." Rev. 19:1-6. This magnificent outburst of music and adoring praise is rendered by the combined groups of all the redeemed, the innumerable company of angels, and the representatives of unfallen worlds who are present on this occasion. Can you picture the scene? Can you hear the music? O, what will it be to be there? Surely, we cannot afford to miss it!

The Marriage Supper of the Lamb. Following the marriage of the King's Son, Matt. 22:2, is "the marriage supper of the Lamb." Rev. 19:9. For this occasion, Heaven has prepared "a table of pure silver…many miles in length," laden with all kinds of fruit from the tree of life. EW 19. We are not told how many miles this table reaches. We sometimes think of it as extending from one side of the City to its opposite side, which would certainly be "many miles in length." But in our mental picture, we must remember that, while we do not know its exact location, we do know that everything else in the City is "round about the throne." Rev. 4:3, 4, 6. As shown in the earthly type, so in the New Jerusalem, the angels surround on all sides the throne which is in the center of the City. The mansions also, which the redeemed will occupy, John 14:2, 3, are located on all sides of the throne. "The tree of life which is in the midst of the Paradise of God" locates the Garden of Eden about the throne. Compare Gen. 2:9 with Rev. 2:7. The redeemed, who will later sit at this table, have entered the City through its twelve gates on the four sides of the City wall and have assembled round about the throne. How meaningful that this table at which all the *redeemed* gather, is of silver, emblem of the ransom paid for their *redemption*! Ex. 30:12, 13. This is the time that Jesus, the *Redeemer*, stepping down from His throne, "shall gird Himself and make them [the redeemed] to sit down to meat, and will come forth and serve them." Luke 12:36, 37.

In one of His parables, Jesus has told us about this "great supper" to which all are bidden. Luke 14:16-24. The last call to the marriage supper of the Lamb is now being heralded: "Come, for all things are now ready." Let us beware lest "a piece of ground" or "five yoke of oxen," or domestic affairs, or some other earthly possession or temporal responsibility so crowd our thoughts that we begin "to make excuse" that we have "*no time*" for eternal realities. Now, more than at any previous time, this call is being given not only to professed Christians, but also to those in "the streets and lanes of the city" and in "the highways and hedges" of heathen lands, and thousands in the darkest corners of the earth are responding and preparing for the "great supper." Soon, very soon, this "compel"—ing message will have accomplished its work and God's house will be filled. vs. 23. If we who live in enlightened lands where the Bible is available to all and where this gospel of the kingdom is preached within our hearing—if we slight the call, will it not be said of us as it was of those in the parable: "None of these…shall taste of my supper?" vs. 24. Can we afford to meet such a tremendous loss and rob ourselves of a place at the silver table in the New Jerusalem? Shall we not rather say with determination and joyful anticipation:—

"I want to be there, I mean to be there,
I expect to be there, I do;
I want to be there, I mean to be there,
I expect to be there, don't you?"

CHAPTER 37 PREVIEW

THE VERDICT OF JEHOVAH'S JURY

- The Descent of the Holy City
- Christ's "Final Coronation," "KING OF ETERNITY"
- The Eyes of the Wicked Opened
- Satan's Acknowledgment
- The Evidence In: The Trial Over
- The Verdict of the Angels
- The Verdict of the Unfallen Worlds
- The Verdict of the Redeemed
- The Verdict of the Universe
- The Verdict Completed
- The Result to Man
- The Result to This Earth
- The Result to Jesus

37

THE VERDICT OF JEHOVAH'S JURY

The Descent of the Holy City. At the end of the thousand years when the judgment of the wicked is finished, Christ again returns to this earth to execute His righteous judgment and cleanse the earth from sin. For this He has put on "The garments of vengeance," Isaiah 59:17, garments "rolled in blood," Isaiah 9:5, "dipped in blood," Rev. 19:13, for this is "the day of the Lord's vengeance, and the year of recompence for the controversy of Zion." Isaiah 34:8. It is the day when in flaming fire, He will take "vengeance on them that know not God, and that obey not the gospel," II Thess. 1:8.

"He is accompanied by the host of the redeemed, and attended by a retinue of angels." GC 662. "His feet shall stand in that day upon the Mount of Olives, which...shall cleave in the midst thereof...and there shall be a very great valley." Zech. 14:4, 5. As the feet of Christ touch Olivet, the mighty plain thus made is purified and made ready to receive the Holy City, which will come down through the open space in Orion, the gateway between the earth and heaven. Then, looking up, the redeemed see "the New Jerusalem, coming down from God out of heaven," See GC 662, 663; EW 41, and a great voice out of heaven is heard saying, "Behold the tabernacle of God is with men, and He will dwell with them, and they shall be His people, and God Himself shall be with them, and be their God." Rev. 21:2, 3. Heaven, God's dwelling place, is transferred to this earth.

When the New Jerusalem reaches this earth, the redeemed enter, and as Satan and the host of the wicked, "the rest of the dead," Rev. 20:5, whom Christ has raised from the grave, surround the City to capture it, "by command of Jesus the gates of the New Jerusalem are closed." GC 664. "Christ again appears to the view of His enemies. Far above the City, upon a foundation of burnished gold, is a throne high and lifted up. Upon this throne sits the Son of God, and around Him are the subjects of His kingdom." Here, "in the presence of the assembled inhabitants of earth and Heaven, the 'final' coronation of the Son of God takes place." GC 664, 665.

Christ's "Final Coronation," "KING OF ETERNITY." Inspiration recognizes three coronations of Christ during His redemptive work, and it is in connection with His *third* and "final coronation" that this work culminates. "Satan...who was once a covering cherub,...sees another standing near to the Father." He sees "the crown placed upon the head of Christ by an angel of lofty stature and majestic presence, and he knows that the exalted position of this angel [Gabriel] might have been his." GC 669. At this coronation, both righteous and wicked are facing eternity. How fitting then that at this time Christ is crowned "THE KING ETERNAL," OR "THE KING OF ETERNITY" as Moffatt has it! I Tim. 1:17.

The Eyes of the Wicked Opened. As the wicked gaze upon this coronation of Christ, they "see in His hands the tables of the divine law, and the statutes which they have despised and rejected," GC 668. As they come face to face with the fact that "sin is the transgression of the law" and that "the wages of sin is death," as they witness the fruitage of evil on every side, and see the total failure of Satan's cause, "the arch deceiver has been fully unmasked," and God stands justified before them. GC 670. Too late, they see that they have been deceived, and with frenzy they turn upon their arch deceiver. "Of all…whom he has allured into rebellion, there are none now to acknowledge his supremacy." GC 672. Then is fulfilled the prophecy of Ezekiel, "Because thou hast set thine heart as the heart of God,…I will bring…upon thee, the terrible of the nations: and they shall draw their swords against the beauty of thy wisdom, and they shall defile thy brightness…. Wilt thou yet say…I am God?" Eze. 28:6-10.

Satan's Acknowledgment. When Satan beholds all about him the ruin that his reign has brought upon the world, when he sees that his own followers have turned against him and "narrowly look" upon him with hatred and scorn, Isaiah 14:16-18, "his accusations against the mercy and justice of God are silenced. The reproach which he has endeavored to cast upon Jehovah rests wholly upon himself. And now Satan bows down and confesses the justice of his sentence." GC 670. His own works have condemned him, and "in the presence of the witnessing universe," he acknowledges "the justice of God's government and the righteousness of His law." PP 339.

But the same old spirit of hatred and rebellion that he has cherished and cultivated for six thousand years, still rankles in his breast, and to live among the inhabitants of Heaven and exercise a spirit of obedience and loyalty to God and a spirit of love to Christ, the angels, and the redeemed, "would be to him supreme torture." GC 670. To one as proud as Lucifer such humiliation would be anything but joy. To him, eternal destruction will be a welcome release. With this final display of determined rebellion and insubordination by Satan and his host, the evidence of God's righteousness, the love and justice of His law are clearly before the universe.

The Evidence In; The Trial Over. When the angels watched the unjust and cruel trial of Jesus before those who were prompted by Satan; when, in spite of all the insult and abuse and torture to which He was subjected, they saw Him without a protest go as a lamb to the slaughter; and especially, when they listened to the last prayer of their beloved Commander, "Father, forgive them; for they know not what they do," Luke 23:34, they understood the amazing love and righteousness of God. With them "the last link of sympathy between Satan and the heavenly world was broken." DA 761. The character of Satan was clearly revealed, and God's character and His law of love fully vindicated. Then was fulfilled this scripture: "Forever, O Lord, Thy Word is settled in Heaven." Ps. 119:89.

The Verdict of Unfallen Worlds. As the unfallen worlds followed Satan in the working out of his wicked and deceitful plans, they concluded that he "abode not in the truth, because there is no truth in him. When he speaketh a lie, he speaketh of his own: for he is a liar, and the father of it." And finally, when they saw him disgracefully and exultantly put to death the Son of God, they knew that "he was a murderer from the beginning." John 8:44. Their decision for Christ and His government is forever settled.

The Verdict of the Redeemed. The redeemed who have gotten the victory over Satan and all his representatives, behold the justice and mercy of God, and with one voice declare, "Who shall not fear Thee, O Lord, and glorify Thy name? for Thou only are holy; for all nations shall come and worship before Thee; for Thy judgments are made manifest." Rev. 15:3, 4. "Every question of truth and error...has been made plain." GC 670. With their own eyes the redeemed have seen the results of rebellion and disappointment; in pain, and sickness, and death; in calamities by land, and sea, and air; in war and bloodshed. They have seen "the working out of Satan's rule in contrast with the government of God," GC 670, a government of love. They have seen God's wisdom, His justice and His supreme goodness, and they are fully convinced. They desire no other Ruler.

The Verdict of the Universe. "In the contest between Christ and Satan, during the Saviour's ministry...nothing could so effectually have uprooted Satan from the affections of...the whole loyal universe as did his cruel warfare upon the world's Redeemer." GC 501. And when the cry "Crucify Him! crucify Him!" came from the lips of those whom he inspired, their decision was forever settled. "With all the facts of the great controversy in view, the whole universe, both loyal and rebellious, with one accord declare, 'Just and true are Thy ways, Thou King of saints.'" GC 671. Everyone, "in heaven, on earth, and underneath the earth" "confess that Jesus Christ is Lord, to the glory of God the Father." Phil. 2:10, 11, *Moffatt*. Before the entire universe, God's wisdom, His justice, His goodness, and the righteous character of His law stand fully vindicated.

The Verdict Completed. At last the trial of Jehovah is over; the verdict of the jury is completed; Jehovah rests in His love. Zeph. 3:17. "In our legal courts, when the attorney has concluded all his arguments for the accused before the law, he announces to the court, 'The defense rests.' He means that he will stake all the evidence he has produced on the innocence of the accused, and on that basis demand an acquittal. Christ as our great Judge Advocate rests the case against us not on our innocence, but on His love, claiming exemption for us on the basis of our acceptance of Him as our substitute and propitiation for sin. He does bail for us too, until the great assize in Heaven judges us not only free from the condemnation of the law, but worthy of reward in His name," *My Lord and I*, p. 325, by H. M. Tippett.

Christ staked his life on the redemption of man. He gave His life, but through that act He lives forevermore. Against the work of Christ, Satan also staked *his* life. He will lose his life eternally, never again to war against God and His righteous government. "That God...renews His intercourse with the fallen race; that Christ could stoop to raise unnumbered multitudes from the abyss of ruin, and clothe them with the spotless garments of His own righteousness, to unite with angels who have never fallen, and dwell forever in the presence of God"—this is "the mystery of godliness." GC 415; I Tim. 3:16.

The Result to Man. "To human beings striving for conformity to the divine image there is imparted an outlay of heaven's treasure, an excellency of power, that will place them higher than even the angels who have never fallen." COL 163. It will "bring the lost into a fellowship with Christ, which is closer than they themselves can know." DA 19, 1898 edition. "By His life and His death, Christ has achieved even more than recovery from the ruin wrought through sin. It was Satan's purpose to bring about an eternal separation between God and man; but in Christ we become more closely united to God than if we had never fallen. In taking our nature, the Saviour has bound Himself to humanity by a tie that is never to be broken. Through the eternal ages He is linked with us.... It is the Son of *man* who shares the throne of the universe...In Christ the family of earth and the family of Heaven is enshrined in humanity, and humanity is enfolded in the bosom of Infinite love." DA 25, 26.

"A tested and proved creation will never again be turned from allegiance to Him whose character has been fully manifested before them as fathomless love and infinite wisdom." GC 504.

The Result to This Earth. "The earth itself, the very field that Satan claims as His, is to be not only ransomed but exalted. Our little world, under the curse of sin, the one dark blot in His glorious creation, will be honored above all other worlds in the universe of God. Here, where the Son of God tabernacled in humanity; where the King of glory lived and suffered and died,— here, when He shall make all things new, the tabernacle of God shall be with men, and He shall dwell with them. Rev. 21:3; DA 25, 26; GC 674-676.

Here on this earth, when the City comes down "from God out of heaven," Rev. 21:2, having the throne of the Eternal, which is in the midst of the Paradise of God, Rev. 2:7, surrounded by the original garden of Eden, here at the very place where Satan caused the fall of our first parents and opened the flood gates of woe upon this world—here, on this redeemed planet, will be the throne of God and of the Lamb. The holy city will be the throne room of the universe, the center of God's universal government, the capital of His entire kingdom, around which circle all other worlds. Thus will be fulfilled the saying: "Suns, and stars, and systems, all in their appointed order, circling the throne of Deity." GC 677, 678. How greatly honored will be this redeemed planet—more honored than any other spot in the universe—more glorious than if it had never felt the blight of sin!

The Result to Jesus. When, at His ascension, Christ was seated on the throne, "At the right hand of God", Heb. 10:12, in *the holy place* of the heavenly sanctuary, and in the presence of all the angels of heaven and the representatives of unfallen worlds, was declared and crowned the KING OF GLORY, Ps. 24:7-10; Heb. 2:9, by "the Father of Glory," Eph. 1:17, 20, He was indeed "exalted." Acts 2:33. This was His *first coronation*.

At the *beginning* of the one thousand years, when probation has closed, when the Judgment of the righteous is passed and they have been taken from this earth to Heaven, He again "shares the Father's throne," DA 832, this time in *the most holy place* of the heavenly sanctuary. Here, in the presence not only of all the angels of Heaven and representatives of unfallen worlds, but also in the presence of the redeemed, He is crowned KING OF KINGS AND LORD OF LORDS. Rev. 19:16. At this, His *second coronation*, He is literally clothed with honor, having His royal insignia written on his vesture and on His thigh. Rev. 19:7, 11, 13, 16. Here again He is indeed exalted.

At the end of the thousand years, when the City comes down from heaven, and Christ is crowned KING OF ETERNITY, He is "highly exalted." Phil. 2:9. Then, "God raised Him high and conferred on Him a name above all names so that before the name of Jesus every knee should bend, in Heaven, on earth, and underneath the earth, and every tongue confess that Jesus Christ is Lord to the glory of God the Father." Phil. 2:9-11, *Moffatt*. This scripture meets its complete fulfillment, not at the first or the second coronation of Christ, but at His *third and "final" coronation*, for on this occasion, not only the angels of Heaven, the representatives of the unfallen worlds, and all the redeemed, but also all the wicked as well as Satan himself—"every tongue" acknowledges His righteous supremacy.

Paul puts it this way: "We see Jesus, who was made a little lower than the angels [margin: a little while inferior to the angels] for the suffering of death, crowned with glory and honor." Heb. 2:9. More than this, "He that descended is the same also that ascended up far above all heavens, that He might fill all things." Eph. 4:10. As a result of His sacrifice He regains not only the command of the angel host, but as the Captain of our salvation, Heb. 2:10, He now becomes King of earth's redeemed. When His redemptive work is finished, He will occupy a position even greater than before He descended to earth. The Father will put all in subjection under Him. "But when...all things are put under Him, it is manifest that He is excepted, which did put all things under Him. And...then shall the Son also Himself be subject unto Him...that God [the Father] may be all in all." I Cor. 15:25-28. Christ becomes Ruler, not only of the new earth, but of the entire universe. He will be given the very highest place of glory—higher than the glory which He had with the Father before the world was. All this is wrapped up in the expression: God hath "highly exalted Him." Phil. 2:9. No wonder all Heaven exclaims, "Worthy is the Lamb that was slain to receive power, and riches, and wisdom, and strength and honor, and glory, and blessing." Rev. 5:12.

CHAPTER 38 PREVIEW

THE TEMPLE ETERNAL—
ITS MOST HOLY PLACE

- Will There Be a Temple After Redemption?
- God's Eternal Throne and the Temple Eternal
- Its Most Holy Place
- The Service in the Temple Eternal
- The Garden of Eden and the Temple Eternal
- The Throne and the Tree of Knowledge
- The Residents of the Holy City
- The Function of the Most Holy Place of the Temple Eternal
- "From One New Moon to Another"
- "From One Sabbath to Another"

38

THE TEMPLE ETERNAL—
ITS MOST HOLY PLACE

Will There Be a Temple After Redemption? We may now ask, will the sanctuary which has fulfilled its mission, first as the earthly sanctuary and then so gloriously as the greater and more perfect tabernacle—the heavenly sanctuary—will the sanctuary be still more gloriously perpetuated when, at the end of the thousand years every trace of iniquity has been forever wiped out of the universe? Answering this question, God has promised: "I will set My sanctuary in the midst of them [redeemed Israel], forevermore." Eze. 37:25-27.

Where will this eternal sanctuary be located? Will it have a court, a holy place, and a most holy place? What will they be like, and how will they function in the Redeemer's wonderful plan? These are legitimate questions that now challenge our study.

God's Eternal Throne and the Temple Eternal. When the work of the heavenly sanctuary—the judgment of both the righteous and the wicked—is finished, will there be a sanctuary? or temple, in "Heaven itself," Heb. 9:25; that is, in the New Jerusalem? Let John answer this question. In his description of the City he says, "I saw no temple therein: for the Lord God Almighty and the Lamb are the temple of it." Rev. 21:22. John saw "no temple" such as he was familiar with, but he did see "*the* temple" which he says is "the Lord God Almighty and the Lamb;" that is, he saw the eternal throne of God occupied by the Father and the Son.

John's vision looked forward to the time when the redemptive work of the Father and the Son, the work of the Holy Spirit, and of the angels as co-workers with them, is finally accomplished. Then the heavenly sanctuary as such, having fulfilled God's purpose, automatically ceases. Like any court of Justice when its work is done it adjourns. But the throne of God and the Holy City, being eternal, remain. The ambition of Lucifer to exalt his throne "above the stars of God" and "be like the Most High," Isaiah 14:13, 14, has crumbled to dust, but [the throne of] "the Lord God Almighty and the Lamb [which] are the temple of it," Rev. 21:22, remains eternally secure. The temple eternal in its fullness will be a complete fulfillment of God's glorious plan, foreshadowed in His word: "Let them make Me a sanctuary; that I may dwell among them." Ex. 25:8. It will be a fulfillment of the prophecy, "The tabernacle of God is with men, and He will dwell with them, and they shall be His people, and God Himself shall be with them, and be their God." Rev. 21:3. It will be a fulfillment of His promise: I will set My sanctuary in the midst of them forevermore.

Its Most Holy Place. We have seen that all parts of the earthly sanctuary typified the various parts and activities of the heavenly sanctuary. Each has a court, a holy place, and a most holy place. God directed that the most holy place of the earthly sanctuary should be a perfect square because it symbolized the most holy place of the temple eternal, the New Jerusalem, which is a perfect square. Rev. 21:16. The ark in the center of the most holy place represented God's eternal throne, which is "in the midst [center] of the Paradise of God." Rev. 2:7, the New Jerusalem. "The King in His glory is in the midst of Zion." PP 87. The cherubim carved on the walls and embroidered on the vail and on the inner covering of the earthly sanctuary, symbolized the *real* angels—"His train that filled the temple." Isaiah 6:1. They were symbols not only of the real angels of the heavenly sanctuary but also of the temple eternal. Their antitypes are eternal; they abide forever.

As already noted, during redemption the heavenly sanctuary in the City is divided into two parts—the holy place where Christ ministered as High Priest, and the most holy where now He officiates as Judge. When redemption is past, these apartments being no longer needed for mediatorial and judgment purposes, the entire city, the "tabernacle of God," His permanent dwelling place with His throne in its center is the final antitype of the most holy place of the earthly sanctuary. It is "the capital" of God's entire kingdom, GC 426, "the throne room of the universe." It is the most sacred and the most glorious place in the entire universe. It is the most holy place of the temple eternal.

The Service in the Temple Eternal. The difference between the heavenly sanctuary and the temple eternal lies chiefly in the service. The service in the heavenly continues *during* redemption; the service in the temple eternal comes *after* redemption; The heavenly sanctuary was set up for redemptive and judgment purposes; the temple eternal functions after both these are past. As the heavenly sanctuary could not begin its service until the work of the earthly closed, Heb. 9:8, so the temple eternal cannot function until the work of the heavenly sanctuary is finished. The ministration in the earthly sanctuary closed at the death of Christ on Calvary; the service in the heavenly closes at the end of the one thousand years when the judgment is past, and the earth is cleansed from sin. Then, when God creates "a new heaven and a new earth," Rev. 21:1, the service in the temple eternal begins. Our present study is to get a mental picture, as definite and as tangible as possible, of the most holy place of the temple eternal and its services.

The Garden of Eden and the Temple Eternal. Now that we have located the New Jerusalem as the most holy place of the temple eternal, let us look about. The throne is on Mount Zion, "high and lifted up." Isaiah 6:1. It is "a glorious...throne." Jer. 17:12. By comparing John's description of the throne in Revelation 22:1, 2, with Moses' description of the Garden of Eden in Genesis 2:8-10, we find several striking similarities.

"The Lord God planted a garden eastward in Eden, and there He put the man whom He had formed... And out of the ground made the Lord God to grow...the tree of life...and the tree of knowledge of good and evil. And a river went out of Eden to water the garden." Gen. 2:8-10. Apparently, this river was the river of life, which was in the midst of the garden, near the tree of life. Originally Eden, with the tree of life and the river of life, was on this earth. But everyone knows that it is not here now. What has become of it? God planted it, and "whatsoever God doeth, it shall be forever." Eccl. 3:14. Therefore, it still exists somewhere. Where?

John says that both the tree of life and the river of life are now in the New Jerusalem, that the river of life proceeds out of the throne, and the tree of life, which is "in the midst [middle] of the Paradise of God," Rev. 2:7, grows on either side of the river. Rev. 22:1, 2. In Eden the tree of life and the river of life were "in the midst of the garden." Gen. 2:9. This locates the throne, with the river of life and the tree of life, in the midst of the Garden of Eden. From these scriptures we learn that the Garden of Eden is now in the New Jerusalem, that it surrounds the throne of God, and that both are in the center of the City.

When and how was Eden transplanted? We are told that "the Garden of Eden remained upon this earth long after man had become an outcast from its pleasant paths…. At the cherubim-garden gate of Paradise, the divine glory [the Shekinah] was revealed. Hither came Adam and his sons to worship God. Here they renewed their vows of obedience to that law the transgression of which had banished them from Eden. When the tide of iniquity overspread the earth, and the wickedness of man determined their destruction by a flood of waters, "the hand that had planted Eden withdrew it from the earth." PP 62.

At that time, God transplanted the Garden which He had made to be the home of Adam, to His own home in Paradise above and placed it in the care of heavenly beings. Here, in the Paradise of God, the most holy place of the temple eternal, it will remain forever. Then, instead of angels around whom "flashed beams of light having the appearance of a glittering sword," PP 60, to guard the way of the tree of life, Gen. 3:24, an angel stands at each gate of the City, Rev. 21:12, not to keep the redeemed away from the tree of life, but to welcome them—descendants of Adam!—to its life-giving fruit. In the days before the Flood the people of God presented themselves *outside the gate* of Eden to offer their sacrifices and to renew their vows of obedience, while in the restoration, those who "do His commandments,…*enter in through the gates* into the city" to worship God and to renew *their* vows of consecration and loving obedience.

A man of wealth, living in Chico, California, once had a tree hobby. He traveled to different foreign lands, collecting interesting trees that took his fancy. These he shipped to his home city, where they were planted in his extensive garden. In a few years he had a very fine collection of rare and beautiful trees which have been the admiration of the city and its visitors. In this garden is one tree of special interest. It is called the "Hooker Oak"—a live oak, estimated to be at least a thousand years old. Under its spreading branches a thousand or more people could find shelter. This tree is listed among the "trees of fame" of our country. The original owner of the garden is now dead, and the garden with its beautiful trees, although still cared for, will sooner or later pass away. In fact, in a recent storm it was broken down, to the deep sorrow of the inhabitants.

Not so with the Garden of Eden. After 6,000 years, this "garden of delight" still lives, "more gloriously adorned than at the beginning." PP 62. Here grew not only a few selected trees, but in it "made the Lord God to grow *every tree* that is pleasant to the sight and good for food"—a marvelous variety. Gen. 2:9. Besides all these He made to grow two other trees of exceptional beauty and value, which might rightly be called "trees of fame." These, the tree of life and the tree of knowledge, grew in the midst of the garden, the most honored location of any of the trees.

"A river went out of Eden to water the garden; and from thence it was parted and became into four heads." Gen. 2:10. Ezekiel, describing this same river, speaks of it not only as "river" but also as "rivers." Eze. 47:9. And John says it proceeds "out of the throne of God and the Lamb." Rev. 22:1. Like a huge artesian well, its water, "clear as crystal," flows from its "four heads" in four directions, down the four sides of the mountain on which the throne is located. Down the mountain for miles, here and there joyously leaping in waterfalls and rushing onward in cataracts, sometimes doubtlessly forming into quiet lakes, from which rivulets flow out "to water the garden," it surely must present a charming picture. David recognized this when he wrote: "There is a river, the streams [plural] whereof shall make glad the City of God, the holy place of the tabernacles of the Most High. God is in the midst of her." Ps. 46:4, 5. The verdure thus watered is "living green" brightened with never-fading flowers of every hue and filling the air with sweetest fragrance. Fruit trees laden with luscious fruit add to the beauty. Lining the river on either side, the tree of life, growing similar to our banyan tree, but "united at the top in one tree," EW 17, takes root all along both its banks. Ezekiel, describing it says, "By the river upon the bank thereof, on this side and on that side shall grow all trees for meat, whose leaf shall not fade, neither shall the fruit thereof be consumed; ["it shall never fade"—*Moffatt*], it shall bring forth new fruit according to his months, because their waters they proceeded out of the sanctuary ["thanks to the water that flows from the sanctuary."—*Moffatt*; the throne of God in the temple eternal], and the fruit thereof shall be for meat, and the leaf thereof for medicine." Eze. 47:7, 12. "The tree of life perpetuates immortality." EW 51, 126.

From the base of the mountain, this tree-bowered river flows on in mighty streams to the jasper wall on the four sides of the City, thence dispensing its life-giving properties to refresh and beautify the Eden homes of the redeemed, located "beside those living streams." GC 675. This garden of unsurpassed beauty, located at least in part, on the slopes of Mt. Zion, may very properly be called the hanging gardens of the New Jerusalem. Long ago in the city of Babylon, which has been called Satan's counterfeit of the heavenly City, the great king Nebuchadnezzar built hanging gardens which were the wonders of earth, but the hanging gardens planted by the King of the universe are among the wonders of Heaven.

The Throne and the Tree of Knowledge. In the City, "there is no cruel deceiving foe to tempt to forgetfulness of God," GC 677; "no tree of knowledge of good and evil will afford opportunity for temptation," Ed. 302, for in that tree the curse of sin first polluted this earth, and in the restoration "there shall be no curse." Rev. 22:3. "But," continues the Revelator, "the throne of God and the Lamb shall be in it." This seems to indicate that God's throne will occupy the place in Eden where first grew the tree of knowledge. Wherever in the Bible the river and the tree of life are mentioned [except at creation, Gen. 2:9], it is significant to observe that the tree of knowledge is consistently ignored as if it no longer existed. Rev. 22:2, 3. In its place is the glorious "throne of God and the Lamb," the fountain head of all true knowledge—the knowledge of good unmixed with evil. How wonderful that in the very place where Satan tried to establish *his* throne, will be located the eternal throne of God and the Lamb! So complete will be the victory of righteousness over sin, of Christ over Satan! Through the redemption of Christ, the garden of Eden first planted in the earth, has been exalted to the highest place of honor, where it stands as a perpetual reminder of the power and righteousness of Christ.

When Eden was transplanted to Heaven, the tree of knowledge was left on earth and finally destroyed, it would seem in the Flood that soon followed; but, like all evil, its influence remains and still pollutes the stream of wisdom falsely so called. Since God planted the tree of knowledge, and since what He doeth shall be forever, how could it be destroyed? God also created this earth, yet because it has been ruined by sin, it will finally be destroyed, or speaking more nearly accurate, *all the sin* in it will be destroyed. Then, out of the ruins of the old, Mal. 4:2, 3, God will create a new heaven and a new earth wherein dwelleth righteousness. Is it not likewise that out of the ruins of the tree of knowledge, God will provide a place in the new earth where the redeemed shall have the wonderful opportunity of delving into the treasures of wisdom and knowledge untainted with evil?

The Residents of the Holy City. Heaven is the home of that vast company of angels who cooperate with Christ in His work. They are the "innumerable company" Heb. 12:22, who from the beginning have been loyal subjects of their mighty Leader. They are "ministering spirits, sent forth to minister for them who shall be heirs of salvation." Heb. 1:14. They have often protected the children of visible human agencies. E.G. White in *My Life Today*, p. 305. While on this earth, the Son of God Himself was ministered unto by certain chosen angels. These loyal angels comprise God's "whole family in Heaven," the family of the "Father of our Lord Jesus Christ," Eph. 3:14, 15. They are the permanent and eternal residents of the City, the most holy place of the temple eternal.

This "innumerable company" does not include "the third part of the stars of heaven," the disloyal angels who joined Satan in his rebellion against God, and with him "were cast down to the earth." Rev. 12:3, 4. It does not include "the angels which kept not their first estate"—an estate more lordly than any ever owned by the most wealthy of earth—"but left their own habitation," Jude 6, left their Father's house, to follow "that old serpent, called the devil and Satan, which deceiveth the whole world." Rev. 12:9. The angels who left their Father's house have no representation in the temple eternal.

According to John, Rev. 4:4-6, 8-10, a multitude of the redeemed are also now in heaven—those whom Christ raised "out of the graves after His resurrection" and took with Him at His ascension, Matt. 27:52, 53; Eph. 4:8, margin, as first fruits of the general resurrection of the righteous. It would seem that these groups—the four living creatures and the four and twenty elders—serving God "in the midst of the throne and round about the throne" will remain in the City as permanent residents. As already noted, certain others who will have part in the special resurrection of Dan. 12:2, will join those "nearest the throne." GC 665. Enoch also, "the first from among men to enter" the gates of the Holy City has his "home—in the City." PP 87; EW 40. The same is true of Elijah and Moses who were taken to Heaven and who appeared with Christ at His transfiguration. Matt. 17:1-3. The rest of the redeemed who are taken from this earth to the New Jerusalem at the beginning of the one thousand years, live in the City until the Judgment of the wicked is past at the end of the thousand years. During this time, as "priests of God and of Christ," Rev. 20:6, they occupy the "many mansions" which Christ at His ascension went to prepare for them. John 14:2, 3. At the end of the thousand years when the City comes "down from God out of Heaven," and the new Heaven and the new earth are created, Rev. 21:1-3, they dwell in their Eden homes outside the City. Here they will "plant vineyards, and eat the fruit of them." Isaiah 65:21. While the "mansions" in the City may be called their city home, these gardens of Eden will be their country home.

The Function of the Most Holy Place of the Temple Eternal. The most holy place of the temple eternal, the New Jerusalem, is "the metropolis of the new earth." GC 676. Having the throne of God, it is the seat of His universal government, "the capital" of the universe. GC 426. It will also be the scene of special occasions for the redeemed, among which will be Heaven's grand reception of all the redeemed—the fourth celebration of Christ's redemptive work. Here is celebrated the marriage and the marriage supper of the Lamb when He is crowned KING OF KINGS AND LORD OF LORDS. Rev. 19:9, 16. Here, also, at the end of the thousand years, will be His "final coronation" as KING OF ETERNITY. And here throughout eternity, all the redeemed, the church of the Firstborn, assemble for divine worship "from one new moon to another; and from one Sabbath to another." Isaiah 66:23. Thus we may call the City the CHURCH of the temple eternal.

"From One New Moon to Another." With Israel, the new moon was a peculiar class of holy days, its arrival being formally announced by the president of the Sanhedrin proclaiming, "It is consecrated." SB Dict. Art. *New Moon*. After leaving Egypt, when the silver trumpets sounded "the beginning of…months," all Israel assembled to offer "burnt offerings and…peace offerings…for a memorial before…God." Num. 10:2,10. Burnt offerings were expressive of a renewal of consecration; peace offerings expressed thanksgiving to God for His care, and His deliverance from their enemies. vs. 9. Both were sweet savor offerings.

The new moon was not only a renewal of consecration but it was "for a memorial" in commemoration especially of their deliverance from Egypt. It was to be "an ordinance forever throughout [their] generations." vs. 8. This ordinance, observed throughout the generations of ancient Israel, will be perpetuated by redeemed Israel when "from one new moon to another," "all flesh"—all the redeemed, God's whole family, the entire church of the Firstborn—shall come to the New Jerusalem to worship the Lord. Isaiah 66:22, 23. Here, as on the original new moon occasion ancient Israel offered burnt offerings and peace offerings, so in its New Jerusalem counterpart, redeemed Israel will bring to God their offerings of heart consecration and thanksgiving for their deliverance from the arch enemy.

With ancient Israel, the special sacrifices of the new moon were followed by a dinner at which the head of the family expected all the members to be present. It was also a time for State banquets, I Sam. 20:5, when all the royal family were to dine at the king's table in his palace. JFB Com. on I Sam. 20:5.

In the restoration, this is memorialized from month to month when the tree of life yields a new fruit. Rev. 22:2. Then redeemed Israel, "the royal family" shall assemble in "the palace" of the heavenly King and dine at His table, that "table of pure silver many miles in length," where the marriage supper of the Lamb they first ate of the life-giving fruit from the tree of life. How fitting that at each new moon, all the redeemed reassemble around this table, here to rededicate themselves to Him who gave His life for them! These monthly meetings will indeed be real feasts from the Fountainhead of love and joy.

Even in this life, we may eat of the fruit of the tree of life, for "its branches hang over the wall" to this world. 8 T 288. The promises of God "are leaves from the tree of life" which are "for the healing [the health] of the nations." MH 122: Rev. 22:2. Its fruit is "the *antidote of death.*" 8 T 288. Our spiritual life is sustained by constantly partaking of the promises of God as found in His Word.

Since the new moon was "for an ordinance forever," how has it been continued from the Mosaic to the Christian dispensation? When do Christians, "the royal family," assemble at the Lord's table, "the king's table?" At the last Passover which Christ celebrated with His disciples on the day of His crucifixion, He established the communion service which like the Passover, pointing forward to His death, was to commemorate His broken body and His spilled blood. From that time, all Christians have observed this ordinance, the emblems of which are placed on the table of the Lord and partaken of by the church.

When Christ instituted this ordinance, He said to His disciples, "I will not any more eat thereof, until it be fulfilled in the kingdom of God." "I will not drink henceforth of the fruit of the vine, until that day when I drink it new with you in My Father's kingdom." Luke 22:16, 18; Matt. 26:29. To what time did He refer? The

Bible mentions only two occasions when all the redeemed meet for divine worship in the Father's kingdom. These are "from one new moon to another" and "from one Sabbath to another." This eternal Sabbath service is a continuation of the Sabbath given by God at creation, and observed on this present earth. Is it not therefore on the new moon occasion that Christ will eat and drink with all the redeemed, "the royal family?"

At this time there is no mention of the preparatory service, feet washing, which was a type of "the higher cleansing" of the soul. DA 646. This soul cleansing which prepares the redeemed to participate at the Lord's table in heaven, takes place on earth. Here and now, is our opportunity to be cleansed in the blood of the Lamb. At each new moon in the New Jerusalem, the redeemed assemble at the silver table in the City, where they dedicate themselves anew to Him whose body was broken and whose blood was shed for their redemption. Thus, while the Sabbath is an eternal memorial of His creative work, the new moon service is a memorial of His re-creative work—an ordinance forever. Num. 10:8.

As with other of God's memorials, Satan, in idolatrous worship, has counterfeited the new moon ordinance. The worship of the moon was extensively practiced by the nations of the East. In Egypt it was honored under the form of Isis [the moon god], one of the only two deities [the other being the sun god] which commanded the reverence of *all* the Egyptians. *Smith's Bible Dictionary*, Art. *Moon*. This the Israelites must have witnessed in Egypt, so they well understood the force of the new moon ordinance instituted by Jehovah.

"From One Sabbath to Another." The Sabbath has always been Satan's special point of attack, because the Sabbath commandment contains the seal of God which validates His law, and pronounces Him Ruler of all. Therefore Satan, thinking to change God's law, Dan. 7:25, has counterfeited the true Sabbath by introducing the observance of Sun-day, the day dedicated to the sun god, as a day of worship in place of the Sabbath which in the beginning God set apart as *His* day, "the Sabbath of the Lord." Ex. 20:10. As a result, heathen religions emphasize the worship of the sun. Osiris, the sun god, the husband of Isis, was the favorite god of the Egyptians. These two idols, Isis and Osiris, were the two deities that "commanded the reverence of *all the* Egyptians"—a complete counterfeit of the new moon service and the Sabbath which will command the reverence of *all the redeemed*.

In the restoration, when Satan no longer dominates the minds and hearts of men, God's law, being eternal, will again shine forth, and the idolatrous practice of sun worship will disappear with its satanic originator. Then from one Sabbath to another shall all the redeemed assemble to worship God in the most holy place of the temple eternal. This is the very same Sabbath that God sanctified for man at creation; Gen. 2:2, 3; the very same Sabbath that He gave to Israel at Sinai as a memorial of His creative work; Ex. 20:8-11; the same Sabbath of which "the Son of man is Lord," Matt. 12:8, and on which as a man He worshiped "as His custom was," Luke 4:16, 20, and taught the people in their synagogues; Mark 6:2. It is the same Sabbath that the apostles and the early Christian church kept holy "According to the commandment," Luke 23:56, and which has been restored to God's people in these last days, Isaiah 58:12, 13,—on this very same Sabbath in the new earth "shall all flesh come to worship before Me, saith the Lord." Isaiah 66:23. Thus the Sabbath, the seal of God's eternal law, is most exalted. How precious will be these Sabbath occasions—the Sabbath, not two or three hours a day, but the entire day from its beginning to its close,—when God's "whole family in heaven and earth" meet together with Him. From the remotest corners of the earth, all are present and on time to welcome its opening hours with lofty choruses of adoration and thankful praise, and to listen to messages of love and joy and peace from the Father and the Son.

During the day, they may have the pleasure and comfort of the "many mansions" which Jesus has prepared for them. John 14:2. Then, at the close of the evening vespers service, spiritually refreshed and strengthened for another week, they "wing their tireless flight" to their Eden homes in the country—a flight more swift than the swiftest plane ever made by man.

Thus the New Jerusalem with the redeemed will indeed be "a crown of glory in the hand of the Lord, and a royal diadem in the hand of our God." Isaiah 62:3. This is God's "Glorious plan" for the most holy place of the temple eternal.

CHAPTER 39 PREVIEW

THE TEMPLE ETERNAL—ITS HOLY PLACE

- The Temple Outside the City
- Houses Resembling Silver Near the Temple
- The Temple of Wisdom
- The "School of the Hereafter"
- Teachers in This School
- The Golden Table in the Temple of Wisdom
- The New Earth University
- The Golden Altar in the Temple Eternal
- The Golden Candlestick in the Temple
- The Witness of the Redeemed
- The 144,000 as Special Witnesses
- Creation and Rec-creation or Redemption
- The "Increase" of Christ's Government
- His "Many Crowns" "Seven in Number"
- The Witness of Those Who Follow the Lamb
- The Fruit of Their Witness
- Visiting the Unfallen Worlds
- Sanctification Eternal
- Quarantined (A Poem)

39

THE TEMPLE ETERNAL—
ITS HOLY PLACE

The Temple Outside the City. We have seen that the most holy place of the earthly sanctuary was a type not only of the most holy place of the heavenly sanctuary where Christ now ministers as Judge, but also of the most holy place of the temple eternal, the New Jerusalem when located on the new earth. We may now ask, Does the *holy place* of the earthly sanctuary, with its golden table, its golden altar, and its golden candlestick, have its final antitype as part of the temple eternal? And if so, where is it located, and what is its nature and its purpose?

When God creates a "new heaven"—and a new firmament—and "a new earth wherein dwelleth righteousness," II Peter 3:13; Rev. 21:1, will there be in it a holy place, or temple *outside* the New Jerusalem, even as in the earthly sanctuary there was a holy place just outside the most holy? Eze. 37:26-28. Does not this include the *entire* sanctuary, its holy place as well as its most holy? Continuing, we read: "And David My servant shall be king over them; [the redeemed]...[he] shall be their prince forever." vs.24, 25.

Who is this king and prince that shall occupy the throne of David forever? Let Gabriel answer—the angel who was sent from God to Mary with a message concerning Jesus, the "Son of the Highest." He says, "The Lord God shall give unto Him [Jesus] the throne of His father David: and He shall reign over the house of Jacob forever; and of His kingdom there shall be no end." Luke 1:26, 31-33. "The throne of His father David" is evidently not "the throne of God and of the Lamb," Rev. 22:1, which is *in the City*. The throne of David is where "the house of Jacob," —redeemed Israel—live.

Through a later prophet God has given quite a detailed picture of the temple which is "outside of the City," "on the way to Mount Zion," "just before" it. It is "a glorious temple," on a mount, and "about it seven other mountains, on which [grow] roses and lilies...There [are] all kinds of trees around the temple to beautify the place; the box, the pine, and the fir, the oil, the myrtle, the pomegranate, and the fig tree bowed down with the weight of its timely figs—these make the place all over glorious." This temple is "supported by *seven pillars*, all of transparent gold, set with pearls most glorious." In it are "tables of stone in which the names of the 144,000 [are] engraved in letters of gold;" in it "only the 144,000 enter." EW 18, 19. These are they who "serve God day and night in His temple," Rev. 7:15, and who "follow the Lamb whithersoever He goeth." Rev. 14:4.

From these inspired authorities, it would seem that while the sanctuary in the new earth will necessarily differ materially from any that has gone before, yet there will be a sanctuary, or temple, in the new earth, outside the City. This temple corresponds, at least in its location, to the holy place of the earthly sanctuary which was just outside the most holy place. The City being the *most holy place* of the temple eternal, the temple just outside the City would be its *holy place*.

Houses Resembling Silver Near the Temple. Near the new earth temple there will be special houses "inhabited by the saints." Unlike the Eden homes that the great multitude of the redeemed build in connection with the vineyards they plant, these houses have "the appearance of silver, supported by *four pillars* set with pearls, most glorious to behold." EW 18. In the earthly sanctuary, the Levites as "ministers of the sanctuary," "lodged round about the house of God" where they served "day and night." I Chron. 9:26, 27, 33. In the temple eternal, the 144,000, successors of the Levites, also serve God "day and night in His temple." Rev. 7:15. They, doubtless, are "the saints" who occupy these "most glorious" houses near the temple. How significant then, that these houses resemble silver, symbol of the ransom paid for the soul! Ex. 30:12, 13. How significant that each is supported by *four* pillars indicating that Christ is the Head of the house! How significant that the pillars are set with pearls, emblem of the great tribulation such as the 144,000 pass through! Rev. 7:14.

The Temple of Wisdom. In Proverbs 9:1, Solomon has described a temple which also is "supported by seven pillars." He says, "Wisdom has built her mansion, and set up her seven pillars." *Moffatt*. Someone has said that these pillars upholding the temple of wisdom represent:

1. Knowledge—Prov. 2:6

2. Understanding—Prov. 2:6

3. Judgment—Prov. 2:8

4. Equity—Prov. 2:9

5. Discretion—Prov. 2:11, 12

6. Prudence—Prov. 8:12

7. Justice—Prov. 8:15

(From *Sabbath School Quarterly on Proverbs*)

Surely this is the wisdom of God, the wisdom that cometh out of His mouth, Prov. 2:6. It is the wisdom that is "from above," which James summarizes in seven words: "first pure, then peaceable, gentle, and easy to be entreated, full of mercy and good fruits, without partiality and without hypocrisy." James 3:17. Job sums it up in these words: "The fear of the Lord, that is wisdom: and to depart from evil is understanding." Job 28:28. This is heavenly wisdom, and while the same righteous principles underlie all true wisdom, it is not perfected in halls of learning in this present world,—it will be found in its perfection only in the temple of wisdom in the new earth. "When this wisdom entereth into thine heart," says the wise man, "knowledge is pleasant unto the soul." Prov. 2:10.

"The School of the Hereafter." Since "in the highest sense, the work of education and the work of redemption are one," Ed. 30, may it not be that this temple of wisdom upheld by seven pillars, and the temple in which are engraved the names of the 144,000, likewise having seven pillars, are one and the same, and that here, at the temple of wisdom, the School of the Hereafter will be conducted? What better place could there be for this school?

The location of this temple which was revealed to the Remnant church in the early days of its history, being outside the City, amid the rolling hills, in a beautiful landscape of ornamental and fruit-bearing trees and lovely flowers, agrees perfectly with later instruction given as to the location of Christian schools at the present time. It is indeed an ideal location for Heaven's temple of wisdom, the School of the Hereafter. And here "in His temple doth everyone speak of His glory," Ps. 29:9,—the natural fruitage of any Christian School.

As in the holy place of the earthly sanctuary, sanctification, the development of Christian character, was symbolized, so in the holy place of the temple eternal in the temple of wisdom, the redeemed, ever learning more and more of the wisdom of God will retain and strengthen a righteous character.

Teachers in This School. Who will be the teachers in the School of the Hereafter? In the earthly sanctuary, the priests and the Levites were the teachers of Israel. Ed. 78, 148: II Chron. 17:7, 8; Neh. 8:9. Is this God-given plan to be perpetuated with redeemed Israel? Let us see. During the one-thousand years when the wicked are judged, *all* the redeemed act with Christ as priests in the capacity of judges. Rev. 20:6; I Cor. 6:2, 3; Dan. 7:22. When the one thousand years are past, redemption being ended, this service automatically ceases. But the 144,000 serve Him "day and night in His temple." Rev. 7:15. Their service continues, but not as priests in the ordinary sense—priests who minister for the sins of the people, neither as judges, for probation has closed and the Judgment is past. How, then do they serve? As successors of the Levites, is it not in the capacity of teachers—assistants of Christ, the High Priest and Master Teacher "in the school above?" CT 209. These may be called the faculty of this school, the redeemed are the students.

Since only the 144,000 "enter" this temple of wisdom, the redeemed from time to time will assemble *at* the temple, [not *in* it where only the faculty gather]. Here Christ "in whom are hid all the treasures of wisdom and knowledge," Col. 2:2,3, assisted by the 144,000, will, throughout the ceaseless ages of eternity unfold more and more to the astonished and delighted understanding of the redeemed, that science of sciences and that song of songs—the science and the song of redemption.

In the type, the Levites, divided into courses, had charge of the earthly sanctuary, I Chron. 23:6, 32, each group "after seven days, from time to time" I Chron 9:25, having an appropriately assigned service. Some were porters who opened the gates and doors. Some were over the treasuries, others had charge of the ministering vessels, still others looked after the fine flour, the oil, the wine, the frankincense, and spices. The Kohathites prepared the shewbread every Sabbath. Others were appointed to make the ointment of the spices. Besides these were the singers who were "employed in that work day and night." I Chron 9:26-33; Lev. 24:5-8. The duties of all these groups were necessary to the sanctuary service.

From this, and from the fact that "the life on earth is the beginning of the life in Heaven; education on earth…an initiation into the principles of Heaven; the lifework here…a training for the lifework there" Ed. 307, may we not learn that, while the grand central theme of the teaching of the 144,000 in the School of the Hereafter will be redemption, this infinite subject will be approached by different groups from various angles according to their "education on Earth?" One group will present it from the wonders and beauties of nature, another from the glories revealed in astronomy, another from the accuracy and perfection of mathematics, another from the "infinite scope" of history, another from all the marvels of the human body, still another from the soul inspiration of music and poetry, and so on? But the purpose of all their teaching will be, as it should be in Christian schools today, to show the wisdom, the greatness, and the power, the goodness and the love of God.

The Golden Table in the Temple of Wisdom. We have seen that in its *location* the holy place of the temple eternal corresponds to the holy place of the earthly sanctuary. We now ask, what about the types in the holy place—the golden table, the golden altar, and the golden candlestick? Of what are they symbols in the temple of the new earth? Take first the table. The bread on the table, the "continual" bread, represented Christ, "the Bread of God … which cometh down from Heaven," the living Word, the Word of God, our spiritual food, of which "if any man eat…he shall live forever." John 6:33, 51. This living Word, the source of all true wisdom, is found in the temple of Wisdom. Here, in the School of the Hereafter, Christ spreads before the redeemed the riches of His wisdom. Thus the "banquet table" of the earthly sanctuary becomes, in the holy place of the temple eternal, the banqueting hall of the redeemed.

The New Earth University. What will be the course of study in this school? "Heaven is a school; its field of study, the universe." Ed. 301. Thus the School of the Hereafter, the school of the new earth, will be a real *universe*-ity in its truest, fullest sense. Here all the redeemed will be privileged to take a full university course of study—one entirely free from error, well worth the best effort of the most talented. Here with "immortal minds" the redeemed "will contemplate with never failing delight, the wonders of creative power, the mysteries of redeeming love." GC 677.

In this university the full beauty of nature of which we now catch only "glimpses through the microscope," "the glories of the Heavens now scanned afar through the telescope," will be opened to the eye of the redeemed. Ed. 303. There "the innumerable worlds in their orderly revolution, 'the balancing of the clouds'", Job 37:16; Ed. 21, the mysteries of sight and hearing and all the other marvels of the human body—all that has puzzled and baffled our study here will be opened to our astonished understanding, for "the vail that interposes between the visible and the invisible world will be drawn aside, and wonderful things will be revealed." Ed. 304.

"All the treasures of the universe will be opened to the study of God's children…and the years of eternity, as they roll, will continue to bring more glorious revelations—'exceeding abundantly above all that we ask or think.'" Eph. 3:20; Ed. 307. A wonderful university! Who would not earnestly desire to attend it?

Not only science in all its phases, but the "infinite scope" of history—history gained through contact with unfallen beings who through ages have witnessed its development—such sources of history will reveal a knowledge of which the wisest of earth have never dreamed. "There will be music there, and song, such music and song as…no mortal ear has heard." "As well the singers as the players on instruments shall be there." Ps. 87:7; Ed. 304, 307.

There "every faculty will be developed, every capacity increased. The acquirement of knowledge will not weary the mind or exhaust the energies. The grandest enterprises may be carried forward, the loftiest aspirations reached, the highest ambitions realized; and still there will arise new heights to surmount, new wonders to admire, new truths to comprehend, fresh objects to call forth the powers of mind and soul and body." GC 677. There immortal minds will contemplate with never failing delight not only the wonders of creative power, but above all, the mysteries of redemptive power and love will be opened to grateful hearts. As we contemplate the wonderful opportunities for true education that await us, we can but exclaim with the Psalmist: "Such knowledge is too wonderful for me; it is high, I cannot attain unto it." Ps. 139:6.

"In this life we can only begin to understand the wonderful theme of redemption. With our finite comprehension we may consider most earnestly the shame and the glory, the life and the death, the justice and the mercy, that meet in the cross; yet with the utmost stretch of our mental powers, we fail to grasp its full significance. …But through the eternal ages, new truth will continually unfold to the wondering and delighted mind." GC 651. Instead of the printed Word from which we now study the science of redemption, Christ, the living word, our Master Teacher, will enable us to comprehend more and more fully "what is the breadth, and length, and depth, and height; and to know the love of Christ, which passeth knowledge." Eph. 3:18, 19. How grateful we should be that this living bread, like the bread in the type, will be "continual!"

Then "the earth shall be filled with the knowledge of the glory of the Lord, as the waters cover the sea." Hab. 2:14. All this is typified in the golden table of the earthly sanctuary; al this, and much more, will be found in the holy place of the temple eternal. How great the privilege to be permitted to feast at this, the true "table of the Lord!" As the most holy place of the temple eternal is the CHURCH of the redeemed, so the holy place is their SCHOOL.

The Golden Altar in the Temple Eternal. As elsewhere in the construction of the earthly sanctuary, so the "gold" of the altar represented "the Almighty." Job 22:25, margin. Here the incense which like the bread was "continual," was burned morning and evening, diffusing its fragrance day and night. The incense represented the never-failing righteousness of Christ which He imparts to those who truly seek it. To those who "hunger and thirst after righteousness" the promise is, "they shall be filled." Matt. 5:6. As in the type the fragrance of the incense not only filled the sanctuary, but it was diffused "without, far around the tabernacle," PP 348, so in the temple eternal, the righteousness of Christ manifest in the redeemed, will not only fill the new earth continually, but its sweet fragrance will extend beyond to other worlds, thus proclaiming the joyful story of redemption.

When the morning and evening incense was offered, all Israel, in sorrow for sin, and in rededication to God, bowed in humble confession and prayer with their faces toward the sanctuary. In the great antitype, the temple eternal, praise takes the place of prayer; "joy and gladness shall be found therein, thanksgiving, and the voice of melody." Isaiah 51:3.

The incense burned on the altar, and that placed on the bread of the table and afterward burned on the altar, illustrates the union of praise and thanksgiving with the wisdom received in the School of the Hereafter. Thus in the temple eternal is fulfilled the promise, "The ransomed of the Lord shall return and come to Zion with songs and everlasting joy upon their heads; they shall obtain joy and gladness, and sorrow and sighing shall flee away." Isaiah 35:10.

The Golden Candlestick in the Temple. In the earthly sanctuary the purpose of the candlestick was to give light. It represented not only Christ, the Light of the world, but also His followers whom He declared to be "the light of the world." Matt. 5:14. While this applies to every true Christian in this present life, it will be most fully revealed in the life to come. In that life, where "everyone doth speak of His glory," everyone reflects in his deeds, in his words, and in his countenance the light of the glory of God. "The theme of redemption will employ the hearts and minds and tongues of the redeemed through the everlasting ages." *Signs of the Times*, April 18, 1906, p. 246.

The Witness of the Redeemed. Light-bearing means service. The last commandment that Christ gave the apostles was, "Ye shall be witnesses unto Me." Acts 1:7-9. "This also we shall be in eternity," Ed. 308, for of that time it is written, "His servants shall serve Him." Rev. 22:3. Of what are the redeemed to be witnesses in eternity? "Ye are my witnesses, saith the Lord ... that I am He; before me there was no God formed, neither shall there be after Me. I, even I, am the Lord, and beside Me there is no Saviour." Isaiah 43:10, 11. Witnessing, ever witnessing of the power and love of our Creator and Redeemer, "and ever as we witness, learning anew 'the riches of the glory of this mystery'; which is Christ in you, the hope of glory." Col. 1:27. In this service will be found "our greatest joy and our highest education." Ed. 309.

The 144,000 as Special Witnesses. Among the redeemed a special witnessing will be given by the 144,000, and for this they receive special preparation. As the result of earnest, faithful, prayerful study of God's Word, this company have a pure faith, "for they are virgins," Rev. 14:4,—a faith untainted with the deceptive errors of Antichrist who is called "the beast and his image," the "dragon," "that old serpent,…the devil, and Satan, which deceiveth the whole world." Rev. 12:9. Through the "little horn" of Daniel 8:9, Satan for centuries has "magnified himself" and "cast down the truth to the ground; and it [the horn] practiced and prospered." vs. 11, 12. But the end of the 2300 days was God's appointed time when His sanctuary—His church—was to be cleansed from all these deceptive errors, vs. 14, and the pure truth of God's Word was to shine forth. During these closing days of probation, those who love and obey God will give special and earnest study to the Word of God, comparing scripture with scripture. As one truth after another is rescued from the rubbish of error under which Satan has buried it, they not only accept these truths and gladly obey God, but they share their newfound faith with others, many of whom also accept and obey. This continues until 144,000 of these faithful students of God's Word have come into the blaze of the pure and everlasting gospel truth. Therefore, they are called "virgins."

As Satan, the "mighty" and "terrible" one, sees his deceptive errors exposed and his "captives…taken away, and … delivered," Isaiah 49:25, his frenzy is so aroused that, says John, he "went to make war with the remnant…which keep the commandments of God, and have the testimony of Jesus Christ." Rev. 12:17. This warfare, grows more and more fierce as the end approaches, yet through it they "have washed their robes and made them white in the blood of the Lamb." Rev. 7:14. They have come forth with praise in their hearts and a song on their lips,—a song of deliverance which "none but the 144,000 can learn" because "It is the song of their experience—an experience such as no other company has ever had." GC 649. This experience has prepared them to witness for God and His everlasting truth as no other group can. Therefore, as teachers, they not only "serve God day and night in His temple," Rev. 7:15, but they also serve Him more widely as they "follow the Lamb whithersoever He goeth." Rev. 14:4. What an infinite and thrilling experience is wrapped up in the words: They follow the Lamb whithersoever He goeth! Where does the Lamb lead them. Let us see.

Creation and Re-creation, or Redemption. When the awful tragedy of sin overtook this newly created world and plunged it into misery and woe, the universe of God was stunned with horror and grief. But, although Satan had brought death into the world, he can not thwart God's plan, for though "the wages of sin is death;…the gift of God is eternal life." Rom. 6:23. "As in Adam all die, even so in Christ shall all be made alive." I Cor. 15:22. Sin has marred this entire world; the image of God in which man was created, Gen. 1:26, has been all but lost, but is the

Omnipotent One discouraged? O no! "He shall not fail nor be discouraged, till He have set judgment in the earth." Isaiah 42:4. "I am the Lord," He says, "I change not," Mal. 3:6. God begins at once the great work of re-creation, or redemption—restoring that which through sin was lost.

Fulfilling the compact which the Father made with the Son before the world was, the three persons of the Godhead—Father, Son, and Holy Spirit—inseparable associates in creation, Gen. 1:1, 2; John 1:1-3, 14, united their divine power in the restoration of fallen man. From this time, "The science of redemption...engages the attention of our Lord and Saviour." *Signs of the Times*, April 18, 1906, p. 246. Jesus, "the Lamb slain from the foundation of the world, "Rev. 13:8, "ever liveth to make intercession for them." Heb. 7:25. Nor does He work alone. "I do nothing of Myself," He says [John 8:28]: "My Father worketh hitherto, and I work." John 5:17. "I and My Father are one." John 10:30; 14:20. Not only God the Father and God the Son are now centering their attention to re-create fallen man, to restore in him the image of God but the Father has also sent "the Comforter, which is the Holy Ghost" to cooperate in this work. John 14:26. The angels, too, are "ministering spirits sent forth to minister for them who shall be heirs of salvation." Heb. 1:14. Redemption "engages the attention" not only of Jesus but all of Heaven.

In the very midst of sin and apparent defeat, God's work of recreation is achieved. He hears the prayer of the contrite soul, "Create in me a clean heart, O God," Ps. 51:10, and "the new man... is created in righteousness and true holiness." Eph. 4:24. Thus, the work of redemption, the recreation of human beings, continues until God's "family...in earth" is made up, Eph 3:15, a sufficient number to "replenish" the earth as He originally planned. Gen. 1:28.

The "Increase" of Christ's Government At the close of the section of eternity which we call *time*, the "attention" of the Creator is no longer "engaged" in re-creating man. This is now fully and successfully accomplished. Sin is abolished forever, Nahum 1:9, and "death is swallowed up in victory." I Cor. 15:54. Time merges into the eternity of the future and the work of creation, interrupted by sin, is resumed, being manifest first in the creation of other worlds of which "there shall be no end." Isaiah 9:7.

Although in the beginning the first Adam failed, and Satan by trickery and falsehood usurped the kingdom and for a time has been allowed to bear sway, yet the government of this earth shall finally be placed upon the shoulder of Christ, the last Adam, its Redeemer. Isaiah 9:6; I Cor. 15:45-47. When Christ becomes "the Governor among the nations" of the new Earth, Ps. 22:23, and new worlds are added to the universe, the prophecy of Luke 1:33 of "His kingdom there shall be no end," begins to unfold. While this prophecy applies to the new earth over which Christ on the throne of David shall reign forever, does it not also have a wider application as stated by Isaiah: "Of the *increase* of His government and peace there shall be no end?" Isaiah 9:7. Through Ezekiel, "the word of the Lord" states it this way: "Moreover I will make a covenant of peace with them [His people] ... and I will...*multiply* them." Eze. 37:26.

This multiplying of His people, could not apply to the redeemed inhabitants of the new earth, because when probation closes, the family of God for this earth is fully made up; the command given at creation: "Be fruitful, and multiply, and *replenish* the earth," Gen. 1:28, has been carried out, and no more inhabitants will be added. This earth has been "replenished" or *filled up* as Webster defines this word. "The number of His subjects is made up." GC 613.

Jesus, answering the Sadducees who were troubled on this matter, explains it this way: "When they [the righteous] shall rise from the dead, they neither marry nor are given in marriage; but are as the angels which are in Heaven." Mark 12:18-25. The finally redeemed make up God's "whole family" for the new Earth, Eph. 3:15, and no more will be born. Quoting from Hebrews 4:3, "the works were finished from the foundation of the world," there are some who conclude that, after this earth is re-created, God's work of creation will cease. These apparently overlook the fact that this text applies to *this world* only, for we read: "As regards this world, God's work of creation is completed. For 'the works were finished from the foundation of the world.'" PP 115. The context of this scripture sustains this truth, for the next verse, vs. 4, reads: "And God did rest the seventh day from all His works." "He rested from all His work which He *had made*," Gen. 2:1-3—not from all the work which He ever would create in the future. The reason these Sadducees did not understand this question, is revealed in the words of Christ to them, "Ye do err, not knowing the Scriptures, nor the power of God." Mat. 22:29; Mark 12:24.

That *we* do not err, not knowing the power of God, let us look again at the prophecies of Isaiah and Ezekiel regarding the unlimited government of Christ. Isaiah states that there shall be an "increase" of His government "of which there shall be no end," Isaiah 9:7, and Ezekiel says He will "multiply" His people. Eze. 37:26. The Hebrew definition of the noun *increase* used in Isaiah is *enlargement*, increase in *territory* or in *number*, and its verb form translated *multiply* in Ezekiel and also in Genesis 1:28, contains the same thought—*to increase in number*. This "increase" or "enlargement" in number or territory in no way diminishes the enlargement of our comprehension and appreciation of God's great work, but rather emphasizes it. But does it not make plain that after this earth has been re-created God will continue His creative work of which "there shall be no end, upon the throne of David [Christ, Zech. 3:8] and upon His kingdom, to order it, and to establish it with judgment and with justice from henceforth even forever?" This work being infinite, finite beings cannot fathom it, so the prophet adds, "The zeal of the Lord of hosts will perform this." Isaiah 9:7. Thus throughout eternity the work of creation will go forward, new worlds will be added to the universe, the kingdom of God will be continually expanding, and Christ "upon the throne of David" will rule over an ever enlarging dominion. And, as the great Jehovah continues His creative work, He becomes continually and everlastingly distinguished throughout His entire universe as the Great Creator, the only true and living God.

His "Many Crowns," "Seven in Number." Is Christ's third and "final coronation" the last of His coronations? So far as this world is concerned, it is. But John saw Him when "on His head were *many* crowns," Rev. 19:12, and another inspired writer, speaking of His crowns, states: "His crown looked brilliant and glorious. It was a crown within a crown, *seven* in number,"—seven, expressive of perfection and completeness. EW 53, 54. When does He receive these "many crowns," "seven in number?" Does this not indicate that after His "final coronation" He receives other crowns? And are these not given when new worlds are created, the "increase of His government," the "enlargement" of His kingdom over which He reigns as "KING OF ETERNITY" I Tim. 1:17, *Moffatt*, over God's entire universe? Paul states it this way: God hath "set Him...far above all principality and power, and dominion, and every name that is named [every title of sovereignty, *Weymouth*], not only in this world, but also in that which is to come, and hath put all things under His feet, and gave Him to be the head over all things to the church, which is His body, the fullness of Him that filleth all in all" [that filleth the universe entirely, *Moffatt*]. Eph. 1:22, 23.

The Witness of Those Who Follow the Lamb. As successors of the Levites, who with the priests, were the teachers of ancient Israel, the 144,000, especially sealed from all the tribes of redeemed Israel, Rev. 7:4-8, act as under-teachers in the School of the Hereafter, Christ Himself the heavenly High Priest being the Master Teacher. This position of "highest honor" is supplemented by another, when, like a bodyguard of honor, they are permitted to "follow the Lamb whithersoever He goeth," Rev. 14:1, 4. As new worlds are created, the 144,000 follow Christ in this work. What a marvelous privilege!—to be with the Great Creator when a new world is called into existence!—a privilege which all the redeemed shall have when the Divine fiat goes forth concerning this world: "Behold, I create new heavens and a new Earth," Isaiah 65:17; "Behold, I make all things new." Rev. 21:5.

What part have the 144,000 in connection with this work of creating new worlds? Let David answer: "They shall come, and shall declare His righteousness unto a people that shall be born," or as Moffatt translates it: His saving deeds shall be declared to generations yet unborn. Ps. 22:31. While this scripture may have a partial application to the extension of the gospel in this world in its present state, does it not also reach forward to all the generations yet unborn—those yet to be created? The newly created worlds, the "increase," or enlargement, of His government, the "multiplying" of His people, the "generations yet unborn," desire to understand the mystery of the "cross of Christ" which will be the science and the song of the redeemed throughout eternity. Ed. 126.

Whenever a new world is created, the 144,000 "follow the Lamb," Rev. 14:4, declaring His saving deeds to generations yet unborn, witnessing of the power of salvation and redeeming love in a mighty and triumphant chorus expressive of their own experience. As they thus witness, these newly created worlds are welcomed into the family of God.

The Fruit of Their Witness. Will sin ever again enter God's universe? Some seem troubled on this point. They think [but without Biblical authority] that when a new world is created, there will be the same possibility that sin will re-enter the universe as when Adam and Eve fell under the power of the enemy. It is true that when Eve was exposed to "the wiles [sly tricks, *Webster*] of the devil," Eph. 6:11, she, being deceived, forgot God and fell a victim to the "Cruel, deceptive foe." But in the restoration, every trace of sin and evil is utterly destroyed, "root and branch," Mal 4:1, Satan the root, his associates the branches. Then the devil, the originator of sin and the source of all evil, "is cast into the lake of fire," Rev. 20:10, where he perishes eternally, never again to mar God's dominion. Then "there will be no cruel, deceptive foe to tempt to forgetfulness of God." GC 677. "No tempter is there, no possibility of wrong." Ed. 302. When the triumphant cry of Jesus, "It is finished" reaches its entire fulfillment, there will be an eternal end of sin, "*It is finished.*" John 19:30. Uriah Smith, generally recognized as a reliable Bible expositor, puts it this way: "The reconciliation effected by Christ not only takes man [those who have been redeemed from this world] out of his actual rebellion, but sweeps through the universe to settle and ground all worlds against any possible disharmony with God [in reference to this great controversy] *in all the ages to come.*" LJ 35, Italics supplied. The death of Christ will eventually make an eternal end of all sin.—"It is finished."

Not only will there be no tempter, and consequently no temptation, on all God's universe, but as new worlds are created, and the 144,000 unfold to their understanding the love and salvation of God manifest in redemption; as they see the wounds that Christ bears in His body—wounds caused by sin; as they learn of the suffering that sin has cost all Heaven; as they grasp the truth that "with the existence of God's law is bound up the happiness of all the beings He has created," GC 671, will they, understanding all this and with no wicked tempter to deceive them—will they, beings of sound mind, deliberately and willfully disobey God and thus bring death and destruction upon themselves?

Moreover, God, who "cannot lie," Titus 1:2, foreseeing the end from the beginning, has pledged His word: "Affliction shall not rise up the second time." Nahum 1:9. This assuring promise is absolute and unconditional. Then will be fulfilled the prophecy of Daniel 9:24 that the sacrifice of Christ was "to finish the transgression, and to make an end of sins [plural] and to make reconciliation for iniquity, and to bring in everlasting righteousness."

Do not these assurances make it clear that sin will never again mar God's universe? If this be not true, but if through some failure to meet a "test" of obedience [of which the Scripture makes no mention], if evil should enter the universe "the second time," would Jesus, "the blessed and only Potentate," I Tim. 6:15, and the only Redeemer, die again to redeem the lost? No! no! "Christ was once offered" "to put away sin by the sacrifice of Himself." Heb. 9:25-28. Never again will the tragedy of sin be re-enacted.

Then, wonder of wonders! will be fulfilled the prophecy of Isaiah: "I will make a man more precious than fine gold; even a man than the golden wedge of Ophir," Isaiah 13:12, for as gold stabilizes an earthly government, so the redeemed by their witnessing will be, as it were, the stabilizers of God's universal government throughout eternity. For this purpose, "He hath raised us up together, and made us sit together in heavenly places in Christ Jesus: that in the ages to come He might show the exceeding riches of His grace in His kindness toward us through Christ Jesus." Eph. 2:6, 7.

Visiting the Unfallen Worlds. When the 144,000 teachers in the School of the Hereafter, follow the Lamb in the creation of a new world, how will the students continue their education? Are the 144,000 the only ones among the redeemed who will have the privilege of going to other worlds? Listen! "Unfettered by mortality, they [the redeemed] wing their tireless flight to worlds afar, worlds that thrilled with sorrow at the spectacle of human woe, and rang with songs of gladness at the tidings of a ransomed soul." GC 677. For 6,000 years these unfallen worlds have watched with intense interest the unfolding of the plan of redemption, and during all these years they have learned more and more fully the mysteries of redeeming love.

With this knowledge of redemption already possessed by these unfallen worlds, what is the special purpose of the redeemed as they visit these worlds? The answer is found in a continuation of the foregoing quotation: "With unutterable delight, the children of earth enter into the joy and the wisdom of unfallen beings. They share [with the redeemed] the treasures of knowledge and understanding gained through ages upon ages in contemplation of God's handiwork." See also Ed. 307. This, then, is the wonderful provision made for the students of the New Earth University to continue their education while their teachers are absent with Christ as He creates a new world.

Thus in the temple eternal, the witness of all the redeemed becomes the light of the universe, the most complete possible antitype of the seven-branched candlestick of beaten gold, with Christ Himself as its central shaft.

Sanctification Eternal. As typified in the holy place of the earthly sanctuary, sanctification is the result of a long, long experience, so in the holy place of the temple eternal, the wisdom of Christ, symbolized by the golden table, the righteousness of Christ by the incense at the golden altar, and the service and of and for Christ by the golden candlestick—all of which as types were "continual"—all these unite in the "continual" and eternal sanctification of redeemed Israel. Thus sanctification becomes an eternal principle in the lives of the redeemed, and the holy place of the temple eternal is a complete and final antitype of the holy place of the earthly sanctuary.

Quarantined

Did you ever stop to think about
    This place we call the earth,
And why you've never left it
    Since the moment of your birth?
And how the folk in other worlds
    Can all go out and in,
While you're restricted to this earth?—
    You're quarantined for sin!
God put up the quarantine
    With a bright and flaming sword,
When the Father drove our parents
    From the "Garden of the Lord."
But His heart was filled with pity
    When He saw our sad estate,
And the world that He had quarantined,
    He moved near heaven's gate.

Then He sent the Great Physician
    To this earth to save the lost,
And reveal the love of God to man;
    Nor did He count the cost
Too great to pay; but gave His life
    A ransom full and free,
So He could lift the quarantine
    That's over you and me.
In the glad time before us,
    When He comes to claim His own,
He will take the ones He's purified
    Back to His Father's home.
When the quarantine is lifted,
    We may all go out and in,
And tell how He redeemed us
    Who were quarantined for sin.

                —*Adele R. Dewey*

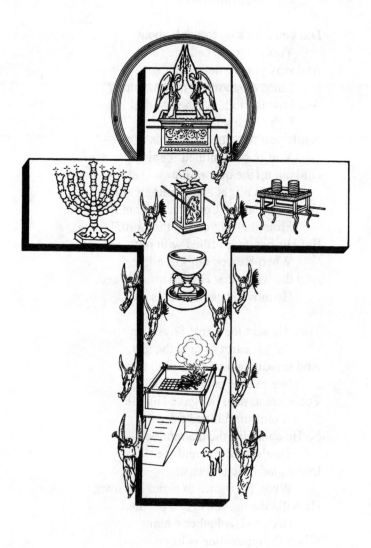

"The Lord Jesus Christ in our own humanity was the true tabernacle." Like Jacob's ladder which represented Jesus, so Christ the true tabernacle reaches from earth to heaven, and angels of God ascend and descend upon the Son of man.

CHAPTER 40 PREVIEW

THE TEMPLE ETERNAL—ITS COURT

- This Earth the Court of the Heavenly Sanctuary
- The New Earth the Court of the Temple Eternal
- No Animals Sacrificed in the New Earth Court
- The "Excellency" of the Court Eternal
- No Trace of Sin Remains
- No Trouble in the New Earth Court
- "Peace on Earth" an Everlasting Reality
- Permanent Homes for the Redeemed
- Eden Homes in the Court Eternal
- God's "Glorious Plan" Realized
- Christ Our Sanctuary

40

THE TEMPLE ETERNAL—
ITS COURT

This Earth the Court of the Heavenly Sanctuary. In the court of the earthly sanctuary, the typical sacrifices were slain and their blood was ministered in the sanctuary for the repentant sinner. The sin offering was then burned without the camp. Lev. 16:27. Likewise, Jesus, the antitypical sin offering, the Lamb "roast with fire," He who suffered and bled and died for our sins, was sacrificed on Calvary, without the camp, and He now pleads His blood in the *heavenly* sanctuary for repentant sinners. Also as the typical sacrifices were washed and cleansed in the court of the earthly sanctuary, so on this earth, the candidates for redemption must be cleansed and prepared for their heavenly home. This earth, then, is the court of the heavenly sanctuary.

Therefore, when John was given a vision of the heavenly sanctuary, he was not shown the altar of burnt offering or the laver—he saw nothing relating to the court of the earthly sanctuary. And when he was given a reed to measure the temple, he was told to "leave out" the court, "which is without the temple, and measure it not." Rev. 11:1, 2. It was "given unto the Gentiles," those who are of the earth, and whose names are "written in the earth" Jer. 17:13—those "who depart from" God and do not accept Christ as their Sacrifice.

The New Earth the Court of the Temple Eternal. As this earth is the court of the heavenly sanctuary, so the glorified new earth becomes the court of the temple eternal. Also, as the court of the earthly sanctuary entirely surrounded the sanctuary proper and was enclosed with the white linen wall, symbol of the righteousness of Christ, likewise the new earth "wherein dwelleth righteousness" II Peter 3:13, will entirely surround the holy place and the most holy place of the temple eternal and will be its court. In the temple eternal, there remains one trace—only one—of the great Sacrifice, as a memorial to the redeemed throughout eternity of what their salvation has cost: He has "horns coming out of His hand; bright beams out of His side;" "and *there* was the hiding of His power." Hab. 3:4, margin. These "horns" and "bright beam," sparkling like brilliant diamonds, or "a lightning blaze" as Moffatt has it, in the glorified body of Christ, have taken the place of the ugly wounds caused by the cruel nails and the soldier's spear.

No Animals Sacrificed in the New Earth Court. In the court of the temple eternal, the blood of animals will not be shed in sacrifice. Oh, no! That all belongs to the court of the first, the earthly sanctuary. In the new earth court God promises to "make a covenant for them [the redeemed] with the beasts of the field, and with the fowls of heaven, and with the creeping things of the ground…and make them [the redeemed] to lie down safely." Hos. 2:18. when this covenant is made, His original plan will be restored, and man will "have dominion over the fish of the sea, and over the fowl of the air, and over the cattle [the beasts]…and over every creeping thing that creepeth over the earth." Gen. 1:26, 28, and as their ruler, he will "subdue" them and they will obey him. Thus will be fulfilled the prophecies of Isaiah regarding the animal kingdom: "The wolf and the lamb shall feed together." Isaiah 65:25. They "shall dwell" together; "the leopard shall lie down with the kid; and the calf and the young lion and the fatling together; and a little child shall lead them. And the cow and the bear shall feed, their young ones shall lie down together." Isaiah 11:6, 7. The animals will roam together, contented and happy. "They shall not hurt nor destroy in all my holy mountain, saith the Lord." Isaiah 65:25.

The "Excellency" of the Court Eternal. In the new earth court "the wilderness and the solitary place shall be glad for them; and the desert shall rejoice and blossom as the rose. It shall blossom abundantly, and rejoice even with joy and singing;…for in the wilderness shall waters break out, and streams in the desert." In the thirsty land there shall be "springs of water." Even "the mountains and the hills shall break forth before you into singing, and all the trees of the field shall clap their hands." "The redeemed shall see the glory of the Lord, and the excellency of our God." Isaiah 35:1, 2, 6, 7; 55:12.

No Trace of Sin Remains. "Instead of the thorn [which is a result of sin], Gen. 3:18, shall come up the myrtle tree." Isaiah 55:13. Instead of decay and death, which first appeared in drooping flower and falling leaf, and which caused Adam and Eve more sorrow than men now feel over their dead, PP 62, instead of these evidences of the curse, the fields will be decorated with never-fading flowers, the grass will be "living green with a reflection of silver and gold as it waves proudly to the glory of King Jesus," and the trees will be "light and all over glorious." EW 18. In the new earth there will be no drought, no floods, no extremes of heat or cold. Instead of weeds, depleted soil, destructive insects and other pests—instead of these blights of sin which now appear on every hand, there will be nothing to hurt or destroy in the court of the temple eternal. "For the Lord shall comfort Zion: He will comfort all her waste places; and He will make her wilderness like Eden, and her desert like the garden of the Lord: joy and gladness shall be found therein, thanksgiving and the voice of melody." Isaiah 51:3.

No Trouble in the New Earth Court. In that land "the inhabitant shall not say, I am sick." Isaiah 33:24, nor will there be any cripples. "Then the eyes of the blind shall be opened, and the ears of the deaf shall be unstopped. Then shall the lame man leap as an hart, and the tongue of the dumb sing." Isaiah 35:6. Weary pilgrims "shall renew their strength, they shall mount up with wings as eagles; they shall run, and not be weary; and they shall walk, and not faint." Isaiah 40:31. In that land there will be no lonely, aching hearts, for "God setteth the solitary in families." Ps. 68:6. Our Father champions the cause of orphans and widows and all who have been bereaved. In our eternal home no one will be harassed by financial worries, "for all things are yours;…and ye are Christ's and Christ is God's." I Cor. 3:21, 23.

Ye are "heirs of God, and joint heirs with Christ." Rom 8:17. Here the redeemed "shall not hunger nor thirst; neither shall the heat nor sun smite them;" Isaiah 49:10;—these experiences are all in the past, never again to be repeated.

Another trace of sin that will be destroyed, is found in the confusion of languages now spoken. In the beginning, for nearly two thousand years, "the whole earth was of one language, and of one speech." Gen. 11:1. What that language was, no one knows, but with all of one speech it would be comparatively easy to acquaint them with a knowledge of salvation. However, this proved to be a broad avenue to lead many away from God. Finally, at the time of the Flood, the wickedness of man had become so great that it grieved God "at His heart," and He destroyed the wicked "from the face of the earth." Gen. 6:5-7.

For many more years, one language prevailed. But at the building of the tower of Babel [which name means confusion], it became manifest that one language in a wicked world was more of a curse than a blessing. Then, in order to save the inhabitants of earth from the tragedy of denying God and thus losing their chance of eternal life, God confounded their language so that they could "not understand one another's speech." Gen. 11:5-9. This confusion of tongues has continued to increase until at the present time, in order to give the world a sure knowledge of God and of salvation, the Bible has been printed in more than a thousand languages and dialects. When this earth is redeemed and every trace of sin removed, God's original plan will be carried out, for then "thou shalt not see...a people of a deeper speech than canst perceive...a speech that thou canst not understand." Isaiah 33:19.

"Peace on Earth" an Everlasting Reality. In this new earth court, Heaven's promise of "peace on earth" meets its complete fulfillment. "He maketh wars to cease unto the end of the earth," and all implements of warfare shall be eternally destroyed. Ps. 46:9. "I will break the bow and the sword and the battle out of the earth, and will make them [the redeemed] to lie down safely." Hos. 2:18. "Violence shall no more be heard in the land, wasting nor destruction within thy borders; but thou shalt call thy walls Salvation, and thy gates Praise." Isaiah 60:18. "My people shall dwell in a peaceable habitation, and in sure dwellings, and in quiet resting places." Isaiah 32:18. This is the promise of the "Prince of Peace." No more need for peace conferences, for "the work of righteousness shall be peace; and the effect of righteousness, quietness and assurance forever." Isaiah 32:17. How blessed is the assurance that in the new earth court, families shall be no more separated by war; the redeemed shall pursue their various occupations in peace and safety!

Permanent Homes for the Redeemed. To those who have left home and loved ones, and have gone to the ends of the earth, moving from place to place to carry the good news of "Peace on earth," how grateful is that other promise: "I will appoint a place for My people Israel, and will plant them, that they may dwell in a place of their own, and *move no more*; neither shall the children of wickedness afflict them any more, as beforetime." II Sam. 7:10. "For as the new heavens and the new earth, which I will make, shall remain before Me, saith the Lord, so shall your seed and your name remain." Isaiah 66:22.

Eden Homes in the Court Eternal. In this court eternal "they shall build houses and inhabit them; and they shall plant vineyards, and eat the fruit of them. They shall not build and another inhabit; they shall not plant and another eat; for as the days of a tree are the days of My people, and Mine elect shall long enjoy the work of their hands. They shall not labor in vain." Isaiah 65:21-23.

"They shall build houses." And such houses! They will be like the Garden of Eden which God built for Adam and Eve, and which He designed as "a pattern for other homes as their children should go forth to occupy the earth." PP 49. In this model home, "the blue heavens were its dome; the earth with its delicate flowers and carpet of living green, was its floor; and the leafy branches of the goodly trees were its canopy. Its walls were hung with the most magnificent adornings—the handiwork of the great Master-Artist." PP 49.

On this present sin-cursed earth, homes are made by destroying the life of stately trees, but in the new earth, where nothing shall destroy, Isaiah 11:9, the redeemed shall "build houses" of *living* trees with wide-spreading branches and glistening foliage. They will make arbors and bowers by training graceful vines, dropping with sweet-scented, never-fading flowers, or laden with luscious fruit. In these homes of delight, "they shall dwell safely...and sleep in the woods." Eze. 34:25.

In the court of the temple eternal, there is "no more sea," Rev. 21:1, no more vast oceans such as now occupy three-fourths of the earth's surface. Instead of these vast uninhabitable areas, will be lovely lakes reflecting the blue sky above, on whose bosom sail graceful, pure white swans, or ducks more beautiful than our bright-colored mallards. In their waters swim fish whose beauty exceeds even the famous fish of Hawaii. Through the air, bright-colored birds fearlessly flit about singing their happy songs; hummingbirds dart from flower to flower, while here and there the lyre bird and the bird of paradise add their rare beauty to the garden. The court of the temple eternal will be dotted everywhere with these beautiful Eden homes, having spacious gardens of flowering shrubs and fruitful trees, and extensive lawns of "living green" watered by streams from the river of life. Gen. 2:10. "Beside these living streams, God's people, so long pilgrims and strangers, shall find a home," a home in the country, "A better country [better than the earthly from which they came out], that is, an heavenly." Also, God "hath prepared for them a city" home. Heb. 11:14-16; GC 675.

Is this mere idle dreaming? Is the picture overdrawn? *Listen*! "Let your imagination picture the home of the saved, and remember that it will be more glorious than your brightest imagination can portray." SC 86. It is utterly impossible adequately to describe these Eden-like homes or picture their attractions, for it is written that "since the beginning of the world men have not heard, nor perceived by the ear, neither hath the eye seen, O God, beside Thee, what He hath prepared

317

for him that waiteth for Him." Isaiah 64:4; "Neither have entered into the heart of man, the things which God hath prepared for them that love Him." I Cor. 2:9. To attempt such a description, we can but exclaim with Paul that to do this we should need "unspeakable words," or as Moffatt translates it, words "which no human lips can repeat." II Cor. 12:4.

God's "Glorious Plan" Realized. In the final restoration when there shall be 'a new heaven and a new earth,' Rev. 21:1, the whole earth will be occupied by homes of the redeemed patterned after the Garden of Eden, that wonderful "garden of delight." As the court of the earthly sanctuary was a "holy place" Lev. 6:26, so every Eden home in the temple eternal will be a holy place. When the new earth is filled with these unspeakable beautiful homes of joy and love and peace, what a magnificent court it will be for the temple itself!

On this earth, HOMES OF RIGHTEOUSNESS where God is daily worshiped at the family altar, where Christ is recognized as the Head of the house, and where His word, daily studied, is the guide in life, are, as it were, types of the Eden homes in *the court* of the temple eternal; CHRISTIAN SCHOOLS are as types of the School of the Hereafter located in *the holy place*; the CHURCH on earth a type of the church in *the most holy place*. The *home*, the *school*, the *church*, are the great and final antitype of the court, the holy place, and the most holy place of the earthly sanctuary. They are the three agencies divinely appointed to continue throughout eternity as God's instrumentalities to promote a more complete knowledge of the Eternal and of the redemption He has wrought. Thus His original plan of peopling the earth with righteous beings, reflecting His own image, will be a marvelous and eternal reality. Then, "though unending ages, the inhabitants of a sinless worlds shall behold the fulfillment of the Creator's glorious plan." PP 62.

Christ Our Sanctuary. "The Lord Jesus Christ in our own humanity was the true tabernacle...Here on earth...He worked out and obtained eternal salvation for us; and now in heaven He is, in His own person and forevermore, all that the heavenly treasures in the earthly tabernacle signified." RH Sept. 2, 1948, p. 4. In Him is fulfilled to His people that most precious and all-inclusive promise, found in Ezekiel 11:16—

> "I will be to them as
> a little sanctuary."

In our study of the *earthly sanctuary*, we have found that in its every part Christ is symbolized. He is the gate to the court through which all may enter; He is the sacrifice entirely consumed on the altar of brass; He is the resurrection and the life symbolized in the laver. He is "the door" to the holy place, and the vail at the entrance to the most holy place. He is the building and its foundation, and its protective coverings. He is the golden table and the Bread which came down from heaven. He is the golden altar and the golden censer, and the incense His righteousness. He is the golden candlestick, the Light of the world, working through the Holy Spirit. His throne is the mercy seat which covers the ark, and He Himself is the law of God drawn out in living characters "a transcript of God's character." PP 52; GC 434. His righteousness is the wall of white linen surrounding all. In the court He is our reconciliation and justification, in the holy place our sanctification, and in the most holy place our glorification. The earthly sanctuary is a complete shadow picture of our Lord Jesus Christ.

Christ is also the great center of the *heavenly* sanctuary; in its holy place He is our sympathizing High Priest and the KING OF GLORY: in the most holy where He now officiates, He is our righteous Judge. In heaven itself, He is KING OF KINGS AND LORD OF LORDS.

The new earth, wherein is located the throne of "the Lord God Almighty and the Lamb," Rev. 21:22, having been redeemed by the precious blood of Christ, becomes the center of God's entire universe, around which circle "suns, and stars, and systems, all in their appointed order." GC 677, 678.

Christ is the King not only of the new earth, but "upon His shoulder" shall rest the government of newly created worlds—"the increase of His government" of which "there shall be no end." Isaiah 9:6, 7. This divine-human King, whose name is "Wonderful, Counselor, the Mighty God, the Everlasting Father, the Prince of Peace"—is not only our earthly and our heavenly sanctuary, but He is our *temple eternal*. In this temple, He is "the KING OF ETERNITY," to whom "be honor and glory forever and ever. Amen." I Tim. 1:17. This King, the Lord Jesus Christ, is "the true tabernacle." To His people forever and ever—

> He is "as a little sanctuary" Eze. 11:16;
> He is "the way, the truth, and the life" John 14:6;
> And "His way is in the sanctuary" Ps. 77:13;

> He is THE PATH TO THE THRONE OF GOD.

We'd love to have you download our catalog of
titles we publish at:

www.TEACHServices.com

or write or email us your thoughts,
reactions, or criticism about this
or any other book we publish at:

TEACH Services, Inc.
254 Donovan Road
Brushton, NY 12916

info@TEACHServices.com

or you may call us at:

518/358-3494

Produced in partnership with
LNFBooks.com